PUBLICATIONS
OF THE
ARMY RECORDS SOCIETY
VOL. I
═══════

THE MILITARY
CORRESPONDENCE
OF FIELD MARSHAL
SIR HENRY WILSON
1918–1922

Field Marshal Sir Henry Wilson.
(From an etching by John Day, 1921.)

THE MILITARY CORRESPONDENCE OF FIELD MARSHAL SIR HENRY WILSON 1918–1922

EDITED BY

KEITH JEFFERY

PUBLISHED BY

THE BODLEY HEAD

FOR THE

ARMY RECORDS SOCIETY

1985

British Library Cataloguing
in Publication Data

Wilson, *Sir* Henry
The military correspondence of Field Marshal
Sir Henry Wilson 1918–1922.
1. Wilson, *Sir* Henry 2. Marshals—Great Britain—Biography
3. Great Britain. *Army*—Biography
I. Title II. Jeffery, Keith
355.3'31'0924 U55.W/
ISBN 0-370-30683-X

© The Army Records Society 1985
Printed in Great Britain for
The Bodley Head Ltd
9 Bow Street, London WC2E 7AL
at The Bath Press, Avon
Set in Linotron 202 Ehrhardt
by Wyvern Typesetting Ltd, Bristol
First published 1985

CONTENTS

LIST OF MAPS

PREFACE

The papers of Field Marshal Sir Henry Wilson which are kept at the Imperial War Museum can be divided into three categories. First there are forty-one volumes of manuscript diaries covering the years 1893 to 1922 when Wilson died. These are exceptionally full and narrate in detail Wilson's thoughts and activities. The second main category comprises a series of numbered files, some 130 in all, containing correspondence with 65 individuals. These papers cover the period from November 1917, when Wilson became British Military Representative at the Supreme War Council, to February 1922, when he retired from the office of Chief of the Imperial General Staff to which he had been appointed in February 1918. The third category includes much additional correspondence and other miscellaneous papers both from the 1918–22 period and also earlier years, beginning with material relating to the South African War of 1899–1902. The Wilson papers have come from two main family sources. Wilson died childless and his literary estate was divided up. The diaries and some miscellaneous papers have been deposited in the Museum by Sir Henry's nephew, Major Cyril Wilson. The numbered correspondence files and other material were given by the late Mrs Marjorie Stevenson, a first cousin once removed of the Field Marshal.

Only the diaries have hitherto been used extensively by historians. Indeed, they achieved notoriety when Sir Charles Callwell quoted substantial passages from them in his official biography of Wilson published in 1927. The selection of documents in this volume covers the years during which Wilson was CIGS and is drawn principally from the numbered correspondence files. These files contain a large proportion of the Field Marshal's personal and semi-official office correspondence. Approximately three thousand letters, both 'in' and 'out', have survived. Holograph or carbon copies of Wilson's letters were retained and carefully filed. Among the correspondents are leading politicians—Lloyd George, Churchill, Curzon, Milner—and senior British soldiers, notably Haig, Rawlinson, Allenby, Robertson and Harington. One section of the numbered files is not open to scholars: the correspondence between Wilson and General Sir Nevil Macready, the General Officer Commanding-in-Chief in Dublin. These letters deal with military policy and attitudes relating to Ireland during 1920–22. When the late Mrs Stevenson gave the papers to the Imperial War Museum in 1973, a fresh bout of Irish 'troubles' had begun, and she felt that no special purpose would be served by releasing papers which might re-open old wounds, particularly in the light of Wilson's own controversial attitudes towards his native land. Mrs Stevenson requested that the letters remain closed for at least fifteen years. No documents, therefore, from the Wilson–Macready series have been included in this volume. Wilson's views on general aspects of Irish policy, however, are fully expressed in the remainder of the correspondence.

I have selected the documents in this volume with the primary intention of illustrating and illuminating Sir Henry Wilson's own work and thought, both concerning the broad analyses and 'cosmic views' at which he excelled, and also relating to less momentous topics of staffing, decorations and everyday routine of the War Office. By including a substantial number of 'in' letters from a wide range of correspondents, I have also attempted to provide a 'cross-section' of British military and strategic opinion during the years in question. There is a general introduction which summarises Wilson's career up to 1918 and short introductions to each year's selection of documents indicate the main themes which arise. Obscure references and other additional information is provided in notes gathered together at the end of the documents. Correspondents and persons mentioned in the correspondence are identified (where possible) in the Biographical Notes and list of senior office-holders in the Appendices.

The documents themselves are reproduced as nearly to the

original as is practicable. Spelling and punctuation have been silently corrected only in a small number of cases where the original would not make sense. A few long, closely-written letters have been paragraphed for clarity. It should otherwise be assumed that any inconsistencies or errors in spelling or grammar derive from the original documents, and not from poor proof-reading. Illegible or doubtful words are indicated [Illegible] or by a mark in brackets [?]. To conserve space the salutation and complimentary closing of letters has in most cases been left out. Substantial omissions from documents are indicated by a row of asterisks; minor ones by an ellipsis. Documents are typescript top copies unless marked [Holograph], [Holograph copy] or [Carbon].

No work of this sort is possible without incurring a large number of debts. Since I began working on Sir Henry Wilson ten years ago I have received assistance and encouragement from Major Cyril Wilson. I should like here specially to mark the very considerable debt which modern historians in many different fields owe to Major Wilson, the late Mrs Stevenson and their family both for preserving the Wilson Papers and for making them available to scholars. This, too, would not be possible without the expert care and preservation provided by Mr Roderick Suddaby and his splendid staff in the Department of Documents at the Imperial War Museum, which is always a most congenial place in which to work. Mr Suddaby and the Imperial War Museum have given very great assistance indeed and have done much to lighten the sometimes heavy burden of working at some distance from home. The quotation of material from the Wilson papers is by permission of the Trustees of the Imperial War Museum. Crown copyright material is reproduced by permission of the Controller of Her Majesty's Stationery Office. I must also thank the following persons who have kindly granted permission for the quotation of other copyright material: the Earl of Cavan, Lord Chetwode, Major A. C. J. Congreve, the Earl of Derby, the Earl Haig, Miss Phyllis Maurice and Sir Austin Robinson, Mr Rupert Murdoch, Mr W. N. Radcliffe, Mr M. A. F. Rawlinson, Lord Sackville and Mr Hugh Sackville-West.

It is not feasible to name all those many people who have helped me with this volume, but a few require special mention. The idea for an edition of Wilson papers came from John Gooch, who has provided constant advice and criticism, as well as much recondite information about dead Italian generals, a little of which is in the Biographical Notes. My colleagues at the Ulster Polytechnic, shortly to be transformed into the University of Ulster, particularly Professor A. J. Anthony Morris, Paul Arthur and Philip Ollerenshaw, have made many valuable suggestions, and forbearingly tolerated my apparently obsessive interest in Henry Wilson. The Polytechnic itself has underwritten my research expenses with generous financial support. Sandra Maxwell and Jacqueline Darrah coped admirably with the typing. Peter Boyden of the National Army Museum helped with obscure references. Dr Christopher Shorley of Queen's University assisted with translation. In London, Lindsay Duguid, John Murray-Browne and Jacquey Visick provided extraordinarily agreeable accommodation. The maps were drawn by my wife, Sally Visick, who has done very much more than that to see the project through to completion.

The Army Records Society, of which this is the first volume to be published, owes its existence to the enthusiasm and energy of John Gooch, together with the hard work of the founding Council and the invaluable assistance of our Appeal Committee, whose particular contribution has been to help in providing an endowment for the Society. Field Marshal Lord Harding and Sir Denis Hamilton have done more than anybody else to secure the Society's future. The pattern of the long-established Navy Records Society has unashamedly been followed. This volume in particular has been modelled on Professor Paul Halpern's exemplary editing of *The Keyes Papers*. Dr Nicholas Rodger, the secretary of the Navy Records Society, has unstintingly helped with the formation of the Society. It is to be hoped, however, that in the future the Army Records Society will develop its own style and character, but that its scholarly standing will soon equal that of its distinguished naval foster-parent.

Keith Jeffery Belfast August 1984

ABBREVIATIONS

(A)AG	(Assistant) Adjutant-General
ADC	aide-de-camp
ANZAC	Australia and New Zealand Army Corps
BEF	British Expeditionary Force
BGGS	Brigadier General, General Staff
Bn	Battalion
CGS	Chief of the General Staff
CIGS	Chief of the Imperial General Staff
CinC	Commander-in-Chief
CO	Colonial Office or Commanding Officer
CRE	Commander, Royal Engineers
(DA)QMG	(Deputy Assistant) Quarter-Master-General
DCIGS	Deputy Chief of the Imperial General Staff
(D)DMI	(Deputy) Director of Military Intelligence
DMO	Director of Military Operations
EEF	Egyptian Expeditionary Force
FM	Field Marshal
FO	Foreign Office
GHQ	General Headquarters
GOC(inC)	General Officer Commanding (-in-Chief)
GS	General Staff
GSO 1, 2	General Staff Officer, Grade 1, 2
IOR	India Office Records
IRA	Irish Republican Army
MA	Military Adviser or Attaché
MEF	Mesopotamian Expeditionary Force
MCC	Marylebone Cricket Club
MGO	Master-General of the Ordnance
MS	Military Secretary
MT	Military Transport
NCO	non-commissioned officer

PM	Prime Minister
PRO	Public Record Office
PS	Private Secretary
QMG	Quarter-Master-General
RA	Royal Artillery
RAF	Royal Air Force
RAMC	Royal Army Medical Corps
RASC	Royal Army Service Corps
RIC	Royal Irish Constabulary
RMC	Royal Military College
RN	Royal Navy
SAA	small arms ammunition
S of S	Secretary of State
SWC	Supreme War Council
TA	Territorial Army
TF	Territorial Force
WF	'With France'
WO	War Office

INTRODUCTION

Henry Hughes Wilson, the second of the four sons of James Wilson, was born on 5 May 1864 at the family home of Currygrane, near Ballinalee, county Longford.[1] He came from a middling family of Protestant Irish landlords who traced their ancestry back to a man reputed to have landed at Carrickfergus, county Antrim, in the suite of King William III in 1690. Four generations later, William Wilson, grandfather of Henry Hughes, using money amassed in the Belfast shipping trade, acquired substantial estates in the counties of Dublin, Westmeath and Longford. These he divided among his four sons, the youngest, James, receiving the property at Currygrane. It was not a very large estate. In 1878 it consisted of 1,158 acres valued at £835 a year.[2] But the Wilson family lived comfortably enough, dividing their time between Currygrane and a delightful eighteenth-century house called Frascati at Blackrock near Dublin.[3]

Henry Wilson began his education at home in the charge of a succession of French governesses from whom he gained a love of France and a useful knowledge of the French language. At the age of thirteen he was sent, like many other sons of the protestant 'Ascendancy', to an English public school: Marlborough College in Wiltshire. There he made no great academic impression. Indeed, at this stage he seems to have been a somewhat carefree youth, keener on games and sports—in which he excelled—than applied study. This was confirmed after his father removed him from the school in 1880 and engaged a series of crammers in order to get the boy into the army. But the effort was in vain. Between 1880 and 1882 Wilson twice failed to pass the entrance examination for Woolwich and three times failed that for Sandhurst.

At this time, however, there was another possible route into the army through the Militia; 'what used in those days to be called the back door'.[4] A Militia officer could gain a regular commission by successfully taking a competitive examination after undergoing two periods of training. This was not an unusual means of by-passing Woolwich or Sandhurst. Sir John French, for example, entered the army in this way. In December 1882 Henry Wilson was gazetted a lieutenant in the Longford Militia. In the summer of 1884 he passed the examination for direct commission and, after first being gazetted to the Royal Irish Regiment, joined the Rifle Brigade. Early in 1885 he was posted to the 1st Battalion, then stationed at Belgaum near Poona in India.

Regimental duties were not very onerous — tiger-shooting and polo figured prominently — but late in 1886 the battalion was moved to Burma to assist in suppressing dacoit guerrilla activity along the upper reaches of the Irrawaddy river. Here Wilson met Henry (later General Lord) Rawlinson, who became a life-long friend. Wilson's spell in Upper Burma was ended by a serious injury sustained when he attempted to arrest two dacoits. One of them attacked him with a previously-concealed dah, or sword-knife, severely wounding him over the right eye. He was invalided home and scarred for life. In November 1887 he returned to Ireland and remained on sick-leave for over a year.

While at home he determined to enter the Staff College and began serious academic study, which he persevered with after he returned to regimental duty, serving with the 2nd Battalion of the Rifle Brigade at Dover, Aldershot and Belfast. During his time on sick-leave, Wilson became unofficially engaged to Cecil Mary Wray of Ardnamona, county Donegal, whom he had known for some time. After he had passed the Staff College examination in 1891, he married Miss Wray, who remained a constant and active support for the rest of Wilson's life. Sadly, they never had any children. The Staff College course lasted two years, during which Wilson developed a particular taste for battlefield tours. In March 1893 he visited north-east France to inspect the scene of the 1870 Franco-Prussian War. Rawlinson, who in India had been aide-de-camp to the Commander-in-Chief, Lord Roberts, was a fellow student at the College. When Roberts came to Camberley for a visit, 'Rawly' introduced Wilson to him. Roberts was impressed and thereafter acted as an important patron for the young officer.

After graduating from the Staff College, Wilson was promoted captain. At the end of 1894 he took up an appointment in the Intelligence Department of the War Office. At the age of thirty-one he was the youngest staff officer in the army. He was attached to the French section of the Department, which was responsible for military intelligence concerning not only France and French possessions overseas, but also Belgium, Italy, Spain, Portugal and all of Central and South America. Wilson seems especially to have enjoyed the political aspects of his work and the frequent liaison with the Foreign Office. Indeed, in later years his real metier was to be in 'staff work', particularly the exposition and analysis of high policy and grand strategy. Yet the duties of a junior in the War Office—desk-bound work in a grossly under-staffed department—also had their tedious side and, when offered the brigade-majorship of the 3rd Infantry Brigade at Aldershot in 1897, he accepted the post with alacrity.

Following valuable experience in the War Office, one of the coveted Aldershot brigade-majorships was certain to advance Wilson's career. But he also longed to see some active service. Ruefully he watched contemporaries—including Rawlinson—take part in the Nile Expedition of 1897–98 and other colonial campaigns. Wilson, however, was soon to achieve his ambition. On the outbreak of the South African War in 1899, his brigade was sent to Natal as part of the Expeditionary Force. He saw action at the disastrous Battle of Colenso during 'Black Week' in December 1899, and also the British defeat at Spion Kop in January 1900. The reverses at the end of 1899 brought a change in the high command. Lord Roberts was put in charge of the British forces in South Africa. For Wilson this was excellent news. His brigade commander, moreover, Major-General (Sir) Neville Lyttleton, had also formed a high opinion of Wilson's abilities, both administrative and in the field.

From February 1900 onwards the tide of the South African War turned in favour of the British. In a series of counter-attacks Roberts secured Cape Colony and at the beginning of June he occupied the Boer capital of Pretoria. The Natal Force, with Wilson's brigade, had meanwhile relieved Ladysmith and joined up with Roberts' troops. In August Roberts took Wilson on to his headquarters staff, first as DAQMG, and later as his own assistant military secretary. In Pretoria Wilson and Rawlinson (then AAG) shared a house with Major-General Sir William (later Lord) Nicholson and Lord Stanley (later the Earl of Derby), both of whom were to be valuable friends to Wilson in the future.

Wilson returned to England with Lord Roberts (who was taking up the post of Commander-in-Chief) in January 1901. He was awarded the DSO for his services in South Africa and in December promoted brevet-lieutenant-colonel. Throughout 1901 he worked with the 'little Chief'. From this time onwards he became less of a subordinate than a friend and confidant to the Field Marshal, who in turn acted almost as a second father to him. Wilson also began to widen his circle of acquaintances. Already he had struck up a friendship with Leopold Amery, editor of *The Times History of the South African War* (which Wilson helped him with) and a Conservative MP from 1911. Amery was one of Wilson's principal early links with the wider world of politics, and in particular that of the Conservative and Unionist Party, with which the young Protestant Irish soldier had a natural affinity.

Since a War Office rule laid down that after five years on the staff an officer must return to regimental duty or command, in February 1902 Wilson took charge of the 9th Provisional Battalion at Colchester, one of the units temporarily created to provide drafts for South Africa. For exactly a year he retained the post and seems to have had a successful and agreeable time as a battalion commanding officer. In February 1903, however, when the unit was disbanded, Roberts brought Wilson back to the War Office to join Rawlinson in the newly-created department of military education and training where they principally worked on a *Manual of Combined Training*. At the end of the year Rawlinson was appointed Commandant of the Staff College, while Wilson became AAG with special responsibility for education.

The South African War, which had rudely exposed many

deficiencies in the British army, both operational and administrative, was followed by a period of army and War Office reform.[5] In 1904 a committee headed by Lord Esher recommended the establishment of an Army Council, a general staff, more or less along contemporary Continental lines, and the reorganisation of departmental responsibilities within the War Office along clear logical principles. The government accepted Esher's report, the post of Commander-in-Chief was abolished—Lord Roberts effectively dismissed—and the new office, 'Chief of the General Staff' (the 'imperial' was not added until 1909), was given to Sir Neville Lyttleton. Under the new regime, Wilson secured an influential position as second-in-command in the Directorate of Staff Duties,[6] responsible for the Staff College, the training and appointment of staff officers, together with Sandhurst and Woolwich. An important innovation which he introduced was the 'General Staff Ride'. This exercise was favoured by the Germans for developing both staff expertise and strategic doctrines. In later years Wilson strongly championed the use of similar 'war games' and simulation exercises as an effective method of military education.

The British General Staff did not suddenly come into being. It took over five years and two Secretaries for War—Arnold-Forster and Haldane—before the new organisation was fully established. In the War Office between 1904 and 1906 Henry Wilson worked assiduously to develop a powerful and efficient staff organisation. He met with some success, although when he changed jobs at the end of 1906 he noted in his diary an 'incomplete and unsatisfied endeavour to get a number of useful and necessary reforms carried out'.[7]

In January 1907 Wilson, with the rank of brigadier-general, succeeded Rawlinson as Commandant of the Staff College at Camberley. Lyttleton had only grudgingly assented to the appointment. Despite their earlier closeness, the two men had drifted apart. Lyttleton mistrusted Wilson's continued close friendship with the now retired Roberts, while Wilson had become exasperated with Lyttleton's indecisiveness while CGS. Wilson, however, was strongly backed for the Camberley job, not only by Roberts, but also by Nicholson (now QMG), Lord Esher and Sir John French. Wilson's backers were fully justified by the striking success he achieved as Commandant. The post admirably fitted his gifts as a teacher: his infectious enthusiasm, his ready wit and his genius for lecturing. At the College he laid special emphasis on practical exercises, such as staff tours and battlefield visits to the Continent. Above all, he sensibly saw the chief role of the Staff College as being to inculcate into the British army a readiness for war. One aspect of this was his keen advocacy of compulsory military service in Great Britain. Lord Roberts, President of the National Service League, was a leading proponent of conscription. Wilson assisted him in preparing speeches in favour of the policy, so much so that his partisanship of a policy not favoured by the Liberal government was criticised in the press. Wilson was beginning to be noticed outside the army.

During his time at the Staff College, Henry Wilson became increasingly convinced that a European conflict between France and Germany was inevitable. In these circumstances he also believed that Britain's duty was to stand side by side with France—an opinion widely shared among the General Staff, although by no means with the same fervour as Wilson. From the beginning of 1906 the Staff began a desultory series of contacts with their French opposite numbers in order to work out arrangements for deploying a British expeditionary force on the Continent. Wilson took no part in these early moves, but they certainly met with his full approval. On a number of occasions he used both Staff College tours of the 1870 battlefields and private visits to north-east France to familiarise himself with the Franco-Belgian and Franco-German frontiers. Over a period of years he reconnoitred virtually every possible route by which the Germans could enter France. He also sought to cement Anglo-French cooperation by making contact with General Ferdinand Foch, Commandant of the *École Supérieure de Guerre* in Paris and his opposite number in the French army. In December 1909 the two men met for the first time. They soon developed a close alliance and deep friendship which lasted for the rest of Wilson's life.

The Staff College appointment was normally for four years. In 1910, therefore, Wilson began to think about his future career. Mindful that he ought to broaden his experience with a period of command, he accepted (subject to War Office approval) the command of a brigade at Aldershot. But Sir William Nicholson—'Old Nick'—who succeeded Lyttleton as CGS in 1908—had other plans, and in June Wilson was appointed Director of Military Operations in the War Office. He left Camberley at the beginning of August after a series of farewell dinners at which speech after speech demonstrated that he had been personally one of the most popular, best-loved and respected Commandants in the history of the College.

Wilson's four years in charge of the Directorate of Military Operations were very largely devoted to perfecting Anglo-French military co-operation. On taking up his new office he discovered that no detailed plans had been made for the mobilisation and despatch of an expeditionary force to the Continent. He therefore immediately set himself to rectify the omission. Wilson visited France often, meeting senior generals and politicians. He cultivated Sir Arthur Nicolson, Permanent Under-Secretary at the Foreign Office, who shared his conviction that the British army might have to intervene across the Channel. The 'Agadir Crisis' during the summer of 1911, when war seemed probable, powerfully boosted work on what became known as the 'W.F.' ('With France') scheme,[8] which provided for the deployment of the British Expeditionary Force (BEF) on the left flank of the main French army. By mid-1911 Henry Wilson had emerged as one of the principal protagonists of the 'Continental Commitment'. In August Colonel Hankey (Secretary to the Committee of Imperial Defence), who did not himself much favour the commitment, observed to the First Lord of the Admiralty that Wilson had 'a perfect obsession for military operations on the Continent. He spends his holidays bicycling up and down the Franco-German frontier.'[9] Wilson, however, brilliantly vindicated his 'obsession' when invited to put his views before the Committee of Imperial Defence on 23 August 1911. Among those present were Asquith, Lloyd George, Haldane, Churchill and Sir Edward Grey. Wilson graphically outlined his proposals for the Expeditionary Force and persuaded the Committee formally to approve a substantial military commitment to France.[10]

Throughout 1912 Wilson's department pressed on with the W.F. scheme. Inevitably the detailed planning of transporting the 150,000-strong BEF across the Channel took up a very great deal of time. Wilson was encouraged by the wholehearted support of Sir John French who became CIGS in March 1912, but he worried about the attitude of Belgium, through which he assumed a German advance into France would probably pass. Anglo-Belgian talks, however, came to nothing since the Belgians were reluctant to jeopardise their relations with Germany by aligning themselves too closely with Britain and France. Still assisting Roberts with his campaign for compulsory national service, Wilson was also concerned about the size of the army. He believed that voluntary recruitment could never provide sufficient numbers of troops. In pushing the case for conscription Wilson extended his contacts among Opposition politicians. During the summer of 1912 he began regularly to meet the leader of the Unionist Party, Bonar Law, and some of his colleagues, A. J. Balfour, Lord Milner, Walter Long and others, whom he impressed with his own military and strategic views. He continued, of course, to do likewise with government ministers. He found both Lloyd George and Winston Churchill sympathetic to the idea of conscription. But, however keen senior politicians might have been, there was no real public enthusiasm for compulsory service and the measure was not adopted until after the war had begun.

Wilson continued with detailed planning for the Expeditionary Force in 1913, but he no longer had to press for acceptance of the principle of continental commitment and he was able to delegate much of the tedious, though vitally necessary, work on the fine detail to his subordinates. As well as his frequent trips to France he was able to travel more widely than before. In September and October 1912 he toured Central and Eastern Europe, visiting Berlin, Warsaw, St Petersburg, Moscow and Vienna. A year later he went to the Balkans and Turkey. In November 1913, at the age of forty-nine, he was promoted to major-general, marking a rise from the rank of captain in only twelve years.

While the European political scene darkened and a major war progressively became more likely, in 1913 and 1914 Wilson and the army were troubled by a problem nearer to home: Ireland. Early in 1913 the Asquith government had decided to introduce a measure for Irish Home Rule. Unionists in Ireland responded vigorously, mobilising under Sir Edward Carson powerful support in Westminster and organising resistance, armed if necessary, in Ulster. Wilson was kept fully informed of developments in Ireland by his elder brother Jemmy (James MacKay Wilson) who was prominent in local politics and had contested county Longford in the Unionist interest in the 1885 and 1892 general elections. In the spring of 1913 Jemmy visited London with a deputation to Bonar Law and told his brother of the plans to resist home rule in the North of Ireland. A 'provisional government' would be established, backed up by 25,000 armed men of the Ulster Volunteer Force. 'As far as I can judge all very sensible', remarked Wilson in his diary.[11] He increasingly worried that the army might be used to crush what he genuinely believed to be the legitimate political aspirations of his fellow-countrymen. This opinion was quite widely shared throughout the army's officer corps. Wilson, nevertheless, was more deeply involved than most in the discussion of contingency plans which senior Unionists from both sides of the Irish Sea almost incessantly conducted during 1913-14. While Wilson's involvement may have raised him in the estimation of men like Bonar Law, F. E. Smith (later Lord Birkenhead) and Milner, it caused some comment within the army and made leading Liberal politicians distrust him.

For the army the 'Ulster Crisis' came to a head during the Curragh 'incident' in March 1914 when fifty-eight officers of the 3rd Cavalry Brigade at the Curragh Camp in county Kildare resigned their commissions rather than obey orders which they believed were aimed at coercing Ulster Unionists into a united Home Rule Ireland.[12] The leader of the so-called 'mutineers' was General Hubert Gough, commanding officer of the brigade, a southern Irish Protestant and a friend of Henry Wilson.

Throughout the crisis Wilson worked behind the scenes to support Gough's action and the Unionist cause generally. Moreover, while stressing to the Secretary for War, J. E. B. Seely, the seriousness of the crisis and the impossibility (in his view) of using the army to break the Ulster Unionists, Wilson also kept Opposition politicans fully informed of everything that happened in the War Office. On a number of occasions he considered resigning, although at one stage confided in his diary that 'I cannot think of a really good way of doing it'.[13]

Such an extreme action, threatened or otherwise, proved to be unnecessary. Gough and his fellow officers withdrew their resignations after they received written assurance from Seely and Sir John French that the army would not be employed to enforce the current Home Rule Bill on Ulster. Seely promised this without any authority from the Cabinet. Asquith afterwards publicly disowned the assurance and both Seely and French were obliged to resign. Seely's action, nevertheless, for the government effectively closed off the option of using military force to support its Irish policy against Ulster Unionist opposition. But before matters in Ireland came to a head again, events in Europe had supervened.

Wilson's equivocal role during the Curragh crisis enhanced his reputation for political intrigue. While Unionists thoroughly approved of him—Milner rather extravagantly declared that Wilson had 'saved the Empire'[14]—Liberals, naturally, did not. Although Wilson's fellow soldiers generally supported his actions, some were critical, believing especially that the Irishman was dabbling a little too much in politics. Hubert Gough's brother John—another general—felt so strongly that Wilson had merely 'led from behind' and had baulked at putting his own career on the line, that, from the time of the Curragh until his death on the Western Front in 1915, he never spoke to Wilson again.[15] Archibald Wavell, then a junior officer in the Directorate of Military Operations, after hearing Wilson declare that the army had done 'what the Opposition failed to do', complained to his father that the army had no right at all to become so involved in politics.[16] Wilson could not agree since he believed that the politicians, not the soldiers, had caused all the trouble in the first place with their wretched Irish policy. A particular worry for Wilson was that the Ulster crisis and its effect on serving soldiers might jeopardise Britain's military commitment to France. Ironically, he himself was sent to Paris in April 1914 to reassure the French that the army was not in danger of disintegrating over Ireland. In this he was, of course, correct. When war came the Irish question temporarily faded into the background.

With the declaration of war on Germany in August 1914, Wilson became sub-Chief of the General Staff of the BEF under Sir Archibald Murray. Sir John French was the Commander-in-Chief. At the War Office Field Marshal Lord Kitchener was appointed Secretary of State and took immediate charge. Although tremendously popular with the general public, Kitchener was less well received within the army. His appreciation of the future—he was one of the few to anticipate a long war—and his immediate call for manpower on a massive scale, ran against accepted military wisdom. Henry Wilson particularly resented Kitchener's interference in the W.F. scheme and characteristically told him so. For some months relations remained cool between the two men. But, on the whole, the mobilisation of the BEF and its deployment in France progressed very well indeed. It was, perhaps, Wilson's greatest achievement.

None of Wilson's pre-war planning, however, had prepared either him or the BEF for the nightmare retreat from Mons in the face of the German offensive which began on 23 August. Murray's health broke down and Wilson effectively took charge of French's headquarters. Wilson also strove to maintain the close Anglo-French co-operation to which he attached such great importance. At the Marne in September the Germans ground to a halt and Joffre's great counter-strike turned them back. By mid-November, with the BEF settled in Flanders, the position had stabilised and the soldiers of both sides began to prepare for a longer war than had been anticipated. French was keen to replace Murray with Wilson. In December he raised the matter with Asquith and Kitchener. Both men opposed the appointment. Asquith mistrusted Wilson's *penchant* for intrigue and blamed him for much of the government's difficulties over Ireland. Kitchener felt that the promotion of Wilson would be objectionable to the many senior officers whom he believed disliked the Irishman. French, therefore, abandoned the idea and in January 1915 Murray was replaced by Sir William Robertson. Wilson was appointed to the new post of Chief Liaison Officer to the French Headquarters, with temporary promotion to lieutenant-general.[17]

Wilson told his wife that his duties would be 'pretty much what I like to make them', but would not greatly differ from what he had already been doing.[18] A lot of his time was spent smoothing relations between the British Commander-in-Chief and his French counterpart, General Joffre. There was no co-ordinated system of Allied command, and while Joffre assumed that he commanded all troops in France, Sir John French jealously guarded the independence of his authority. It was a fruitful source of friction, and also frustration for the intensely Francophil Wilson, who began to favour the notion of some supreme Allied command structure.

One of the chief difficulties in the Anglo-French military relationship was the persistent French belief that the British were not fully pulling their weight on the Western Front. The French High Command continually called for more British troops, which in Wilson's view could only be supplied through the introduction of conscription. The French also resented any dispersion of effort in 'sideshows', such as the costly Gallipoli expedition. But Gallipoli reflected a certain desperation among politicians and generals. With apparent stalemate in France and Flanders, policymakers cast about for any alternative means of defeating Germany and her allies. The gradual realisation that it was going to be a long war—a view which Wilson had not held in 1914— also contributed to the healing of his relations with Kitchener and his at least partial rehabilitation in Asquith's eyes. It seems that neither man could afford to ignore as articulate a soldier as Henry Wilson.

In May 1915 Asquith formed a coalition government and brought into the Cabinet a number of the Unionist politicians who respected Wilson's views. In any case, Sir Henry—he was knighted in July—was never short of a lively opinion on current events, an attribute which many politicians apparently found attractive. This was certainly true of Lloyd George who began to develop a high opinion of Wilson's abilities. Sir Henry was also perhaps the best-informed man in the British army about French military thinking. Kitchener began to consult him regularly; Asquith gave him a private interview—'He listened very attentively and in the end was very civil';[19] and Wilson was invited to speak at a Cabinet meeting. In August he was offered the command of a corps, but he turned it down after French told him that both he and Kitchener particularly valued the liaison work and would prefer that Wilson continued in his existing position.

Meanwhile the war of attrition continued on the Western Front. In the late summer of 1915 Joffre promised victory after a fresh offensive. When it began Sir John French's forces at Loos gained some initial success, but the major French attack in Champagne made no significant progress. The whole enterprise turned out an expensive failure, which prompted changes among the high command. In December French, by now in indifferent health, was appointed Commander-in-Chief Home Forces and replaced at the head of the BEF by Sir Douglas Haig. There had been some gossip that Wilson, despite his relatively junior rank, might become CIGS, but in the end Robertson was given the post. Wilson could not continue as liaison officer for Haig. The two men did not get on well together and the new Commander-in-Chief regarded Wilson as a malicious intriguer.[20] On Kitchener's recommendation, and with Asquith's approval, Wilson was given command of the IVth Army Corps. He took over the Corps from his old friend Rawlinson on 22 December 1915.

Wilson held the command of IV Corps for almost exactly a year. It was not a very distinguished formation. Deployed around Béthune, his troops saw comparatively little action. During 1916 all British efforts were concentrated further south on the Somme. Wilson himself worked hard at training and his celebrated lectures came to be much in demand. In May, when his immediate superior, General Monro, went on leave, Wilson temporarily took over command of the First Army. He gained a black mark when an enemy attack captured three-quarters of a mile of his line on the slopes of Vimy Ridge and a counter-attack failed to regain the position. Haig certainly seems to have counted this—among other things—against Wilson, for when Monro was posted to Mesopotamia in August Wilson was passed over for command of the Army. In October, moreover, the Corps was reduced to a headquarters only and put into the Reserve.

Throughout 1916 Wilson kept up his political contacts. Lloyd George, who became Secretary for War in July after Kitchener went down with the *Hampshire*, thought increasingly highly of Wilson, whom he afterwards described as having 'undoubtedly the nimblest intelligence amongst the soldiers of high degree . . . He had also a lucidity of mind and therefore of expression which was given to none of his professional rivals.'[21] The two men had much in common, although not their politics. They were both quick-witted, articulate and jesting, and found each other good company. They also shared a low opinion of Douglas Haig. Exasperated by the apparent feebleness of Asquith, Wilson came to believe that the war could only be won by a 'real fighting Government' under Lloyd George.[22] He was not the only person to hold this opinion. Dissatisfaction with Asquith's administration had been building up for some time and, in December 1915 after a short political crisis, Asquith resigned and Lloyd George formed a new coalition government.

Shortly before he became Prime Minister, Lloyd George had secured Cabinet agreement to Wilson's appointment as British military representative on a full-scale Anglo-French Mission to Russia. The job carried with it temporary promotion to full General and it marked the beginning of Wilson's rise to high military office in the train of Lloyd George. The purpose of the Mission was to investigate the supply of war material provided to Russia by Britain and France. But it stayed in Russia for only a comparatively short time during January and February 1917 and in retrospect the exercise was almost completely futile. The Mission left St Petersburg on the eve of the February Revolution. A fortnight after they arrived home the Czar abdicated. Although

Russia nominally remained in the war for some time, it could no longer realistically be counted as an asset to the Allied cause.

Immediately on his return Wilson was asked to become Chief Liaison Officer between Haig and Nivelle, the new French Commander-in-Chief. Relations were poor between the two, and this was proving to be a serious impediment to Nivelle's planned spring offensive in Champagne. After some reflection, Wilson agreed to take the post and succeeded remarkably in promoting Anglo-French co-operation. But the Nivelle offensive failed badly, setting off widespread mutiny in the French army. Nivelle was sacked in favour of Pétain, whom Wilson found much less accessible than his predecessor. The new Commander-in-Chief characterised Wilson as a Nivellite. Wilson, for his part, mistrusted Pétain's cautious, not to say pessimistic, outlook. Even Foch felt that Wilson would do no good by remaining Liaison Officer and so in June he resigned the appointment.

For the next two months Wilson was unemployed, on half-pay. He felt himself that if he remained without a job for very long he might get 'into mischief'. Yet he ridiculed a suggestion that he might enter Parliament. Wilson was not yet ready to join the 'Frocks'.[23] Lord Milner, who was a member of the War Cabinet, begged him to be patient and assured him that employment equal to his abilities would soon be found. Wilson meanwhile went home to Ireland for the first time since before the war. There he found widespread nationalism and anti-British sentiments. Acutely conscious of the pressing need for men in France, Wilson thought that conscription (effective in Great Britain since 1916) should be applied in Ireland. Not only would it fill depleted British ranks but he believed it would also help to counteract the growing strength of Sinn Féin, the Irish republican movement.

Another problem which exercised him at this time was the old difficulty of co-ordinating Allied policy. Late in August he pressed Lloyd George to establish some some sort of inter-Allied body to supervise policy at a high level. Lloyd George, who as usual was restlessly searching for some way out of the continual, and to his mind needless, slaughter on the Western Front, was taken with the idea, which he thought might at least make the prosecution of the war more efficient. He also seems to have regarded it as a possible way of supplanting either or both of Robertson and Haig whom he personally held responsible for the inconclusive progress of the war in the West.

In late August Wilson turned down an offer from Lord Derby (Secretary for War) to join a mission to the USA on the grounds that he felt he could not work with the head of the mission, Lord Northcliffe. At the beginning of September, however, he accepted the Eastern Command at home from Robertson. With its headquarters in London, Wilson remained at the centre of affairs. He was, moreover, left with a considerable amount of free time. At this stage in the war domestic Commands (apart from Ireland) involved no very onerous duties. During the autumn of 1917 Wilson in effect became a regular, though unofficial, military adviser to Lloyd George. In October the serious Italian reverse at Caporetto brought the matter of Allied co-ordination to a head. A conference was hastily organised at Rapallo in early November. Here Lloyd George secured French and Italian agreement to the creation of a Supreme War Council. It was to comprise two representatives from each Great Power, together with Permanent Military Representatives. Lloyd George and Milner were the political members; Wilson was nominated to the military post. All plans were to be submitted to the new body for approval. Robertson, thus, had to forward British proposals to Wilson who in turn would present them to the Council for consideration in the light of inter-Allied needs.

The Supreme War Council was located at Versailles, where Wilson quickly set up a staff. His relations with the War Office began awkwardly since Robertson, with reason, resented the new institution. He realistically asserted afterwards that the politicians' object in setting up the Council 'was not so much to provide effective unity of military command as to acquire for themselves a greater control over the military chiefs'.[24] For Lloyd George one of the strongest arguments in favour of the Council was that he could use it to circumvent the gruff and inarticulate CIGS in favour of the more congenial advice proffered by Wilson, who was much more the Welshman's type of man than Robertson.

Over the turn of the year 1917–18, the Supreme War Council completed much useful, mostly prosaic, work towards the promotion of an efficient and well co-ordinated Allied war effort. Little of this was particularly contentious, but in January 1918 Wilson developed a scheme for a general reserve of troops for the entire Western sphere—not just France and Flanders—which provoked a lively debate on the question of who should control it. Wilson believed that the reserve should come under a single authority—Versailles—while Robertson forcefully argued that it should be commanded by the CIGS and his counterparts in other countries. Early in February, with Lloyd George powerfully in favour, the Council accepted Wilson's plan amd set up an 'executive War Board', comprising the Permanent Military Representatives, to control the General Reserve of troops for the whole of the armies on the Western, Italian and Balkan Fronts.[25] Robertson refused to work under this new arrangement. He also rejected the suggestion that he might become Military Representative at Versailles while Wilson took his place in London. His intransigence gave Lloyd George the opportunity to replace him. Although the Prime Minister offered the post of CIGS to Sir Herbert Plumer (who unhesitatingly declined) it seems that he really wanted Wilson. After a week of confusion and indecision, Sir Henry Wilson was appointed Chief of the Imperial General Staff with effect from 18 February 1918.

1918

1918

Very few letters survive in the Wilson papers which refer specifically to his taking office as CIGS. Perhaps the circumstances did not conduce to congratulations, or even very much comment. The letter from Foch [Document 1], however, clearly demonstrates the satisfaction with which many French leaders greeted the appointment. Foch remained one of Wilson's closest military friends, and after he became General-issimo in March 1918, his co-operation with Wilson for the rest of the war—although not entirely untroubled—represented the apotheosis of that Anglo-French alliance on which they had both worked before 1914.

At the Supreme War Council Wilson was succeeded as Permanent Military Representative by Sir Henry Rawlinson [2], whose conception of the General Reserve, however, does not seem to have been quite the same as Wilson's. A letter from Sackville-West, whom Rawlinson inherited as chief of staff at Versailles, reflects both this and some of the strains within the British high command [4]. Rawlinson was suspect in Sackville-West's eyes because of his apparent closeness to Haig. This does not seem to have troubled Wilson whose own relations with Haig, for the most part at least, were quite amicable. Haig, indeed, told Rawlinson 'how much easier he found it' with Wilson as CIGS, 'instead of Wullie'.[1] One of the main concerns which Haig and Wilson shared during March 1918 was the problem of supplying manpower to the Western Front, especially in view of an anticipated German push [6, 7]. Manpower remained a major worry for what turned out to be the last year of the war [11, 19, 25, 29]. It was widely assumed that the conflict would continue until 1919, or even 1920, and the steady Allied advance which began in August [26] caught many people by surprise. In September London were still so anxious to conserve manpower [29] that Sir Douglas Haig believed they must have some ulterior motive. As late as mid-October even Wilson thought that the German army was '*not* beaten' [34].

The great German spring offensive which began on 21 March 1918

[8, 9, 11] drove the Allied forces back almost to the limits of the German advance in 1914. So serious was the reverse that the British at last agreed to the establishment of a unified command with General Foch as Commander-in-Chief of the Allied Armies. We find Wilson thereafter dealing directly with his old friend [12, 13] and in August once more taking on the role he had played four years before in reassuring the French of Great Britain's full commitment to the Allied war effort [27]. Another aspect of inter-Allied co-operation was the urgent need to utilise fresh American manpower to stiffen the front line [17]. Wilson, too, had to deal with occasional problems arising from the employment of Australian troops, even after the Armistice [22, 36, 37, 38, 40, 41, 43].

Manpower difficulties also lay behind the 'Maurice case' during April and May 1918.[2] Sir Frederick Maurice, who was DMO until April 1918, strongly disapproved of Lloyd George's war policy and thought that the Prime Minister had deliberately starved Haig of men. This, he believed, had left the British forces vulnerable, a fact strikingly demonstrated by the initial success of the German offensive. In April both Lloyd George and Bonar Law defended the government's policy in the House of Commons, prompting Maurice, after ascertaining opinion in France, to complain to Wilson [19]. The CIGS did not apparently respond and so on 6 May Maurice wrote to the press. This letter certainly provoked a flurry of excitement [21]. On 9 May Asquith moved a vote of censure in the Commons. Although it appears that there was some truth in Maurice's specific assertions, and also that Lloyd George deliberately misled Parliament during the 9 May debate, the government comfortably defeated the censure motion and Maurice was discredited. He was retired from the army and never got the posting to command a division in France for which Wilson had recommended him [5].

Staffing and appointments was one of the matters Wilson busied himself with. In one respect—the problem of Sir William Robertson's future [13, 15]—this reflected the slightly awkward circumstances accompanying Wilson's appointment as CIGS. King George V, moreover, had a high opinion of Robertson and had not favoured his replacement by Wilson.[3] Following the change of CIGS the King continued to take a keen interest in Sir William [14, 16] who at the end of May succeeded Lord French as Commander-in-Chief, Home

Forces. Another aspect of the CIGS's functions—and one which suited Wilson very well—was the giving of advice on large questions of strategy and military policy. Wilson thus had to balance the needs of the Western Front with those of the campaigns in Italy, the Middle East and elsewhere [10, 21, 30, 34].

One far-flung commitment lay in Russia [23, 24, 31]. Allied troops intervened in various parts of the former Russian Empire during 1918 in order to sustain so far as was possible those anti-Bolshevik forces committed to war against the Central Powers.[4] The Russian Bolsheviks formally withdrew from the war with the Treaty of Brest-Litovsk on 3 March 1918 and this released German troops for service in the West. The spring offensive seemed to confirm the importance of reviving the Eastern Front. But in the end intervention did nothing to assist the prosecution of the war. What it did do was to embroil the Allies in domestic Russian politics and enlarge the scale of the civil war between the Reds and the Whites.

During September and October 1918 both the Allied armies on the Western Front and Sir Edmund Allenby's Egyptian Expeditionary Force in the Middle East began to advance strongly. Yet, reflecting a continual wartime worry that the British were too involved in 'sideshows' even as late in the war as October, Clemenceau opposed the deployment of any additional resources in the Middle East [32]. But as the war against Turkey moved to a close—the Turks sued for an armistice at the end of October—Allenby began to encounter the problems of rival regional ambitions—French, Arab, Zionist and British—which were to bedevil the establishment of a lasting post-war settlement [33, 44]. This was also true for Sir George Milne (GOC of the British Salonika Force) whose first impressions from Constantinople indicated some of the likely future difficulties [45].

In the West, after a brief pause for congratulation [39, 42], Wilson and his colleagues had to begin tackling the problems of the peace. As soon as the war ended Lloyd George called a general election, the first since 1910. During the campaign he promised that there would be a rapid demobilisation of the armed services. With the ending of hostilities soldiers themselves naturally expected to be sent home as soon as possible. But from the army's point of view substantial forces were required to secure the peace and Wilson thought that conscription should be extended [47, 48]. So, as had been the case during the war, the problem of supplying manpower to meet Britain's manifold responsibilities continued to exercise the army during the peace.

I

General Foch to Wilson

[Holograph]   20.2.18

Je vois dans les journaux que les projets de M. Lloyd George se réalisent et sont approuvés. Ce n'est pas sans une grande satisfaction de ma part. Elle est encore plus grande du fait que vous devenez Chef d'Etat M^{or} Impérial. Notre entente continue, en particulier dans les circonstances difficiles me laisse penser qu'il en sera de même, dans l'avenir et surtout si ces circonstances se reproduisaient.

Pour le moment je pense qu'il faut *sans perdre une minute* nous mettre *tous* en travail à Versailles, et en liaison avec les Commandants en Chef. Qu'il faut dans ce but voir arriver sans retard le Gal Rawlinson à Versailles, s'il est désigné.

Qu'il nous faut avoir à Versailles des officiers de liaison sûrs, intelligents et actifs pour communiquer avec le M^{al} Haig et tel qu'était le Gal Wilson avec le M^{al} French en 1914.

Dans une autre ordre d'idées, je vous demande de hâter le retour d'Italie, des troupes que vous en faites revenir, et de me tenir au courant des dates de leurs mouvements afin que je puisse faire préparer le transport de certaines troupes françaises qui auraient également à en revenir[1] . . .

[I see from the newspapers that Mr. Lloyd George's plans are being carried out and gaining approval. This gives me great satisfaction—the more so because you are to be Chief of the Imperial General Staff. Our sustained mutual understanding, particularly in difficult circumstances, gives me reason to believe that it will continue in the same way in the future, especially if similar circumstances were to recur.

24

For the moment I think we must *all* set to work at Versailles *without wasting any time*, in collaboration with the Commanders in Chief. With this end in view we must see General Rawlinson at Versailles without delay, if he is designated. And at Versailles we must have reliable, intelligent and energetic liaison officers to communicate with Marshal Haig—officers who will conduct themselves as General Wilson did with Marshal French in 1914.

On another subject, I would request you to expedite the return of the troops you are bringing back from Italy, and to keep me informed of the dates of their movements, so that I can have preparations made for the transport of a certain number of French troops who would also have to come back from there[1] . . .]

2

Wilson to General Sir Henry Rawlinson

[Carbon]   London
                                                    1st March, 1918

I got your telephone message this morning which the "Lord"[2] gave me and I see you expect to be at G.H.Q. tomorrow or Sunday.

I shall be anxious to hear what the C.-in-C. [Haig] says about being relieved by those two Belgian Divisions. I have not written to him myself, because I think it might complicate matters as you are already dealing with the subject, and I think a windfall of that description might fairly fall to the General Reserve.

I have already discussed your establishment with some of the Army Council and directly the official paper begins to circulate I will push about and try to get it through.

As regards Plumer's return,[3] there will still be some little delay in recalling him, because he is engaged, or will be within a few days, on certain operations for which he is responsible, and therefore it seems to me that, for the moment, both he and Tim Harington will have to remain in Italy. I daresay another week or ten days will see them back at Cassel.[4]

I think that we must be a little cautious about speaking over this telephone, because I got another hint today that the French tap all our messages. I will see if we cannot get something much more direct than we have at present; in fact, as I write I hear that, amongst other people, our telephone wire passes through the French War Office exchange . . .

3

Wilson to General Diaz

[Carbon]   1st March 1918

You will have heard that I have succeeded General Robertson as Chief of the Staff in London.

I was personally opposed to the change, as I looked upon Versailles as my own child and was most anxious to remain there until the end of the war; however the authorities thought otherwise and I had to obey orders . . .

4

Major-General Sackville-West to Wilson

Supreme War Council,
British Section,
Versailles.

[Holograph]   March 5 [1918] 10 p.m.

Rawly has just come back from G.H.Q. full of the idea of calling a meeting of the M[ilitary]. R[epresentative]s. tomorrow to discuss the question of the "General Reserve". Well this may or may not be a good idea I don't yet know what resolution he may or may not want to put *but* the idea is not his but either D.H.'s or more likely Bob Whigham's, who was there and who is coming to stay tomorrow. I want to show you the difficulties with which you are going to be confronted — Honestly I am doubtful whether R.

ought to stay here. I saw Boy Capel and he confirmed what has been long in my mind that the Tiger⁵ never meant what you meant by the General Reserve but *manpower* and that is what I fancy L.G. meant: otherwise all that talk at the last meeting of the S[upreme]. W[ar]. C[ouncil]. in Paris really if you read it is incomprehensible. The Tiger is convinced that the offensive is imminent and therefore is not prepared to "hamper" the two C. in C.'s.⁶ There was much nonsense talked at the Ex. Board⁷ conference yesterday and I foresee much more. Meanwhile do you think it wise to have the S.W.C. in London with the possibility of the offensive beginning in the middle it will be like the news of Napoleon's escape from Elba reaching the Conference at Vienna! But what I want to urge on you now is that Rawly cannot be in a position to give any independent advice if he is so lié with D.H. I am inclined to think he is better employed in commanding the IV Army?

March 6

As an instance of what I have said before re G.H.Q.: R. sent by the open Rolls to D.H. the other day his complete files of the minutes of the S.W.C. Session—now strictly speaking these minutes are his personal property and I pointed that out and said he could do as he liked but I could not send the office copies—on getting to G.H.Q. they were all copied—now I know I am loyal to any master I serve and I am loyal and like Rawly but as this seems to make my point I tell you though of course I know you won't mention it to R. or my position would become difficult.

He is now issuing suggestions to the other M.R's. of a modification of the Executive war board—these really amount to little more than the powers the M.R's. always have had & a certain control of such Reserve Divisions as may at any time be available. This last seems quite impracticable but D.H. agrees—
Perhaps I'm becoming unduly suspicious . . .

5

Wilson to Field Marshal Sir Douglas Haig

[Holograph copy] 7.3.18.

Many thanks for your letter received last night. I delayed answering until I had seen Peyton. We have had a long talk and he knows all that I do about the subject of circulation of promotion and so, as he will explain it all, I won't burden you with a letter. I think both Whigham and Maurice would do well as Divisional Generals, and really of the two I think Maurice would almost be the best. He is a gallant fellow and in some ways has more sides to him than Whigham. If you will agree to this I shall have to [illegible] for two men to replace them. The two that I should like would be Tim Harington and P. de B. Radcliffe. Tim to succeed Whigham and thus become an Army Councillor and Radcliffe to succeed Maurice. I know I am asking for two amongst the best Staff Officers in your Armies but I am really doing it as much in your interest — I mean the interest of the Army in France — as for any selfish motive. I am afraid Plumer will never call me "Harry" again! and yet it will be a rise for Tim both in standing and in pay and we shall have the benefit of Tim's great experience and knowledge and be able to help all the more. All I have said about Tim applies also to Radcliffe. But I have talked it all over with Peyton so he can tell you . . .

6

Wilson to Haig

[Holograph copy] 18.3.18.
Private

I am a little nervous of all this praise and newspaper boasting about our aeroplanes, our guns, the strength of our positions, the inferiority of the Boches etc. etc. I am a little nervous of the effect this has, and will have, on the recruiting, because it leads quite naturally to men—and employers—thinking that we are quite safe and quite sure to win the war and that no great effort on their part in working in Munitions, in Mines and in the Shipyards is necessary.

It leads also to constant demands being made to withdraw men from the Army in France, for Munitions, for Shipbuilding, as Clerks, Civil Servants etc., in the belief that you can easily spare them. The truth being, of course, the exact opposite, viz. that you are deplorably short, dangerously short, of men and that the workers at home are only putting in half, or at most threequarters, time.

Will you think this over and if you agree will you ponder what we can do? . . .

7

Haig to Wilson

General Headquarters,
British Armies in France.

[Holograph]   20 Mar. 1918
Private

Yours of 18th

Only quite recently the W.O. told us that too much was being made of the enemy's possible offensive! People at home were being nervous etc.!!

Where does the happy mean lie? I have seen Macdonogh today and mentioned this to him, so you might have a talk with him. Also please remember many papers are read in the Trenches so we must not say our guns are insufficient.

Good luck to you . . .

8

Rawlinson to Wilson

British Military Representative,
Supreme War Council,
British Section,
Versailles.
22nd March, 1918.

I rang you up on the telephone this morning to tell you that we were very anxious to get the proposals arrived at yesterday by the Executive War Board sanctioned by the British Government as soon as possible. I hear they have already been approved by Clemenceau, and, in view of the situation on the Western Front, we want to get the divisions back from Italy as soon as possible.

The Bosche appears to have put in a really serious attack, (in which 37 of his divisions have already been identified) and which might well have penetrated deeper into our line than it actually has done. I hear, however, this morning that Goughy's line is back to the CROZAT CANAL, to which position he withdrew during the night.

There is a rumour started by an Alsatian deserter that the Bosche means to attack this morning with ten fresh divisions at the junction between the British and the French Armies, but, so far, there is no confirmation of this attack having been launched.

It is quite clear that the Bosche means to press here on the Western Front, and we shall be short of men before many months are past. I am, therefore, strongly opposed to undertaking further side-shows like Archangel and the Adriatic, which will make further claims upon our manpower.

I was unable to visit the Italian Front, as I had to come back in a hurry yesterday from Turin for a meeting of the Executive War Board, without which we could not have sent you the telegram which you received this morning. I am sorry, for I should much like to have seen the Italian Front.

However, I had a long talk both to Cavan and Maistre, who are quite confident that no Austrian attack will be made, and who take

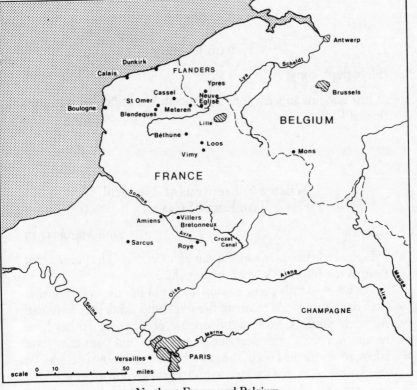

Northern France and Belgium

a very different view of the general situation there from that which Diaz expressed in far too pessimistic terms. Of course, he did this with the object of inducing us to leave all the French and British divisions in Italy, but, in view of the situation which is likely to supervene here in France, I am strongly of opinion that we must withdraw certainly two French and one British division, if not more.

* * *

9

Wilson to Haig

[Holograph copy]   24.3.18.

Just one line to wish you God speed. We will do all we can at this end . . .

10

Wilson to Lieutenant-General
The Earl of Cavan

[Carbon]   29th March 1918

I am a little uneasy about the situation in Italy. The picture that I see in the future is something like this:

We are presently going to stop these old Bosche in this terrific rush they have made to break the line, but I think they have had sufficient success, both in the amount of ground that they have recaptured and in the number of prisoners and guns they have taken, to justify the cost of the experiment to their own people. By that I mean—even if they fail to pull off a big 'coup' like the taking of AMIENS—they will still be able to claim sufficient victory to allow of the German people—and especially the German women—continuing the war. Now, if that is so, I think their next move will be—or in my judgment, at any rate, ought to be—an attack on Italy. They can do this by a serious increase to the number of Austrian Divisions, with an addition of say 10 or 15 of their own German Divisions.

I am not quite clear in my own mind whether, with our present distribution, we can withstand an attack of that sort.

I do not think that you were present when Plumer came down to Italy last November, and when I told him that, in my opinion, the best way to use the British and French troops would be to incorporate them with Italian troops, or if you like to put it the other way, to incorporate Italian troops with French and British, and the reason I gave Plumer in November for suggesting this course seems to me to hold equally good today. The reason was this: If we—that is to say we British and French—go together and hold a bit of the line the Bosche will take damn good care not to attack that particular bit of the line, but will fall on the parts of the line held by pure Italians, and my object in incorporating the Italians with ourselves and the French was to lengthen that part of the line over which we could exert an influence.

There seems no doubt that the bit of the line that we and the French are now taking over is a much more important bit than the Piava; it is in fact a part of the line which I urged Plumer to take over in November, but in spite of that the total front which we both occupy is exceedingly small compared with the total front on which the Bosche can attack. What then can we do to make our influence felt on a greater length of line than the one we are now taking over? I see no way of doing this except by the proposal which I have just made to you. Will you let me know what you think of this plan? If you agree with it, how do you think we ought to approach Diaz with a view to getting it carried out? . . .

II

Wilson to Haig

[Holograph copy]   30.3.18

The position seems to get increasingly steady though the strain on our poor divisions must be increasingly great, especially S. of the Somme until the French come up in greater weight. Maurice will tell you all our news and once we have got arrangements here *finally fixed* about combing out and about Ireland I hope to run over and pay you a visit. Does all go well with Foch? Can I help in any way?

Will you make sure about your communiqués reaching Paris at night in time for the next morning's newspapers; apparently the absence of such a communiqué one day shook the little Frenchmen to their foundations! I think this rain ought to help?

Don't dream of writing but tell Maurice your news so that we can help with all our weight. What are you doing with Goughie?[8] . . .

12

Wilson to Foch

[Copy]   17.4.18

My old friend,

I submit these notes for your consideration. I am only anxious that you should see the picture as I see it.

Ever
Henry

[Enclosure]

NOTE BY C.I.G.S. FOR GENERAL FOCH.

1. After our conversation this morning[9] I want to put the following on record:
2. It seems to me essential that we face the facts as they really are and that we look a little more into the future than we have been doing.
3. Two courses are open to us if the enemy challenge us in battle along our present line South and East of YPRES.

   (a) We can accept battle on our line of today.

(b) We can shorten our line by withdrawing altogether from where we now stand and gradually reach and hold a line with our left on the inundations of Aire—St. Omer—the Sea.

4. You favour (a).

5. That being so I think you must act in accordance with that decision and bring up sufficient troops to defeat all the enemy's attacks.

6. How many Divisions this will require I can't say nor can anyone except the enemy.

7. If he brings up 10, 15, 20, 30 divisions then you will have to bring up whatever number will be required to defeat the attacks of these divisions as they are brought into action.

8. But I think, if this is your policy and the decision rests with you, that you should so inform the Field Marshal[10] so that there may be no doubt in his mind as to your wishes. You will find that he will accept and carry them out in the most loyal manner.

9. Just one word more—General Plumer is of opinion that he cannot hold his present line much longer with the troops at present at his disposal if the enemy continues to attack as he has been doing.

The Field Marshal agrees—I do also.

I have already told you all this in conversation this morning but I think it right to repeat it here.

(Sd.) Henry Wilson.
C.I.G.S.

Blendecques[11]
17.4.18.
10.45 a.m.

13

Wilson to Haig

War Office
[Holograph copy]   17.4.18

I am anxious to hear what Foch said on his return from his visit to the Belgians today. In the very rough & hasty note I wrote to Foch this morning, copies of which I sent to you and Plumer, I tried to show the picture as I saw it after my conversation with him. It seemed to me that he was not taking a sufficiently long view of the situation, and in my opinion our present hand to mouth existence can only lead to disaster. I spoke to P.M. about Robertson and he agrees that if you would like to have a talk with him by all means do. I told him that I had suggested Robertson as a possible Chief of Staff or Q.M.G. but that you thought your present C.G.S. and Q.M.G. could not be bettered. Nor did you wish to give Robertson a command; and that being so I told P.M. that it was not easy to see how Robertson could be employed, but he quite agreed that if in spite of this you wished to talk matters over with him you were at full liberty to do so. As far as I am concerned I am absolutely indifferent. I do so hope that Foch will focus the present situation and see things as they *really* are. Tell me if there is any mortal thing I can do to help you . . .

14

Wilson to Colonel Clive Wigram

War Office
[Holograph copy]   18.4.18

There seems to be, from what I hear, some misapprehension about the inclination or wish on my part—or somebody's part—to make use of the services, in some capacity, of Sir W. Robertson. It is inferred that because Robertson is not employed in France the State is the poorer.

This may or may not be so, but his non-employment in France is not due to any fault at the W.O. He was offered to the C. in C. for a Command, as his Chief of the Staff, or as his Q.M.G. Sir Douglas did not see his way to putting him in any of these posts. Robertson's seniority precludes his employment in anything but the higher appointments.

I spoke to Sir Douglas about all this the day before yesterday and wrote again last night to ask him if he could think of anything else or if he would like Robertson to go out to talk matters over as between two old friends. I hope this is all clear.

One other thing. I gather from from Price Davies just now that the King was nervous lest I should withdraw some of our Divisions from Italy if I sent down some of our skeleton Divisions there. This was never in my mind . . .

15

Haig to Wilson

General Headquarters,
British Armies in France.

[Holograph]   Sat. Morning
Personal   20 Ap. 18

Many thanks for yours of 17th which reached me last night.

Foch has ordered more French Divisions to our 2nd Army and intends to hold the present positions, and to retake "the foot hills" if it possibly can be done i.e. Neuve Chapelle [corrected by Wilson to 'Eglise'] Spanbroekmolen, Meteren etc.

Our IXth Corps is being entirely relieved by French troops.

This is all satisfactory.

As regards Robertson, he has written me that "I (R) can conceive nothing you could offer me or that I could appropriately and usefully accept" . . . "I specially wish to avoid anything of the nature of a faked billet".[12]

Then I wired and asked him to stay for a few days, but have

received no reply.—I don't know what else is to be done for him . . .

16

Wilson to Wigram

[Holograph copy]   21.4.18

Many thanks for your letter.[13] I am glad the King knows the facts as to the question of Robertson's employment in France. I confess I know of no sects, schisms, or dissensions in the General Staff, even though some people and some newspapers conceive it to be their patriotic duty to insult Robertson and me alternatively.

Because he and I sometimes differ in our honest military opinion it does not necessarily follow that either of us is a blackleg . . .

17

The Earl of Derby to Wilson

General Headquarters
British Armies in France
[Holograph]   21.4.18
Confidential

My dear Long Job,[14]

Pershing was here when I arrived and stayed the night. He is I think quite genuine in his wish to help, and he and D.H. have come to an arrangement with regard to the brigading of his troops with ours which is satisfactory to both—but I am certain you have got to leave it to Pershing to say *when* he considers the troops sufficiently trained to take them out for his American army. I had a private talk with him and found him very firm as to his having this power. I don't think you need be afraid of his being in a great hurry to do this as he sees very clearly how bad his generals and their various staffs are, and therefore he will be anxious to leave them under our people. He was very frank about this.

Well I hate leaving the War Office and can't help feeling that I have been pushed out. I may like my new job, but if I don't I shall not hesitate in chucking it. I haven't been treated with much consideration but I suppose Ll.G. is happy now he has got Milner at the W.O.—he has wanted it some time, I am sure.[15] As you know I don't trust Milner much, but he may run straight. I hope he will. This is only for your own eye, as I feel it is somewhat a bitter letter . . .

18

Rawlinson to Wilson

Headquarters, Fourth Army
[Holograph]   April 24th 1918

The Bosche attacked on my front south of the Somme at dawn this morning with two fresh Divisions (4 Grs and 77 D. from Russia) and after failing in his first rush came on again at 7 a.m. and gained a footing in V[illers] Bretonneux. He used tanks of two kinds; one about the size of ours and another of a larger size with an armament of ten 5 pounders and 4 Machine Guns. I do not think he had more than 8 or 10 altogether of both sorts. The weight of this attack fell on V.B. and some 2000 yards to the south and during the heavy fighting he succeeded after heavy losses in gaining possession of the whole of the Village. My 8 and 58 Divisions which were defending this portion of the front are both made up Divisions which have been fighting more or less continuously since the 21 March and the reinforcements they have received are composed of young boys who were under fire for the first time. I fear that the heavy bombardment which he put on before the attack for 4 hours with a certain amount of gas shell must have shaken these children a good deal hence the success of the second effort. The weather was foggy and the clouds have not been more than 150 feet high all day so that any assistance from the Air has been impossible. I have scraped together three fairly fresh Brigades from the Australian and 18 Division to put in a determined counter attack at 8 p.m. tonight in the hope of regaining the Village but after that I have only one Brigade of Australian and one Brigade of the 18 left in reserve so I am pretty short.

Du Cane and the Chief were over here this afternoon and we have put the situation to Foch. If we succeed tonight in recapturing the Village I shall have no fresh troops to hold it with as I have already reduced the Australian front to a dangerous extent should the Bosche elect to attack there next. So in my view as well as in that of the F.M. there is no alternative but for the French, who have quite a large number of fresh Divisions available, to take over the front as far North as the Somme, that is the front of the III Corps. In no other way can we keep the enemy out of Amiens for D.H. cannot give me any more fresh Divisions and we must depend on the French to assist us. If the enemy does not put in another attack before 8 p.m. tonight I think we have quite a good chance of recapturing the Village which is situated on a spur overlooking the Somme Valley right down as far as Amiens and is therefore of the highest tactical importance.[16] We *must* get it back whatever happens.

The Chief who was here today tells me that in the North things are steadying down but that there are indications of an offensive in front of the Belge. Such an attack is likely but it is by no means an easy one for the Bosche to carry out in view of the inundations. If the Belge will only stop on their trenches and shoot along the causeways through the floods the Bosche should have no chance. I got yours of the 21st this morning. I have no doubt that you are run off your legs. We are crying for rain here to hamper the Bosche but cannot get a drop only low cloud . . .

Major-General Sir Frederick Maurice to Wilson

[Endorsed by Wilson in holograph: 'Received 30.4.14 [*sic*]. Maurice never mentioned this when he was DMO']

[Holograph]

20 Kensington Park Gardens, W.11
30.4.18

When I was last over in France I was told by many officers both at G.H.Q. and elsewhere that certain of the Prime Minister's statements in his speech of April 9th had had a very bad effect in the army because a very large number of all ranks knew them to be incorrect. The two statements chiefly quoted to me were those in which it was stated that the Army in France in 1918 was stronger than in 1917, and that all except three of the infantry divisions in Egypt & Palestine were either Indian or contained a very very small proportion of white troops.

As you know the first of these statements is literally true because the Prime Minister referred to the date of the 1st January, but very shortly afterwards, as you also know, the Army in France was reduced by 2 cavalry divisions & 140 Infantry battalions. This is perfectly well known to the Army which regards the statement as very misleading. The second statement as to the troops in Palestine is incorrect & is known to the Army at large to be incorrect. I now hear that a somewhat similar impression has been produced by Mr. Bonar Law's answers on April 23rd to questions as to taking over the line. The statement that this question was not referred to Versailles is, as you know, incorrect & other statements in Mr. Bonar Law's reply are misleading. The general effect has I am told been to produce a feeling of distrust & lack of confidence in France. You probably know this already but although I have ceased to be your D.M.O. I think it right to make certain that you are aware of it . . .

[Added by Lord Milner in holograph: 'Similar representations have been made to me. There is, of course, something in them.']

20

Note from Sir Douglas Haig

[Holograph]
S. of S. for War

Would you very kindly send me *as soon as possible* the following for the French Troops fighting under Plumer *to encourage them.*

100 D.S.O.
200 Mil. Crosses
500 Mil. Medals

D.H.
1 May 18

21

Wilson to General Sir Edmund Allenby

[Holograph copy]   9.5.18

What wretched weather the 60th Division seems to have had for the Amman enterprise.[17] It really does appear to me that we have had bad luck in our weather. Mud all autumn in Flanders, no snow in Italy; heavy snow rain and gales in Persia to hamper Dunsterville, and fog in the Somme for Goughie and mud on the so called Amman Plateau. It is odd to say the least of it. I wired a couple of days ago asking you for rather more detailed an account of what had happened over the Jordan, and then I wired later asking for an appreciation of what you saw likely in the future. The War Cabinet is, on the whole, very good but occasionally fusses rather and wants to know rather more of the inside story and your inside thoughts than appear in the usual official wires. I am proposing to send C.B. Thomson to Versailles if you can spare him. I think he will be of more value in that sort of work than as CRE Division?

I think we are coming near the time now when the old Boches

will make another formidable attack of 40–60 Divisions. In my opinion he ought from his own point of view to throw the major part of his weight on to the British and try to knock another 10 Divisions into Cadres and yet another 5 or 10 into a very tired condition. This would reduce the value of the BEF to about ½ what it was in Feb. and would be a serious affair. The Americans are at last beginning to come in and from this month (inst.) we ought to ship some 150,000–200,000 men a month. This will give us very real support even if only half of them come to us and the other half to the French. They come in Battalions and we are putting 1 Battalion into each of our Brigades to start with.

The excitement at the moment here is Maurice's letter in the newspapers a couple of days ago. He is still under me in this Office but I knew nothing about it until I saw the letter in the M[orni]ng Post. The curious thing is that he is incredibly inaccurate. The taking over of the line by us was *not* decided by the Supreme Council as D.H. and Pétain had agreed before the Council met. Maurice was not present. The figure of 3 white Divisions was given by *me* one day at a Cabinet meeting in March. It ought to have been 5. But Maurice was present and corrected the proof sheets the next day as I was in France. The total strengths of Allies and Enemies was given by L.G. from a W.O. table and 9 days *after* the speech Maurice agreed they were accurate. So what the man is thinking of I can't imagine. Nor can any of us. As I write, your letter of Ap. 20th has just come in. Many thanks for the nice things you say. I hope you get a large mounted force over the Jordan. I am sure that would be wise. All sorts of good wishes. Tell me if there is anything in which I can help? I still mean to give you troops enough with which to thrash the Turks but for the moment I can't . . .

22

Keith Murdoch to Wilson

United Cable Service
(Australasia)
London Office,
162 Queen Victoria Street,
E.C.
Private & Confidential   Jun 20, 1918.

Many thanks for your brief note of today. I was delighted that you were able to come on Monday evening and meet Mr. Hughes, who I can assure you will be found amongst your supporters during the next few days. I need say no more.

I had a long talk with him on the Western Front, and like everyone who comes over the seas, he had much to learn.

I do trust that during his visit he will be able to carry out what is his most earnest desire, which is to put in some solid strokes against the Boche.

I have been intending to write to you to clear up a point touched upon in our conversation the other night. We had, of course, heard whispers about your intention in regard to our Light Horse,[18] but I confess I was rather caught unawares when you mentioned it on Monday. Possibly I gave you a wrong idea of what would undoubtedly be our strong view. It is this: we have always tried to carry out the desires of the C.I.G.S. unquestioningly, and we should be of course very much swayed by your recommendations. At the same time, we would feel that as our Light Horse has made such a distinctive place for itself amongst the cavalry of the world, and as, moreover, it is the arm towards which we look for much in the defence of Australia, we would urge that it should be the last cavalry to be broken up. That is to say, if it is brought West we would think it should be broken up only after all the British cavalry, which has nothing like such work to its credit, has been put into the infantry formations. This would be our very strong opinion. A further consideration with us is that our Light Horse so far has escaped the shattering experience of infantry, although it has had the heaviest casualties among British mounted troops. We should rather feel, therefore, that we have a right to these men, unless and until all units are sharing the fate of filling the infantry's camps.

All this, of course, in closest confidence, and with kind regards . . .

23

Major-General F. C. Poole to Wilson

Murmansk
[Holograph]   29th June 1918

I talked over matters very fully with the First Lord[19] when he was here, and he has now gone home quite "au fait" with the situation.

The Hun is a little anxious about us and has been getting busy at Archangel in anticipation of our landing. I'm quite sure I could have got in there but I should have had very little sting left in me, so I decided to wait till I get the French and American reinforcements & make a proper job of it. Since then matters have developed here. Lenin & Chicherin sent up a string of fulminations against our brutal conduct in occupying this place. Natsaremus, the Special Commissar from Moscow sent to control all the White Sea District, wired to the local Soviet to tell them they were to make a formal protest to us re our occupation & then to wait his arrival & he would take steps.

Meanwhile I have been taking steps to bring the local Soviet into a reasonable frame of mind. They have been "wobbling" for some days as to whether they should support us or not. Last night however they definitely took the plunge and have decided to denounce Moscow as pro-German and throw off their allegiance and come in on our side. It is, in any case, only a question of a few days before we bump up against the govt. as I hear from the French Intelligence that Natsarenus has left Petrograd for here with 1500 men. These men can only be intended to enforce his threats to push us out. I consider his action unfriendly. I have therefore instructed Maynard to prevent his movement North by force if necessary. Thus the fact of there being a "counter-revolution" started here doesn't complicate matters at all. They will declare martial law today. Tomorrow they will have a mass meeting—allies and all—and declare their resolve. They will have to go through with it now as they have placed the rope around their necks. Also I have them fairly well in hand now and can guide their footsteps if they try to falter.

We shall mobilise at once here, I shall try to weed out and get more quality & less quantity in the army. I hope 6000–8000, but we shall see how everything goes on. The crux of the whole movement will be the success or otherwise in the other provinces.

* * *

I have great hopes that we are going to pull off a big thing. If there is any doubt—and of course there will be—as to the desirability of sending more troops out here, I would most strongly urge that now that the Americans are coming over so well you could easily afford the loss if the show comes unstuck; but, if it is a success then you will gain a prize quite out of proportion to your stake, not only immediately from the military point of view, but also in the future from a Political point as we shall ensure the Allies a comfortable "place in the sun" in Russia. It's well worth while to carry it through—quite independently of intervention in the East. We have made a good start now and only want a very slight push to get us really going. I wish you could see my Russian officers company—they are so strong so far—I have a Major General as a Corporal, but I have promised to make him a 2nd Lt. when its strength reaches 100!! I keep very fit & very optimistic!! . . .

24

Wilson to Poole

War Office
[Holograph copy]   26.7.18

The 1st Lord gave us all your gossip, but much has changed,
even since then. Yours of the 29th June just received. We are
pushing about all we can. The Pres. (USA) Pershing & Foch *at
last* all agree to 3 Battns of Americans & some Engineers going to
you, but not guns so we must look elsewhere for these. A French
Battn. is on the water, an Italian Battn is ready & goes as soon as
possible. Our Battn will sail as soon as we can collect it & the
Americans ditto.
At last also I hope to see the Japanese going in by Vladivostock.
Knox started last week. Foch is doing *well* on the Marne. I watch
your work daily . . .

25

Wilson to Lieutenant-General
Sir J. P. Du Cane

W.O
[Holograph copy]   1.8.18

My dear Johnnie,
The more we look into the question of our manpower the
uglier it seems to be. Agriculture, Vital industries for ourselves
and our Allies, Coal, Shipbuilding, Aeroplane & Tank Construc-
tion—& personnel—& so on & so forth all show such formidable demands that little remains for the fighting services. The
Cabinet therefore are anxious about the future. They do not want
to end the war in an absolutely exhausted condition, if this can be
avoided. They asked me to find out therefore whether Genl. Foch
was going to call on the British troops for any major operations
this year, for if so they would like to know what was intended and

what the estimated cost would be. Of course the Cabinet have no wish to ask about minor operations unless they lead to major operations. Will you let me have an answer as soon as possible.

Ever

H.W.

26

Du Cane to Wilson

Marshal Foch's Temporary HQ

[Holograph]   8th Aug.

At the earnest request of Marshal Foch and the CinC I refrained from giving you particulars of the offensive which began this morning[20] up to the last moment.

I sent Gen Grant over yesterday with all the information available, so that he could explain to you the intentions of the General in Chief & what he hopes to gain by this attack.

The secret appears to have been very well kept. The troops assembled up to time without interference from the enemy and the attack seems to have been a complete surprise. This should justify the precautions taken to maintain secrecy.

According to the reports received at the time of writing, 3 p.m., the advance seems to have been very rapid, particularly on the front of the Australian Corps. Unconfirmed reports have been received of the action of cavalry and Tanks ahead of the infantry.

Marshal Foch hopes by a rapid advance in the direction of Roye to gain possession of the heights overlooking the valley of the Avre & so to compel the enemy to abandon the ground between the Avre & Les 3 Dones [?]. If a serious breach is made in the enemy's defences he hopes to extend the front of attack by exerting pressure both to the North & South. The gains of to-day if held will free Amiens & the St. Just railway, which was the primary object of the operations.

As regards the effect of these operations on the question of man power, about which you have recently written to me, you will note that the attacking troops are principally Australian and Canadian. It is too soon to say whether these operations will develop into a great battle involving a considerable body of British troops. Crown Prince Rupprecht had about 20 fresh Divisions in reserve when the battle began & in a few days time he may counter attack without using up his reserves. At present all that can be said is that the battle has opened very favourably for us . . .

27

Wilson to Foch

War Office

[Holograph copy]   12.8.18.

I hope & believe that you did not think I was rude in my interview with you at Sarcus[21] yesterday; but you touched me in a very sore place when, I thought by what you said you implied that England was not playing the game of a good & loyal comrade.[22] Because England *is*, & she has difficulties and anxieties and commitments which in a degree, & to a certain extent, limit her purely military effort on the soil of France. All I can say is this that everything that can be done *will* be done, every strain that can, with safety, be put on the British Empire *will* be put, every sacrifice that can be made *will* be made in the cause of this War & to the end of victory.

No one can, in justice, accuse me of indifference or of half-heartedness in this matter; for 27 years I have worked for one object & one object only & that was, & is, the safety & greatness of my country. If then I have to say, & to do, things which are distasteful to my friends I hope they will credit me with the fact that these things are *at least* as distasteful to me as they are to my friends. I know you will understand the spirit in which I pen these few lines to the oldest & the greatest friend I have in the French Army . . .

28

Wilson to Haig

[Holograph copy]   21.8.18.

No indeed you owe the Cabinet the thanks for the wire which
you so well deserved . . . The old Boche is learning the art &
science of retiring & with more practice he will become perfect. I
wish to goodness we had 4000 or 5000 more Tanks to give you
now as we ought to have had we looked more into the future.

I hope the Honble Byng will have a great success.[23] I will try &
run over at the end of week . . .

29

Wilson to Haig

[Holograph copy]   2.9.18.

No, it isn't really want of confidence in you it is much more the
constant—and growing—embarrassment about man power that
makes the Cabinet uneasy;[24] it is the curiously hostile attitude, on
several points, of both the French & the Americans; it is the
uneasy spirit in this country as evinced by the Police Strike; it is
these & other cognaté matters which make the Cabinet sensitive
to heavy losses especially if these are incurred against old lines of
fortifications. Of the total 77,000 loss since the present offensive
began some 50,000, have come in the last 10 days, & a considerable proportion (16,000) up Bullecourt way. No, it is not want of
confidence in you so much as the feeling that, when the end
comes, we must still possess a formidable Army. My wire
therefore was only intended to convey a sort of distant warning &
nothing more. All so easy to explain in talking, all so difficult to
express in writing.[25]

* * *

30

Wilson to Allenby

Just a line by Waterfield who starts back tomorrow. Yours of Aug. 14th reached me two days ago. Many thanks for your good wishes which I value very much, but in truth I have had very little to do with all these recent successes and only wish I could have helped more. The credit must go almost entirely to Foch but much credit is also due to D.H. who has accepted his altered position in an admirable spirit and who has played up in the most loyal way to the new C. in C. Our men also have been wonderful and during the month of August we have taken close on 60,000 prisoners with a total loss to ourselves of under 80,000 casualties. This speaks volumes for the altered conditions on the Western Front.

I hope you will have the best of good fortune in your coming attack and that you will get a real good haul of Turks and also secure and keep Haifa. We have done all we could to help you but it has all fallen far short of what I had originally hoped and intended. Still I know you will understand that our limitations were imposed and were not of our own making.

As regards outside theatres we are conducting several gambles at Petchenga, Murmansk, Archangel, Baku, Krasnovosk and Vladivostock but I believe under the present conditions all these gambles are worth their prices even though in some of them we may end in disappointment or even disaster.

Waterfield will take you all our gossip.

The Police strike is over,[26] but it was a disgraceful affair and it has cost us Macready, who succeeds Henry, and Macready's successor may be "my" Macdonogh.[27]

Never hesitate to wire me an H.W. wire if you think I can help you.

The best of good luck . . .

31

Sackville-West to Wilson

British Military Representative,
Supreme War Council,
British Section,
Versailles.

[Holograph]   Sept. 19. [1918]

No I didn't suppose you would be pleased with our decision as regards Archangel but I don't see what else you could expect. President Wilson may say what he likes no doubt—The M.Rs. can scarcely advise sending troops to Archangel from America so long as the probability of the American programme being fulfilled for France is in doubt. Foch of course let us down by saying two apparently different things. He is no more consistent than most people. Meanwhile I dont think you give us credit for thinking out the problem. Poole naturally asks for more men & is like the "daughter of the horse leech". Furthermore you rightly say you are doing all you can to provide "effectives" & we back you up but we can't really suggest you can send or America can send men until the principal theatre is satisfied which it won't be.

Meanwhile the battles are going well in most theatres. Let the French run Russia—they'll squeeze the brutes as we shall never be allowed to do by our humanitarians (peuh) and they will bump up against your cousin's[28] pretty ideals which will unite America & what you call now the English—the future is with us because we have the same mentality & cleanness. Why do you hurry so to answer peace notes which you haven't received? You have deliberately played into the hands of the Boches again—Milner was very charming as usual—his judgment as regards Boches is worth listening to because he is ½ Boche as Clemenceau says. The affaire Spears is perfectly childish it is absurd for the C.I.G.S., Milner, Ambassador & Winston to spend hours over the wishes of an intelligent & very ambitious young man. Poor Eddy D[erby] is so worried he doesn't know where to turn . . .[29]

32

Brigadier-General E. L. Spears
to Wilson

Mission Militaire Britannique,
Près le Gouvernement Français,
4bis, Boulevard des Invalides,
PERSONAL & SECRET.   PARIS.
M.S. 1713.   4th October, 1918.

I had a conversation with M. Clemenceau on general subjects this morning. I gathered the following points, for which I can vouch:

1. Clemenceau will oppose a purely British expedition in Turkey with Constantinople as objective.

2. He thinks the mere threat of an expedition against European Turkey, which should be prepared and announced, will cause Turkey to ask for terms.

3. He is very alive to what he calls French interests in the Mediterranean and is certainly on the look out to take up the cudgels for these against England.

4. As in the case of Bulgaria, he is opposed to a peace with Turkey, but desires to conclude an armistice such as has been concluded with Bulgaria. His words are "No peace until the general peace."

5. Clemenceau is not desirous of seeing Constantinople occupied by Franco-British troops, but would sanction this measure were it necessary.

6. His mind is, as ever fixed on the western front; he says that he considers the Balkans as subsidiary, and his one idea is to create a situation in the Near East that will render possible the transfer of what he considers a decisive number of troops to the western front. This, he added, was all the more necessary, now that the Americans were not giving us the help we were entitled to expect of such good troops. *He added that this situation would not be allowed to last long.*

Clemenceau ended the conversation by saying—"Voyez, je

vous ai tout raconté". This is probably true, as he made various unflattering statements on a variety of subjects, which are not worth recording . . .

33

Allenby to Wilson

General Headquarters
Egyptian Expeditionary Force
[Holograph] 19.X.18

I returned yesterday after visiting Haifa, Saida (Sidon), Beirut and Damascus. Haifa has settled down, quietly and happily, under a British Military Governor.

At Saida is a French Military Governor, subordinate to the French Military Governor at Beirut. The Military Governor at Beirut is Colonel de Piépape who commands the French detachment in my force. He is a good soldier, but has not much idea of how to carry on a Civil Administration. I am sending Money over, from Jerusalem, to give him a little advice & help; and I have also sent Colonel Huggett, my financial expert, to advise him on the currency question and financial administration.

I impressed on de Piépape that he has nothing to do with politics; and that he is an officer of mine, responsible to me for the Civil Administration of Occupied Enemy Territory North of Palestine. His inclination has been to congratulate the inhabitants of Syria on coming under the protection of France. This I have forbidden. My policy in Syria is the same as in Palestine; viz.—I, in Supreme Military Command, am responsible for the Civil Government and Administration of all Occupied Enemy Territories. For this purpose, I have appointed Military Governors— British in the Southern Territory; French in the Northern; Arab in the Eastern. These Military Governors are my officers, and responsible to me alone. The French have a sort of idea that their Government has already a voice in the Administration of Syria. Of this idea they must be disabused. While I command, in active operations, I must control everything, including sea ports. The suggestion of a special base in Syria for the French Detachment is inadmissible. That Detachment is part of my Army; and I must have power to employ it anywhere, if I think it necessary.

At Damascus, the Arab Government is getting to work satisfactorily; and the Military Governor, Ali Pasha, is a clear headed, hardworking man. I informed Feisal of the communication which Wingate was authorized to make to the King of Hedjaz[30] regarding the Administration of Occupied Enemy Territory;[31] and I had some long talks with him.

He, like every other Moslem in Syria, is convinced that the French mean to get hold of the country; and the fact that French Military Governors have been installed in coastal areas has deepened their suspicion.

I told him that these were Military arrangements; and that all the present temporary organization was liable to revision and alteration at the Peace Conference—where the Arabs, as a recognized belligerent nation, would doubtless be represented. What he feels most is that all access to the sea is banned. Haifa, Beirut, Tripoli, Alexandretta closed to the Arabs. He said—"I am in a house which has no door". I told him to turn his mind to the Administration of the great areas which have been conquered by our allied arms; and to trust, for the future, to the good faith of the British and French. I added that the French were our Allies, an honourable nation, fighting for the same cause and with the same ideals.

This dislike & distrust of the French is universal among the Moslems in Syria. It cannot be abated by anything I say or do. If a statement, by the two Governments French and British, could be published to the effect that after the war, the wishes of the inhabitants would be considered in deciding on the form of Government in conquered territories—it would do much to restore confidence. Cornwallis, who is my British liaison officer with Feisal, is a first rate man, wise and tactful. Captain Mercier, the French liaison officer with Feisal, has, I hear, informed his Government that his position is impossible, owing to Arab obstructiveness. I've only just heard this. It is typical of the

French attitude. Mercier is, of course, my liaison officer—just as much as Cornwallis is. He should have communicated with me. He has nothing whatever to do with the French Government. I am looking into the matter; but it is only a trifle, & no trouble should ensue.

Congratulations on all your victories . . .

34

Wilson to Cavan

[Copy]   19th October 1918.

Many thanks for your private letter of October 13th just received. You say that you are sure that Comando Supremo mean business.[32] This is *good*. The flooding of the Piave is most unfortunate but we must hope it is only for a week or so though even 10 days unnecessary delay is tiresome.

I am glad you think well of Caviglia of the 8th Army since you have to work so closely with him.

I am quite content to your leaving the 48th Division under Italian Command for the time being. I think it is a wise and a very necessary precaution but I hope the division will rejoin your command when the reason for its detachment is over.

The position in France, as I see it, is this. The Boch Army is *not* beaten. It has been roughly handled and is sore and tired, but it is still well able to extricate itself from awkward angles and corners and to fall back in continuous and unbroken line to the Lys, to the Scheldt, to the Meuse—in short to wherever it *must* fall back.

All the more important therefore that we should under-cut the Boch Allies. The real truth being that our occupation of Damascus and of Homs; of Uskub, Nisch and Sofia is a more deadly cut at Boch ambitious hopes and aspirations than the occupation of Lille, Roubaix, Bruges, and Ostend.

Anything you can do over the Piave will add enormously to Boch difficulties and Boch embarrasments. You will see by this that although I am a Westerner of 27 years standing (a *much* older

Westerner than any living soldier) I am also a convinced believer in the enormous importance of success in southern and Eastern theatres.

Therefore any help I can give you whether in Staff or in personnel or material I will give—willingly.

Every sort of good wish . . .

35

Sackville-West to Wilson

British Military Representative,
Supreme War Council,
British Section,
Versailles.

[Holograph]   Oct 22. [1918]

I have slowly & after much gazing at the map come round to your view as regards Turkey. I think the Turk is the best door keeper we can find for the Bosphorus & Dardanelles these latter in peace must be internationalised I see no way out—so was the Suez Canal before this war. I admit the differences but by keeping the Turk in C. we can give the islands & Smyrna to Greece. Poland seems an almost insuperable difficulty—I have been studying this as well as the Yugoslav question & its a muddle. Russia is the great danger—I dread Bolshevism for Europe—I don't at all agree with that paper of the French General Staff. We can't conquer Russia—the fact is the French want back their francs—If I could I would get out of Europe if I could & the Mediterranean also.

Meanwhile we must insist on disarmament for the Boche this side of the Rhine . . .

36

W. M. Hughes to Wilson

Commonwealth of Australia
Prime Minister
[Holograph]   Nov 4/18

I should be glad to learn the result of your representations, the
Australian Corps being again ordered to take up position in the
line. As you will remember I pointed out that the army was worn
with constant & heavy fighting extending over a period of many
months & was badly in need of rest.[33]

The matter is very important & very urgent.

Awaiting your reply . . .

37

Wilson to Hughes

[Copy]   7/11/18

I only got back from France last night. I saw the C. in C., also
Sir Henry Rawlinson and also General Monash and we went
carefully into the whole matter. An arrangement was, I believe,
finally reached which was satisfactory. I have not heard the details
of it yet . . .

38

Hughes to Wilson

Commonwealth of Australia
Prime Minister
[Holograph]   Nov 11/18

Now that the armistice has been signed its terms must be given
effect to. I am writing to ask that the Australian Corps shall be

given an opportunity along with other of the Empire forces of holding the bridgeheads and such other territory as in the disturbed state of Germany it may be necessary to occupy in order to safeguard Allied interests . . .

39

Rawlinson to Wilson

Headquarters
Fourth Army.
Nov. 11th 1918.

[Holograph]

I never thought we could bring down the Boche Empire so quickly when I began hammering him on Aug. 8th. It is really wonderful—We have now secured for the Empire a really firm foundation on which to build, all we have now to do is to work hard at it, and crush self advertising asses like Hughes—I hear from D.H. that Plum and I are to lead the Armies of occupation and are to start on the 17th so I shant be able to run home—Can you come and see me before that date? . . .

40

Wilson to Hughes

[Holograph copy]   12.11.18.

I am sure that Australian troops will form part of the Army of Occupation. They won't be too tired? . . .

41

Hughes to Wilson

Commonwealth of Australia
Prime Minister
[Holograph]   13/11/18

I did not think it possible that a man like yourself—a soldier—
who knows what the Australian troops have done, would have
referred to these brave men in such sneering fashion . . .

42

Wilson to General Pétain

[Copy]   13/11/18

There are no words in my vocabulary to express my feelings of
admiration for the French Army and the women of France. As I
think of all the brave men who have passed since the middle of
Aug. 1914 and of all the brave women who never faltered or
spared themselves, I find myself, with my cap in my hand and with
tears in my eyes, marvelling at the greatness of France. How
proud you must be to be the Commander-in-Chief of such an
Army.

No British officer sends warmer greetings to you and your
Armies than

Yours very sincerely
(sd) Henry Wilson.

43

Wilson to Hughes

[Holograph copy]   Nov. 14th [1918]

I did not refer to your splendid men, but to what you have so
often impressed on me as to their condition.

However, as you know, four of the Divisions are going to move forward with the 4th Army, so we are all happy . . .

44

Allenby to Wilson

General Headquarters
Egyptian Expeditionary Force
[Holograph]   16 Nov./18

I have your letter of the 16th Oct.; and I thank you for looking into the matters to which I have from time to time referred in my letters to you. My congratulations to you, on final victory. Yourself, Lloyd George, Clemenceau & Foch have organized and accomplished it; and I have placed you in order of merit. It looks as if there will be a lot of police work to be done in Europe and Asia before the new little nations settle down, or they will all be tearing each others eyes. Mark Sykes has arrived here, and will be helpful. He is quite subordinate and loyal; and his ideas appear to be sound. He will do nothing without reference to me, but will be useful in talking to Picot on matters of international policy. I am glad that Feisal is to attend the conference at Versailles.

The French will have to allow the Arabs a port on Syrian coast—probably Tripoli—or there will be awful trouble. If the French are tactful, they have a chance of placating the Arabs. Politics in Palestine & Syria are not going to be too easy in the future. Jews, Arabs, French, Italians, English & other nations, all think they have special interests & special claims & rights;[34] and every known religion asserts itself, and adds knots to the tangle. However, I maintain the attitude of Gallio; and I concern myself only with the maintenance of order, and the establishment of an impartial, non-political administration . . .

45

General Sir G. F. Milne to Wilson

Salonika.
December 1st 1918

I have only just returned from Constantinople, and you may care to hear my impressions formed by my visit there. I am afraid this letter may be rather sketchy, as it is being dictated with a view to catching the evening's mail.

What strikes one most in Constantinople is the peaceful and every-day appearance of the town. The streets are crowded, the shops are open, and everybody seems to be doing a thriving trade. Turkish officers and men in uniform are everywhere, and there seems a very very slight sprinkling of British, chiefly prisoners of war just released. The only difference from previous appearances is seen in the small number of ships in the Bosphorus. Food seems plentiful; prices are enormous. My hotel bill for myself and nine officers for one night was £100. Needless to say I did not pay it; nor was the hotel proprietor in the least perturbed by the ruthless way it was cut down by my A.D.C.

In the Bosphorus are a few ships of the Allied Navies, the Sultan's yacht and the "Goeben"[35] still, I regret to say, flying the Turkish flag. The great absence of martial or naval display has had its natural effect on the Turkish population. All news of the war has been kept from them. They have not heard of their losses in Palestine or Mesopotamia, and they are totally ignorant of the fact that Turkey has been beaten. A few of them resent the presence of the few Allied soldiers in the vicinity of Constantinople, and they are always ready to quote the terms of the armistice to the effect that no occupation of the town is legal. It is most unfortunate to my mind that the occupation of strategic points was not insisted on in the armistice terms. The fact that the Turk does not really realise that he is in disgrace may give trouble in the future, and if the peace terms are going to be severe, it appears to me essential that our forces in the town are strengthened before they are promulgated. This, even if it is allowed, I can do only when I get more troops.

The impression of defeat is not strengthened by the numerous Allied officials with whom the Turk now deals. There are now three High Commissioners—British, French and Greek; a British commanding General, the Allied Headquarters at Salonika, and myself, for which reason, on my recent visit, I declined to see a single Turkish official. This naturally assists the Turk in his ancient method of playing off everybody against everybody else when anyone wants anything done. One strong man in sole charge would have easily wheeled him into line by this time, and he badly wants it.

I am sorry you were unable to agree to communications being made on military matters direct between the military authorities as it is the one method the Turk fully understands.

The Government seems to be composed of weak men. The Committee of Union and Progress[36] is still going strong under other names, and though they may have taken a back seat for the moment, they are only biding their time. Apparently the Germans ran their army, and the result of their departure from the War Office has left everything in chaos. The Turkish War Office officials do not know what army they have got or where it is. To disentangle the tangle and to sort out what units and classes can be left after demobilization will take some time. I do not know— nor do I want to know—what the after policy in Turkey is going to be, but if we are endeavouring to make the Turk our friend in the future we seem to be trying to do it very nicely, at least we take the greatest care to do nothing to hurt his tender feelings or susceptibilities. Naturally the Turk himself adopts a tone of the poor ignorant boy who was led away by the naughty Committee of Union and Progress whom he would now like to see punished, while everything is forgiven and forgotten. What he really seems to require is to understand that he is thoroughly in disgrace and that he is going to be well punished for his misdeeds, and that in the meantime he has got to do everything he is told, whether it is in the conditions of the armistice or not; and that even then his punishment will be pretty severe. I am certain that unless this is made pretty clear to him he will resent his punishment later on. The attitude of leaving him "to stew in his own juice" as a reward for his misdeeds is ridiculous as the only persons who suffer for the "stewing" are the Allied troops in occupation. Unless such minor trifles as railways, waterworks, hospitals, etc. are kept going we suffer; they don't.

There seems to me little difference in the crimes of the Turk and the German. Unfortunately for the Germans they committed their crimes on sea and on land. Fortunately for the Turk his crimes were committed only on the land.

The above impression, formed during a stay of only 36 hours may assist you in realising the state of affairs on the Bosphorus. What I want to bring out is that the Turkish people in their own capital do not realise either their defeat or their iniquities.

This week a portion of my Intelligence staff moves to Constantinople. Next week I move myself. Probably there will be a wail from the Turk on the occupation of his city, but I am certain the more he sees of British soldiers during the next two months the less trouble there will be after the Peace Conference.

[Added in holograph]

Dont imagine this is a complaint, though it sounds like one. It is solely a first impression on a purely unbiased mind, which I thought might interest you . . .

46

Wilson to Allenby

[Copy]   7th December 1918.

Very many thanks for your letter of Nov. 16th just received and your much too flattering remarks about myself and the part I have played. It is the simple and the bare truth to say that my role has been a very small one especially when it is remembered what a lot of opportunities I had for helping and how many of them I let slip.

The main credit is due to Foch, to you and to Franchet d'Esperey and the Serbs. The advent of the Americans and the blockade and work of our sailors both in the Fleet and in the Mercantile Marine were also tremendous factors. The picture of this war that I have seen for a great many years now has been this:

The Boch had set his mind on two things—

(a) Command of the Sea

(b) The Near and Middle East.

When in 1917 and early in 1918 it became clear that he could not get command of the sea and that therefore his first objective was lost to him I was always casting about in my mind how his second objective could be frustrated.

You and Franchet did that. The collapse of the main theatres followed almost automatically.

With the loss of both Prizes the Governing Class of the Boch lost heart—as well he might—and was no longer able to buoy up his Army and Navy.

Hence this indescribable crash. It is a wonderful story.

I hope Mark Sykes behaves himself. He is a good fellow but cracked and his blessed Sykes–Picot Agreement must be torn up *somehow* . . .

47

Cavan to Wilson

General Headquarters
British Force in Italy
[Holograph]   Dec 14 [1918]

* * *

Demobilization people are not quite fair to us. They wire for our A.7. Z.8.[37] Urgent—on which all depends—but they have never sent us any but a couple of specimen copies!

Consequence is that at this moment only six men have left Italy!

I am sending you a very select list indeed of officers of "outstanding merit". If other fronts are sending you enormous lists—I hope my boys won't suffer by my making a list of absolute "peaches" & not even including "plums" of which I have a good few.

You will see that only about ten or a dozen Officers will say that they intend to resign their commissions—Others may if terms of batta etc are good—

As regards myself I shall wait till I am demobilized & then you shall have my papers resigning commission at once—as I shall go "back to the land"—& House of Lords—but to be honest with you I shall never vote for conscription—I am *positive* you can get all the men you want, if you pay them well—

I suppose you take up yr. residence in Paris shortly & I don't envy you your job! . . .

48

Wilson to Cavan

[Copy]   18/12/18

Yours of the 14th just in. I will tell A.G. about your demobilization points and I will see to your "peaches" when your list comes in.

I am sorry you are against conscription because I have always held:

1. That it is the only *fair* way of solving the problem.
2. That even if there was never going to be another war it ought to be enforced as a part of necessary moral and physical training.
3. That it is truly democratic . . .

1919

1919

The most urgent problem facing the War Office at the beginning of 1919 was the demobilisation crisis. Pressure within the army, which frequently verged on mutiny, built up at home [49, 50], in France [52] and further afield, such as in Egypt [66], where Allenby observed that 'nothing will convince the troops that military operations did not end on the signing of the Armistice' [70]. But this was precisely the misapprehension which Wilson and his colleagues wished to correct. Early in January the Military Members of the Army Council resolved that the government 'must make it clear to the country that the war is *not* over, that we are demobilising quite fast enough'.[1] Lloyd George made a statement embodying the Army Council's requirements [51], but the difficulties with demobilisation were really only resolved through the energetic policy adopted by the new Secretary for War, Winston Churchill. Although the demobilisation scheme had been elaborately formulated so as to avoid mass unemployment, its effect was demonstrably unfair since it favoured those who had most recently enlisted. Churchill quickly replaced it with a much more straightforward 'first in, first out' system. In order to meet the army's need for manpower, however, compulsory service was partially extended and some of the most recently-conscripted men were retained until 1920.[2]

While the Army Council were sure that they needed more men, there was less agreement as to where they should be deployed. A strong lobby led by Churchill believed that substantial and sustained assistance should be given to the anti-Bolshevik 'White' Russians. Wilson disagreed. Although he was as ardently anti-Communist as the Secretary of State, from a practical military point of view he recognised that the Allies did not have sufficient forces available to intervene directly in Russia and 'declare war formally on the Bolsheviks'. The best that could be managed was to offer as generous support as possible—but preferably not direct military involvement—to the independent republics which had established themselves along the frontiers of the Soviet

Union [56, 82]. There was pressure from the French to help out in Eastern Europe where they had extensive political and economic interests. Yet despite his pro-French bias, even Wilson had to resist demands from Paris for Britain to contribute towards Allied peace-keeping forces of one sort or another [79].

During 1919 Lloyd George, undoubtedly reflecting British public opinion, determined that British troops should be withdrawn completely from Russia [60, 77]. He told Churchill that 'an expensive war of aggression against Russia is a way to strengthen Bolshevism in Russia and create it at home'.[3] There was a chance that the French and the Americans, who also had troops in Russia, might abandon the country and leave Britain supporting the Whites on her own [63]. The anti-Bolshevik Russians, moreover, were not themselves particularly rewarding allies and it was reported back to Wilson that they were hardly grateful recipients of British largesse [84]. Churchill eventually gave up the struggle and the evacuation from North Russia was achieved relatively painlessly. During September 1919 the last British troops embarked at Archangel.[4]

British intervention in South Russia proved to be more intractable. There was a greater strategic interest in the Caucasian and Transcaspian republics since, however remotely, they lay on the borders of India [94, 96]. Lord Curzon was among the most vigorous proponents of retaining a strong British presence in the Caucasus [85]. This, and Wilson's steadfast opposition to the policy, surfaces frequently in the correspondence in 1919 and 1920. In the post-war period, indeed, Curzon became something of a *bête noire* for the War Office, frequently demanding troops, which Wilson claimed he could not spare, to support expansive policies in the Middle East.

Sir George Milne, the British GOC in Constantinople, who had the lowest possible opinion of the local inhabitants, certainly favoured Wilson's desire to evacuate British troops from the Caucasus [53]. Colonel Toby Rawlinson, however, represented another body of opinion who felt that the British should remain in the region for humanitarian reasons. Withdrawal would inevitably be followed by the massacre of Armenians by Turks [84]. The matter was complicated by the existence of French troops in the area and an apparently serious offer from the Italians[5] to take over the Batum–Baku line from the

British [62, 63, 69, 72]. In Constantinople itself, reflecting the position throughout the Near and Middle East, there was simmering rivalry between the British and the French which made life particularly difficult for Milne [54, 55, 59, 82].

Allenby in Cairo, who was responsible for the administration of an enormous swathe of occupied enemy territory along the Eastern Mediterranean littoral, found that the French had local ambitions, especially with regard to Syria. This sharply challenged Arab national aspirations and promised to be an abundant source of discord. He noticed, too, the unpopularity of Zionism and predicted that its imposition on Palestine 'at once would result in riots and massacres' [54, 70]. In Egypt itself there was a period of nationalist unrest in the spring of 1919[66], although by the autumn the GOC, Congreve, reported that matters had improved noticeably [89]. Nationalism seemed to be spreading throughout the Empire. From India General Monro warned that nationalist politicians might cause trouble in the future [96].

During the first half of 1919 Wilson, as chief military adviser to the British government, was heavily involved in the Paris Peace Conference. His correspondence reflects the apparently endless round of meetings and the frustrating difficulty of reaching agreement, even among the Allied Powers [59, 60, 61]. The Treaty of Versailles with Germany was eventually signed on 28 June, but even in the weeks before the signing it was not absolutely certain that Berlin would accept the Allied terms. Contingency plans, therefore, were prepared for direct military action in the event of the Germans refusing to sign [72, 74, 78]. The continual negotiation of the 'frocks' and the painful slowness of peacemaking— the German agreement was followed by treaties with Austria, Bulgaria, Hungary and, eventually in August 1920, Turkey—did nothing for Wilson's good humour. Nor had he very much faith that the decisions of the Paris Conference would guarantee peace for any great length of time. He remained convinced that the only certain means of maintaining peace was to enforce it [93].

A proportion of the 1919 correspondence illustrates the regular work of Wilson's department in the War Office, for example, the exchange with Harington (Deputy CIGS) while Wilson was in Paris during April [64, 65]. Wilson himself regularly attended Cabinet meetings and frequently reported them to his correspondents. When Churchill was on holiday in September, he sent him a particularly full account of Cabinet business [85]. There was an air of competition between Churchill and Wilson in the War Office. Both men were very forceful characters and Wilson's concern to 'keep tabs' on Churchill is clearly demonstrated in correspondence with Generals Asser and Holman [71, 90, 92, 95]. Wilson and Churchill clashed directly over the retention of General Knox as Head of the British Military Mission in Siberia [75, 76]. As had been the case in 1918, the question of employment for Sir William Robertson proved a little troublesome, not so much because of any apparent antipathy between Wilson and Robertson, but because Wilson was not sure that his predecessor was entirely suitable for the Irish Command which Churchill had offered him [88, 97]. When the question of the 'peace' honours list came up [67], Wilson argued that both Robertson and other senior officers were 'much too decorated already'. He was, however, anxious that soldiers who had served in theatres other than the Western Front were suitably honoured [68]. He himself was rewarded with promotion to Field Marshal, a baronetcy and a grant of £10,000.[6]

Wilson wrote many wide-ranging letters of what he called 'gossip', both to close friends, such as Sackville-West [86] or Lord Esher [91], and also to less intimate colleagues, such as Milne [93] and even Robertson. His motive was evidently to keep all his colleagues well informed about events and policy-making at home. He even apologised to Robertson for not writing more often [72]. It was in one of his letters to Sir William that Wilson briefly raised the subject of domestic unrest in Ireland. This matter was increasingly to dominate all aspects of his thinking. 'Ireland', he wrote in June 1919, 'goes from bad to worse and it seems to me', he added presciently, 'that we cannot get out of it, and ought not to get out of it now, without a little bloodletting' [74].

49

Wilson to Cavan

[Carbon] 6th January 1919.

I write to say that with the very greatest regret I had to take away Shoubridge from command of the 7th Division.

You may have heard of the trouble we have had at Folkestone, the result of which goes to show clearly that we want a senior officer with recent experience of command of troops to command at Folkestone.[1] I think there is no doubt Shoubridge is just the man for the job and the Army Council have decided to appoint him to command at Folkestone, although Shoubridge himself has most strongly protested that he wants to go back to his Division.

I of course see clearly his point of view that he would like to say good-bye to the troops he has commanded throughout a good deal of fighting during the past two years, but I am afraid that the public interest will not allow this. Shoubridge is also naturally very much upset at the idea that anyone should think that he has taken advantage of his leave to get himself placed in a billet at home. This is very far from being the case, as I am sure you will recognise. We have taken Shoubridge absolutely against his will and entirely in the public interest for this job . . .

50

Wilson to Derby

[Holograph copy] War Office.
7.1.19

The heart of our present troubles in the Army lies in the reckless speeches & promises made during the recent elections, & in constant civilian & therefore ignorant & dangerous interference in our de-mobilization scheme. Exactly where we are drifting to—for we are drifting—I don't know. At the present moment there are rows of lorries outside this Office & 1000 lorrymen up from Kempton with demands of sorts. The P.M. came back at 9 p.m. last night from Criccieth.[2] It is now 4.15 p.m. & he has summoned neither Milner nor me. Meanwhile unbridled abuse of the W.O. & all its works by Daily Mail (Northcliffe) Daily News (Beaverbrook)[3] Westminster (Squiff)[4]—one thing is certain that unless P.M. buckles to & makes it quite clear that he & the Govt. are solid behind the W.O & the Officers of the Army we shall lose the Army, & then the Navy & then the Air Force. The times are eminently suitable for Leagues of Peace! . . .

51

Philip Kerr to Wilson

8th January 1919.

I enclose copy, as arranged, of the notice going out to the Press to-night . . .

[Enclosure: Carbon]

The Prime Minister has been giving careful personal attention to the speed at which the process of demobilising the army is being maintained. He considers that his first duty is to make sure that the fruits of the victory which has been won by the sacrifice of so many lives and by so many brave deeds are not jeopardised by any apparent weakness on the part of Britain during the critical months of the Peace negotiations. For this purpose it is imperative that we should maintain a strong army on the Rhine and of course the necessary services behind the front both in France and at home. Although the fighting has stopped the war is not over. The German armies have not yet been demobilised and are still very powerful. No one can tell what the Germans will do, nor whether they will agree to the terms of Peace and reparation which we seek to impose upon them. Impatience now might lose in a few weeks all that it has taken years of heroism and sacrifice to gain. During these next few months we must be strong and united in order that a firm settlement may be made with the enemy and our country may exert its proper influence among the other nations at the Peace Conference.

Demobilisation cannot be carried out in any way that would undermine the military strength of Britain until final peace is secure. No less however than 300,000 men have already been demobilised and steps have been taken to increase the speed as far as is possible without injuring vital British interests in the world or impairing the safety of our troops in Germany. No doubt there will be a great many hard cases and personal grievances. The troops may rest assured that everything possible will be done to listen to and remedy individual grievances of whatever nature when presented through the authorised channels. Instructions have been issued to ensure sympathetic hearing of all legitimate complaints. But inequalities and hardships are sure to remain and the Prime Minister is confident that these will be endured in the same way as much harder trials have already been borne in order to make certain of a lasting & just peace. The men who have fought and shed their blood in this war would rightly hold the Government responsible if, after all the work they have done, it allowed the results to be frittered away; and the nation as a whole has unmistakeably expressed its sentiments on this point.

Furthermore, fair and even treatment must be noted but as between men bearing the hardships of the field and those whose duty is discharged at home.

One thing is certain the work of demobilisation is not going to be quickened, on the contrary it is bound to be delayed by the men trying to take the law into their own hands. It is not by these irregular assemblies or marches that anything can be put right. The reason why public opinion has been tolerant of these demonstrations is because the country knows that all ranks would have cheerfully done their duty if actual fighting had been going on. But a point has now been reached where real harm is being done to the national cause and to the reputation of the British army, and it is therefore essential that discipline should be maintained.

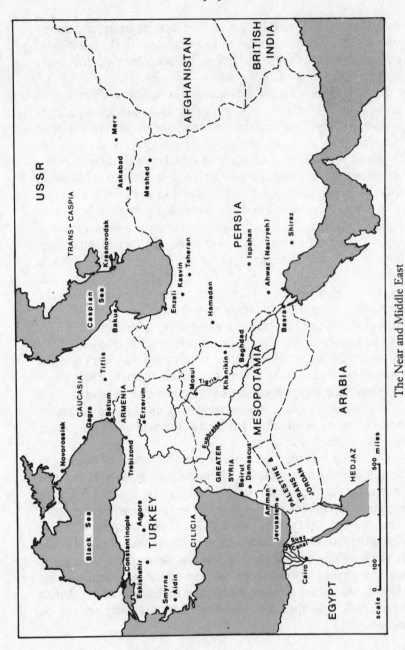

The Near and Middle East

52

Wilson to Haig

[Copy]   10/1/19

I have shown your telegram A.Z.310 (re unrest amongst your troops) to both Milner and Churchill.[5] With all these games of musical chairs going on you can imagine there is not much real business being done. We have, however, got the Press into a better mood, and P.M.'s letter in the newspapers saying the war is not over and discipline must be maintained is something. I have to go to Paris tomorrow with P.M. but hope to be back early next week.

I watch anxiously for the coming of the Post Bellum Army . . .

53

Milne to Wilson

[Private & Confidential]   22nd January, 1919.

I am writing to you in the train from TIFLIS to BAKU, and shall send my letter by fastest possible route in order to give you my impressions of the CAUCASUS after discussions with various authorities and from what I have personally seen.

It must be remembered that the various States in the CAUCASUS for the past 100 years have been practically ruled by an autocratic regime, kept in force only by armies. The result has been to develop a fierce hatred of Russia and in fact of all elements of law and order. The country has now been allowed to split up into so-called republics, each ruled by men of very advanced socialistic ideas little removed from Bolshevism at the head being one or two educated men in Georgia & Azerbaijan but not elsewhere. The remainder are illiterate and dishonest demagogues of the worst type with no ideas of administration, and with the one idea of making hay while the sun shines. The inhabitants of Georgia, Armenia and Azerbaijan cordially loath each other only a little less than they loathe the Russians. They all keep up armies at great expense though they avoid it by not paying their armies. These armies are intended to assert the rights of each State against the other, though possibly they would all combine against Russia. Were the Entente to guarantee protection against Russia and for each State against the other it might be possible to get these armies reduced everywhere, otherwise the tendency is to increase them, with a view to each State being better able to grab a bit from its neighbour. So long as we are not in a position to guarantee security of these newly formed republics, they will keep these armies going, not that I for one moment advocate guarantee-ing such security. I wonder if it is realised that every piece that has been chipped off Russia, at least in this part, will require to be administered by a civilised power for at least one generation if not for two, and even then one will get no thanks from the inhabitants for having done so, who will look on the organised power in exactly the same way as they regarded the Russians. I put this quite plainly because I doubt the advisability of any one Power accepting the onus of assisting these States. Economically their condition is rotten. The Georgians have secured all the rolling stock of the railway and have command of the bulk of the traffic, they put every difficulty in the way of railway administration, though they cannot run their railways without the assistance of the oil from BAKU.

Georgia especially is living on its capital. Its finances are rotten and on the verge of bankruptcy. Trade is nil and everything is being nationalized. Food everywhere is becoming very scarce, in fact, famine is likely to arise all through Trans-Caucasia unless some arrangements can be made for getting in grain. The railway difficulty is such that even if all the Austrian and German prisoners in Trans-Caspia should surrender I don't see how we can pass them through for some months. BAKU is especially difficult as there are many thousands of Russians, upholders of Russia as against the Republics of Caucasus, and they are now in a position by striking to suspend the whole of the working of the railways, electric light etc., etc., Hence the necessity of a strong force there.

From a purely military point of view I cannot see what we are to gain by remaining in Trans-Caucasia, except to keep the railway communication open to Malleson's Force on the other side of the Caspian, the situation of which appears daily more difficult. The country and the inhabitants are equally loathsome and we seem to be accepting an enormous responsibility which will incur great expense for no very great reason. If the ASKABAD Republic must be bolstered up surely it will be better to do so by a line of communication from BALUCHISTAN in preference to keeping a big force in Trans-Caucasia. I am fully aware that the withdrawal of the British troops would probably lead to anarchy but I cannot see that the world would lose much if the whole of the inhabitants of the country cut each other's throats. They are certainly not worth the life of one British soldier. The Georgians are merely disguised Bolsheviks led by men who overthrew Kerensky and were friends of Lenin. The Armenians are what the Armenians have always been, a despicable race. The best are the inhabitants of Azerbaijan, though they are in reality uncivilised.

I think it wants to be clearly understood at home that if we accept responsibility to help these countries we will have to retain troops here not only for one or two years but possibly for 10 years, while the education of the people to manage their own affairs will be the work of several generations. Even then I cannot see that these little republics will ever be able to stand on their own: they are so dependent on each other that some form of federation seems essential.

I hope to be able to cross the Caspian tomorrow and shall send my views regarding the situation there with as little delay as possible . . .

[P.S. holograph] I have never seen a more miserable country or people. GFM

54

Spears to Wilson

SECRET.
L.S.W. 86.

Mission Militaire Britannique,
Près le Gouvernement Français,
4bis, Boulevard des Invalides,
PARIS.
23rd January, 1919.

The French public is beginning to recover from the state of
semi-coma into which it had sunk during the last 18 months of
the war. The French are realising that they are victorious and in
this realisation of victory are being tempted to exaggerate the part
which they have played in the war. It is most difficult to foresee
developments, as practically no one has seen the French as they
are to-day—that is to say, with a real belief in themselves. Today, perhaps the first time for fifty years, the French are taking
themselves seriously as a first-class power.

With a cheerful disregard to the small and shrinking population and to the economic weakness of FRANCE, many Frenchmen are giving free rein to violently imperialistic ideas. As
"moderate" a politician as FRANKLIN-BOUILLON told me a
day or two ago that he thought that the French had committed a
gross error in permitting voting for the German Constituent
Assembly, to take place in the occupied regions on the left bank of
the RHINE, and most of the French do not seem to recoil before
the idea of entirely detaching the German territories on the left
bank of the RHINE from the rest of GERMANY.

Some of the French are now expressing fears that a German
Republic may constitute a greater menace to FRANCE than the
Empire! If this means that the Germans, having learnt that
militarism does not pay, will still remain Germans with their old
social and economic organisation, and with their old aggressive
commercial qualities, they are probably right. It is however
difficult to see how they can prevent the Germans from being
German.

It is however on these international and imperial questions that public opinion is fastening. Internal politics are at a standstill—and if the Clemenceau Government is indeed losing ground, as it certainly appeared to be a fortnight ago, it is by its attitude at the Peace Conference, and not by its internal policy that it will stand or fall. (This is not to say that it can afford to go on mis-handling economic questions, and it appears to be running grave risks in this direction). For the present, at least, it seems to be pursuing a fairly aggressive policy, which adequately reflects the opinion of the French nation as a whole.

It must, however, be clearly realised that there is very little material force behind this aggressiveness. The exhaustion of the war has weakened FRANCE to an extent which nobody has any difficulty in realising. The French are, however, for the moment, conscious of their greatly increased prestige and of little else, and they are beating the national drum louder than ever.

There are no indications of definitely anti-English tendencies—as opposed to anything else. The indications which do appear of rivalry with and jealousy of English influence are merely one side of the chauvinism, which is the keynote for the moment of French public opinion. In this connection, however, it is interesting to note that criticism of British action in policing CONSTANTINOPLE has been very acute and expressed in terms indicating suspicion of British aims and a rather exaggerated imperialism. The press has evidently been "inspired" in this connection so that the Government can claim that its hands are being forced. With regard to the SYRIAN question, the imperialists such as BARRES seem to think that FRANCE should not only have SYRIA and CILICIA, but also the control of the territory to the north of MESOPOTAMIA, i.e., the DIABEKR-MOSSUL line. FRANKLIN-BOUILLON, who seems rather scared at the proportions which the Syrian agitation has taken and foresees that it may lead to trouble with us, tells me that he does not think that the agitation can now be stopped as it has gone too far. In all the comments that have been made with regard to the German merchant fleet, it seems to be assumed that FRANCE should be given the largest share to compensate her for not having one!

There is no reference to our great losses and our legitimate claims for compensation.

It should also be remembered with regard to the single command that FOCH regards himself first and foremost as a French general taking his orders from the French Government—M. Clemenceau's relations with him are practically those of master to man . . .

55

Lieutenant-General Sir T. Bridges
to C.I.G.S.

CONSTANTINOPLE,
February 9th, 1919.

We arrived here this morning after a capital trip through the Dardanelles, and landed with due pomp. All the troops were out, and our own contingent looked extraordinarily well, better than anybody else. Franchet made his entry on horseback. As Allenby had had a procession the day before, this fell perhaps rather flat, and it was just as well.

Franchet and Allenby met and had a talk, and I just caught Allenby before he left this afternoon for Haifa. The "Bull" looks well; his crest has thickened. Calthorpe told me that he pulverised the Turkish War and Foreign Ministers when he delivered them his ultimatum. I wish he were staying here.

Franchet has taken Enver's house at Ortakeui, having Madame Enver, who was expecting a little Enver, evacuated. He proposes to establish a small personal reserve of a regiment, a squadron and a battery; he brought one battalion along with him. His idea is that the Turks may give trouble, and there may be religious riots, when they come to know what the terms of peace are going to be.

He was very annoyed to hear that Liman von Sanders had been allowed to leave, as he desired to have him court-martialed, having got good evidence from Venizelos as to his complicity in Armenian and Greek murders. Calthorpe has telegraphed to

Malta to have him stopped, and has asked the Foreign Office for instructions.

I hope we shall get along here all right, but there are too many chiefs. Milne is back here from a short visit to the Caucasus, where I understand he had a fight at Merv, and hostilities are still going on while we are trying to entice the Bolsheviki to Prinkipo.

As you know, Franchet d'Esperey is very restless, and it may save trouble if we get him travelling, and I propose to try to coax him off to Odessa before very long. He wants to go to Trebizond, and I think this is bound up with some French policy, but we may be able to head him off.

* * *

56

Note by the Chief of the Imperial General Staff on the present military situation in Russia with a proposal as to the best military action possible under the circumstances

1. There appear to be two military solutions to the present chaotic situation in Russia—

(a) To declare war formally on the Bolsheviks and to move into Russia in sufficient force to overthrow the Bolshevik Armies and then allow Russia to determine her own form of Government.

(b) To define the new Russia by delimitating the eastern and northern frontiers of all the new States; to order all Russian forces outside her new boundaries to retire within them and then to treat the Russia so described as a Neutral State until she herself goes to war with the Allies or joins the League of Nations.

2. After a careful and detailed examination of proposal (a) I have come to the distinct conclusion that the Allies do not dispose of sufficient forces to warrant the attempt being made. I therefore rule it out.

3. As regards proposal (b) I am of opinion that apart from the fact that both our interest and our honour insist on its adoption the allies possess sufficient force and power both moral and physical to adopt it as their course of action and with good hope of successful issue.

4. From the military point of view the following Allied action is necessary:

(a) The frontiers of the states which have seceded from Russia must be clearly defined.

I understand these States to be:

Finland
Esthonia
Latvia
Lithuania
Poland
Ruthenia
Bessarabia (to include the Bukovina)
Caucasus

(b) The sovereign rights of the Russian Government shall cease in these new States and all Russian troops etc. shall be at once drawn back behind the new frontier thus defined.

(c) By this means one continuous land frontier will be established from the Arctic Ocean to the Black Sea to the east of which Russia will lie and to the west these young States, and a clearly defined line from the Black Sea to the Caspian to the north of which Russia will lie and to the south the young States. It will be for the Allies to determine their respective responsibilities as regards economic, financial and, if necessary, military assistance to these new States; thus Great Britain might be responsible for Finland, Esthonia, Latvia, and Lithuania; France might be similarly responsible for Poland—and so forth.

(d) Pending the acceptance by the Bolsheviks of the arrangements previously suggested and the execution of the terms laid down the Allies should continue their present policy of giving every assistance to those Russian elements (such as Denikin) which have been called into being by recent events.

5. It is probable that the Bolsheviks will agree to a decision presented to them by the United Allies and will withdraw behind their new frontiers leaving all these young States in peace and quiet and if they do it seems to me that we may have to withdraw our troops from Archangel, Ukraine, and Siberia and our further assistance from Denikin etc., but this would be a gradual withdrawal and we would have time to make the best arrangements we could for our Russian friends.

6. It is possible on the other hand that the Bolsheviks may refuse to retire behind their new frontier. In this case the Allies will have no option but to force them to carry out their orders. They will have to declare war on Bolshevik Russia for being in occupation of territories of some of the Allies or Protected States.

7. What would be the issue of such a war?

The populations of the States mentioned in para. 4(a) amount to 46,180,000 whereas the population of European Russia (less the new States) amounts to 124,000,000. It would seem therefore at the first blush that a contest between these young States and European Russia would be a hopeless undertaking but this is far from being the case. The Bolsheviks have only got some 270,000 troops in European Russia; the railways in this theatre are in a state of great disorganization and in a hopeless state of repair with no power of amelioration; the power of making munitions etc. is very limited; the output of aeroplanes and tanks is negligible. The Bolsheviks possess few big guns, a limited amount of ammunition, poor gas appliances or protection etc. and no means of increasing production; added to the above will be complete isolation from the outside world while poor power of production, poor power of manufacture and still poorer power of transportation will make the conduct of war on even a moderate scale impossible. On the other hand the Border States will have behind them the whole support, moral and material, of the Allies—and in Allies I of course include America since America is at least as responsible as anyone else for calling these States into being. The Border States would also have the assistance of such Allied voluntary effort as it may be thought possible and advisable to give. There can be no doubt as to the final issue of such a war.

8. What would be the cost of such a war?

It is not possible to form an estimate of the cost until the frontiers have been delimitated and until the total front of operations has been divided up and allotted to each of the Great Powers, but so far as Great Britain is concerned we are still possessed of vast stores of munitions of all sorts, of clothing, boots etc. the grant of which would not form a fresh charge on the Exchequer. It is true that we should have to nurse those Border States which fell to our care with food, agricultural implements, and other necessities of peace life which tend to make a people busy, thriving, and contented and which are therefore some of the surest means of preventing the spread of Bolshevism, but it does not appear to me that all this put together would mean anything very formidable nor indeed, since the war material and clothing is already available, does it appear that the charges will be much greater than the responsibilities we have already undertaken—*vis à vis*—these young States—would necessarily entail.

9. I have not touched on the question of unity of Command in the Border States, this is a matter which can be dealt with later, nor have I referred to Bolshevist Propaganda—a most important matter—because I deem it a little bit outside the scope of a military paper.

10. In conclusion I submit the following clean cut proposals:

(a) An advance into Russia with a view to the defeat of the Bolshevik Armies and the occupation of the country followed by a new Government to be set up by Russians is not, under present conditions, a possible operation of war.

(b) If the frontiers of the Border States are delimitated, if the frontiers and States thus defined are divided up amongst the Great Powers for the purposes shewn in para 4(c) it is in my opinion an operation of war to force the Bolshevik troops back over the newly defined frontiers should they not agree to go peaceably, and then to maintain those frontiers against any attacks which Russian forces can bring to bear against them.

Paris   Henry Wilson
19th February 1919.   C.I.G.S.

57

Wilson to The Prime Minister

[Carbon]   19th February 1919

It is a year today since you appointed me Chief of the Imperial General Staff. In that period we have been through many anxious and difficult times, and I want to thank you for your constant support and most courteous treatment of me. If your recollection of our work is as pleasant to you as it is to me I am well satisfied and fully repaid.

58

Message from Prime Minister to C.I.G.S.

21st February 1919

Felicitations on your first birthday as C.I.G.S. You have turned out a fine infant and in every way fulfilled the highest expectations of the anxious parent. What a time we have been through! Your foresight, resource, courage and good cheer contributed materially to the ultimate triumph.

59

Wilson to Churchill

[Carbon]   [Paris]
SECRET   13th March 1919.

Yesterday we spent discussing the question as to whether the ex-Emperor of Austria should be allowed to go to Switzerland or not—the Swiss not wanting him there unless the Great Powers will guarantee that they will not later on ask for extradition. The question was referred to a Committee.[6] We then went through the Air conditions for the Germans, which in my opinion are much too severe, and unnecessarily so, but which on the whole were endorsed by the Supreme Council.

The Prime Minister, Wemyss, Maclay, and I had a long talk about the conditions to be offered to the Boche today at Brussels. I got a wire from Haking last night which on the whole was rather re-assuring and my opinion is that the Boche will agree to our terms re their shipping.

This morning we discuss the question of Constantinople, and a memorandum put in by the Admiralty on the League of Nations Covenant. I have been asked to draw up a short military memorandum on our military view of the Covenant and I am engaged on that at the present moment; but I find the Articles of the Covenant so obscure, so vague, and to me so contradictory, that I am afraid my effort will be of little practical use.

This afternoon we were to have discussed the final draft of military terms for the Boche but for some reason or another the Supreme Council don't propose to meet. I am not even sure if they are going to meet tomorrow. These delays prevent my getting away, which is most annoying, as after the military terms have been discussed I am wanted to be present at the discussions on the Rhine front and the demilitarisation of the Palatinate. If we meet neither today nor tomorrow and only pass the military terms on Saturday it means that the Rhine front cannot possibly come up until Monday or Tuesday. Allenby arrives on one of those days when the question of Syria will have to be examined and God knows when I will get over.

Curzon has sent me a wire re six hundred thousand War Office rations and medical comforts which are now at Copenhagen and which were put there for the repatriation of our prisoners. I am going to ask Chamberlain for permission to use these for the Boche ['altered to Russians' added in margin] in our occupied territories.

Nothing definite has been settled about Franchet d'Esperey's position at Constantinople. I hope to bring it up to this morning's discussion, which is by the way only a meeting of the British Delegation, and I should think perhaps we had better wait now until Allenby arrives before pushing the matter through.

I spoke to Bob Cecil about Allenby succeeding Wingate, but that appears to be off for the moment as Mr. Balfour thinks it not opportune to make any change . . .

60

Wilson to Churchill

[Carbon]   [Paris]
SECRET   15th March 1919.

I see by your wire received last night that you have selected Travers Clarke as Quartermaster General. I am sure he will do the work well and be a great help in clearing up the Q.M.G. business in all theatres. I think on the other hand that DuCane would have strengthened the new Army Council more than Travers Clarke will do.[7] However, that is in the more remote future and perhaps the pressing needs of the present are more important.

Yesterday we did practically nothing. The Prime Ministers with President Wilson had a three hours' talk in the afternoon, resulting I believe in no decision. Hankey was not present and therefore there is no record of what passed.

This afternoon we take up the military terms for the Boche and hope to get them through, but I understand there is a chance of President Wilson once more raising the question of giving the Boche a Conscript Army in preference to a Voluntary Army. I am sure if he does the P.M. will down him at once, and whether the Voluntary Army is right or wrong it will really be intolerable if decisions reached one week will be reversed the next.

* * *

The questions of Reparation and Indemnity are giving great trouble and so far as I can make out we have been quite unable to see daylight up to the present. Klotz's position is becoming intolerable nor does it appear to me that any Minister of Finance will live a week in France if he imposes heavy taxation on the people.

I will add a line to this this evening after we have had our meeting on the military terms.

Later—5.p.m.

We went to the Quai d'Orsay this afternoon. President Wilson did not appear and so the whole meeting was postponed for 48 hours until 3 o'clock on Monday. This seemed to be a stroke of genius on the part of somebody, I do not quite know who, but whether it means that we shall have our Peace Terms ready by the end of this coming week or not I much doubt.

I saw Foch about the proposal to train Russians to send to Murmansk and Archangel in order to stiffen up those garrisons when we come away. He was entirely opposed to the idea saying that he saw no good in trying to bolster up Russians under those conditions and therefore he did not propose to help us in either collecting Russians or training them for that purpose. Our Prime Minister also spoke to me on this subject. He is very apprehensive that we may be starting another very expensive 'Denikin' and 'Kolchak' in Archangel and Murmansk, and there is certainly something to be said from that point of view. I think that before you take action, either in sending a mission to General Judenitch or in beginning to collect up the Russian officers and men with a view to shipment to Northern Russia, that it would be well to wait for the decision of the Supreme Council as to future action in Russia. When this decision will be given I have no idea because as I have told you the subject of Russia has never been considered, and so far as I know is not yet over the horizon, but the Prime Minister is so averse from spending more money, either on a mission to Judenitch or in training the Russians, or in as it were starting another 'Denikin' in Northern Russia, that I think it will be wise to pause before you do anything further in the matter. I am sending Radcliffe a wire to say that Foch will not help us in the matter, and telling him that I have written to you on the subject . . .

61

Wilson to Churchill

[Carbon]   [Paris]
SECRET   22nd March 1919.

The P.M. is going down to Fontainebleau and has asked me to go down there with him to spend a couple of days in reviewing the position of affairs here in Paris, and in attempting to outline a policy for him to pursue in the future.[8] I find M. Clemenceau decidedly older and with distinctly less grip either of his colleagues or of the general situation. This of course greatly adds to the difficulties because, as Chairman, if he cannot hold the Meeting to their point and insist on decisions being reached, the usual result, which you know so well, follows—discursive debates, minor points fastened on; red herrings dragged across everybody's path; and at the end of hours, in a room with a temperature of one hundred, the result is nil. This is what happened yesterday. We spent three hours trying to draft a short telegram to the Boche telling them that they were to allow Haller's Divisions to pass through Danzig to Warsaw.[9] At the end of three hours the telegram was not in fact drafted.

The P.M. is very much alive to the danger that he sees in front of him and so wants a couple of days' quiet to consider what course of action he ought to pursue. I had meant to have crossed last night and to have been in London this morning. I do not suppose now I shall get over until Tuesday or Wednesday but you may be sure I will take the first opportunity I can to get back.

The D.M.O. has sent me a short note containing a proposal to send a rather big Mission to the Baltic States. I have written to him to say that I hope that after this Fontainebleau trip to be in a position to let you know the P.M.'s views on the Russian situation generally, but my own feeling at the moment is that we are unwise to undertake further responsibilities until combined effort is made on the part of the Allies to solve the Russian problem. As I said to Radcliffe, one thing is quite certain and that is that England alone is incapable of solving the Russian problem.

A curious thing happened at yesterday's Meeting. When it was found that we could not arrive at some decision as to passing Haller's Divisions through Danzig to Warsaw Foch proposed that he should, within the very limited capacity of the rolling stock, pass Haller's troops through Italy and Austria to Cracow and thus to Warsaw. The Supreme Council would not agree to this proposal!

We have not yet so far as I know had an answer to the two telegrams we sent, one to the Commander-in-Chief in Poland and one to the Commander-in-Chief in the Ukraine, to cease fighting at Lemberg.[10] I do not quite know what the Supreme Council will do if these two Commanders-in-Chief pay no attention to their telegrams. It will only be another proof of the really hopeless position into which Paris is allowing itself to drift.

I hope your Dinner last night to Jack Cowans was a great success.[11] I was really sorry not to be present. How did Jack acquit himself as an orator? . . .

62

Wilson to Milner

[Carbon]   [Paris]
SECRET   28th March 1919.

I got your letter and enclosure of Hankey's which I return to you. During the few hours that I was in London the day before yesterday I was so hustled that I had not the time to telephone nor to write you a line . . . You may have seen a rather unfair attack which Foch made on Denikin at one of the Meetings here four or five days ago. This attack was due so far as I can see to two things: first to a certain soreness about the French mis-handling of the South Russian problem and their now being kicked out of Odessa,[12] and secondly from a very pessimistic report furnished by a young fellow called Berthelot, himself I believe a nephew of the fat General. However, I really do not think Foch did Denikin any harm, and Denikin is getting all the supplies which according to Briggs he can handle and digest.

You know of course that the Italians have agreed to take over from us the Batoum-Baku line, an agreement which to me appears somewhat sanguine ['or cynical!' added in holograph], and I have settled with Diaz that the Italians shall send out a General and a Staff, both military and naval, to go round all our dispositions and then to come to a fixed plan as to the relief, both of our Caspian fleet and of Milne's troops in the Caucasus. This will no doubt take two or three or four months, and will be constantly hung up for lack of shipping.

Meanwhile, yesterday it was settled that military action in Central Europe, outside Roumania and Poland, was not an answer to Bolshevism, so the plan for such action which was put up by Foch was negatived. If military action is not an answer to Bolshevism then I do not know what is, and if there is none then hang go all the terms of peace.

When are you coming over here again? . . .

63

Wilson to Churchill

[Carbon]   [Paris]
SECRET   2nd April 1919.

I gave the Prime Minister your telephone message of last night re asking the President for permission to disembark the sailors from the two American cruisers at Murmansk if the situation requires it and if Richardson approves. The Prime Minister saw the President this morning who said that he had no objection but wished me to discuss it with Bliss. I have just been to see Bliss who again on his part says that he has no objection but must inform Benson and get his approval, and I am writing at the present moment for a telephone message from Bliss to say that Benson approves.

This morning in talking with the Prime Minister I suggested to him that in view of the unsatisfactory state of the moral of the French and the Americans we ought to let both Ironside and Maynard inform all their commands that their troops would be relieved by fresh troops as soon as the ice permitted. Bliss came to see me last night with some alarming telegrams from his people in Archangel and he was very nervous of what the Americans up there might do, hinting that it was just possible they might even join the Bolshevists. I asked him whether he thought a promise that these men would be relieved would steady them for the time being and he said he could not help thinking that it would be a very wise thing to do. The Prime Minister when I told him of these facts agreed that it was probably the best course open to us at the moment, so I have asked Radcliffe to telephone over now to Kirke to get your approval for telegrams in the above sense to be sent to both Maynard and Ironside.

Foch is off to Spa tonight.[13] He wanted me to go with him but it is impossible for me to be away at the moment. The Boche now seem to be going to try to take charge of the situation by making offers to us as to the course we should pursue; thus we hear it likely that they will offer to transport the whole of Haller's Polish troops from France across Germany and put them into Poland, thus obviating their going via Danzig, and, as it appears to me, incidentally challenging Paris to enforce its views as regards the passage of Polish troops from Danzig into Poland. The Boche also seem to be going to make an offer to rebuild with their own men and their own material all the towns and villages in France which they destroyed. Both these proposals seem to me to be in the nature of an attempt to take the conduct of the future out of the hands of Paris and to put it under the roofs of Berlin.

I expect the Italian officers who are going to go out to Constantinople and on to the Caucasus to turn up here in the next couple of days, when we will show them all the information we possess as regards Milne's and the Caspian naval dispositions, and push them off with all speed to Constantinople. I am personally in a hurry to get out of the Caucasus because I am not quite clear that the Turks and the Bulgars are not going to combine and make it very difficult for us to maintain our position, either in the Caucasus or in Constantinople. It is a pity that the American Constitution is so cumbersome because if it is settled that the Americans take over Constantinople it will be a great convenience if they will do it at once, whereas, apparently, there is no possibility of such a thing because any proposal of that description has to go before Congress before it can be adopted by the President[14] . . . I have asked for a ruling as to which country is responsible for enforcing Armistice or Peace Terms on to the Turks, as if we are the people we ought to set to work at once to make our plans.

Bliss has just telephoned that Admiral Benson has told the 2 cruisers to land what men they can if so desired . . .

64

Major-General Sir C. H. Harington to Wilson

War Office
6th April, 1919.

Many thanks for yours. I am afraid you are having a most difficult time and we quite understand that it is hopeless to expect you back under these circumstances, and I hear you have had to put off the dinner again.[15]

Things are going all right here.

Horne was very angry at not getting Southern Command but he was a little quieter when I saw him yesterday. Maxse has accepted York but I do not think that anything has been fixed about Chester. Winston saw Congreve and I understand was not greatly impressed and Congreve said that he always suffered from Asthma in that part of the world. Winston has not mentioned anything about a new M[ilitary] S[ecretary] so I hope he is sticking to his bargain with you that he would not touch it till you came back. There is a feeling that other theatres have been left out in these new commands. Marshall tells me that he would like to get a command in India—for instance, the Southern Army if there is a chance,—and I have told Winston. The latter was very good with the Lords-Lieutenant over the reconstruction of the T.F.[16] and quite carried them with him, and the same thing with the Military Members of the House of Commons who much appreciated his address. I went with him on both occasions and I am convinced that he did a lot of good. I do not think there will be any difficulty in getting men for Russia.[17] I am trying to make quite sure that those strengthened ships—the "Czar" and "Czaritsa" are back in time from Port Said where they tranship Australians and are ready to start again by the 1st May.

I lectured at the Staff College a few days ago. They are a splendid lot and of course all want to go to Russia . . .

I am a little worried about the command of these Territorial divisions. The Lords-Lieutenant, Derby, and Esher are very anxious that officers who have commanded Territorial divisions in the war should get these. I agree that their claims should have great consideration, but all, including those on the Rhine, must be considered. It would be grossly unfair to give these fourteen permanent jobs simply on that reason. We badly want a Selection Board, and I am sure as soon as you come back you ought to get Sir Douglas, the Army Commanders, Cavan, and Marshall, to settle these things and many others. M.S. is writing to you.

I have put up a small Committee to go into the question of Permits for officers' wives. It is monstrous that all these bankers and butchers wives and peeresses are allowed to go anywhere while the soldier's wife is not, and this Office must be made more human.

* * *

65

Wilson to Harington

[Carbon]

[Paris]
8th April 1919.

Many thanks for your letter received last night. I do not see any immediate prospect of returning home, but as Paris lives from day to day, not to mention the nights, one never knows when writing a letter that one won't walk into the room of the man to whom the letter is addressed before the letter is delivered.

I am sorry Horne was angry at not getting the Southern Command but I have very little patience with those gentlemen who pick and choose their jobs, and I wrote and told him that I was mainly instrumental in Harper being appointed. I see that Maxse has accepted York but that nothing has been finally settled about Chester nor about the new Military Secretary, and I am sure Winston will not do anything about the latter appointment without having a further talk with me. As regards the outside Commands, I put in, as you may remember, George Milne for one of the Home Commands and suggested also that Marshall should be considered for India. I am quite certain that we ought not to forget those outlying people, and in our Honours Gazette make sure that neither Ironside nor Maynard are forgotten.

I am sure Winston was admirable with the Lords Lieutenant over the reconstruction scheme for the Territorials. I quite agree with you that although the claims of those Generals who commanded the Territorial Divisions during the war must be very carefully considered it would be very unfair to exclude the consideration of all the other officers, and your proposal that we should start a Selection Board at the first moment is perfectly sound. Now that we have got a new Commander-in-Chief in England and new Commanders at Aldershot and Salisbury we have quite enough material with which to work.

I am glad you are going into the question of the permits for officers' wives. It is a positive scandal the way both highly placed social individuals and pushful bagmen, with their wives or other people's wives, are allowed out into the different countries at the present moment. Only yesterday I was told of a number of people, all of military age, none of whom have been out of England since August 1914, who are now trafficking in all the different countries, trying to make contracts, and picking up money to the exclusion of sailors and soldiers and their wives who have been fighting right through the war. I do not mean that the soldiers and sailors have been fighting their wives but I do mean that the soldiers and the sailors and their wives have been fighting the Boche.

* * *

66

Allenby to Wilson

The Residency,
Cairo
[Holograph]   21st April 1919

* * *

The situation in Egypt has not improved. Outwardly there is quiet; and, in the Provinces, order prevails. This is due to the presence of my troops. The Strike continues, however, under terrorism.[18] All Government offices are practically at a standstill. The law courts are closed in Cairo. An irreducible minimum of trains are running on the main lines & worked by military staffs. I have given the Ministry every chance to exert their influence, but they have none left and have completely failed to stop the strike. I am now going to arrest the leaders of the movement—many of them lawyers & notables—and tomorrow I issue a proclamation ordering all back to work. I should have done this last week; but the week has been one of holidays, for all creeds, ending today with a big Moslem holiday. I may have to arrest 70 to 100 leaders; but it has got to be done.

22nd April. The Prime Minister has resigned, and the fall of the Ministry will possibly have no bad—even a good—effect. Rumours are that officials return to work tomorrow. If so, good. If not, then I must make the arrests.

The Americans have recognized the Protectorate of Gt. Britain over Egypt. This was communicated to me, this afternoon, by the American Consul General, & I shall publish this letter in the papers tomorrow. The recognition will, I believe, have a calming effect on public opinion, as it was hoped & expected that Wilson (President) wd support Nationalists.

I'm sorry to say that some 3,000 men at the Demobilization Camp at Kantara have refused to allow men to come on as helpers on the railways. I am working the railways by military personnel & had formed some railway companies for Kantara. Some trade union microbe has got into them; & they are obstinate, though polite, in their refusal. I can't shoot them all for mutiny; so I must carry on as best I can, & I must resume demobilization. I have wired the situation to Troopers;[19] and hope that you will hasten on my promised reinforcements. The reasons given by the men was that to work on the railways wd be "strike breaking". However, the real reason is homesickness, & distrust of the War Office and their promises. They don't believe that reinforcements are coming; or that, if they do come, demobilization will be resumed.

23rd April—Most of the government officials have returned to work this morning; & I hope the remainder will return during the day. My Proclamation, the resignation of the Ministry—wh had become unpopular—& Wilson's recognition of our Protectorate have all contributed to the result; and each will, probably, eventually claim the whole credit! Martial law will have to rule the country, for months to come, & I don't see much prospect of reducing the number of troops now garrisoning the country. Demobilization must go on, or my troops will mutiny—so I reiterate the necessity for a steady flow of reinforcements & drafts . . .

67

Lieutenant-General Sir F. J. Davies
to Wilson

War Office,
Whitehall,
S.W.1.

[Holograph]   7.5.19.

Thanks for yours of the 5th and for the list with your notes which will be most useful. I will not forget the independent Commanders.

What about people in the W.O. who can't recommend themselves i.e. Army Councillors? They have all got a K. of some kind so I really think they can rest with that.

I am going to take [?] the list with the Military Members tomorrow but it will be a miracle if we get it all out on the Birthday.[20]

What can we do for Robertson? He is a G.C.B. Perhaps he would like a G.C.M.G. or do you think he ought to be a Field-Marshal? Winston wants to make some more, but I thought Plum and Allenby were the ones which stood out . . .

68

Wilson to Davies

Paris
[Copy]   8th May 1919.

I think the Army Council is much too decorated already. We are a mass of orders &c. Yes I think this applies also to Wully.

I am sure Plumer and Allenby ought to be made Marshals and I spoke about this long ago to Winston and I think he quite agreed.[21]

I wired Winston proposing, as I have also done before, that Chester be kept for Milne.[22] We really must watch the outside theatres, and D.H. of course won't do that for us!

So the Boches gave our Frocks a little touch of Boch yesterday and frightened them![23] . . .

69

Wilson to the Prime Minister

[Carbon]
SECRET   9th May 1919.

1. You asked me this morning for a note on the situation in the Caucasus with reference to our relief in that theatre by Italian troops.

2. The present position is as follows:

(a) We (British) are making arrangements to come away as soon as we can and are aiming at commencing to embark our troops at Batoum on June 15th.[24]

(b) I have informed Baron Sonnino and General Cavallero of the above.

(c) The Italians are getting their two Divisions ready and will be in a position to commence shipping at Taranto on June 1st.

(d) I have impressed on the Italians the necessity of taking over our Caspian Fleet at the earliest possible moment.

(e) The Italians say that we must find most of the tonnage for the shipment of their two Divisions and the tonnage for the upkeep of these troops in the Caucasus for some months until they can make their permanent arrangements.

(f) I now propose to tell Denikin of the contemplated change.

(g) An Italian Staff is now being taken round the Caucasus and is making the local arrangements for taking over from us.

3. The plans for the whole movement are therefore well advanced and when I get the shipping programme I can fix exact dates . . .

70

Allenby to Wilson

[Holograph]   Cairo
                                                  17th May/19

My telegram to Troopers will have kept you fully & well informed as to our affairs. Byron, your liaison officer, has come and has shown me your memorandum on the state of the Armies.[25] He appears to be an intelligent & helpful officer. I am sending him back, in a few days, with notes on our condition here. Egypt is quiet now; and agriculture and business are getting back to normal conditions. It will, however, be necessary to picket the Country—as at present—under Martial Law for certainly some months to come. Meanwhile, I have been forced to resume demobilization on a large scale.

There is great unrest and discontent throughout my Army; and, in the case of the Administrative service, unrest verges on mutiny. Nothing will convince the troops that military operations did not end on the signing of the Armistice; and they do not think the W. Office intends to deal fairly with them—by sending drafts & reinforcements which will facilitate their demobilization within a reasonable period of time. I have, as you know, a very large proportion of /14 & /15 men. These men would, most of them, have been dead by now—no doubt—if their services had been in France—but they take no comfort in that consideration. I know you are doing your best for me, and I know also your great difficulties; but it is no use my trying to hide from you the gravity of the situation as it appears here.

I am thankful that you have given up the idea of our withdrawing from Syria. If I withdraw my troops, I am pretty sure that the Arabs would at once declare an independent Syria and attack the French. The Emir Feisal is as bitterly anti-French, after his stay in Paris,[26] as he was before he left Syria for Europe. I saw him at Damascus, on the 12th inst., and had long talks with him. He told me, plainly, that he would have no French in Syria. There was a great demonstration in my honour—which practically took the form of a mass meeting. The streets were filled with processions of all sorts, bands & flags, troops & civilians, pell mell, yelling & singing. Hundreds of the lower class population were around with naked swords, knives and sticks wh they brandished round my car, in the wildest way, but in perfect friendliness. My wife was with me, and thoroughly enjoyed the experience. The least hint from Feisal would turn all this mob the other way. At a big dinner given to me by him there were the leading Sheikhs of all the Bedouin tribes of Syria & Trans-Jordania. He had brought them in to see him, on his return from France; and I think that, possibly, the accident of my visit prevented a Coup d'Etat and the declaration by him of the Independence of Syria. All these tribes are Feisal's men, & would obey him to the death; & they have many rifles & much ammunition.

Supposing that I withdrew to the proposed strategical line Dera'a–Haifa, and that these Arabs were against us. My right, at

Dera'a, is in the air, threatened by all the Druzes & Bedouin tribes who are based on the Hauran, rich in corn and all supplies. My long line of communications is open to attack from Es Salt, Amman, Kerak, by Arabs longing to plunder Palestine & to kill Jews who defile the Holy City of Jerusalem. Further south, the tribes of the Sinai Peninsula could attack Beersheba & El Arish; & cut my railway, or at any rate try to do so.

Zionism is more & more unpopular; and I am sure that any attempt to force it on Palestine at once would result in riots & massacres. The only chance for a peaceful settlement of the Syrian & Palestinian questions lies in the speedy arrival of the promised Commission from the Peace Conference.[27] Every day it is delayed makes the situation more difficult & dangerous. Lord Curzon, I know, is trying to stop it. If it is stopped, the Arabs will have been deceived, and their anti-French sentiment will become anti-European. The Zionists & French dislike the Commission, and so do our politicians in Mesopotamia; but it is the only solution for Syria & Palestine . . .

71

Wilson to Lieutenant-General
Sir J. J. Asser

[Carbon]
PERSONAL 24th May 1919.

I very much like your proposal to send me a weekly letter on the lines of the one I received last night. It is a great help to me to know what is going on in your Command. Of all the Commands under the War Office yours is the one I know least about and get the least information from.

I am picking up several of the points you mention and will just enquire how they are being dealt with at home.

Do not take too seriously conversations with the Secretary of State. I do not mean by this to disparage what he says but he has a habit of throwing out schemes in conversation, and in writing, which when examined are found in many cases to be unworkable, and which he himself, when the counter-case is put to him, is the first to admit. Therefore, do not act on anything he says until it has been endorsed from the War Office. I only give you this hint because in one or two places in your letter I see you refer to his wishes, which of course must receive every consideration, but which, as I have said are sometimes unworkable, and no one is quicker or more generous in admitting the fact than he is himself.

* * *

72

Wilson to General Sir W. R. Robertson

Dictated
SECRET & PERSONAL 5th June 1919.

I have not so far kept my promise to you with regard to writing you a weekly letter because every week since you went to Cologne I have sent you either Johnnie DuCane or Charlie Grant and as I saw them just before their departure, on each occasion, and told them the whole of my gossip, I thought it was only burdening you with more labour to write you a letter in addition. DuCane, who came back the day before yesterday, is off to Aix tonight for a three weeks' cure but of course he is available at twelve hours' notice if you want him at any time.

As regards the position of affairs here in Paris we have reached a point where within the next week we Allies must submit our second lot of Terms to the Boches, and this second lot must clearly be final. I think the "Frocks" will be ready to send the Boches these Terms some day next week. I imagine they will give the Boches about a week in which to sign. Of course there will be no question of any further talks. Therefore, with any luck, by the 13th or 20th of this month we shall know finally whether or not we are going to have a signed Peace. My own opinion is that when two people want to sign a paper as much as do the Allies and the Boches it will take more than all the Powers in all the Capitals to prevent them from doing so. Therefore I personally think there is very little chance indeed of your having to move forward. It is because of this that I keep on refusing to allow you to have the railway personnel etc. from France which you otherwise would undoubtedly require.

The Italian Mission that went out to look round the Caucasus arrived back in Paris last night, and Stokes, who I sent with them, tells me that they are going to report to their Government the advisability of taking over the Caucasus from us. I was very glad to hear this last night as I am fussing a good deal to get our troops out of the Caucasus, partly in order to let the demobilisables get home, partly in order to strengthen our force at Constantinople, and partly in order to send some battalions of natives to help Allenby.

The Afghan position is still very ill-defined but from all I can see there does not appear to be much heart or weight in the Afghan Jehad. If this is so our advance to Jalalabad will probably knock the bottom out of the whole thing and incidentally do an infinite amount of good to our prestige in Mesopotamia, Persia, and Trans-Caspia.[28]

As regards Russia there does not seem to me to be much chance of Petrograd falling, unless the Bolsheviks walk away from the place without fighting, in which case perhaps Hubert Gough will drive in a motor! Our arrangements up at Archangel and Murmansk are working quite satisfactorily and if Kolchak's Northern Column can get hold of Viatka and stretch up to Kotlas we ought to be able to make a junction at that place in the course of the next month.

We are in all sorts of difficulties with our good friends the French, our better friends the Arabs, and our best friends the Jews and Syrians in Palestine. The series of agreements entered into by gentlemen like Sir Edward Grey, Mr. Asquith, and the present Government have so completely boxed us up that it matters not in the faintest degree what we do we are bound to cast somebody. Our great object therefore at the moment is to fall as lightly as we can on the gentleman who is least likely to turn round and scrag us.

What a pity Johnnie French published those letters in the Daily Telegraph. It was bound to bring reprisals. Smith-Dorrien of course has asked to be allowed to reply.[29] I have advised the S. of S. on no account to allow him because if we once allow officers on full pay to get writing to the newspapers it seems to me there will be no end to the amount of damage it will do to the Army; each of us setting out to prove that our superiors are really our inferiors. I see Asquith had a special lunch at which he denounced the Field-Marshal, and meanwhile the Northcliffe Press keeps jobbing him in the ribs all the time. I am waiting for a suitable opportunity to sell my diary to the highest bidder, whether that bidder will be a man who will publish it or suppress it I am not yet quite clear . . .

73

Bridges to Wilson

Personal
No. C.S. 33/1.
Constantinople,
8th June, 1919.

You will not have received a letter from me for 3 weeks but I do not expect you have noticed this.

The past fortnight I spent in hospital with an infantile complaint—"mumps"—but am now back at the Mission.

Franchet d'Esperey . . . is preoccupied about the political situation in Bessarabia, where he thinks the Roumanians by their methods are antagonising the people and driving them to deal with the Bolshevists. From all I could gather in Bucharest 3 weeks ago this view is exaggerated. The Bessarabians appear to be for the most part backward clods who will accept anything in the way of a government if it is applied with force and consistency. Anyway the Roumanians appeared to be quite confident that they could handle them.

Franchet d'Esperey is also concerned about the Hungarian situation and the fact that we have allowed the Red Army time to form 7 divisions.[30]

For people who declared war after everyone else had finished fighting, I found the Roumanians very hard to satisfy. Like the Greeks, they want the fruits of everybody else's victories. They are particularly opposed to any kind of concessions to Bulgaria. The King of Roumania with whom I have had conversations, does not realize the danger that continual hostility or a revolution in Bulgaria would mean to his own country.

In this connection Franchet d'Esperey is to meet Teodoroff, The Prime Minister of Bulgaria and General Chrétien and discuss the advisability of an immediate reduction of the Bulgarian Army by the disbandment of 4 divisions. As this lies outside the terms of the Armistice it must be done by the goodwill of the Bulgarian Government. Personally I do not agree with the advisability of this measure. The Bulgarian Army is well in hand and is a factor of law and order. There are no police worthy of the name and if it is further reduced the Government will find it very difficult to control Bulgaria if she gets what she considers a "bad peace", and it will be an added temptation to her neighbours to pay off old scores. In a word the reduction will increase the risks of revolution, and a revolution in Bulgaria at the present time is to my mind most undesirable.

King Boris is gaining in influence every day. He is popular and deservedly so. An attractive personality, cultivated and accomplished, a good sportsman, and keen soldier, he has at the same time all the dignity of race that gives him a strong ascendancy over his entourage. He is apparently entirely without his father's duplicity. He is an asset to the future peace in the Near East and to monarchies in general. If he has to go we will have ourselves to thank for mismanaging the problem.

Though she cannot do quite all she would like with her own Government, I found the Queen of Roumania had all the foreigners, not excluding our own representatives, under her influence. A good instance of this was afforded me in the case of Colonel Anderson, the American Red Cross Commissioner for the S.E. He has fallen a victim to the Queen's charms and lays everything he can collect at her feet. Even Red Cross stores and a hospital train destined for Denikin had been handed over to the

Roumanians. In answer to my enquiries about this, Anderson said that the Roumanians had informed him that Rostoff would soon be in the hands of the Bolshevists and Denikin off the Map. I tried to put him straight.

You will observe that even the correspondents of the Foreign Press in Bucharest take the same blatant "won the war for you" tone and they remind one of the old Scotchwoman's prayer "Oh Lord take everything from everybody and give it all to me".

It is worth remarking that Roumanians, Serbs and Greeks are all following the same policy as regards Bulgaria, i.e. trying to show that Bulgaria has not demobilized, is in a state of anarchy, is engaged in comitadji activities, is creating depots on the frontier, secretly arming etc, and generally not playing the game. This is in order to afford pretexts for occupation of territory and to depreciate as much as possible Bulgaria's chances at the Peace Conference.

I hold no brief for the Bulgarians but must in justice say that since I have had dealings with them they have been correct and have done everything that was asked of them.

* * *

Confidential [holograph]

You will have remarked that the chief reason given by Franchet d'Esperey for the planting of his flag at Constantinople—to keep touch with the troops in S. Russia—has now disappeared.

The communications with Bucharest and Belgrade, the H.Q. of the Armies of the Danube & of Hungary, respectively, are bad and the situation on either of these fronts would justify the closer attention of the C in C.

Add to this the fact indicated in my telegram T.B. 821 of 12.5.19 (H.W. personal) that d'Esperey's prestige has considerably fallen & it would seem that you have an opportunity, should you wish it, of pressing for a change of command.

At the same time it would not be desirable to dispense with the French troops here. The general situation, though much improved in the last two months, does not warrant any reduction of the troops of occupation. The advent of the Caucasus division would be to my mind only a medium [?] addition.

Another reason which would make d'Esperey's exit from Constantinople desirable is that he is coquetting with the Turks on his own account simply, I believe, for want of something to do. (The advent of Madame & Mlle. d'Esperey, now expected, may help to keep him out of mischief!)

The ideal would be for d'Esperey to move his H.Q. to one of the Balkan capitals & leave the British in command in Turkey but this too much to expect.

No doubt the greater changes are so near at hand that you will not think it desirable to move in the matter.

Much as I dislike criticising my chiefs I thought I should put it up to you.

We have not had a hot day yet. Hailstorms and gales . . .

74

Wilson to Robertson

[Carbon]   [Paris]
SECRET & PERSONAL   13th June 1919.

I had to go over to London on Tuesday night for a meeting there on Wednesday and I came back here again yesterday.

I hear that it is proposed to hand the Boche his final Terms on Sunday and he is to sign or not sign, whichever he pleases, by Friday. This will give you what I fancy is a fairly accurate forecast of the date by which we shall know whether or not we have to take further military action. I am writing to the War Office to inform them of this and to tell them to let Asser know he may have to send you up the railway personnel at short notice. I do not know that I have much other gossip for you this week.

We hope that Ironside will be in his forward movement on Kotlas in the first week of next month. Meanwhile Koltchak seems to be steadily falling backwards, and if he continues to do this I am afraid our hope of a junction between Ironside's force and Koltchak's right by way of Viatka and Kotlas will be disappointed.[31]

The Boches continue to be most truculent in the Baltic States and so far I have been unable to persuade the 'Frocks' to take drastic action. It seems to me that we are losing such a good opportunity of measuring swords with the Boches over this question of the Baltic States—not over the Terms of Peace but on forcing him to carry out the Terms of the Armistice. However, the "Frocks" seem to think otherwise and as they are the responsible people there is nothing more to be said.[32]

Down in the South Denikin is doing very well and if he can go on for another fortnight or month he may get both Tsaritsin and Astrakhan, which will be really good business. We hope that Italians will begin shipping their troops from Taranto on the 20th, for the Caucasus, and by the end of July or middle of August our troops ought to be clear of that cursed country.

Monro calls urgently for the 20 battalions which we have ready to send to him, so directly we can get the shipping, somewhere towards the end of the month, they will begin to go out.[33] We hope to ship at the rate of two battalions a week, so that the whole movement will not be over until the middle of September. It is very unfortunate that these poor boys have to go out at the very height of the hot weather but we are doing all we can in the way of greatly increased tonnage to make their journey as bearable as possible, and I hope they won't have to go up country until the cool weather has set in.

Ireland goes from bad to worse[34] and it seems to me that we cannot get out of it, and ought not to get out of it now, without a little blood letting . . .

75

Churchill to Wilson

[Copy]   War Office, S.W.1
VERY SECRET   13.6.1919

On other papers I have commented on the poor quality of the reports and messages we receive from General Knox. The telegram from General Janin dated 30th May throws into painful contrast the military quality of the information with which Knox has supplied us. Here is a terse and comprehensive staff paper drafted in admirable military form and presenting a clear impression of the situation as a whole. Surely there are officers in our service capable of similar work. We should have at this most important centre an officer of the highest attainments in whose judgement we have the utmost confidence, and not merely a good energetic man who is clearly out of his depth.

I have been wondering whether we could spare Macdonogh for this extremely important service. Maxse is another man who would be adequate. There is no doubt that we require a figure of a certain size at this centre. Already Gough is making a considerable difference in the theatre where he is working clamping things together and keeping us well informed. The paramount importance of these Russian matters require us to employ officers of proved capacity possessing unimpeachable military credentials.

Pray let me know if you have any alternative suggestions to make, and generally what you think . . .

76

Wilson to Churchill

[Copy]   Paris
                                       15/6/19

I do not like the idea of changing Knox at the present time, nor indeed could a successor reach Omsk before the end of July or beginning of August.

Knox's position is a very difficult one. He is subordinate to Janin who again is a man of quite inferior quality. I fought at the beginning to get Knox a stronger position but M. Clemenceau was so much opposed to this that the P.M. felt constrained to give in. But not only is Knox subordinate to Janin but in addition he has nothing to [do] with operations. It says much for Knox that he has been able to convey the purport of our many telegrams to Kolchak and still keep friends with Janin. These are some of the reasons why I think we would be unwise to send out a senior officer—we have definitely accepted a seat in the second row in this theatre and although I was against this at the beginning—and am still—there is nothing to be gained I fear by re-opening that question. But there are other points we must remember. Neither Macdonogh nor Maxse so far as I know speak Russian, nor do they know nor understand the Russian mind. Knox not only talks Russian like a native but he knows everybody in Russia and some of his despatches during the war when the Russians still kept the field were very remarkable documents.

I am inclined to think that now that attention has been called to the fact that we want more front line information he will give us as much as he can collect.

I hope you will agree[35] . . .

77

Wilson to Churchill

[Carbon]   [Paris]
SECRET & PERSONAL

16th June 1919.

I have now had two talks with the Prime Minister about your proposal to get the Czechos, who are now in Siberia, to fight their way out to Viatka and Archangel,[36] and I think he will do all he can to further this scheme. I will, however, jog his memory day by day and will lose no opportunity of pressing your proposal.

This morning at and after breakfast the Prime Minister and

Lindley, who as you know is back from Archangel, and myself had
a long talk about Northern Russia. The Prime Minister is rather
frightened and very much averse from getting in any way much
mixed up by a too forward advance from Archangel, and the
paragraph which particularly caught his eye was Ironside's proposal (Telegram E.1426 dated June 6th. Ironmay) under certain
eventualities to go 30 miles south of Kotlas.[37] Lindley gave
Ironside the highest character as a man of sober sense and good
judgment and this had considerable weight with the Prime
Minister, but he asked me to send a wire to Ironside making two
points quite clear; first, that under no circumstances whatever
was he to get himself so embroiled that it would be necessary to
send an expedition to pull him out, because no expedition would
be sent; and secondly, under no circumstances whatever was he
to run any chance of not being able to withdraw the whole of his
force from Archangel before the ice set in. I pointed out to him
that in Ironside's telegram (above quoted) both these questions
had already been answered, and I made him read this telegram
again, but he still expressed so strong a desire for me to send a
telegram to Ironside that of course I at once agreed I would do so.
I enclose you a copy of what I propose to send and I am sending it
off to the D.M.O. to despatch from the War Office after you and
he have seen it.

I wrote you a line early this morning which will reach you at the
same time as this letter telling you that I hope to get over to
London for the best part of next week if I possibly can. There are
several important questions which I want to discuss with you and
in which I want your help. I am going to base my claim for the four
or five days in London on the fact that in any case I have to be at
Oxford tomorrow week, Tuesday, to receive the honour 'D.C.L.'
from the University.

This morning after discussing Archangel the Prime Minister
and I had a long talk about the Italian occupation of the Caucasus
and our attitude generally speaking towards the Italians. I told
him that I personally was much in favour of keeping friendly with
the Italians and of helping them in small ways to any of their
legitimate or possibly even illegitimate aspirations. His own mind

was travelling in the same order of ideas and he sent for Sonnino to have a quiet talk with him after I had left. I will let you know what the result was if I hear anything.

This afternoon I have to discuss Bulgaria and Poland with him, and tomorrow Turkey. The Four 'Frocks' are seeing the Turkish Grand Vizier tomorrow at the Quai d'Orsay.

It is a blessing to know no matter what happens we shall know the Boche attitude by the end of this week.

It is very hot over here and the country is parched and crying for rain . . .

78

Wilson to Lloyd George

[Carbon]

[Paris]
16th June 1919.

As I was not present at the Meetings in May when Marshal Foch laid out his plans for the march into Germany and the occupation of Berlin much of what I heard this afternoon was new to me.[38] I want without a moment's delay to give you such advice as I can without having had the time to go deeply into the problem.

I think our Force of 39 Divisions is enough to accomplish the operation you wish carried out, viz the march on and the occupation of the Capital, but if such a manoeuvre is not instantly successful in attaining your object I would be very anxious indeed as to what might follow.

The Allied Forces will consist of four different nationalities and starting from a long base will require—at any rate for a great part of the distance—four different Lines of Communication; these Lines of Communication will be German railways with German personnel. I need not enlarge on the danger of this, but it is obvious that a great many of our men will be required to protect these hundreds of miles of railways. In addition our men will have to be billeted on a population which may prove hostile and which in any case is almost starving.

The forward march does not frighten me but if this does not immediately bring us the desired result the straggling occupation of an enormous country where our troops can nowhere be strong, and in which we shall probably have to rule by martial law fills me with apprehension.

I advise therefore that while proclaiming that we are going to move forward until our end is achieved we should make our first bound only to the R. Weser (say 150 to 200 kilometres) and when we have got ourselves firmly secured up to this line then see what further action we can advantageously take, calling on the Poles, Czechos, and Italians to help and co-ordinating their assistance into one good sound converging military plan . . .
Copy to Marshal Foch (thro Gen Grant) DMO

79

Wilson to H. W. Moggridge

9.7.19.   [War Office]

I forgot to tell you what Bill Thwaites told me on the telephone:

1. Balfour said I *must* go over tomorrow (Thursday) to be present with Foch at a meeting on Friday about:
   Danzig,
   Siberia,
   Bulgaria.
2. Franchet said he *must* have 2 Battns of ours in Sofia. I said he could have a Platoon.
3. Clemenceau said he would withdraw his 2 Divs in the Balkans if we did not supply equal numbers. I said the sooner he withdrew his Divs the better as they were no use.
4. The Americans will (apparently) find the shipping for any Czechos from Vladivostock. I said "so best".
5. The 'Frocks' thought an Allied Divn. would be necessary at Danzig. I said we would not find a man.

6. The Frocks contemplated an Allied Force in Siberia pending a Plebiscite. I said not one British soldier.

Will you show these notes to D.M.O. . . .

80

Wilson to Lloyd George

[Holograph copy]   31/7/19

I am rather fussy about the future of the Army, its size, its composition, its distribution, etc. etc. and its relation to the Navy and the Air.

You know all these problems and their close ever inexplicable interdependence. And I am warmly anxious to lighten your load.

As you know I am much in favour of a Defence Minister and so is Beatty and so is Trenchard but if this is not practical politics at the moment couldn't you set the old C[ommittee of] I[mperial] D[efence] on its legs again with a Vice-Chairman (yourself of course Chairman for great decisions)[39] . . .

81

Sackville-West to Wilson

PRIVATE.   British Delegation,
                                                       Paris.
                                                       5th August 1919.

When you were in Paris you had a definite policy. This policy you gradually got adopted by the Conference. Now that you have gone away a situation has arisen where Paris and London, to a great extent, adopt divergent views. As I understand your policy it is to this effect — that we, the British, should clear out of Europe, concentrating our efforts upon the East. Unfortunately, when we get to the question of Russia the two cannot be so clearly differentiated. I have sent Colonel Beadon over this afternoon to see M.O.5[40] on the subject of Russia. The various telegrams the War Office send to me are to some extent conflicting on the subject. Demands are made by Russia on the Allies for material assistance. If I knew exactly to what extent the British Government was prepared to meet these demands I could go to my colleagues at Versailles with a statement and ask them to what extent they can make up the deficiency. I gather that the present policy is to back General Denikin, but if we supply General Denikin with all his requirements can we supply those demands put forward by General Gough? Would it not be wiser if the Powers divided up the various people whom they propose to supply and concentrated their efforts only upon them respectively? For instance, could we not say that we, the British, would, so far as we are able, satisfy the demands of the Baltic Provinces and General Denikin, leaving the French to deal with the Poles? Koltchak formulates demands but I am under the impression that we at least do not propose to send any more material to him, and I do not think anybody else is prepared to do so.

During the last few days the Quai d'Orsay has been somewhat agitated over the question of Bulgaria. Personally I do not believe that Bulgaria is going to make trouble, but many of the authorities concerned think they will.[41] In any case I understand that we, the British, are not going to send any troops there.

As regards Turkey, I do not think myself that the British Delegation in Paris realises the attitude that I think you wish me to take up. Mr. Balfour, more than even the Prime Minister, is realising that diplomacy without the support of the military is a somewhat frail reed to rely upon. If I understand rightly, we have sufficient troops, or we shall have sufficient troops by, say, April next, to fulfil the commitments which we, the British, have taken upon us as regards our own possessions, but we have no troops to carry out the policy in Europe. Mr. Balfour is realising this situation but he is realising it from what either General Thwaites or I myself have said to him rather than from an authoritative statement of policy by the British Government.

As regards Malcolm in Berlin. The job for which he was originally sent out, i.e. looking after Russian prisoners of war, has now come to an end. I am sure you want him to stay on in Berlin and he is being told by Mr. Balfour that he is required in connection with the Baltic Provinces and evacuation of German troops. It is most important, I think, that he should stay there, and the reason for which he stays is immaterial.

I am finding myself in a somewhat serious difficulty in so far as my duties at the Astoria[42] take up practically the whole of my time. From 11.30 till 1 o'clock every morning I attend a conference with Mr. Balfour and from 3.30 in the afternoon till about 7 o'clock I am at the Quai d'Orsay. Meanwhile an increasing number of subjects are referred to Versailles, where I am asked to sit in conference on them. I am delegating Studd to replace me at Versailles so far as I can, but the French somewhat resent this attitude. This must be interesting to you as you know the situation at Versailles as well as I do.

This letter does not require any answer as I can imagine that you are absolutely snowed under with letters, both of congratulation and of request. I merely send it to you to let you know the situation and I propose to send you letters of a similar nature from time to time.

I think I know your policy, generally speaking, and I will try to carry it out, but it is not made easier by the fact that I do not think the British Delegation as a whole sees eye to eye with what I imagine are your, and the Prime Minister's, ideas on many matters . . .

82

Wilson to Sackville-West

[Carbon]   6th August 1919.
Private

I have just received your letter of yesterday for which I am much obliged. You rightly interpret my frame of mind as regards our military action in Europe. Ever since November I have been struggling to get out of the scrum and concentrate on the mufflers

which we licked up round the outside railings. On the whole the
Cabinet has allowed me to do this although the process has been
very slow, and when we come out of Archangel and Murmansk,
and out of the Caucasus, we shall have no troops, properly so-
called, in Europe except—

A Mixed Brigade on the Rhine;

A small mission under Gough in the Baltic;

A battalion at Fiume;[43]

Probably about a division at Constantinople;

About a thousand officers and men with Denikin; and

Our commitments with Kolchak reduced probably to 100 to
150 officers and men.

There remains the question of giving stores and equipment to the
different people who are constantly shouting. I have proposed,
and the Cabinet has agreed, that we should put the weight of our
effort in helping Denikin. But such odds and ends of things as we
were going to send to Archangel and Murmansk and which are
not now required or which we withdraw from those parts when we
come away I propose to send to Gough for the Esthonians and the
North Russian Army. As regards Kolchak, you have seen the wire
in which we said we have nothing more which we can send, and
when our two battalions come away and our Mission is greatly
reduced all temptation on our part and all temptation to invite us
to send on Kolchak's part will probably disappear.

As regards Malcolm remaining in Berlin, by all means for the
present. But I see that Mr Balfour has been telegraphing to him
direct and giving him certain other duties to perform without
reference to us. Obviously if he wants Malcolm to perform those
duties Malcolm must do them, but it tends to confusion if Mr
Balfour telegraphs to him about some things and I telegraph to
him giving him orders about other things which may possibly
clash with the duties Mr Balfour wants him to perform. I have
written a long letter to Philip Kerr, a copy of which is being sent to
you, and you will see how easy it is to get into a muddle when I am
not fully informed of the wishes of the supreme Council. The
case of Milne really rather frightens me. He is put in a position
which no officer of his standing and seniority should be asked to

fill.[44] I am greatly amused at the fact that your Versailles friends are cross with you that you do not do your work down there. I quite sympathise with you but even "Roche's Bird" you will remember could not be in two places at once[45] . . .

83

Wilson to Churchill[46]

[Carbon]   *SECRET*
                                                  7th August 1919

1. Before the war the Military Forces were directed to fulfil three functions, viz.:
  (a) Peace garrisons throughout the Empire.
  (b) Drafts from Home to keep those garrisons up to strength.
  (c) The organization of those draft-finding units into formations up to divisions, inclusive—making a total in point of fact of 6 Regular and 14 Territorial Divisions—and thus constituting a force which when the Reserve was called up could intervene in small wars and guarantee Home Defence.
2. Three things must be noted:
  (a) The Army was raised on a voluntary basis, and it must be clear that an army so raised will in all probability have no relation to the policy of the Government. It happened by chance that the voluntary effort of these Islands, amounting to some 30,000 recruits a year, did give us Peace Garrisons; draft finding units; and a small Expeditionary Force. But the Expeditionary Force of 6 Divisions had no relation to any wars that could be conceived—it was too big for some and it was too small for others.
  (b) There was no real intention on the part of England to intervene in any great war on the continent of Europe —that this was so was abundantly clear from the size of the Armies that the Great Powers could place in the field as compared to those which we disposed of.

(c) There was, in the minds of many people, a real danger of an invasion of these islands.

3. Now that the war is over we are faced with a somewhat different problem:

(a) We still have to find Peace Garrisons for the Empire.

(b) We still have to keep draft-finding units to keep those Garrisons up to strength.

(c) We still require a small and very efficient force capable of moving at short notice overseas.

but

(d) There is no longer any possibility nor any danger of another great European war for some years to come.

(e) There is no longer, for years to come, any danger of invasion.

4. If the foregoing very short review of the situation before the war and the situation today is correct, and I confess that it seems to me to be irrefutable, then it follows, dealing with the immediate future only and taking a short view of our present necessities, that—

(a) We do not require any power of great expansion.

(b) We do not require any troops allotted for Home Defence only.

5. Although the conclusions arrived at in para. 4 follow logically on the position we are now in, as stated in para. 3, I have to observe one other fact in which we differ somewhat from our position in 1914 and that is we are much more likely to need troops of an expeditionary nature for our oversea possessions today than we were in 1914.

6. It is true that in 1914 we narrowly escaped civil war in Ireland; it is equally true that the state of Ireland now is at least as bad as at any period in 1914. But we have today much more danger facing us in Egypt, in Mesopotamia, and in India than anything that we could have foreseen in 1914.

7. I am now working out the minimum number of troops and of aeroplanes which in the opinion of the General Staff might be required to deal with a crisis in Ireland, a crisis in Egypt, a crisis in Mesopotamia, and a crisis in India. It is possible, it is even

probable, that if we get into difficulties in any one of those theatres we shall get into difficulties in all four. When I have arrived at rough figures I shall be able to make an estimate of the total annual cost. I can then submit a short paper showing those two items, i.e., the total force required for all the peace garrisons and for the reinforcements of those peace garrisons in case of deliberations, and the same paper will show the cost of this effort. But I shall have to put in a saving clause pointing out that my proposals are only for the immediate future and that taking a longer view of the military situation of the world it will probably be both necessary and wise to re-organize the forces of the Empire on a broader basis and one which will admit of considerable expansion in the case of a large war.

84

Wilson to Rawlinson

[Carbon]   1st September 1919.

Many thanks for your two letters dated August 13th and 16th the latter of which enclosed me a resume of events drawn up by Ironside, which I found very interesting.

I sent you a couple of days ago a long H.W. Telegram giving you my own personal opinion about affairs in your theatre. Since I sent that I have had further talks with Gough and also with Bowes who is just back from Siberia. They are both sceptical, almost hostile, to the Russians. They both tell me the same story, which, indeed, I hear on every hand, that the Russians only remain grateful as long as you pour in everything that they want, but that the moment the stream of benefactions ceases they turn round and curse you. With the single exception of Denikin I confess I see no use whatever in trying to bolster up the other Russian theatres. They have not got a leader in these other theatres who is worth a damn; they have not got a Corps of Officers who are either patriotic or knowledgeable; they have not got the slightest power of administration, and, in short, to put the thing bluntly, with the single exception of Denikin there is no doubt that Lenin and Trotsky and those round them are far the abler men. What Denikin will be able to do in the end I do not know, but we are continuing to send him large consignments of arms and equipment.

Toby [Rawlinson] who arrived here two or three days ago has been to see me two or three times. His account of the state of affairs in Armenia and the Caucasus is deplorable, and he himself advocates our leaving troops in those countries because he says, and I am sure with considerable truth, that when we leave the Caucasus the Turks will massacre the Armenians. But on his own showing the Armenians deserve to be massacred, since under our aegis they have for the last six months behaved in the most brutal manner to every Turk man, woman and child they could lay their hands on. Again in this theatre as in yours I am perfectly clear that our proper course is to clear out bag and baggage. I do not believe in these half measures of small Missions or small forces—either one thing or the other. Either, in your case, take Petrograd and move on Moscow or shell out altogether, and in the case of the Caucasus put in another 2 or 3 Divisions and effectively occupy Georgia, Azerbaijan and Armenia, or else, in this case also, clear out root and branch. There is no middle course—there never is—in these sort of countries.

Your last little attack on Ironside's front seems to have been quite successful. I am sure you are very wise in gaining these local successes before commencing your retirement in real earnest. I can quite believe that when the Russians realise that we are going to clear out they may turn nasty and even try to do some shooting, but I hope that if they try a game of this sort you will put it down with an iron hand. There was a time when I had some sympathy with the Russians but I have devilish little at the present moment . . .

85

Wilson to Churchill[47]

[Carbon]

[War Office]
2nd September 1919.

At the Cabinet this morning we began by discussing the question of the Caucasus, and Lord Curzon advocated the proposal to leave a Brigade of 4 Battalions spread over the towns of Tiflis, Batum and Baku. In this, on the whole, he was rather supported by Lord Milner, but Mr Bonar Law, Mr Montagu, Mr Austen Chamberlain and, I think, Mr Barnes were opposed to this. As you know I also am opposed to it because I think that a force of that strength is not strong enough to impress all those unruly people with the might of England. On the other hand, it is weak enough to tempt a lot of wild cut-throats and excitable natives who will be urged on to commit excesses of all sorts by men of the type of Enver and Kiamil. Further, it will cost us an enormous sum of money to keep up, and I am afraid it will be a very unpopular service both amongst the British soldiers and the natives. It is one thing to be a member of a considerable force dominating a country like the Caucasus, which we have hitherto been able to do, but it will be quite another thing to be a member of a poor miserable Brigade scattered over vast distances and therefore feeling continually both lonesome and forgotten.

However, this discussion of what we are to do in the Caucasus got presently mixed up with the next point which Lord Curzon brought up, namely, the despatch by the French of 12,000 men to Alexandretta. Lord Curzon agreed with me in thinking that it was fantastic to imagine that 12,000 French or native soldiers landed at Alexandretta could ever by any conceivable means get to Armenia and prevent massacres taking place there, and a suggestion that I made was agreed to by the Cabinet, Lord Curzon promising to telegraph to Mr Balfour in that sense. The proposal was this, that as the French were very anxious to stop massacres in Armenia and as they had 12,000 men to spare—which we have not—to send there, we would facilitate their going by every means in our power including even the loan of some shipping, but in order to get there they would have to go either to Batum or Trebizond. Further, we will agree to remain on in the Caucasus until this force of 12,000 men have got safely established in Erivan and Erzerum. The fact that the bulk of these 12,000 men were going from Constantinople or Bulgaria and were part of Franchet D'Esperey's force made it all the easier to transport them from Bulgarian and Turkish ports across the Black Sea to Batum and Trebizond. I pointed out that if this proposal was agreed to and a telegram sent we really would find out what was in the French mind, because if they refuse to go to Erzerum and Erivan it is quite clear that they have no intention of trying to stop massacres in Russian Armenia. If on the other hand they accept this it would be well worth our while to remain on a little longer until their force got established and then pass the onus for law and order on to the French shoulders. As you know, my own opinion is that M. Clemenceau proposes that this force should occupy Cilicia, Aleppo, Nisibin and possibly Mosul, and then claim the Sykes–Picot agreement.

The other subject we discussed this morning was whether or not Gough had made good his case by his paper, and whether or not he should return to the Baltic. Lord Curzon read a letter which he had received on the subject of the Baltic from the Prime Minister, and it was quite clear to me that neither the Prime Minister nor Lord Curzon would support Gough if he did return, and as he himself does not wish to return without full support I think we may take it that he will not go out again. When I see the minutes of the Cabinet I think I will find it recorded as the Cabinet decision that he is not to go out, in which case I will send for him and tell him . . .

86

Wilson to Sackville-West

[Carbon]   25th September 1919.

Many thanks for your three letters received in the last few days.
I quite agree that we should drop the question of pressing for the
return of the Bulgar prisoners. It is a very small matter and it is not
worth running contrary to the other Allies.

I have had a long talk with Allenby about Syria. It is perfectly
clear to me that a division such as is suggested by the Prime
Minister, that is to say, to allow the French to take over Cilicia and
the coast of Syria, and to allow the Arabs to remain on the railway
Aleppo-Damascus without having an exit to the sea will directly
lead to a war between the Arabs and the French. Moreover,
Clemenceau's careful caveat shows that he will still fight for a
place like Mosul, so that the Prime Minister's proposal does not
seem to me to solve anything, and this is certainly Allenby's
opinion also. Allenby says that if the Prime Minister's proposal is
carried out he, Allenby, will require all the troops he now has, that
is to say, roughly, two cavalry divisions and two Indian divisions
for Palestine, and one cavalry brigade and six infantry brigades for
Egypt.

As regards the Caucasus you will have seen that we have agreed
to leave one white and two black battalions in Batoum until a little
more daylight is visible. I raised no objection to this so long as we
had free issue and access through the Straits and the Bosphorous.
Personally I am all in favour of making friends with the Turks and
I cannot understand our Foreign Office view of backing perfectly
rotten people like the Greeks, who cannot possibly help us against
the Turks who can do us infinitive damage. I have just written a
minute in this sense to Winston on the question as to whether we
should maintain or withdraw our troops from the Anatolian
railway. I am all in favour of withdrawing them and in doing
nothing at all which would start a quarrel with the Turks. If we
had a friendly Turkey and we managed her properly we would
have a real buffer between the West and the East. If we have a

hostile Turkey she will throw herself into the arms of Germany and we shall have instead of a buffer a conduit pipe from West to East.

As regards the Baltic we really have got ourselves in an amazing position. Today is the 25th September. On the 22nd November last, just 10 months ago, I pressed very hard for a solution of the Russian and the Baltic States question, and the Cabinet agreed that when the Peace Conference opened the Prime Minister would not discusss any subject until a settlement of this question had been reached. As you know of course nothing whatever has been done in the ten months, or rather a good deal has been done, everybody jumping about in any direction like fleas on a blanket, now it is solemnly proposed to eject the Boches by bringing the Poles against them. I do not mind laying a wager of ten to one that if the Boches fight the Poles they, the Boches, will wipe the floor with them—in that case what position would the Allies be in? The real fact of course is Paris has crashed, nobody cares a damn what they say, their wisest course now would be to shut up shop and say nothing because otherwise they will simply be turned into ridicule. As I wrote to Winston this morning on another subject, you have only got to look at questions like Danzig, the Baltic, Poland, Hungary, Roumania, Greece and Smyrna, Italy and the Eastern Mediterranean, and now Fiume to see how little anybody in Europe cares what Paris says. But I am all in agreement with you that if the Poles are going to be used to clear the Boches out of the Baltic States, let the French do it and let us clear out bag and baggage, that is to say, Gough and Marsh and all our Mission.

Now as regards the troops for the plebiscite areas.[48] I daresay your proposal based on my original suggestion is the best, that is to say, areas should be allotted to the different Powers, on that area where a Power commanded, the bulk of the troops should belong to that Power with a small detachment of the Allies to show the Allies' flags—that would work all right, a small detachment I presume will be a company or battalion. But the first thing to do is to get Paris to allot the areas. Do you think you would be able to get that through?

Lastly, I quite agree with you in thinking that all these civilians ought now to get out of uniform and if possible leave their rank with their caps in the cloak-room. I will write a note on this subject to the A.G. I also agree with you that officers returning from these various missions should report to the War Office and should not be allowed to go and gas to responsible and irresponsible 'frocks' in Paris on their way back. I will see that this [is] done also.

I have still got this cursed cough[49] and am going down to Bagshot[50] on Saturday for a few days, but the medicines greatly relieve me and there is no doubt I am decidedly better . . .

87

Wilson to Sackville-West

[Copy]   11/10/19

Fight all you can against supplying any troops which that idiotic Paris want to put in some Zone along the Aidin Ry. as a "pneu" between the Greeks and Turks.[51] It is surely obvious that the Greeks can't remain in Smyrna without Allied assistance. It is surely obvious that the Allies can't give assistance, ought not to give it, won't give it. When that vain old ass Venizelos—Paris thought him a Statesman!—goes by the board his fantastic idea of taking over Asia Minor will go with him. Our business is to stand by the Turk. Meanwhile does George Milne command in Asia Minor or does he not! Will you get Eyre Crowe to find out. What did A.J.B. settle that time? when I was so angry with the old fool.

I am afraid my language is getting rough, but you must put it down to the whooping cough which however is getting better and F.O. incapacity which however is getting worse . . .

88

Wilson to Churchill

[Carbon]   12th October 1919

How do we stand about Robertson going to Ireland? He wants to know and I don't know what to tell him. Have you arranged with Lord French? And in view of the fact that we are—apparently—going to have some sort of Home Rule Bill this autumn which, if I know my country, will lead to serious trouble this winter, don't you think you ought to consult P.M. before finally settling?[52] . . .

89

Lieutenant-General Sir W. N. Congreve to Wilson

[Holograph]   Cairo
                                             Oct. 19 1919

I am just back from Cilicia & Syria & have had an interesting time. You are I am sure filled up with the opinions of politicals & want to hear no more. I am inclined to think them alarmists & to exaggerate things for the increase of their own importance & I am not at all sure that they all always do all they can to promote the Entente. I saw Picot & Brémond & both expressed themselves satisfied with us now, bar the matter of Armenians who we have been flooding Cilicia. Poor devils, no one seems to want them anywhere & yet despite all they have gone thro' I did not see a thin one amongst a good many thousand I saw & most looked cheery too. The massacres seem to have been a good deal exaggerated but the destruction of their villages is v. complete for hardly a stone remained on another. The women & children seem anyway to have survived & the former are reported content to live with Turks & have children by them. I don't know what there is about the Armenians, but no one, not even the missionaries, seems to have a good word to say for them.

Our troops seem on the whole pretty well. There is tho' too much malaria still & horses suffer from want of green food in Syria. 16 Lancers are in a bad way, very bad. Only 5 officers at duty, a large number of men sick, quite out of proportion to other Regts, & their horses very bad for want of proper attention. They are full of recruits & had no officers to look after them. I hope some are on the way for the Regt. now is not fit for service of any sort. Of course it is a most interesting country, but I have seen nothing in it I would exchange for Chartley.[53] My family always says I am rather "insular"!

Here are all the usual rumours of strikes, boycotts & rebellions in full swing—on the surface no signs of anything out of the common, but it all keeps poor Cheetham on the jump & he will be 100 years younger when Allenby returns. He came up here yesterday from Alexdria but the Govt still remains, chiefly because it draws detention allowance whilst there!

A lot of women seem to have come out in the short time I have been away & already they are dancing & balling several nights a week. I shall be glad when the Bull returns for I do not like Cairo any too well—it is hot & relaxing & there are too many people & the country too far away, but I am v. glad to have seen it.

My congratulations to you on yr. strike breaking arrangements wh. seem to have been wonderfully good.[54] But why oh why didn't yr. friend the P.M. make a real victory of it instead of allowing them to go off calling themselves victors & talking of "next time". It looks as if he had had the chance to free us from labour's tyranny for many years. Why did he throw it away? Papers so far with us have not reached the date of the end of the strike so I can't tell what happened but if he has let them off defeat then I shall find it hard to think well of him for he had a worse enemy than the Bosch to deal with.

I keep well & I hope you do, but I wish you would come out here for a rest & to see the situation for yourself. It would do you a world of good. I am wondering what is to be the future of Palestine. Weizmann lately here talks big. I fancy he will want

British bayonets to keep his head on his shoulders for many years to come & I am not sure that it would not be interesting to be High Comr & C in C of Palestine in the immediate future . . .

90

Wilson to Major-General H. C. Holman

[Carbon]
Private   25th October 1919.

Our present Secretary of State takes a very keen interest in many subjects but chiefly in Russia and in anything bearing on Russia, with the result that he has asked several of the Commanders and heads of Missions to telegraph and to report direct to him. Although of course any Secretary of State is quite within his rights to do this it is obviously somewhat outside the ordinary routine and military precedence. However, Mr Churchill always shows me anything that is sent to him and your telegrams to him are of course always repeated to me.

As regards letters I think your best plan will be always to send me a copy of the letters you write to the Secretary of State—that will make certain that I know what you have written, in case the Secretary of State forgets to show me your letter, and puts me in the position of letting you know at the earliest possible moment whether the views you express are those of the General Staff or not. If then I get copies of telegrams and letters there is not much harm done in this method of conducting business. But of course the fewer telegrams and the fewer letters you write the better it is . . .

91

Wilson to Viscount Esher

14th November 1919.

You will be pleased to hear that I have got rid of the whoopings; but not of the cough. All the same the cough though still tiresome at night is steadily getting better and another four or five years ought to see the end of it.

Meanwhile we are getting on with the post-bellum Army and we have at last settled such knotty questions as Communication Companies, Machine-Gun Corps, and Tank Corps. As regards the Territorials and the Yeomanry, although there has been as you rightly guess a babel of tongues we are making steady progress towards the solution, which like every other solution after a war of this magnitude, must be tentative. On the whole I am not displeased with the advance we have made in the last three weeks. The problem as you know well is very complicated and when we soldiers are not informed of the high policy of the Government nor of how much money we may have our military problem is very nearly insolvable. We have therefore, as we did before the war, taken on ourselves to decide on the high policy and are pegging away and putting ourselves in a military position to ensure and to enforce that policy if need be.

I must remind you that when you and the other 'Frocks' in Paris all last spring and summer made your Peace on a false base you did not simplify the military problems that we soldiers have to solve. When you and my sanctified cousin from the 'Dis-United' States of America thought fit to establish a permanent world's peace on 'Balkanised' Europe and a Soviet Russia, and when on the top of that you proposed to decide the fate of nations, both small and great, by a League without any power to enforce decisions, you did as far as your limited capabilities permitted you, establish the reign of eternal wars. Being in the military profession I make no complaint; being a taxpayer I hate you all like Hell. I have seen nothing more shameless nor more pathetic than the proposal from Paris to re-set up Versailles with executive powers at exactly the same moment when the League of Nations comes into being by the Terms of the Treaty and takes over the World, the Flesh, and more particularly the Devil.

Our Prime Minister seems to have thrown a Prinkipo fly into the turtle soup, with the result that the the City Fathers vomited up the whole dish.[55] It is again pathetic to realise that one year and three days after the Armistice we have between 20 and 30 wars raging in different parts of the world . . .

92

Holman to Wilson

[Holograph]   Taganrog
Private   28/11/19

The Secretary of State told me before I left England to write to him and he has since ordered me to telegraph to him at least 500 words a week. Just recently he has asked me for detailed information on a number of points which necessitated long telegrams in reply.

I think, if I remember right, that I have only written to him on the two occasions in which I have sent home the reports by officer messengers. I will certainly not fail to send you, in future, a copy of anything I write. My difficulty at present is to furnish the Secretary of State with information sufficient to enlighten him on all the many questions which arise.

This is in reply to your instructions dated 25th October which I have only just received. The ordinary post beat the W.O. bag in this case by at least a week.

I trust you have quite recovered from your cough and that you are not overworked.

I do not like the look of the Bolshevik game in Afghanistan, Persia, etc. & have endeavoured to represent the situation in my telegram of today's date to the Secretary of State . . .

93

Wilson to Milne

It is quite a long time since I wrote you a letter of gossip. I have been so sorry for you all these last few months because in spite of repeated and strenuous endeavours to get your position defined by the Paris authorities we have so far been quite unable to do it. Paris was never a very strong combination except indeed for evil but Paris now is 'pour rire'. How the different frock-coated gentlemen can go on issuing their impotent ukases, finding as they do that even the smallest States now ignore not only their wishes but their commands, I cannot imagine. To me the whole peace proposals were based on false assumptions and were built on false foundations, and I am not in the least therefore surprised to see the whole great fabric coming crashing down, and in my judgment the sooner it crashes the better we shall be because it will force us to return to realities and what you Scotch call 'verities'. It is an amusing state of affairs that after $12\frac{1}{2}$ months of Armistice and 5 months after the signature of Peace, two or three months after the ratification of the same by England, France and Italy we are still unable to finish off the Peace with the Boches.

As regards the Turks as you know we have not even commenced to consider the terms of peace, and all this time we keep on interfering with everybody's business. Paris is now sending quite considerable forces to plebiscite areas — we have to furnish 11 battalions, some cavalry and guns — then we advise the Italians to give up Fiume, and advise the Czechs to pass coal into Austria, and we advise the Poles not to fight the Lithuanians, and we advise the Roumanians not to fight the Hungarians on the one hand or Denikin on the other. If instead of spreading our energies all over Europe and doing nothing but irritating everybody thereby we devoted ourselves to governing our own countries we would I think be on much safer ground, but I confess that the present way of conducting an Empire fills me with alarm. I seem to see that the power of governing is slipping out of the hands of the English and that under ridiculous terms like 'devolution', 'self-determination', and so forth England is in reality saying, on the one hand to Ireland, on the other to Egypt, on yet another to India "I am sorry to have to tell you that I am quite incapable of governing you and under the title of devolution, federation, self-determination, sympathetic treatment, or some other nostrum you will be good enough to govern yourselves". If this is so it means the end of our Empire, because one thing is quite certain, if we cannot govern other people then other people will come and govern us; if we cannot govern the Sinn Feiners then the Sinn Feiners will govern us, as they are doing; if we cannot govern the Egyptians then the Egyptians will govern us as they are commencing to do; if we cannot govern the Indians then the Indians will govern us as they are commencing to do. Why the English who are by far the finest race in the world should suddenly begin to think that they have lost the art and power of governing I cannot imagine.

Touching things nearer to you we have asked for the recall of Franchet after the signature of Peace with the Bulgarians. I have no doubt that the French will refuse to do this but they will have to give some reason for their refusal and it is not easy to see what they can say except as an indication that they propose to take over Constantinople itself. As you know, my wish and intention ever since the Armistice has been to pull our troops out of the scrum of Europe and concentrate them in areas which really belong to us; now I find myself being driven by Paris to send crowds of troops back into Central Europe on some fantastic scheme of plebiscite. It is enough to make an angel cry when we have not got anything like enough troops to go round our own possessions.

I see that you have a poor opinion of Denikin. I am not quite sure that in this you are right. To me he would indeed be a wise man if he was what the democrat calls a 'reactionary', because I think we have proof enough already that a democracy, even in a most enlightened country like the United States of America, is rather a broken reed, but a democracy in Russia is nothing short of a danger to the world, so that some form of autocracy in Russia will probably be the best for that unfortunate country. The more I see of democracies and republics the more inefficient, callous, and disagreeable they appear to be.

I wish I could induce Downing Street and Paris to come to some reasonable terms with the Turks. It is a pitiable fact that after these eleven months we have not even begun to consider terms. Everything that we do so far as I can see tends to throw the old Turk into the arms of the Boches and the Bolshevists on the French! I have always thought that we were mad to allow, and indeed to encourage, Venizelos to go to Smyrna, and I am quite sure the old man would like to get out of it now if he could with any sort of credit because he has ruined himself and is going to ruin his country . . .

94

Wilson to Viscount Curzon

[Copy]   20/12/19

Undoubtedly a combination of Bolsheviks and Afghans would be a serious menace in the first place to Persia and in the second place to India, and I am not at all happy at the way events are shaping.

You will remember at our last Committee Meeting[56] I was insistent on the need, the necessity, of making friends with the Afghans as otherwise Malleson and his small force will have to be recalled in the event of a Bolshevik-Afghan attack. With the retirement of Denikin I think we may soon see the Bolsheviks in command of the Caspian and then our troubles will begin . . .

95

Wilson to Holman

[Carbon]   23rd December 1919.

Many thanks for your letter of the 28th November received a few days ago. I was sure you would understand my wish to have copies of anything you may write to the Secretary of State, not in order to interfere in any way but to make sure you were not advising one thing out there whilst I might be advising something different at this end. As you know the Secretary of State takes a tremendous interest in the Russian problem and has done an enormous deal to help the Russians—much more than any of us—and so long as we do not get ourselves involved with the Foreign Office or committed to anything not agreed to by the Cabinet I am all in favour of the Secretary of State's action.

Poor Denikin is being severely pushed about for the moment but from all your reports and from what Briggs told us on his return there seems no reason to think that he will not be able to bring the Bolsheviks to a standstill. The weak point of course is that he alone is conducting active operations against the Bolsheviks and the whole front from Murmansk to Odessa lies quiescent, whilst on the extreme east of the Baikal side things go from bad to worse, with the result that Denikin has to stand the shock of the great bulk of the Bolshevik hatred and forces . . .

96

Wilson to General Sir C. C. Monro

[Carbon]   29th December 1919.

Many thanks for your telegram just received in answer to my wire to you relative to the effect on India of Montagu's Bill.[57] I quite realise from what you say that later on when India begins, under the Montagu Bill, to "sit up and take notice", she may have something to say to the employment of Indian troops outside the Indian frontiers. This was a side of the question which I confess I had not realised but it is obviously one which may come to pass in the not distant future and which may affect very materially our position both in Mesopotamia and in Egypt.

I send you by this bag a copy of a little war game I am having played here in the War Office by the D.M.O. and D.M.I., assisted by Cobbe from the India Office and by Trenchard from the Air Office. I will let you know the result of our workings. The whole

problem in its larger aspect is for the decisions of the Foreign
Office and the Indian Office together, because, in short, it
amounts to this, whether we are to defend India in India, or under
our new obligations to Persia and under the dangerous threat of
the Bolshevists, we ought to attempt to defend India along the
northern boundaries of Persia and by retaking the command of
the Caspian, should it fall out of the hands of Denikin, and by the
occupation of Baku, Tiflis, and Batoum, cause the Bolshevist
threat to stand right back from the Indian frontier. The answer to
many of these questions will turn on the detailed examination of
ways and means, of roads and railways, and of transport in all its
different forms, and if as a result of our labours we can get something that is really sensible I will, as I say, send you a copy, and I
will also put the whole thing up to the Cabinet as a Cabinet Paper.

Last week I asked the Foreign Office to let me know where the
Command would lie if we get into trouble in Persia, pointing out
that Malleson at Meshed was based on Simla whilst MacMunn
in Baghdad and Hamadan was based on London. This is one of
those ridiculous anomalies which so often happen between
England and India.

All sorts of good wishes for 1920 . . .

97

Wilson to Robertson

[Copy]   31st December 1919.

There is no change nor further development about Ireland.
Winston is away till next week. The moment I catch him I will
discuss and write you again.

There never was a more ridiculous idea than that of sending a
Devonshire boy to East Prussia where balancing a tin hat on his
head with a bayonet fixed on his gun he is to stand at the mouth of
a Polling booth making certain that a Balt Baron votes according
to his conscience!

All good luck in 1920 . . .

1920

Wilson began 1920 with a general letter to Churchill (who was in the North of England) touching on four main themes of importance in the post-war years: intervention in Russia; the defence of India; the problems accompanying the peace settlement; and the apparent threat of violent domestic upheaval [98]. By the beginning of 1920 it had become clear that there would be no wholesale counter-revolution in Russia. All that was left for the British was to disengage from the remaining White forces as decently as possible. By the end of March Denikin had withdrawn his army from Novorossisk and had taken refuge in the Crimea. Soon after, he resigned his leadership of the White armies in favour of Baron Peter Wrangel who held out for a few more months before he and the remnants of his force were evacuated to Constantinople.[1] The progressive collapse of anti-Bolshevik forces in Russia put in jeopardy the hoped-for 'cordon sanitaire' of independent republics in the Caucasus and Transcaspia. Curzon favoured increased British support for the republics, but although there were some desultory talks with representatives from Georgia and Azerbaijan [99, 109], nothing came of these. Wilson was certainly quite opposed to any further British commitment.

A passing observation made by Wilson, that three-quarters of the Caucasian politicians were Jewish, illustrates a strain of anti-Semitism prevalent among people of his time and class. Jewishness was identified with Communism, or, as Wilson put it, 'the international view of German origin' [99]. Sir Tom Bridges remarked on the influence of Communist Jews in the Austrian government [102]. The appointment of a Jew, Sir Herbert Samuel, to be High Commissioner for Palestine came in for particular criticism. Both Curzon and Wilson disapproved [115, 117]. A noteworthy feature of the anti-Semitic sentiments expressed in the Wilson correspondence is their casual nature. For the most part they occur as a matter of course and clearly as if such opinions were commonly-held, as no doubt they were. Sir Henry Wilson was not given to self-analysis, but his old friend from South African days, Sir Walter Congreve, attempted to explain the attitude in April 1920. In the first place he noted the unattractive aspects of militant Zionism, and 'when you add the complicity of the Jews in Bolshevism and the centuries of aversion to Jews born in us it is hardly to be expected that private feeling can be pro-Jew' [106].

The experience with Denikin and the transitory leaders of weak new republics on the fringes of Soviet Russia boded ill for any 'forward' policy for the defence of India. Over the turn of the year, Wilson set his staff to play a 'War Game' on the question of Indian defence [98]. The exercise demonstrated to Wilson's satisfaction the impossibility of holding a defensive line through any part of south Russia. The best that could be managed was to fall back on the railheads in Palestine, Mesopotamia and India [115, 123]. Armed with these conclusions, the CIGS set about securing a complete withdrawal from the Caucasus. Since the autumn of 1919 the only British commitment of any significance comprised a small contingent of troops at Batum. Although at a ministerial conference in January 1920 Lloyd George agreed with Wilson that they should be withdrawn, Curzon's stubborn opposition and his touching faith that France and Italy might share responsibility for the Caucasus ensured that the men remained in Batum for the meantime.[2] Throughout the spring Wilson and Curzon sniped at each other over the commitment [101, 103, 108, 109, 112]. Wilson thought that he had won when he discovered in May that the French proposed to send only a colonial unit and that the Italians had dropped out altogether [115, 116]. Curzon managed to temporise [117], but when a small British detachment at Enzeli in north Persia had to withdraw in the face of a Bolshevik advance from the north, the pressure to quit Batum became irresistible [119, 120, 121, 122, 123]. After some last-minute delays, the British finally withdrew from the town in July 1920.[3]

One of the problems of the peace settlement which Wilson mentioned to Churchill at the start of the year was the need to provide troops to supervise League of Nations' plebiscites along Germany's eastern frontier [98]. The supply of these troops, and units to keep order in places such as Danzig [146, 150, 152], was a real thorn in Wilson's side, especially since he regarded it as a very low priority. In this matter, as with Batum, Lord Curzon disagreed [108, 150]. Post-war policy-making also put strains on Anglo-French relations. Although Wilson and Foch remained close [147, 152], the French, with reason, believed that the British were not as fully committed as they might have been to enforcing the terms of the peace settlement on Germany [99, 109, 149]. One successful instance of Anglo-French co-operation, however, was the joint Mission to Poland during the summer of 1920 [141, 144]. Nevertheless, as illustrated by Wilson's letters from the San Remo conference in April 1920, the process of international decision-making remained as long-winded and frustrating as it had been during the Paris conference in 1919 [108, 109, 110, 111].

The fourth theme in Sir Henry's letter to Churchill was that of domestic British unrest. Fear of civil disorder at home developing out of industrial action, especially in the coal mines, was shared by many politicians and generals. The need to retain troops at home placed yet another strain on Britain's scarce military resources. A constant theme in Wilson's writing was the 'necessity of securing our base',[4] and in January and November he used this argument to justify holding back troops earmarked for overseas [100, 147].

Wilson's domestic preoccupations were amplified by the apparently inexorable growth of violence in Ireland where, he wrote in May, 'we are getting into a filthier and filthier mess' [115]. The government's Irish policy—or, as Wilson would have had it, their *lack* of policy— prompted an extraordinary series of minutes between Wilson and Churchill during June and July [125–129, 132, 134, 136–138] in which the Secretary of State sought policy advice from the CIGS. Wilson was inexplicably reluctant to oblige. In normal circumstances he was never slow to offer an opinion on any topic, but concerning Ireland he confined himself to generalities, asserting that he could only assist at the policy level if and when the government handed over the administration of Ireland to the military. At the end of the year, indeed, the government decided to introduce Martial Law over part of Ireland and this raised Wilson's hopes that they might allow the army to apply it 'thoroughly' over the whole country [153]. The peculiarity of Ireland's military needs did for Robertson's hopes that he might get the Irish Command. Sir Nevil Macready was appointed to the job. Wilson complained that he had not been consulted, but Churchill told him that neither had he and that Lloyd George had insisted on Macready [105, 107].[5] The Prime

Minister argued that with his special experience of police work Macready was the general best suited to command in Ireland.[6]

During 1920 an unexpected crisis blew up in Mesopotamia. On 20 June the GOC in Baghdad, Sir Aylmer Haldane, sent Wilson a general report concerning his command. He noted that the Civil Commissioner was 'anxious regarding the situation', but stressed that he himself was not 'and have never been' thus [124]. Ten days later the Mesopotamian rebellion broke out, putting an immediate strain on military manpower reserves [145]. The insurrection dragged on until the early autumn, and illustrated all too graphically the slender margin of manpower available to the army. In December the DMO reflected that in Mesopotamia 'we ran things too fine and that a great disaster was only narrowly avoided'.[7] For Wilson an advantage of the Mesopotamian crisis was that it increased the pressure to evacuate the British garrison from Persia [140, 142, 145]. In other parts of the Middle East affairs were slightly less critical. Congreve glumly contemplated Palestine, for which he had little affection [106] and Allenby raised the unsettling possibility that Egypt might turn into 'another Ireland' [148].

In Constantinople the British and French occupying forces settled down more or less amicably. There was, nevertheless, much activity, as Bridges' and Harington's letters at the beginning and end of the year indicate [102, 151]. The Peace Treaty of Sèvres with Turkey retained the Sultan's government, but with reduced powers. It also transferred territory around Smyrna to Greece. But Turkish opposition to the treaty was beginning to build up in Anatolia where Mustafa Kemal had established a nationalist government at Angora [123]. In the meantime the Greeks, backed by Lloyd George but not favoured by Wilson or the army generally, had decided to carve out a larger empire for themselves in Asia Minor. By November their armies had conquered a large part of western Turkey. But a change of government in Athens during the same month left the Greek position somewhat uncertain [150].

One event in 1919 which had serious repercussions in 1920 was what became known as the 'Amritsar massacre'. On 13 April 1919 troops under the command of Brigadier-General R. E. H. Dyer fired without specific warning on a mass meeting in the Jallianwala Bagh, an enclosed square in the centre of the city. An estimated 379 Indians died. There was widespread disorder throughout the Punjab at the time and the immediate effect of Dyer's action was to quieten the region. The general was widely applauded in Britain and British India for his firm policy. But the Hunter Committee of Enquiry into the incident, which reported in May 1920, divided on racial lines. The white members of the committee largely exonerated Dyer; the Indians roundly condemned him. The government determined that the general should be ordered to retire, but this had to be approved by the Army Council who considered the matter in early July [133, 135]. Eventually they decided that Dyer should not be offered any further employment. The affair had an enormous impact in India and served to alienate a substantial part of Indian political opinion from the Raj.[8]

On a much more trivial level, one of the issues with which Wilson had to deal was the abolition of the rank of Brigadier-General. This upset a number of officers, but Wilson had no sympathy for those who appeared to desire status as an end in itself [106, 111, 113, 114, 118]. Perhaps a similar estimation lay behind his low opinion of politicians. A particular characteristic of the 1920 correspondence is Wilson's growing disenchantment with the 'frocks'. Throughout the empire he saw Lloyd George and his colleagues giving ground before nationalists and revolutionaries of one sort or another. Perhaps a little extravagantly, he deplored the 'total and absolute lack of any power to govern' [104]. But his acute frustration was partly caused by his growing estrangement from the Prime Minister. His advice was no longer so regularly sought or taken. This was especially so regarding Ireland where 'owing to the fact that I am a Protestant and an Ulsterman I am obviously untrustworthy and biassed' [115]. It is possible, moreover, that his odd reluctance to advise Churchill on Irish policy stemmed from a bleak appreciation that no advice he could give would be acceptable to Lloyd George. For a man like Wilson, who had sat with the great during the last year of the war and at the Peace Conference, such a rejection must have been very hard to take.

98

Wilson to Churchill

1st January 1920.

I got your three notes this morning—one about the future of Russia; one about 20,000 tons of coal for Denikin;[1] and one about Wardrop's fantastic idea of some British sailors taking over the Caspian.[2]

As regards the 20,000 tons of coal, I had a talk last night with the First Sea Lord who told me that the Commander-in-Chief of the Mediterranean had already given Denikin 2,000 tons and could give him more if the Cabinet so desired, and he went last night to see Lord Curzon with a view to getting an expression of opinion. If I hear any further gossip on this point before I send this letter I will add a line. I told Beatty that we here in the War Office would be only too delighted to back him in any way in his endeavours to get permission to give some more coal—even if we could give some 8,000 or 10,000 tons it would probably do for some months.

As regards your other two queries, I think I can best answer them by telling you what we are doing here. When Denikin's position became quite clear I set a War Game which is now being played by the D.M.O. and the D.M.I. Staffs. It runs on the following lines:

Denikin is back again on his line of last May, viz., Rostoff—Manytch River.

The Bolsheviks are in Astrakhan and Krasnovodsk.

The Turks and the Kurds are thoroughly unsettled and are hostile.

Allenby has sufficient troops in Palestine and in Egypt to secure law and order.

Persia is weak and vacillating, watching which is going to be the stronger party.

The Afghans are hostile.

India is suspicious and restless and requires all her internal troops plus one division to keep her quiet.

Now I have asked the D.M.I., who dates all his orders and despatches from Moscow, being the head Bolshevist, and the D.M.O., who dates his from the War Office, being the head Englishman, to work out carefully and in detail a plan for the attack and defence of Mesopotamia and India. I have asked Trenchard to help with the Air, and Beatty to help us as regards the Black Sea and the Caspian, and Cobbe to help us as regards India, and we are hard at work. It will take another 10 days or fortnight before we begin to see what is and what is not possible.

Turning to another subject, I am sorry to see that the Boches are now inclined to sign the Protocol, because this will mean that we will have to send all those battalions to the Plebiscite areas,[3] and in view of the condition of affairs in this country and in Ireland, in Egypt and in India we can very ill spare 11 British battalions. As you know I have fought against this ridiculous idea of garrisoning Plebiscite areas to get Balt Barons and other gentlemen of that description to vote according to their conscience but I have always been over-ruled by Paris.

I spent an hour yesterday with Mr Bonar Law enlightening him as to our position in the event of a Triple Alliance strike.[4] I pointed out to him that no body of men were ever so willing to help, and as a matter of fact always had helped, as the soldiers but that it would be criminal folly to allow the Cabinet to remain in ignorance of the condition in which we now find ourselves, especially after we have despatched the seven battalions to the Rhine, the battalions to Egypt and India, and the battalions to the Plebiscite areas. It is not at all that we do not want to help; it is not at all that we won't help: it simply is that there are certain things we can do and there are others that we cannot. I thought it would be good for Bonar to realise our position and not to go on in that sort of comfortable frame of mind which I am so afraid many of the Government departments are in which consists in saying "Ah, I know that when the pinch comes those soldiers will produce soldiers, lorry drivers, wireless, telephonists, etc. etc.". Beatty got nothing out of Curzon last night and has now wired to De Robeck to tell him not to give any more coal to

Denikin until he (Beatty) has laid the matter before the Cabinet. A thousand good wishes for 1920 . . .

99

Wilson to Major-General Sir W. Thwaites

[Carbon]   17th January 1920

Marshal Foch is a good deal upset by the delay in our sending out our plebiscite battalions because owing to the arrangements which he has made with the Boches as to the dates on which they retire their troops there will be a hiatus of five days during which there will be neither Boches nor British troops in those areas. I telephoned over last night to find out if there was any possible way of hastening but was told that no change could be made. I accordingly informed the Marshal. I think the initial fault was mine in allowing the men of the plebiscite battalions to remain too long on Christmas holidays.

We discussed in the Cabinet here for three hours last night the question of Denikin and the Caucasus but beyond a sort of preliminary clearance of brushwood we did nothing. I am personally, as you know, very anxious to avoid sending any troops out of England at the present moment but whether I shall be able to get the P.M. round to my way of thinking or not I do not know.

Today Beatty and I are going to discuss with the Georgian and Azerbaijani Delegates who are in Paris, their proposals for holding the line of the Caucasus, which they say they can do unaided provided we arm them and feed them. It will be amusing to see what sort of military gentlemen these civilians are and what sort of proposals they put up. Winston was very anxious to further support Denikin but the others would not hear of this and I was not able either to support his proposals or the proposal that we should hold the line Batoum-Baku with less than two divisions. I hear that three out of the four Georgian and Azerbaijani Delegates who are coming to see me are Jews. Do you think just by chance that it would suit the international view of German origin if we scattered our forces over the world and left England undefended? You might ask the first Jew boy you meet in Whitehall on your way to lunch . . .

100

Wilson to Congreve

[Carbon]   23rd January 1920
Personal

I am sending you a telegram to tell you that of the five battalions for Egypt and one for Palestine, total six, I am keeping back four for the present. I hope to let you have these later on, but the unrest in this country is so great, and the number of troops which are left to us is so few, that I was able to persuade the Prime Minister to refuse to send eight out of the eleven battalions due to go to East Prussia and Silesia, and I am pinching four others from you. You know how sorry I am to break faith with you like this at the last minute but I am sure you will realise that I have not done so without strong and sufficient reasons which I do not like to put into a letter. For the same reason, i.e., because of the unrest in this country I have given up all idea of going out to Egypt for the present. I am just back from Paris where great and far reaching decisions to do nothing were come to and no doubt will be adhered to until the enemy make us do something for a change . . .

101

Wilson to Curzon

[Copy]   16/February/1920
                                                              3/pm

I am so distressed you should think I was not playing fair about Batoum.[5] Several times on Saturday [14 February] and several times today I have tried to see you but with no sort of success.

My position is that I want to get the Batoum garrison away from that place as quickly as I can but I also want to use it to reinforce Constantinople which has been made dangerously weak by Franchet's action in withdrawing 4 battalions from that town, with a view to making the British position there untenable. The Prime Minister told me that on no account was Franchet to be allowed to take over the direct command of that town, and to show you how urgent I deem it that the troops now in Batoum should be shipped to Constantinople with all speed I may say that I have told Egypt to hold 2 battalions to be in readiness as reinforcements and I have ordered 4 more battalions here at home to be ready to move at short notice.

It is some weeks now since the S. of S. informed the H. of C. that the Batoum Garrison are coming away, and as you know I have been pressing for this move for a long time and on February 3rd the Cabinet decided that the evacuation might take place. It was not till Feb 14th that a telegram was sent to Mr Wardrop asking him what he thought should be done when the soldiers leave. I have not had an answer from Milne as to the date of the shipments but I cannot alter my advice to the Cabinet which is that I am anxious to get clear of Batoum as soon as possible and I am still more anxious to reinforce our garrison at Constantinople . . .

102

Bridges to Wilson

Constantinople,
24th February, 1920.

I arrived here on February 14th having crossed Franchet en route somewhere about Belgrade.

Communications, instead of improving, appear to get worse. Once beyond Vienna one launches into a sort of "no man's land" where time tables are unknown. People steal rolling stock and live in the trains to alleviate the "crise de logement". The so-called

Orient "Express" from Belgrade to Sofia, a distance of 350 kilometres and a 9 hour journey in peace, now takes 48 hours if you are lucky enough to coax an engine from the Bulgarians on their side of the frontier, but usually the journey takes 60 hours and 3 to 5 days to Salonika and the transit of goods is calculated in weeks. People seldom arrive anywhere with their baggage unless they are lucky enough to have an armed guard for it. At the present time of the year there is no other means of transit. The roads are such as to preclude motoring. Mud on the aerodromes and clouds on the mountains make flying an impossibility nine days out of ten. I shall come back by the diligence.

There are one or two items en route that may be of interest. I spent three days at Vienna waiting for the train. There had been a blank week in the service to Budapest owing to peevishness of officials and lack of coal. Fortunately at Vienna the winter has been a mild one so far but in spite of this the old people are dying off fast. The children are being fed by the Allies, the British taking them up to 6 years and the Americans from 6 to 15. We cannot feed them all but the Americans deal with at least 250,000 a day and our own work of more recent origin should rapidly grow. It is all well organised and the Cuninghames are doing good service in this direction.

The kroner was at 1050 to the £1. I was told that the Communist Jews are hastening the debacle of credit on a definite bolshevist plan. The Jew element in the Austrian Government, which is practically Communist, seems to be predominant at the present moment but the population themselves have little tendency to Bolshevism cold and hungry though they are. The police are extraordinarily good. The Volkswehr is a public danger, hooligans with rifles.

I spent one day at Buda-pest. Admiral Horthy, who I am glad to see has been duly elected Protector of Hungary, is anxious about the prospects of a big concerted Bolshevic movement in the spring. He says that communists at Vienna, Milan, Buda-pest and Moscow are working industriously for a united effort that will cut off South East Europe from the Western world and bolshevize it. I found that neither the French nor the Italian Generals

(Grazziani and Mombelli) favour Horthy's dictatorship so it is probably a good thing.

At Belgrade I took up the Hungarian food question with Alban Young, our Minister, Plunkett being away at Agram. It is too involved a question to bother you with but the gist of it is that Hungary has paid for food that the Serbs have not delivered for paltry reasons and the Serbs are demanding additional payments to compensate for the fall in the exchange though the delays have been deliberately caused by themselves. Alban Young unfortunately takes the Serb part though it is all against our ideas of business and fair play which makes me think that he has been too long in Guatemala whence he recently emerged. I hope however that he will be converted.

* * *

Here in Constantinople, as far as Anglo-French relations are concerned, calm reigns. General Claudel commands the French Army of the Orient, i.e. all French troops remaining in Turkey, Bulgaria and Macedonia and Thrace. He is temporarily in Franchet's seat. I tried to extract from him what his position was in regard to General Milne or what executive command he was expected to exercise if there was trouble in the country. He would not give me a direct answer, chiefly because I think he did not know. As I have telegraphed to you the position is nebulous. [Added in holograph: 'telegram held back as we have just heard from Franchet that he will be back early in March'.] I presume that under the original charter (which I never saw) a French General commands the Allied Armies of the Orient. Your telegram 72134 of 5th December, 1918 said "it was decided yesterday that all forces in the Balkans, including Turkey-in-Europe, should remain under general command of General Franchet d'Esperey." Presumably therefore, a French general must exercise general command in this sphere until the command of the Allied Armies in the Orient is dissolved. No doubt Franchet's visit home will clear up these matters. I was very glad to get your telegram 350 of February 19th and to hear that you had had it out with him. We will keep our eyes open for any sign of

interference in the way of detaching troops from General
[H.F.M.] Wilson's command.

* * *

The Atlantic Squadron is here under Fremantle and there is
much junketting. There are five ships of the R class and the effect
of their presence is certainly salutary although I am told the Turks
think nothing of them as they have only one funnel apiece. The
sailors some 2–3000 strong—a brave show—do a parade march
daily round various quarters. They did Stamboul this morning.
The Turks turned out in force but with oriental passivity. The
squadron was to have made a couple of trips up the Bosphorous
and into the Black Sea before it leaves but there have been some
mines about at the mouth of the Bosphorous, put there we think
by the Turks, and these trips will probably not take place.

* * *

103

Curzon to Wilson

[Holograph]   1, Carlton House Terrace,
S.W.1.
Feb. 25 1920

You will be relieved to hear that I brought the question of
Batoum before the Peace Conference this afternoon and
obtained the consent of the French & Italian Premiers to send 1
battalion each to Batoum provided we keep one also—preceding
the ultimate constitution of Batoum as a Free Port under the
League of Nations. The garrison will therefore consist of 3
battalions which should suffice.

I hope you will be satisfied with this decision as it will enable
you to release one battalion for your sorely pressed position at
Constantinople . . .

104

Wilson to Allenby

[Copy] 28th March 1920

I have owed you a letter for ever so long but I find it difficult to get time for letter writing other than dictated. Your wires about the recognition to Feisal's claims to Crownship[6] have fluttered the Democrats! To accept a Mandate—whatever that may mean—from a King would be quite beneath the dignity of a Democrat or a Republican or an "Allied & Associated Member!" These gentlemen can give each other whatever they want out of other peoples properties whether it be Fiume or Constantinople or Mosul or Palestine or Cilicia or German East Africa or Islands hither and thither. It is a funny world and inhabited by odd people. I confess the "goings on" of our friends The Frocks terrify me. There is a total and absolute lack of any power to govern, whether in England against the Unions, or in Ireland against the Sinn Feins or in Egypt or in India.

We used to be told when we were children that the Bourbons learnt nothing. It is quite unnecessary to go so far afield or so far back as the Bourbons for examples of people who know nothing and learn nothing. Poor things, it is pathetic to see them struggling and drifting and sinking without principles without knowledge without determination without character. Just look at Ireland. Was ever a more disgraceful and pitiable sight. They (The Frocks) will have to hand over before long to the soldiers. It is d——— lucky you are already installed in Egypt. Poor Squib Congreve I am always robbing him of troops and he is behaving like the gentleman he is. The troops here at home are very very young and wholly untrained. When I tell you that there are in every battalion some hundreds of men who have not yet fired a recruit's course it will show you how we stand and the training is very difficult. The Administrative services being very short—we have 3,000 civilian lorry drivers and mechanics in England alone and all members of Unions, and the guards and duties everywhere very heavy, for example the 7 weak battalions on the

Rhine find 1167 O[ther]. R[anks]. on guard every day, and the 30 battalions in Ireland have an average of only 2 nights in bed. You can see our difficulties. Still if we can get peace and quiet for the next 6 months we will shake down a good deal.

I hope to see Milner this week and hear all your gossip.[7]

My best wishes to you both . . .

105

Wilson to Churchill

[Copy]   29th March 1920

I am sorry you thought it necessary to appoint Macready as G.O.C. in C. Ireland without letting me know.[8] I know that the right of selection rests with you but as your chief military adviser I should have welcomed the opportunity of discussing with you an appointment which vitally affects the security of Ireland and the training of the troops quartered there, two matters for which I am greatly responsible.

106

Congreve to Wilson

[Copy]   1st April 1920

I have lately sent you several telegrams direct. I never do it without a feeling of shame in bothering you with details, knowing how many bigger things you have to occupy your attention, but I find it is the only way in which anything ever gets done and so I am sometimes driven to it. Telegrams to War Office remain weeks unanswered and sometimes absence of answer drives me into a hole from which you are the only ladder. So think as kindly of me as you can.

Newman has arrived vice Wavell who is a great loss to me. He is an exceptionally good staff officer—strong—quiet—sound—a great worker—and exceptional memory for details and figures, and popular too. He is worth your keeping. I don't think you can put him to any job he will not do well in. I know nothing of his power of command, but should expect it to be good . . . It is too early to speak of Newman, his successor here; he seems quite a nice fellow and he works hard.

I have named 20th Hussars for Constantinople if wanted. It was a choice between them and XIth Hussars, both being about the same, but the 20th are more easily moved being in camp at Tel el Kebir, whereas XIth are in barracks here. I can get on all right without them but their going accentuates the shortage of machine gun fire and of men for employment in essential services and departments.

I am rather held up by the M[achine]. G[un]. organization not being laid down yet but I am making a temporary one for something must get into being at once capable of taking the field. If no Indian units may be armed with M.Gs I shall have only 88 guns in an Army of 10 brigades which is sadly little. We already arm the Indian units with Lewis and Hotchkiss guns so why not with Vickers?

All seems fairly quiet both here and in Palestine, but the Sultan and P.M. have been agitated by rumours of withdrawal of troops from here to fight the Arabs in Palestine, where we are reported to be at death grips, and so I am told to play Chinese tactics with infantry and aeroplanes here in Cairo. As I have always told you I do not see any signs of a rebellion. The fellaheen wherever I go seem glad to see us and I have never heard a rude word. If there is discontent it is with their own landlords who exploit every rise in prices by increasing their rents and never spend a penny on their estates to better the condition of the fellaheen.

In Palestine there is a good deal of anxiety as to Zionism and very natural that there should be for to the Arab it means being ousted and nothing anyone can say will make him see any other view of it. Weizmann and the other Zionists accuse us all out here of being anti-Zionists and I do not doubt that in our hearts we are, but everyone has accepted the Government adoption of Zionism loyally and there have been no acts which can be interpreted as hostile to it. To people living amongst the Jews in Palestine it is difficult to dissociate the theory of Zionism from the actual man on the spot who is anything but attractive and when you add the complicity of the Jews in Bolshevism and the centuries of aversion to Jews born in us it is hardly to be expected that private feeling can be pro-Jew. You are quite likely to hear from Herbert Samuel and Weizmann that the Palestine Administration is anti-Zionist. It is not true. I know pretty well all that is going on and I say without hesitation that everything is done to make the Administration impartial and fair to all creeds and interests. It is because it is impartial that the Zionists dislike it—they want preferential treatment and won't display any tenderness to the Arab in their use of it. You will say I am an anti-Zionist! But I dislike them all equally, Arabs, Jews and Christians in Syria and Palestine, they are all alike, a beastly people, the whole lot of them not worth one Englishman. I of course speak of them collectively and not as individuals.

As regards the military position in Palestine I have nothing to add to what I have already told you. Our force for the present area and situation is more than enough, but once we begin to extend N or E we may want all we have, or even more, unless we have the Arabs for our friends, which I fancy we can if we acknowledge an Arab Kingdom of which Palestine is a province, paying an annual contribution to the Central Government. All the Arabs want is money and a nominal sovereignty to sop their pride. Money we already give them. The other will cost us nothing and save a great deal for they can be troublesome enemies.

There is a good deal of searching of hearts over the newspaper report that the title 'Brigadier' is to be abolished. Personally I think it should be retained by those who commanded brigades, but by those only. The apparent reduction of such here will not be understood by natives with whom the Brigadiers have chief dealings. But I don't doubt there are excellent reasons for the change. Today I have had an old gunner who is time expired in September proposing to leave at once in order to be able to remain 'General' for the remainder of his days, for he thinks if he stays on till September he will become Colonel and remain so in retirement.

It is beginning to get hot here now but we have it much later than usual. The oldest inhabitant does not remember so cold or prolonged a winter. I go to Palestine for 10 days on 7th to see about summer locations for troops to hold the Jordan Valley, which is a difficulty on account of fever. We are very well. Geoffrey[9] attached to XIth Hussars for a month to learn to ride and to soldier. Goodbye. My love to her Ladyship . . .

107

Churchill to Wilson

Private

Mimizan,[10]
LANDES.
4th April, 1920.

Macready's appointment was, as you know, virtually made over my head. The Prime Minister repeatedly pressed me on the subject, and the increase of the crime wave in Ireland raised the question entirely outside the scope of a purely departmental decision. When I sent for Macready before I left London and asked him whether he would undertake the task, I learnt from him that he had already seen the Prime Minister that day and regarded the matter as practically settled. In these circumstances I gave the necessary directions, and as Robertson had been offered this command, I also directed that a submission should be made to the King securing him his baton. What else could I do?

I should very much have liked to have told you about what was taking place had I been able to see you on Monday or Tuesday, the 22nd and 23rd. I learnt on the Monday that you intended to come to see me on the Tuesday before I left for my holiday, but, unhappily, this did not materialise. I do not, therefore, think that you have the slightest ground for complaint in the matter; or, if you have, it is no more than my own complaint, for the question has been dealt with as one of high policy and not as a War Office matter at all. As you know, my wishes were of an entirely different character, but having regard to the development of the Irish situation, I cannot presume to set myself in opposition to the views of those who bear the direct responsibility; and I think it is quite possible that in this matter they are right.

You will observe from the curious communication which I enclose that Macready is apparently settling up his financial arrangements through the agency of Mr Long in his capacity, no doubt, as Chairman of the Home Rule Committee of the Cabinet.

With regard to Plumer's telegram, you should ask my Private Office to show you the message which I sent him, which explains itself. There was no question of offering him the appointment, though that would be a matter entirely in my discretion, but only of finding out whether among various moves this would be one agreeable to him. Had he been willing to take it, Robertson might have gone to Malta. The Prime Minister was, however, quite set on Macready and would not hear of any alternative. Also, Plumer is a good judge of what to avoid.

I am indeed thankful that the evacuation of Novorossisk has been so successfully achieved. I cordially concur in your congratulatory telegram to Milne. It seems to me that we should send an official letter from the Army Council to the Admiralty expressing our appreciation of the brilliant support accorded by the Navy to the Army in these difficult circumstances. There are several telegrams bearing on this subject in the file. Perhaps you will have them collated and give directions which will enable the official letter to be written. It should be sent without further reference to me.

I have had a very pleasant ten days here alone with Rawlinson, who is a very good companion. We have had some very good hunts, but unhappily have been baffled by an evil manoeuvre of these pigs which consists of swimming a river too deep for us to ford and thus separating us from the hounds. I expect to be back on Thursday or Friday. I may stay a night in Paris *en route* . . .

[Enclosure: holograph]
S of S

Ch of E's P.S. rang me up this morning to say that 1st Lord has written to Ch of E. forwarding the terms on wh. Macready will consent to accept the Irish Command. They are, in addition to his pay, £1400 table allowance (instead of the former peace-time allowance of £1150, or what poor Gen. Shaw has been drawing, £500) and a lump sum of £5000 as compensation for disturbance!!

No one here knows anything of this & J. T. Davies says he doesn't know of the P.M. having come to any understanding.

It is supposed that Macready wrote to W. Long as Chairman of the Home Rule Bill Ctte!!

Austen Ch. is replying to say that he cannot act except on a recommn. from the S of S for War.

So far as W.O. are concerned, the present stage of the appt. is that M.S. wrote yesterday offering it to Macready, whose answer is not yet in.

E[dward] M[arsh]
31/3

108

Wilson to Harington

[Carbon]   [San Remo[11]]
18th April 1920

Coming down in the train yesterday I had several talks with Lord Curzon, and I pressed once more for the removal of our troops from the Plebiscites and from Batoum. I think that if we stick to it with great pertinacity in the end we shall get our way.

In his letter to me which Farnham brought Mog tells me that there is a wire from Milne saying that he is getting anxious about the safety of the Mission in the Crimea. I hope you will press for the Mission to come away. I do not know what the hell they are doing there, and when we got our chance of clearing out, lock, stock, and barrel from Novorossisk I have never been able to understand why we did not do it; so I trust the Secretary of State will not put any impediment in the way of our coming back from the Crimea to Constantinople.

Lord Curzon told me that on several occasions he had asked for the loan of some officers for Georgia, Azerbaijan, and Armenia. I told him that I had no recollection of such a demand but I would make enquiries. Did the Foreign Office so ask?

This morning it is raining hard; some courtesy visits have been paid from 'Frocks' to 'Frocks', and from what I hear it seems likely that the afternoon will be spent in discussing Coal. Curzon told me that just before leaving London he received a wire from Buchanan from Rome giving a most alarming account of the situation in Italy owing to the lack of coal for the manufactories.

You will be sorry to hear there are no golf links but glad to hear there are some lawn tennis courts and that I propose to play when the rain stops.

I telegraphed last night about sending out a cipher officer with a War Office cipher. The Foreign Office who were to do the deciphering have only brought two unfortunate fellows and they have no War Office cipher. If you send one, and I am borrowing one from Paris, that would give us four cipher officers, which once we get started will not I think be a bit too much.

So far as I can find out no definite arrangements have been made for getting our letters back from here to you, or from London to San Remo . . .

109

Wilson to Moggridge

[San Remo]
23rd April 1920

Yours of the 20th arrived last night. I have now put in a letter to Lord Curzon on the subject of the 'Milne Command'.

I am not quite sure where we stand, here in San Remo, as

regards the Turkish Treaty. The whole problem is in such a pie that it is quite impossible to say when it will come out of its mould and what shape it will be when it does.

Yesterday I again raised the question of withdrawing the two battalions from Batoum. This was hotly contested by Lord Curzon and by Berthelot, both of whom thought it would be a disaster to come away. I reminded both the French and the Italians that some two months ago they promised each of them to send a battalion and had not sent one single man, and moreover had no intention of sending any: I did not see therefore what they had to do in the matter. The discussion was fairly warm and ended in the matter being referred to Foch and myself for a report. He and I met last night and drew up a short paper, a copy of which goes to you today, and plumped for a minimum garrison of two divisions. That I think will knock the whole damn thing out and we shall get our battalions back to Constantinople before we have another disaster.

Although Erzerum only appears to have three Armenian inhabitants the 'Frocks' are determined to give it to the Armenians. They do not mention the date on which these three Armenians will take over the town!

The so-called representatives of Georgia, Azerbaijan, and Armenia represent those countries just as much as Barnes and Thomas represent Labour or Johnny Redmond and Dillon represent Sinn Fein.

We have not yet tackled the French proposal for occupying the Ruhr if the Boches disobey orders. Last night Foch, Badoglio and I had a long meeting in conformity with the wish expressed by the 'Frocks' that we should produce "une demi-douzaine" of solutions to a recalcitrant Boche! After much talk, which indeed has been going on between us for the last three or four days, we threw out proposals for putting pressure on the Boche by occupying either Leipzig or Munich, either Dresden or Berlin, either Hamburg or Emme, and we plumped solidly for the occupation of the Ruhr with four divisions in the first line and four divisions in close support. Foch was able to account for six out of these eight divisions in the following manner:

1 Belgian
1 Franco-British
4 French

but he admitted that the other two were difficult to find and he invited me to find one or both, which I said I would be delighted to do if the 'Frocks' would give me the men and the money. That paper will come before the 'Frocks' this afternoon and what they will do with it I have not the slightest idea, but so far as I can see if military action is necessary as against the Boche then the only place to take it is in the Ruhr.

The Danzig situation appears to be very obscure and I will press again for permission to withdraw those troops of ours.

I am sorry for this row between Allenby and Meinertzhagen.[12] I have read the latter's letters with great interest and a certain amount of sympathy. I think we shall have to send out some impartial person to see exactly how best to run that show . . .

110

Wilson to Lieutenant-General Sir R. C. B. Haking

[Carbon]   San Remo
                                              25th April 1920

Many thanks for your private note and appreciation of the German Situation as you see it. With much of what you say I agree. A steady, well-ordered Germany, in full working order would be the cause of great stability to the rest of Europe, and this time last year when I was asked for an estimate of the forces required to keep Germany internally quiet I worked out a scheme showing that the minimum was 200,000 in addition to the police which they had in the year 1918. This was cut down by the wisdom of the statesmen to 100,000 with the result that Germany, even if possessed of the best will in the world is incapable of keeping law and order. The result has been that she has started all sorts of illicit and illegal forces to try and bolster up the Police and the Army of 100,000 which is allowed her. She has now written officially asking for her Army to be raised to 200,000 and this is the subject of consideration at the present moment.[13] I am in agreement with Marshal Foch in thinking that we ought not now to change the Army of 100,000 into one of 200,000, but I am strongly of opinion that we ought to largely increase her police force, not giving them guns, large formations, staffs etc.

But there is another side altogether to the problem which faces us and it is this; with the withdrawal of America from any form of active co-operation in the affairs of Europe is there, as a matter of fact, enough money and enough raw material available to put France, Germany, and Russia on their feet at the same time, and if there is not, and I believe the answer is that there is not, then in what order ought these countries to be re-established? As you know as well as anybody, in the re-establishment of these three countries coal plays a predominant part. With our miners at home doing less and less work and getting more and more wages; a large percentage of the French mines ruined by the Boches; with the Silesian mines being squabbled over between the Boches and the Poles, there remains only the Ruhr Valley from which large quantities of coal can be obtained. If then it be true that there is not enough money, raw material and coal to put the three countries on a sound footing at the same time which country I ask again ought we to begin with? My answer to that is that we must commence with France, and if it is necessary for France to obtain more coal, more money and raw material to prevent her crashing then she must obtain these three things before any of them go to Germany. After France in my mind comes Germany, and after Germany, Russia. As regards Italy, it really seems very doubtful if we can prevent the country from collapsing, chiefly again from want of coal. But the collapse of Italy, bad as it would be, would be nothing like as serious to Europe as the collapse of either France or Germany. You might ponder over this aspect of the problem and let me know what you think.

We have been down here at San Remo for the last 8 or 9 days and hope to get away in another couple. We have been, or at least the 'Frocks' have been bitterly engaged in trying to regulate the affairs of Russia and of Turkey and of the Adriatic, and tomorrow we tackle the question of the disarmament and demobilisation of the Boche forces, and the critical position in the Ruhr Valley. But I have a horrible feeling all the time that the 'Frocks' having shown that they are incapable of taking charge of events, events are now taking charge of the 'Frocks' and are dragging them hither and thither to their great discomfort and to the danger of their various countries. For the moment the Polish question to my mind sinks into a second or third place. It is these great Empires of France, Germany, Russia and Italy which require all our thought and all our forethought . . .

III

Wilson to Congreve

[Carbon]   San Remo
                                          26th April 1920

Yours of the 1st April reached me here the day before yesterday. I have been here for the last ten days on this so-called 'Peace Conference' where the 'Frocks' succeed in muddling things to such an extent that there is no possible way of getting out of the mess. As I often say to them, there is not a muck heap in Europe, and when I say Europe I mean the world, into which they have not got right up to their necks.

Do not hesitate to send me H.W. telegrams whenever you think I can help. I think there was an inexcusable delay by the Q.M.G., about which you telegraphed to me before. But as regards the General Staff, our delays, which I am afraid are often both serious and annoying, are generally caused by having to refer matters to the Foreign Office, and so the blame lies only partly on us and partly on them.

Since you wrote your letter of the 1st April we got you out of sending the XXth Hussars to Constantinople. But I hope that before now you will have received a machine-gun organization which as a temporary measure we have had to bring in. It is of course India who objects to their natives being armed with machine-guns, though why they draw the line at machine-guns and include all manner of other quickfirers I do not know. I think it is more a matter of moral than of anything else.

At this Conference the 'Frocks' have finally decided the fate of Palestine under the Zionists, Syria under the French, Arabia under the Arabs, and Palestine under a British Mandate. The actual boundaries have still to be fixed but I understand that the experts are getting on fairly well.

A couple of days ago Weizmann came to me in a great state of excitement complaining bitterly of the attitude taken up by Allenby, by you, and by Bols, and he produced a great file of charges by Jews against Arabs, Jews against Christians and so forth. I let him run for some ten minutes or a quarter of an hour and then I fell on him with real violence. I asked him what the hell he meant by coming complaining to me about three miseries of Jews having been shot when I belonged to a country where the British Government allowed loyal citizens to be shot at the rate of half a dozen a day! I said that after he had had one hundred years of that he could come back and make his complaints, pending which he had better get out and mind his own business. I think he was surprised at the line of my attack and has been immensely civil ever since. The Meinertzhagen incident is unfortunate, and I have not seen all the papers yet although I have read Meinertzhagen's letter to the Foreign Office, on which, so far as I understand it, Allenby has asked for his recall. But curiously enough in his letter Meinertzhagen says that he has Allenby's permission for writing as he did. However I shall hear all about it when I return to London during the week. You may be quite certain of one thing and that is that I am not going to allow anybody to say that either Allenby or you or Bols are not as impartial as three men can be. I quite agree with you that the whole lot, Arabs, Jews, Christians, Syrians, Levantines, Greeks etc are beastly people and not worth one Englishman.

The word 'Brigadier' was abolished because we had got some hundreds of these so-called Generals who were turning the rank into a laughing stock. We first of all thought we could limit the word to those who actually held command of troops but we found on investigation that it was absolutely impossible to define this position owing to the curious and varied posts we have all over the world. So in the end we came to the conclusion that we had better abolish the thing altogether.

I hear that the recruiting for the Territorials at home is very indifferent but I imagine that this is more because the machinery we have set up has not yet got going.[14] The recruiting for the Regular Army, on the other hand, is good.

In Ireland we go from bad to worse and no sign of government at 10 Downing Street. I was over three weeks ago and I never remember seeing my unfortunate country in so parlous a condition.

You will be glad to hear of an event far more important than all the treaties, or so-called treaties, that have been made by the 'Frocks' with the Boches, the Austrians, the Turks etc. and that is that I think I have bought a yacht of some forty tons from Dundonald. When next you come home by hook or by crook, or with your crook like Captain Cuttle,[15] you must come sailing. You had better get Geoffrey[16] to teach you how to burnish the binnacle . . .

112

Curzon to Wilson

[Holograph]   1 Carlton House Terrace,
                                                                S.W.1
                                                        May 3 1920

Rumours reach me from more than one [?] quarter of a WO draft telegram ordering the evacuation of Batoum.

This cannot be done without a Cabinet decision as important questions of policy are involved, nor could I consent to the despatch of such a telegram until a Cabinet decision had taken place.

I believe the subject is down for a Cabinet on Wednesday

morning, but I am myself ready at any time should other arrangements be preferred.

F.O. told me I should receive your draft tonight. But tho' it is now midnight it has not so far arrived.

113

Lord Hardinge to Wilson

Foreign Office,
May 7th, 1920.

I understand that with the abolition of the rank of Brigadier-General it is proposed that de Wiart should return to Warsaw, when he goes, as a Colonel. If this intention is carried out I think it will certainly have a very serious effect on British prestige and on de Wiart's own personal position. Indeed, I very much doubt whether it would be possible for him to return under such conditions.

De Wiart is of the very greatest service to us at Warsaw and his departure would be a correspondingly great loss; I therefore very much hope that something may be done to enable him to remain. If it is out of the question for him to retain the rank of Brigadier-General, perhaps he could be promoted temporarily to Major-General, the rank which is held by his French and Italian colleagues, and which would consequently be preferable even to the retention of his present rank . . .

114

Wilson to Hardinge

[Carbon]   8th May 1920

With reference to your note of yesterday about Brigadier-General Carton de Wiart. We are abolishing the rank of Briga-dier-General throughout the whole Army, and as far as I am concerned all present holders will revert to Colonel. You think that such reversion will affect his usefulness in Poland! I cannot agree. I have personal experience of this class of work myself, having been reduced to rank just before I was attached to a Foreign Army in somewhat the same position that Carton de Wiart is now and far from doing me any harm it did me good.[17] No soldier who is worth the name likes to assume a rank to which he is not properly entitled, nor does any foreign soldier treat with reverence a rank which he knows quite well the holder is not entitled to. We have discussed this question of the abolition of 'Brigadier-General' for months, and we soldiers here in the War Office are unanimous on its total abolition. I do not think you will find that anything serious will happen. If you want a Major-General in Poland we can replace Carton de Wiart by a man of that rank any day you like . . .

115

Wilson to Milne

[Carbon]   14th May 1920.

It is ever so long since I wrote you a letter. I always have the feeling that it is rather a waste of time because you get so many telegrams from us that you are fully posted in what we are doing and thinking, and any letter written being some three weeks old when received must come as stale news. However, I will send you a little of our gossip in amplification of our wires.

As you know when last January it was decided not to hold the line Batoum-Baku-Novorossisk, nor even the line Batoum-Baku-Enzeli[18] I did all in my power at that time, and have done ever since, to withdraw completely from the Caucasus. I cannot for the life of me understand what good two miserable battalions in Batoum can do, and I realise very fully into what trouble they may drag us. To hold the line Batoum-Baku is a clear policy; to come away altogether is a clear policy; to hold Batoum with two battalions is nonsense. I live therefore in hopes that I may receive a wire from you saying that the position of those two battalions is no longer tenable, and that you are withdrawing them. I would have sent you an order to do this any time for the last five months if it had not been that the Foreign Office has over-ruled me every time.

As you know, the French propose to send a black battalion. On drawing Lord Curzon's attention to this fact he wrote a very strong letter to Paris saying that he could not understand such a proceeding when he had been specifically promised a white battalion. As regards the Italians I have no clear news up to date.

You have already seen the Terms of the Turkish Treaty, and you know as well as I do that if they refuse to accept we are quite unable to enforce our terms. This is the universal story since the peace Treaty began to be drafted. The great statesmen who assembled in Paris eighteen months ago first demobilised and disarmed themselves and then proposed to their enemies that they should demobilise and disarm. It seemed to me at that time, and it seems to me still, that the better plan would have been to disarm our enemies first and impose our terms, and then to disarm ourselves secondly.

In Ireland we are getting steadily into a filthier and filthier mess with the result that if the Government continue their present policy of vacillation and funk we shall have to regularly reconquer the country or lose it. To reconquer the country will be a serious matter; to lose it would mean the end of the British Empire. One of these days perhaps the Cabinet will be able to make up their great minds on this subject. For two years, in my small way, I have been trying to impress them with what was coming, but owing to the fact that I am a Protestant and an Ulsterman I am obviously untrustworthy and biassed, and so my advice has never been taken, and the contrary advice has always been acted on.

In Egypt and Palestine matters remain more or less stationary, but the Cabinet's appointment of a Jew Administrator for Palestine appears to me to be about as silly an arrangement as could possibly be devised. On a Plebiscite return they ought to have appointed an Arab Administrator for the Jews, since the Arabs in Palestine stand to the Jews as about six to one.

India is calling for more battalions and more cavalry regiments, and Mesopotamia with her ill-defined boundaries is continually scrapping on her Northern borders.

Ever since the Armistice I have never ceased advocating the withdrawal of all our troops from those places which do not concern us but I have been totally unable to persuade the Cabinet that this course was the only safe one, and in my opinion long before this year is out we shall be raising fresh troops on a thoroughly unsound military basis, scrambling to meet each eventuality as it arises, or more probably after it has arisen . . .

116

Wilson to Curzon

[Copy]   17 May 1920

You will see by the attached[19] that the Italians will not send any troops to Batoum, and, as you know, the French propose to send a black battalion.

May we come away now?

117

Curzon to Wilson

Confidl.
1, Carlton House Terrace,
S.W.
[Holograph]   May 18 20

Batoum: Bolt! most certainly not! The French battalion is Algerian not actually black. We cannot bolt just as they are going in. Of course the Italians refused. We expected nothing else. 3 battalions however:
1 English
1 Indian

1 Algerian
can hold up our end a little longer until we know what is going to happen.

The Georgians are standing at *Gagra*, a regular Thermopylae, which can never be forced if they stand fast. They can similarly hold the *Dariel Pass*.

All they want is rifles & cartridges, and yet Milne who would make an angel weep or the Deity swear, went & sent back the only cargo of arms that arrived! He is the kind of man that renders any foreign policy impossible. See Wardrop, who is back, and get a few sidelights on the soldiers in the Caucasus!

Milne has got his orders to withdraw the moment there is any real danger & that is surely enough. Of course in his eyes everything the Georgians do is wrong. De Robeck takes a much sounder[?] view [?].

I am much obliged for your letter about the Zionists.

I largely agree. But the PM dashed in & appointed Samuel without telling anybody . . .

118

Wilson to Haking

[Carbon]   20th May 1920

I have received your letter of the 17th May enclosing a letter from Carton de Wiart to you. I saw Carton de Wiart on this subject when he was here, and I explained the situation to him. I am afraid I was quite unable to persuade him of the wisdom of our proposed step in abolishing the rank of Brigadier General. He took up what to me was the fantastic position that he would rather leave the Army than lose his temporary rank of Brigadier, although he had no answer to make when I asked him if he thought it was fair for the man who is commanding a brigade in the field to be called 'Colonel' whilst he, who was commanding nothing, should retain the title. In my opinion he ought to be ashamed of himself for going on shouting about a thing of this description. I have not had one single word of complaint from any of those who are actually in command of troops, whereas all those people like Carton de Wiart, Spears, and other fellows who are out on side-shows have not only complained to us here in the War Office but many of them, including Carton de Wiart, have both written to and seen Winston, and have got all manner of other people to bring pressure upon the Secretary of State, and I told him here in my room that he ought to be ashamed of himself for so unsoldierlike a proceeding.

I understand that as a matter of fact it is not so much poor Carton de Wiart as his wife, but of course we cannot take any notice of that sort of thing . . .

119

Wilson to Curzon

[Copy]   20 May 1920

Thank you for your letter in answer to mine re Batoum. Perhaps the 'regrettable incident' at Enzeli which has now occurred[20] and which will be followed by others may lead you to change your mind and even trust, a little, in the advice of the responsible military advisers. I see that on January 12th I began to urge the withdrawal of our troops from the Caucasus and from Persia for the very simple reason that we were not strong enough to remain there.

Meanwhile to judge from the wires to the F.O. it appears as though the brave Georgians were going to make peace, or have made peace with the Bolsheviks. If this be so surely we can come away from Batoum? . . .

Curzon to Wilson

1, Carlton House Terrace,
S.W.1
[Holograph]   May 20 1920

Enzeli is emphatically a case in which I have listened to 'the responsible military advisers'.

Who was it who wrote the telegram of Feb 25 telling the Enzeli force to hold on & offer a bold front there?[21]

Not the FO but WO.

Who was it who told us only a week ago that 'it was impossible for the Bolsheviks to shift him from Enzeli by direct attack *either by* land or sea'?

Not the FO but GOC Norperforce.

Who was it who wrote 'The withdrawal of the British advanced detachment from Enzeli will most probably be *speedily followed* by a corresponding advance on the part of the Russians'?[22] Not I but you, and I so heartily agreed with your words that my policy was 'Hold out as long as you can'.

Who was it who came repeatedly to E[astern] Conference & told us that the Bolshevik policy in Persia was *not invasion* but propaganda? Not I but General Radcliffe. Therefore do not, my dear Field Marshal, accuse me of being indifferent to Military advice. I have trusted it too implicitly! . . .

121

Curzon to Wilson

1, Carlton House Terrace,
S.W.1
[Holograph]   May 23 1920

I am bound to tell you that your telegram no. 8488 to Milne does not appear to me fairly to carry out the instructions of the Cabinet on Friday.

You asked if you might repeat the former instructions to Milne about withdrawal [from Batum]. The PM distinctly said that this was unnecessary and the Cabinet concurred with him. You were authorised merely to ask Milne his views on the present situation as affected by the recent arrival of a French battalion and the present position of

(a) Soviet troops

(b) Georgians

You have gone beyond this and have given Milne a direct tip to withdraw at once & this telegram was sent off without reference to me or to anyone.

I hold that this telegram went beyond the authority given to you by the Cabinet and I am telegraphing to de Robeck to explain the real situation.

I find it almost impossible to conduct any [?] policy when the W.O. put their own views into telegrams which they send off without any consultation . . .

122

Wilson to Curzon

36 Eaton Place[23]
S.W.1
[Copy]   24th May 1920

I only got your letter (of the 23rd) today.

I am so sorry but the case is not so bad as you think. On Friday evening, after the Cabinet, I drafted the offending telegram. I sent you a private note enclosing a copy before I sent it. You had gone to Kedleston.[24] I then called up Hardinge. He had left the Foreign Office. I then called up Eyre Crowe. He also had gone.

I then sent the telegraph to the cypher room for despatch seeing no chance of getting it sent before Tuesday when I was told you would be back. But funnily enough close on 8 o'clock Winston went to see the P.M. and told him of my wire and P.M. said he thought I ought to show it to you in spite of the delay.

Winston told me of this at 8 o'clock and I at once sent to the cypher room and recovered my original wire which I have here on my table. How, then, the wire was sent I can't imagine and I am very sorry and will find out about it in the morning.

That is the story, and I am not so much to blame as you, very naturally, thought at the first blush . . .

123

Wilson to Milne

[Carbon]   2nd June 1920
PERSONAL

Your letter of the 22nd May with enclosures has just reached me—many thanks. I was only too delighted to put you up for promotion to General. Nobody in the Army has deserved this promotion better than yourself for you have not only seen a great deal of fighting but single-handed you have had to deal with one difficult situation after another and have always kept the Flag flying for the good of England.

Last night, as a result of your telegram G.C.727 I wrote across to the Foreign Office proposing that you should withdraw at once from Batoum, and long before you get this letter I hope you will have received the wire. As you know I have been agitating repeatedly and without ceasing since January for the withdrawal of the force at Batoum. When we decided that we had not sufficient troops to hold the line Constantinople-Batoum-Krasnovodsk-Merv nor even the line Constantinople-Batoum-Baku-Enzeli-Teheran-Meshed I urged that we should there and then fall back to the line Gibraltar-Malta-railheads in Palestine, Mesopotamia and India; but in spite of my representations the Foreign Office has so far beaten me with the result that we still have two unfortunate battalions in Batoum and we still have commitments in Persia which will lead us to one disaster after another. I am now putting up a paper[25] showing the distribution of our forces over the world, the dangerous situation which this distribution carries with it, and I am asking for permission to be allowed to withdraw the three battalions that we have in the Plebiscite Areas in Germany, the two battalions from Batoum, fifteen out of your twenty one battalions from Constantinople, and the eight battalions now in Persia; this would give me, even after the Indian battalions have been disbanded—those at least that have to be disbanded—a small reserve in hand with which to play, for at the present moment such is the distribution that we are strong nowhere, we are weak everywhere, and I have not got in any single theatre, not even in England, any reserve to stop a gap or to carry out a mandate.

The position in Turkey is as you graphically describe in your letter. It matters not a button whether the Turk in Constantinople signs the Treaty or whether he does not—all power has passed out to the Anatolian side.[26] We on the General Staff have pointed this out over and over again to the Cabinet but without any result whatever, the Foreign Office being particularly determined to engage in all sorts of enterprises without having any force at all to carry them out. There is absolutely no connexion whatever between the policy of this country, which does not exist, and the armed forces of the Empire which practically do not exist either.

Meanwhile, whilst these outlying theatres like yours, Palestine, Mesopotamia and Persia are in a state of extreme unrest we are right up against it in Ireland. The Cabinet have thought fit to pursue in Ireland the same policy that they pursue all over the world, that is to say, without the faintest idea of where they are going they sometimes threaten, they sometimes run away, with the result that in Ireland, even more than in any other theatre, chaos reigns supreme. The Irishmen who are clever enough are gradually looping into their toils Labour in England[27] and if the Cabinet do not take a stand, and a firm stand, and if they do not take that stand in the very near future the Irish question will be so complicated with the Labour question in England that it will become insoluble, and this would mean the loss of Ireland to begin with; the loss of the Empire in the second place; and the loss of England itself to finish up with. I have not been so nervous about the state of affairs in regard to the British Empire since July

1914, and in many ways I am more anxious today than I was even that fateful month.

As you will have seen from a telegram I sent you yesterday I am very loth to send you a cavalry regiment seeing that my whole strength is being used in withdrawing from those positions which do not belong to us back to those which do in order that in the latter we may be sufficiently strong to stand the bumps that are coming. As I have said, I want to reduce the whole of the Black Sea Force to six battalions in Constantinople and I want to clear out altogether from the Plebiscite Areas and from Persia. I fully realise that such a course will hand over most of the Near East to Bolshevism. I am very sorry but I cannot help it. When the 'Four Immortals' at the Peace Conference a year ago decided in their wisdom to disarm themselves first and then proposed to their enemies that they should disarm next it can easily be seen where unfortunate England will be landed . . .

124

Lieutenant-General Sir J. A. C. Haldane
to Wilson

ARMY HEADQUARTERS,
MESOPOTAMIA.
[Holograph]   20th June, 1920.

I have replied to the W.O. telegram but the situation may change quickly, that is to say before this letter arrives, and anything in it may be entirely superseded by telegrams sent in the interval. The Civil Commissioner[28] still says that he is anxious regarding the situation. I am not and have never been, but he has not been opposed to Germans for $4\frac{1}{2}$ years. His underlings are mostly young and inexperienced people and seem to me to be too ready to jump to conclusions and take counsel of their fears. The result is a continued cry of "wolf". For instance 2 days before I left for Persia he wrote to me expressing grave anxiety regarding the districts about Hillah. The following day I heard accidentally though I knew that he had flown there to see his headmen, that he had a most satisfactory interview. He did not inform me until I sent for him that this was so, when he stated that his Sheikhs had said there was no fear of trouble now or later. I left for Persia with a clear conscience and what followed you know from his telegram to the India Office. This kind of thing makes it difficult to decide satisfactorily as to movements of troops and one has to follow ones own experience and judgment rather than accept political guidance. But that is so everywhere, the politician always pressing for dispersion while the soldier knows he must concentrate. My candid opinion, but circumstances may alter it, is that the situation is no worse than when I arrived in March. The Arab may be influenced by religious motives but is mainly out for loot and does not want to get killed. A quiet show of force is the best way to cool his ardour, but he is mobile and transfers his attacks elsewhere. I have no fear of a general rising. Tribes have diverse interests, and I do not think that the combating force, be it Sherifian or Turkish, is capable of organising a general movement or a continuous series of raids on our communications such as might paralyse the question of supply.

The climate of this country and the extreme monotony of its aspect—i.e. the miles and miles of b- all as described so aptly by T.A. [?]—undoubtedly reacts on the nerves of those who have been here some time; senior officers who have served mainly in India are however not as bad as those at home to accept responsibility and the result is that though I have two good level-headed Scotsmen as divisional commanders they get worried unnecessarily. I am flying to Mosul tomorrow where the G.O.C. thought a few days ago he was going to be besieged, which I confess sounded ridiculous to me, considering that he has plenty of troops south of the place and should be grateful to the Arabs if they would assemble in a large body and give him a chance of a good blow.

* * *

125

Wilson to Churchill

[Copy] 23/6/20

These reports show an increasingly unsatisfactory position and this in spite of considerable reinforcements of troops.

I have absolutely no faith in the present regime as a semi-military semi-police operation, and I think before long we will find that the soldiers do not like the work . . .
[Enclosed with this minute were copies of the Weekly Report on the Situation in Ireland.]

126

Churchill to Wilson

[Copy] 24/6 1920

Have you any definite proposals to make of a practical character? . . .

127

Wilson to Churchill

[Copy] 24/6/20

You will find my answer on the attached paper 'A' . . .
[Paper 'A': copy]
SECRET No. 15
Daily Report from G.H.Q. Ireland, 24th June
1920
2/22597 G. 24/6/20 Operation Report

Guard of one NCO and six men H[ighland]. L[ight]. I[nfantry]. marching through streets were held up and disarmed at Ennis yesterday at 1830. Corporal wounded with a knife. No arrests. At Londonderry heavy sniping on troops early night 23/24th. Armoured cars returned fire and silenced snipers. Situation this morning much quieter.

S. of S.

These are very deplorable incidents and are very bad for the troops. They will continue until the Government realize that they are at war with the Sinn Fein and say so and *act* on the fact.

(id) H.W.
24/6/20

128

Churchill to Wilson

[Copy]   25/6/20
Private and Secret

I do not think it is any use simply saying that the Government should "declare war on Sinn Fein and act accordingly", unless you show by a series of definite illustrations the kind of measures you think should be adopted. It is in this field of practical suggestions that your military knowledge would be of the utmost advantage, whereas, so long as you confine yourself to generalities, it is impossible for me to carry the matter any further.

I suggest you should draw up a paper showing exactly the kind of military regime appropriate to a state of war which you recommend should be enforced in Ireland, or in such parts of Ireland as were specially disturbed, with definite detailed illustrations of the kind of thing which would be done under this regime which cannot be done under the present Defence of the Realm Act.[29]

I have now become a member of a Cabinet Committee specially charged with the duty of watching over Irish affairs and suppression of crime and disorder in Ireland.[30] Therefore I shall be in a position to bring any recommendations you may make to the notice of this Committee at the earliest moment. It is no use, for instance, answering the question, 'What would you do in Ireland', by saying 'I should shoot', or 'I should shoot without hesitation', or 'I should shoot without mercy'. The enquiry immediately arises 'Whom would you shoot?'. And shortly after that 'Where are they?' 'How are you going to recognise them?'. If by acting as if a state of war existed you mean that an incident such as that which occurred at Ennis should be followed by burning down a dozen houses or by shooting a certain number of the inhabitants, drawn by lot or otherwise, you should say so plainly so that the matter may be considered. Then if your suggestions are not adopted by superior authority, you will at any rate have left them in no doubt of what your views are. Everyone knows that the situation in Ireland is unsatisfactory, that it is bad for the troops and full of potential dangers for this country. I do not myself believe it would be bettered by the kind of methods the Prussians adopted in Belgium, but if you think so you ought to say so . . .

129

Wilson to Churchill

[Copy]   28th June 1920

I am not quite sure that I understand your minute. Do you wish me to give you my views on how to govern Ireland? This, being political, is a subject outside my province . . .

130

H. W. Moggridge to Wilson[31]

[Holograph]   War Office
                                                        1 July [1920]

It is only an hour or two since you left; & I have to send now for the first bag.

I enclose Irish letters & telegrams. S. of S. was in a great rage, & sat down & orated to Gen. Harington, saying he will try Lucas[32] by Court Martial, that Jeudwine's career would be ruined if he were captured; & that you didn't trouble to read what was written, that you always said "Peace or War", & were not helpful!

I am afraid Gen. Knox (Flurry) has written a stupid letter to S. of S. complaining in uncensored [?] terms about his non-promotion to Major-General. I have not seen the original, only a summary; but that said that Maj. Gen. Ironside, 9 years his junior, had most unjustly been promoted . . .

131

Harington to Wilson

[Holograph]   War Office
                                                               1 July [1920]

Great fun—Winston furious at your memo & mine. He made me speeches purple in the face! He has been properly drawn this time. He says you always talk of war & peace & never even read his minutes! Not at all helpful! He is going to try Lucas by Court Martial if he can!

If Jeudwine or anyone else is captured it will ruin his career! He says he has sent me a memo as to what instructions shall be issued to officers. Revolvers, bombs etc. in every pocket. He says he is winning & is gaining ground daily. Meantime the enemy have poured 3000 gallons of petrol into the Canal at Mullingar! . . .

132

Churchill to Secretary War Office, and C.I.G.S.

[Copy]   2/7 [1920]

Your responsibility is to make definite and practical proposals for the handling of the troops and police who are working with them and to show in what directions further latitude or powers are required.

Questions of improved mobility, of concentration or dispersion, of better communications, of measures against ambushes and surprises all fall properly in your sphere. If you are satisfied with what is being done, there is no need for me to trouble you. But if you are not satisfied you should furnish a series of detailed proposals and improve matters!

You are not called upon to advise officially on the political aspect: but of course I am ready to listen to any helpful view you may wish to express . . .

133

Notes by Harington[33]

[Carbon]   *SECRET*

THE CASE OF BRIGADIER-GENERAL DYER.

I have considered Brigadier-General Dyer's case very closely and I am of opinion—

(a) That he certainly acted for the best and had reasonable ground for action.

(b) That he was faced with a most difficult situation on arrival at Amritsar.

(c) That he appreciated the situation with sound judgment.

(d) That he dealt with it firmly and well.

(e) That he gave ample warning.

(f) That it is ridiculous to suppose that he was faced by an innocent assembly.

(g) That he was the best and only judge of how much force to use.

(h) That he was right to consider the effect of his action in other places.

The situation demanded it.

(j) That he should be exonerated from any charge of inhumanity.

His previous actions and action on 12th and subsequent action proved this.

(k) That he was justified from a military point of view in safe-guarding the lives of his small force, before attending to the wounded rebels. They were wounded in consequence of their own action.

(l) That he was faced with "open rebellion" or "insurrection" and not "unlawful assembly".

(m) That it was in substance the same mob which had defied all law and order during the previous two days.

(n) That if he had not taken strong and firm action his own force and the women and children would have been overwhelmed.

(o) That previous half measures had failed.

(p) That from a tactical point of view he was right to take firm and prompt action.

(q) That the so-called "crawling order"[34] was an error of judgment but has been much exaggerated.

(r) That he was warned . . . that a meeting was being summoned in spite of his stern proclamations.

(s) That the C.-in-C. India should be called upon to explain—
   (i) Why no Court of Enquiry was held.
   (ii) Why a year's delay.
   (iii) Why Dyer was promoted if to blame.
   (iv) Whether A.G. gave his approval of action, with C-in-C's approval.

(t) That Dyer certainly lost neither his head nor his nerve . . .

(u) That he did not fire all his ammunition.

(v) That he acted in good faith and on reasonable grounds.

(w) That he should be freed from blame and censure.

(x) That he should be freed from charge of inhumanity.

C.H.H.
D.C.I.G.S.

4th July 1920
[Added in holograph: CIGS.
These are my views after 4 Hours study of Dyer's report.]

134

Wilson to Churchill

[Copy] SPA
6/7/20

I am so sorry to be at variance but as you said, and quite rightly I thought, on another paper, the conduct of affairs in Ireland is political and not military. This being so it does not appear to me that I am responsible for making definite and practical proposals for the handling of the troops and police.[35] This is a matter entirely for the Civil Authorities in consultation with the C. in C.

As regards questions of mobility you will remember how often we have put forward the present state of immobility of the Army, and how little success we have had in remedies—and this is not only in Ireland but in every theatre in the world. And this applies equally or with greater force to our communications, our wireless, our telegraphists, our railway personnel and so forth!

If the Cabinet decide to place the conduct of affairs in Ireland in the hands of the military you will not find me slow to move in these matters, but until this is so it would surely be an impertinence and an unwarranted interference on my part to intervene in and interfere with the powers and discretion of the Civil Authorities . . .

135

Harington to Wilson

[Holograph] War Office
July 7 [1920]

Mog. has given me exactly 5 minutes to write to you. Re Dyer. We have had a very difficult task. Held several meetings ourselves. We told Winston we were doing so in the interests of the Army generally. We prepared a written document but he would not receive it and he sent us a message to say that we should incur a grave responsibility if we went against C. in C. India! However we went to the A[rmy]. C[ouncil]. yesterday. He started on me as I expected he would but I kept my end up. I was rather well placed as I was faced with the same sort of task 22 years ago in Belfast.[36] Brigg's (Dyer's Bde Major) was my own subaltern and my father was nearly massacred in 1857. I gave my views strongly and dead against further action—M.G.O. came next—then QMG and AG. All on same lines. Williamson & Peel both agreed with us.

Then Winston talked for an hour. He agreed with us on (1) necessity to shoot hard (2) that Dyer was right to look after his force before the wounded (3) That 'crawling' was a minor issue. We eventually drew up a document with which we are generally satisfied. We agree that there was an error of judgment. We can't get away from the fact that he went all out & meant to, as he condemns himself by saying if he had had more troops he wd. have inflicted more. We cannot get away from C in C having removed him, sent him home, sent him a 'D' letter etc. This is his business. The censure of the Govt is not our business but we gained our point, which is really all that affects us, that we do *not* agree that he shd be retired, though we shd. not employ him. Winston was reasonable throughout. There will of course be a howl in the Press as the public no doubt think we could override the Govt. censure etc. I think the whole case was handled disgracefully by India. However there it is. We are generally satisfied & I think did better than we expected.

S of S has flatly refused Milne's leave in spite of your wire.[37] Just heard from Macready. He wants 3 more Battns.—a Brigadier vice Lucas & a complete Bde HQ for the South West. They want to divide S.W. into 2 Bde areas. I think we will send Livesay & staff temporarily & offer C in C a choice of some Colonels to act vice Lucas. The latest is that Lucas has gone on hunger strike! Had my old Cheltonian Dinner last night & made 2 speeches! . . .

136

Churchill to Wilson

[Copy]   10/7 [1920]

You—not I—first began this series of minutes by your minute of 23/6.

After every endeavour to elicit from you your opinion, or some indication of what you wish done I find myself without any information.

I don't understand what was the object of your minute of 23/6, if you had nothing to suggest; or what comment you expected me to make.

We can all agree that the situation in Ireland is unsatisfactory. When you have some remedy to propose I shall be glad to receive it . . .

137

Churchill to Wilson

[Copy]   July 14th 1920
Private

I do not understand your statement that you have "no knowledge of the policy being pursued in Ireland". So far as I am aware you have seen every paper which has been circulated to the Cabinet and every decision taken by that body. You are in direct communication with the Commander-in-Chief in Ireland and he sends you weekly reports which, at your request, are addressed direct to yourself. You are in frequent personal consultation with General Macready and with General Tudor. I have frequently invited you to express your views freely on the subject of the military measures required to maintain order in Ireland, but I have not been fortunate in securing from you any advice of a practical character but only general statements that the situation is 'unsatisfactory' and 'deplorable'.

I feel I am entitled to call upon you now for definite advice in regard to this question of transport. Is good use being made of what is there? Is it true, as the Quartermaster-General states, that sending more transport out of proportion to the artificers would only result in general inefficiency and in a large quantity being out of repair? Is the policy of increasing the mobility of the troops and police in Ireland by means of mechanical transport a sound one from a military point of view? Do you recommend its continuance or expansion?

You have had daily opportunities during the last fortnight of talking to the Prime Minister at Spa, and in that respect you are more fortunate than I am or almost any other member of the Cabinet. I must say that I think it extremely unhelpful in these circumstances for you to deal with the long and carefully detailed memorandum of the Quartermaster-General in the spirit of your minute of the 12th instant . . .

138

Wilson to Churchill

[Copy]   18th July 1920
Private

I said I had 'no knowledge of the policy being pursued in Ireland' because I have no such knowledge.

I do not see the Cabinet papers on Ireland.

I have no idea what the Cabinet Committee recently established discuss or what decisions if any they reach.

You yourself have never once given me any idea of what the Government policy consists of.

But on the other hand I see, by the newspapers, that men arrested one day are released the next. I am told by the C. in C. Ireland that proposals made by him, after the capture of General Lucas, were turned down by the Secretary for Ireland. I see battalions sent to Belfast to quell a coming disturbance kept in Ireland when no disturbance takes place in Belfast; I am assured by the C. in C. that if we hold 8 battalions at short notice he will ask for as few as he can, he hopes he may not have to ask for any but he is fairly confident he will not ask for more than two, and these within a few weeks; not only have all the eight battalions been sent over but eight more have to be put under orders and these also are rapidly disappearing across the Channel, as well as a small matter of four cavalry regiments. I know that a proposal to raise eight Garrison battalions, which were considered necessary, was abandoned; I know that an attempt to recruit 3,000 war-trained men has signally failed; and I believe that an effort largely to increase the R.I.C. is not meeting with much success. How then am I to grope for and to find a policy in all this tangle of contradictions.

It is true that "I am in close touch with the C. in C." but he has never yet been able to tell me the policy of the Government beyond calling on me for troops and transport without limit to either.

I never see General Tudor who is not under my orders and with whom therefore I have no concern beyond helping him in every way to find officers for his needs.

No! I warmly resent the statement that I am "extremely unhelpful". On the contrary I have helped in every possible way and there has not been a demand made by the C. in C., whether for personnel or for material, that we in the War Office have not strained every nerve to meet. But on the other hand it is my duty to point out to you that these urgent and repeated demands from Ireland, demands which go on increasing, leave us with far too few troops in this country to meet a civil disturbance and with no troops at all to answer the call of other theatres.

It is the uncertainty of the present and the impossibility of forecasting the future, especially for this coming winter, which makes me profoundly uneasy . . .

139

Wilson to Churchill

[Carbon]   29 July 1920

On another paper which I am putting up to you for submission to the Cabinet I show in detail the dangerous military situation into which we are drifting owing to our Military commitments being altogether beyond our Military strength. I am always examining our position with a view on the one hand to increase our effective strength and on the other hand to diminish our liabilities, and I have already advised a complete withdrawal of troops from Danzig and Allenstein and also from Persia and a large reduction in our garrison at Constantinople.

It has struck me that in view of the pressing need of a Reserve of troops in Great Britain, the Government might allow Ulster to keep order inside the boundaries (6 Counties) laid down by the Home Rule Bill now before Parliament.

This would allow me to withdraw some 6 Battalions and bring them back to England. This, of course, is a matter of Policy on which it is not my province to advise, but in view of the dangerous position in which we stand I submit the proposal for your consideration . . .

140

Wilson to Churchill

[Copy]   30 July 1920

As you know I am very strongly opposed to reinforcing our Persian forces except—as was the case in North Russia—such reinforcement as is absolutely necessary to effect a withdrawal. This is not the case at present. I think it is sheer madness for our people (civilians and women and children) to remain on in Teheran . . .

141

Lord D'Abernon to Wilson

British Legation,
WARSAW.
31st July, 1920.

Of all the forlorn hopes on which man was ever sent this is certainly one of the forlornest,[38] but I am consoled by your having been good enough to send with me General Radcliffe, whose advice and support are of the greatest value.

He will have told you better than I can the exact military position. I think we have done the best thing possible to improve it by putting Weygand in as confidential Adviser to the Chief of the Staff, with access to all papers, orders, etc. Radcliffe is assisting. Weygand naturally meets with a good deal of jealousy and opposition. Marshal Pilsudski, who is a dangerous conspirator by trade and a Napoleon by ambition but not by capacity, gives rather luke-warm and intermittent support, but the best of the Ministers realise that their only chance of success is to get in greater capacity than this country produces. It would be difficult to rate too low the ability of the Polish Generals as shown in the recent campaign, while the inferior officers have also been beneath contempt. The men, on the other hand, have been rather good whenever they were well led.

Although the military situation is still very critical. I am hopeful that Weygand and Radcliffe may be able to pull it together. Whether they will do this in time to save Warsaw is a matter of doubt.

In this country military considerations are very much mixed up with politics and the appointments to the various commands are frequently given to very incapable soldiers, by political favour. Happily the Bolshevik Army is not really of much account; its rapid advance has been due more to the weakness of the Poles than to its own strength. One proof of this is to be found in the fact that I have not yet seen a wounded man. Most of the important commands were given to men previously in the Austrian Army or with Austrian training. It would be difficult to devise a surer way to failure.

It looks as though the Bolsheviks intend to spin out the Armistice negotiations, with a view to securing a further military advance before the time comes for signature . . .

[Holograph]
P.S. Your suggestion about living in the train was brilliant.[39]

142

Wilson to Curzon

[Copy]   'White Heather'[40]
COWES
2nd August 1920.

I hear you have written me a letter about the withdrawal of the Persian Garrison. There is of course no question of my sending an order for withdrawal until the Cabinet give their approval, or until, which seems to be the more likely event, the garrison withdraws to avoid a disaster. As you know I have urged concentration for months and months without any success whatever.

Telegrams of July 30th from Mesopotamia tend to show that my advice was sound.[41]

I am trying to get a couple of days sailing in foul weather . . .

143

Field Marshal Lord Plumer to Wilson

[Holograph]   The Palace
Aug. 7th 1920   Malta

Dear Harry,

Many thanks for your "appreciation" of 26th July.

Not very cheerful reading, but all too true I am afraid.

It is inconceivable that after 4 years war statesmen, or even politicians, should not realize that edicts and manifestoes without the power of enforcing them are not worth the paper they are written on!!

Now of course any people who can organize and use force can do as they please.

It is rather a bitter situation to face isn't it?

The politicians were all frightened at their "home" situation and desperately afraid of losing their own offices and places.

What is to get us out of the mess? I think a Labour Government in the first instance don't you? to bring all one's domestic trouble to a head. A few good rows at home on a big scale to clear the air and then a reaction with sensible men closing up their ranks and joining together.

You are having an anxious time and a pretty bad one I am afraid . . .

144

Major-General Sir P. P. de B. Radcliffe
to Wilson

[Copy]
                                        WARSAW
                                Wednesday Aug 18/20

Since my last letter, dated 12th, the situation has developed as outlined in my daily wire. Winston sent me a wire saying I was not sending him enough information, but during the week previous to the 13th there was little to say beyond what Carton de Wiart's daily telegrams told you and Lord D'Abernon's telegrams to Lord Curzon, which no doubt you see.

On the 13th de Wiart and I got back about 8 pm from the front line near Seroch, where we had gained a distinctly good impression, to find little short of a panic reigning in Warsaw! The Frocks all packed up and intending to leave that night!!

The scare was started by that rotter Henrys, in Weygand's absence, and the latter when he came back and heard that "les civils" were going did nothing to stop them as he is frightfully bored with Jusserand and was only too glad to see him go. So off they went—the whole Corps Diplomatique, tacked on to our train—except Tomasini the Italian who, though the biggest coward of the lot has strict orders from the Government to stay— as they are very lié with the Bolsheviks.

Incidentally Lord D'Abernon took my (or rather Tit Willow's) excellent clerk with him, so I am reduced to M.S.S. letters. The ambassador suggested my coming too, but of course I would not think of it and he did not press the point, so I have remained on with the Legation all to myself.

There has been a wonderful change in the complexion of affairs in the last few days. The Polish plan of a counter offensive by the IV and III Armies was decided on as far back as the 6th and for that reason one has always had hopes that the situation might be saved, but the question was whether it could be brought off *in time*. When you hear of the Army Commander of the Warsaw sector telling a French journalist that it was useless digging trenches as his troops would never stand, it made one doubtful as to whether the first, i.e. the Warsaw defences, would hold long enough to enable the counter offensive to take effect. However they have done so, and the astonishing mobility displayed by the Polish armies, rendered possible by the immense number of little country carts and excellent country bred horses, has enabled the 4th Army, starting from the river WIERDC, E. of Ivangorod—or Deblin as the Poles call it, to cover 45 miles in about 36 hours.

The situation on the left wing too has been saved by the energy and vigour of Sigorski [*sic*]—of whom I had great hopes which have been fully justified. He has beaten the XV Bols. Army, but still has the IV i.e. the extreme right wing of the Bolos to deal with. To-day should pretty well decide this, and if things go well, as there is good reason to expect, I think we shall see a general retreat of the whole Russian northern front. It will then be time to turn attention to the South, where the great Buddennie's Cavalry Army is having things pretty well its own way. Fortunately however, the bait of Lemberg is proving so tempting that he is occupying himself there while the decision is being obtained up here—200 miles away.

Much the same on a smaller scale is happening in the case of the Bolo 3rd Cavalry Corps, which is having great fun shelling Wloclawek and the trains to Danzig from the opposite side of the R. Vistula, instead of fighting Sigorski in close touch with IV Army.

I think Lord Haig would be interested in these operations, as it was one of the lessons he always used to drive into us when he was training the Cavalry Division — 10 or 11 years ago.

This war is a *most* interesting study, and comes as a useful corrective after 4 years of trench warfare. It is curious how in both theatres the chief failures have been brought about by the inability to appreciate the limitations of the local conditions.

In the West we persisted in the idea of "breaking through", regardless of the fact that the numbers available in relation to the whole extent of front and the absence of any open flank must inevitably bring any penetration on a relatively small fraction of the front to an ultimate standstill.

Here on the other hand they have been trying to hold a continuous line on a front greater than that from Switzerland to the sea — where we had a million and a half rifles — with about 150,000. They have thus been helplessly weak everywhere and abdicated all power of manoeuvre.

Weygand most modestly disclaims any credit for the recent successes, but I am certain that both from the technical and moral point of view he has made just all the difference. His tact, loyalty and firmness have been beyond praise and I have the greatest admiration for him in a most difficult situation. Pilsudski is said to have admitted that he had learned more about war from Weygand in a fortnight than he had acquired in 6 years campaigning!

Weygand has been perfectly charming to me and taken me completely into his confidence. I meet him daily in his office where he interviews his own Operations and Intelligence Staff (of the French Mission) and it is quite an education to see him at work.

His idea now is that directly the military situation is definitely cleared up he had better leave and in this I think he is quite right. About another week should see the end of the present phase.

This is a great life and especially the last week intensely interesting. Now that the front is so close one can get out to the front line every day, between breakfast and lunch, or go out after lunch and be back for dinner and the local "Travellers" is full of excited individuals every evening, who come back with tales of desperate adventures. The Italian Staff are specially graphic in their account, but as I happened to see the effect of a single spent bullet on them, (and all the other crowd who were watching the start of yesterday's attack) I take their stories with a great deal of salt.

This attack, by the way, was like nothing on earth! A Division ordered to attack from the trench line aside the Brest–Litovsk road, with objective NOWO MINSK—$7\frac{1}{2}$ miles distant, advanced 2 hours after the advertised starting time, on a front of 1 Company, straight up the road—and—most amazing of all— actually got there!! It shows how little is required to start the ball rolling in the opposite direction.

We have had no news or letters or papers for 10 days, so I don't know whether we are still in Ireland, Mesopotamia, etc or have been kicked out!

I must apologise for this long scribble, but I am telling Mog. to get it typed before giving it to you . . .

145

Wilson to Haldane

[Carbon]   24th August 1920

Your letter of the 20th June, received here only some fortnight ago, has remained a long time unanswered. You move, or at least events move, so rapidly in Mesopotamia that I always feel that a letter written here is so much out of date by the time you receive it that it is like 'pinching Queen Anne'.

There is no possible doubt now that you are in a very difficult position, at the same time your telegrams have been uniformly of a steadying character, and I hope that when your villainous hot weather is over and you can get moving about more freely you will take tea with the rebels. Whether in the end the Government come out of Mosul, or Mosul and Baghdad, or only Persia, or whether they try and remain in all three, the first essential is undoubtedly to re-establish our prestige and order, more especially on the Lower Rivers. We are trying in every way we can to help you but our resources, both here and in India, are already so strained that we cannot do nearly as much as we would like, and I see by your telegrams received today, that the slow arrival of the troops from India has not allowed you to keep pace with the increasing unrest. I hope that India will agree to send you forthwith the three British battalions you want, and for which we wired some days ago, offering at the same time to India to replace them by three battalions from here as soon as we can get them through the Red Sea.

As you know, I have been warning the Cabinet for a great many months that our policy was quite out-running our power of enforcing the same, and we stand today weak in every theatre, strong in none, and with absolutely no reserves in any part of the world, including England, on which to draw. In fact, so short are we in troops that we are contemplating withdrawing 10 battalions from Ireland and 4 from the Rhine to meet this threat of a miners strike which some people here think may develop into a strike of the Triple Alliance, i.e., miners, transport workers, and railways, not to mention, possibly, the Post Office.

As regards M[echanical]. T[ransport]. personnel, we are in a truly parlous condition, and only last night I saw a return where the Q.M.G. had invited some 8,000 M.T. drivers who had been with us in the war, to return to the Army, with the result that he got only 174 acceptances. We are now going to try a bounty of £40 and see whether that will do us any more good. We have already had to 'bounty' wireless up to £100.

I personally am very much in favour of coming out of Persia, partly because this would increase your force in Mesopotamia, and chiefly because it would give you much more mobility after withdrawing all the M.T. now on the road between Khanikin and Kasvin. But the Government won't hear of it, and so I have to keep on telegraphing to you to remain there, although I always put in a proviso, to the great annoyance of the Foreign Office, that you have absolute power to come out of Persia if you deem it essential to save the situation in Mesopotamia. I hope you realise that I really mean this and that if at any time you think it necessary to withdraw the troops and the transport from Persia in order to re-establish yourself on a sound basis in Mesopotamia you won't hesitate to do so. I have told the Cabinet this over and over again and any time that you decide to do so I will back you at this end, nor would the Cabinet be in any position to resist.

I hope to see Sir Percy Cox this morning—he is by way of sailing tomorrow—and I propose to show him your telegrams suggesting that he postpones his departure from here for another month or so until you have quietened the country. I think your proposal to this end is eminently a sound one. I will add a line if I see Cox.

Ironside as you know has been ordered out and we are telegraphing now to George Cory offering him the other post. I do not know whether you know Ironside but you will find him an absolute pillar of strength. He is beyond question one of the most rising, if not the most rising, of the young fellows in the Army, a very fine headpiece, wonderful linguist, great physical strength, and infinite courage and resource . . .

[Added in holograph]

I have seen Cox and have shown him your telegram. He thinks that, although there is much in what you say, it will be best for him to go out so he is off the day after tomorrow.[42]

146

Wilson to Haking

[Carbon]   25th August 1920

I do not wonder at your being "fussed" with the confusion of affairs in Danzig. Last night I sent you on copies of telegrams which we had received here sent by the Prime Minister in

Lucerne to Mr Balfour who is God knows where. This will in a sense have answered your telegrams.

The Cabinet having come to the conclusion that the great probability is that there is going to be very serious work here in England in the shape of formidable strikes next month immediately went on leave—some abroad, some to Scotland, the others scattered about in different parts. You know how difficult it always is to get a decision when the Cabinet is sitting over it, you can imagine the difficulties which exist now when the Cabinet is scattered over the face of Europe. But the complete collapse of the Bolsheviks in front of the Poles makes the urgency of the transport of war material into Poland, from the military point of view, less great, although of course, from the political and international point, Tower's position, and yours, are as difficult as can well be imagined.

I got this morning a telephone message from Mr Balfour's Secretary, Mr Balfour himself being away, sent through Mr Bonar Law's Secretary, Mr Bonar Law being in Dinard sent through Mr Churchill's Secretary, Mr Churchill being at Rugby, to tell me to move the troops in Allenstein and Marienwerder, to Danzig. I asked my Secretary to give my Compliments to Mr Churchill's Secretary and to ask him to add his Compliments and telephone to Mr Bonar Law's Secretary suggesting that this latter should include his Compliments by telephoning to Mr Balfour's Secretary and, with the accumulated compliments of four secretaries, to give as my answer to Mr Balfour, the suggestion that he should "put his head in a bag and keep it there for the present". I have heard nothing more, and what shape that message will take by the time it reaches Mr Balfour, who is God knows where, I have no idea. We were lucky however in getting our Allenstein men on to the Rhine in good time. But, joking apart, if Labour in Danzig takes a firm attitude as regards the forbidding the transport of any war material, either personnel or material, through Danzig to Poland, I am bothered if I know how we are going to tackle the subject because your estimate and Radcliffe's of the number of troops required to enforce this transport is, as you well know, prohibitive. We must trust to your being able to persuade the Danzig recalcitrants, a task rendered perhaps a little easier by the complete upset of the Bolshevik forces. Was ever anything more amazing in history than the running away of the Poles followed by the running away of the Bolsheviks.? . . .

147

Wilson to Foch

[Copy]   26th August 1920
Private

This is for your private eye only.

There is some chance, I do not believe there is much danger, but there is *some* chance that we may get into real trouble with our Labour Party and with the miners, the railways, the transport workers, and the Post Telegraph and Telephone Operators—a formidable combination if it takes place.

You know how few battalions we have got in England and how young and inexperienced are the officers and men. In view of this possible danger I am making preparations and amongst these preparations I have ordered plans to be drawn out for 10 battalions to be brought from Ireland and 4 battalions from the Rhine. I write therefore at once to tell you. You will understand that I am only preparing plans and that I hope and believe I will not have to carry these plans into execution . . .

148

Wilson to Churchill[43]

6th September 1920

There is not much news. An elaborate paper is being got out by Bonar on the subject of which you know, and meanwhile the decision as to publication etc has been postponed until the return of the P.M. who so far as I can make out will be back here either tomorrow night or Wednesday night. After that I hope something may be done as time presses and the daily disclosures continue to show an ever increasing and intimate association.[44]

Macready had a long talk with me this morning. He says that if we withdraw 10 battalions from Ireland we may as well put up our shutters there. Hamar Greenwood is still away and Macready can get no touch with him and therefore no decisions. It seems to me a most scandalous thing that a man in Greenwood's position should be absent weeks from his post in Ireland at a crisis like this.

The Lord Mayor of Cork is still alive but all the reports continue to say that he is continuing to sink. The hungerstrikers in Cork, who started apparently some 4 days before him, are still a lap ahead, and from what Macready told me this morning, are being well looked after, and properly fed.[45]

Allenby was in also this morning. He does not return to Egypt until the middle of next month. He tells me that if the Government is not very careful Milner's scheme, with the propaganda which is now in full swing in Egypt, will end in turning Egypt into another Ireland.[46]

* * *

Allenby was very strongly of opinion that neither in Palestine nor in Egypt could we reduce any troops, more especially in Egypt where he thought it was quite possible with this Milner scheme in full blast we might have to reinforce the place . . .

149

Lieutenant-General Sir T. L. N. Morland
to Wilson

[Holograph]   General Headquarters,
                                    British Forces on the Rhine.
                                    4th November 1920

I had a visit yesterday from Gen. Degoutte who has just returned from Paris where he has been discussing Rhine affairs with Foch. He is disturbed at our weakness here owing to the withdrawal of 2 Bns. He appears obsessed with the views of so many Frenchmen, including I fancy Foch himself, that the Boches are only waiting a favourable moment to spring at our throats. According to his view troubles in Ireland, or a serious labour movement in France would be sufficient to make the Boches go for us. He thinks Cologne a vital & dangerous spot & wants to send French troops into or close to Cologne as a precaution. Whether this is the real reason or that he wants them nearer the Ruhr I am not sure; but he is a genuine little man & has got the wind up so perhaps he really thinks the position dangerous. I told him that I had every reason to believe that the 2 Bns would shortly return, that at present I saw no reason for having French troops in our area. Luckily we gave the French Bensburg 12 kilos E of Cologne when the new areas were arranged, on reduction of our army. They had an Algerian Bn there, which was withdrawn recently, when they sent troops to Syria. I said Bensburg was excellently situated vis à vis Cologne & that I shd be pleased if he would put a Bn there again. The way he received this suggestion made me think that he wanted to get into our area & that Bensburg did not satisfy him. However it was so obviously suitable (as a glance at the map will show) that I choked him off other places for the time.

I think he wants to get French Troops into Cologne itself. I am dead against this & our High Commissioner looks upon the suggestion with horror.

I told Degoutte that I personally did not think that the mass of the German people wanted to fight again yet, whatever the Junkers & officer class might want.

I further said that if there were a question of the occupation of the Ruhr I had no doubt there might be serious trouble & that strong forces would be required; he did not pursue this subject! ? suspicious.

Things here are quiet enough now but there may be labour troubles later on in the winter. I know what your views were as to our strength when you were here in the summer. We have reports from time to time of "tall talk" at various meetings to the effect that arrangements are in hand for the sudden disarmament of our troops in Germany. However unlikely such an attempt may be, one has to be prepared for it & our guard duties must always be heavy.

I think our 7 Bns are the minimum force necessary for reasonable safety. To bring French troops into Cologne would be in my opinion politically most undesirable if not disastrous, & I would only agree to it under grave threats of disturbance. Therefore I shd like the 2 Bns back soon.

* * *

As you know I am not pro Boche. I dislike them & mistrust them & I feel much sympathy for the French. I get on very well with the French & like Degoutte & always do what I can to meet his views, but there are limits!

A German paper the other day said the British CinC was very "sympathetic" to the Germans. I am not sure that this is quite correct but it shows that I am just anyhow.

I am afraid this is a long rigmarole but I want to let you know exactly how things stand . . .

150

Wilson to Rawlinson

[Carbon]   23rd November 1920.
Personal

Your letter of the 10th November from Port Said has just come in. You seem to have had a rough passage across the Mediterranean, otherwise you were both comfortable on the ship[47] . . .

Nothing much has happened in Persia since I last wrote. In Ireland, however, we had a bad set of murders, the day before yesterday, of 14 officers,[48] and yesterday of another officer and two of the R.I.C. This of course gives the lie direct to the Prime Minister, who at the Mansion House on the 9th November claimed that he had the murderers by the throat. In spite of this most scandalous affair the Cabinet funk taking over the responsibility of the government of Ireland on to their own shoulders and still leave it to the 'Black and Tans', to Tudor, to Macready, to anybody whom they can throw to the wolves at a moment's notice. I had hot words with Winston last night but I cannot flatter myself that I made the slightest impression.

At Vilna and at Danzig I have been carrying on a most amusing battle single-handed against the Cabinet, against Bob Cecil, against Balfour, and against the League of Nations. By a system of lying back in the traces and of asking questions which I knew these idiots could not answer I am almost inclined to think that I am going to win. These prime pippins ordered me to send two companies from Danzig to Vilna. I pretended of course that nothing was nearer to my heart but at the same time said that it was impossible to so order them until four questions were answered—

(a) Who was going to command?

(b) Where were the companies to go to?

(c) What were they to do?

(d) How long would they remain?

Meanwhile the sagacious Ambassadors' Council in Paris decreed that all troops were to be withdrawn from the Free City of Danzig by today (23rd); of course I acted, as Old Nick[49] would have said, with the greatest acumen, vigilance and celerity, and the British battalion and French battalion are beginning to ship their stores away today and tomorrow, and I hope on Sunday and Monday next we will have them back on the Rhine. Meanwhile I have got Richard Haking to telegraph to say that typhus has broken out in Vilna and the neighbourhood, and I raised a further point this morning with the Lord Chancellor[50] as to whether so dastardly a thing could be done as to make a military base for military operations to the great FREE City of Danzig! F.E. said that this would be illegal but pointed out that there were many other illegal acts being done by other gentlemen in other parts of the world and that one more or less would not make much difference in the sum total. The League of Nations feel that they are so nearly 'bust' up already that they must do something to show their authority and so they propose to have a plebiscite in Vilna while Zeligowski[51] is in occupation, the troops for the plebiscite to be found from England, France, Italy, Belgium, Spain, Holland, Denmark, Norway, and Sweden,—what our French friends would call a "Salade de russe".

Now, further down on the map, at Constantinople, Tim [Harington] has got himself into a mess—obviously not Tim's fault but a mess all the same. One hundred and twenty thousand starving, naked, verminous refugees are passing his hall door. Poor Tim is trying to give soup and underclothes where he can, and I am trying to get him £10,000 or £20,000 out of the Cabinet to run a soup kitchen.[52] The French, as they were good enough to back Wrangel, have now the responsibility for looking after these precious Russians. Where they will put the unfortunate devils I have no idea, and I think myself their best place would be Algiers—but that is for the little Frenchmen and not for us.

Meantime, M. Venizelos has taken this inopportune moment to fall off his perch,[53] with the result that I expect we shall see all the Greek troops in Asia Minor "hopping it". If they do Tim will be left as naked as a Russian refugee and as empty as a basin. I send you a copy of an Aide Memoire that we have drawn up, and of a paper that we drew up in Paris nearly two years ago. I really think it will be worth your while to read these and see how wise we were all the way through about Turkey and how unwise have been the P.M. and all the other 'Frocks'. Our proper course, even at the eleventh hour is to let the Greeks clear out and to make love to Kemal, stick him in Constantinople, and try and make the Turkish nation a buffer between ourselves and Russia. Whether the 'Frocks' will have the pluck and the intelligence to do a thing like this I do not know.

Further south on the map you will see a place marked Egypt. A General called 'Allenby' has asked us to strengthen the force we propose to leave there by a matter of eight battalions, in view of the fact that Lord Milner's scheme has upset the whole place . . .

151

Harington to Wilson

[Constantinople]
                                                            Dec 13th [1920]

So many thanks for your letter of 26th Nov. which arrived only yesterday & also please thank the "D.C.I.G.S." for his which I will answer. Your letters tell me what you are saying & thinking at home. Its difficult to know here as Rumbold is told nothing by the Foreign Office and I haven't a notion of what your "Frock" friends are intending to do. I suppose nothing till after the Xmas holidays. It's such a long time since they had their summer holidays, which we spent in the W.O., that they must need good long Xmas ones. I am most awfully grateful for all the help being given to me by all branches of the W.O. & I should be very glad if you would thank the Mily Members. The help about the 6 gun batteries & disposing of surplus animals is splendid & now enables me to square up this Force & get rid of the surplus & fix up those who remain in as much comfort, warmth & light as I can. I see evident signs of improvement on all sides and I also hear of much joy on the part of the men. Thinking of the men first seems to have been forgotten in this part of the world. I couldn't have dropped into a more glorious job from that point of view and everyone is hustling hard.

I have had to send home damages against Tom Bridges' house in Smyrna for £2900—you had better look at it as it's a pretty serious state of things. It is pretty hard to make junior officers pay when seniors allow these sort of things. I am having a jolly careful inventory made of what is in my house & I understand they gave Milne a clean bill of health. All I know is that items such as 5 carriages & a dinner service of 80 pieces are completely missing & I shall be interested to see the complete list! I'm not going to pay & its unfair that the public should. Rank robbery & no supervision went on here.

Am glad to hear the French High Commissioner is pleased so far. That is because I fell in love with his wife & also his married daughter. I am very sorry De France is going. They have been awfully kind to me. Helping the French run the refugees & spending $3\frac{1}{2}$ hours burying Gen. Foulon!, who Milne would not recognize gave me an excellent chance of putting things square. As far as I am personally concerned (nothing to do with politics) I am on excellent terms with all the Allies, civilian knuts & the Navy & all the foreign navies & our High Commission. I had to be very careful over the latter but I have won in the end & now all barriers are removed and I think they will show me everything of importance. Charpy arrives tonight & I have written him a letter which he cannot refuse. He particularly asked that I should not meet him & should send no Guard. Just as well as he arrives 1 a.m. I cannot make out from the wireless whether General Pellé or Marshal Joffre is coming as Ambassador—anyhow its a soldier which is pretty artful.

I am having awful fun summing up all these people. Shuttleworth who has been in the Turkish War Office & who hates the High Commission is trying hard to make me butt into politics & deal direct with Izzet over the heads of Rumbold & Co. Block is trying to make me beat the Minister of War over the head for spending too much money. Block himself having no power till the French appoint the President of the Finance Commission. They only amuse me & there is no danger of my falling into politics! De Robeck evidently thought the Navy were not doing enough so I had a meeting with Webb yesterday & gave them 10 tasks to perform all of which they agreed to. It made me laugh when I sat down to think how to employ the Navy. They are simply falling over me with offers of Battleships & Destroyers.

* * *

I don't think there is any danger in the Dardanelles except from the French who fire at every ship! The Orient Express is much too risky to put our money on so you may be certain we shall keep our only other means of escape well open!

I wired you about Wrangel's army—of course he has the only force in the neighbourhood and I doubt very much that the disarming was very well done but I am trying to find out. Anyhow many arms were sold for bread I am sure. I am sure there is no danger about Wrangel's army at present and I only wish I had it on my side!

* * *

Don't forget to come out when you have settled Ireland. Tell Trenchard to send someone in an aeroplane so that I may see what an aeroplane looks like. This force would like to know. We are very happy in this house & have at last got it warm & 3 dinners a week and an afternoon dance once a fortnight so we are not downhearted. I haven't felt as fit for years. Remember me to the other good people . . .

152

Wilson to Foch

[Copy]   December 27th 1920

Many thanks for your kind letter about my wife. She is slowly but I hope steadily getting stronger and I hope to be able to take her to Paris about the 13th January, and then on to Biarritz about January 15th.[54] I want to go round by Cologne if I can and see General Morland and our troops there but I don't know whether I shall be able to do this as it would mean leaving here about January 7th and I don't know if Cecil will be strong enough by then.

Last night I received, through the Foreign Office, a letter from Le Rond asking for the help of British troops in Silesia. I had to refuse—a thing I hate doing when the French ask for help—because I really have no troops to spare. I am sending another 10 battalions to Ireland this week and this leaves me dangerously weak in England and my only possible reserve for England are the battalions on the Rhine. I have one battalion here in England (Middlesex Regt) so weak owing to its having sent big drafts to India that I am thinking of sending it to Cologne. The battalion is only 250 strong and I think it could recuperate and train better at Cologne than anywhere else.

Many thanks also for your note on Danzig. We are agreed that it is vital to Poland that Danzig should remain open but we seem to differ a little as to the best means to this end. You think that Poland should be allowed to occupy and defend it and I think that an almost better chance will be to do it by the Allied Administrator and his local forces, for in that case if either the Bolsheviks or the Boches attacked it they would really be declaring war on the Allies whereas if Poland held it they would only be attacking Poles which is not so serious an offence. The Poles succeeded in making themselves very unpopular in Danzig which would add to their difficulties if they occupied that town, and the behaviour of the Polish Armies in the field has not given me a feeling of great confidence. For these reasons it seems to me that the better chance of keeping Danzig open and free for communication—a *vital* necessity for the Poles—is to put it under the Allies rather than under the Poles.

I do not however feel very strongly on the subject and if you still think a Polish occupation the best I am quite ready to agree.

Will you please thank "le petit Weygand" for his kind messages and to you and Mdme Foch and Mlle Anne and all your family I send you my warmest, closest and most affectionate greeting for 1921 . . .

153

Wilson to Rawlinson

[Carbon]
Personal & Private   28th December 1920

I have four of your letters to answer, but as events have answered many of them I need not labour the different points you have raised.

So far as I know *nothing* has been settled about the Viceroy. In the 'Morning Post' this morning it was categorically stated that four people had been offered and had refused the Viceroyalty, to wit, Austen [Chamberlain], Willingdon, Reading, and the Duke of Devonshire. Whether this is true or not I cannot tell you, but it certainly looks as though there was great difficulty in getting somebody to serve under Montagu—a pretty pass indeed for the Government to have reduced the highest post under the Crown to such a state—to hawk it about amongst Gentiles and Jews and get nothing but refusals. George Lloyd, as I told you, is a very good young fellow but he is 10 to 15 years too young for Viceroy.

Yes, your first big snag, as it always is in every public office, is the snag of finance. India can very well stand a good deal more taxation before she approaches to anything like what we are undergoing here at home, and a Budget of 70 crores[55] I should imagine could easily be carried on her back. The 'Frocks' are always afraid of imposing taxation on anybody except the unfortunate Englishman. They are even frightened of taxing Ireland; they are frightened of course of taxing Egypt; they are frightened of taxing Mesopotamia; and they are terrified of taxing India; but the poor unfortunate Englishman gets done in every time for the benefit of these other Dagos. Of course, if out in India Montagu and Chelmsford have built up a Legislative Council with so powerful and dangerous an element of black men that they are afraid to tax up to a reasonable capacity, then Montagu and Chelmsford have nobody to thank but themselves, and it is no use flinging at your head the cry that the Council might give an adverse vote if called upon to increase the taxes in India. The right people to kick out for such a state of affairs are not the Council but Montagu and Chelmsford.

Since you wrote it has been decided that Dobbs' Mission should go to Kabul, I think rightly so in spite of Montagu's hesitations and scheming to put the onus on the Viceroy, and from all I gather Dobbs appears to be a first-class fellow[56]. If we do not take steps to draw the Ameer to us he will most undoubtedly go across to the Bolsheviks and, just as in the case of the Turk any far-seeing man would adjust his policy so as to make friends with the Turks and put a solid block of friendly Mahommedans, *from Smyrna to Baku*, between us and the Bolsheviks, so the same man, if he was not a damn fool, would put a solid block of friendly

Afghans between us and the same Bolsheviks. With these two friendly 'Buffer' States we could, so far as India was concerned, Mesopotamia was concerned, Palestine and Egypt were concerned, laugh at the Bolsheviks. But if, as the Cabinet at the present moment seem determined to do, we throw the Turks and the Afghans into the arms of the Bolsheviks, then goodbye to Palestine, Egypt, Mesopotamia, and India. As Winston said in a short and admirable paper he wrote last week to the Cabinet,[57] so far as the Near and Far East are concerned we have succeeded in making enemies of all the four people who count—the Greeks, the Turks, the Arabs, and the Bolsheviks, a truly magnificent piece of foreign policy on the part of the present Government. I see no sign of either the P.M. or the Cabinet realising in the faintest degree the vital necessity of making love to the Turks. On the contrary, the last speech that the P.M. made—last Friday before the House of Commons rose—was in favour of the Greeks and against the Turks.

What a funny old council you must have to be terrified at War Office interference and War Office control in Indian affairs, and how well you and I know what rubbish all that is.[58] But I will find out from D.M.O. and D.M.I. whether some of their subordinates have been inclined to write letters making ugly faces and terrifying noises from behind the War Office screen. I think that even such great men as you and I used to make these faces and these noises in old times, especially if we saw some poor old lady with a gamp that we were not afraid of.

Your last letter which I have received, dated December 9th, reached me today. I hope you were able to get through your Committee with the Finance Member and another, and work out the details for the Viceroy about the Esher Committee.

I am sorry to see that your Q.M.G's Department is in such chaos. This letter appears to explain a telegram which I got from you today in which you ask for Holman to be sent out at once. In this letter dated December 9th you refer to some telegram that you were sending on that day asking for Holman by January 1st. Neither Philip [Chetwode] nor I have ever seen this telegram and we have sent round the office now to try and find if it arrived. I wired to you this morning asking you for the status, grading, pay, and length of tenure of the post you are offering to Holman, and I have sent Holman a copy of your telegram asking for him to be sent out, and a copy of mine, showing him that I was trying to get further information for him. Directly I get your answer I will get Holman up here and let you know what happened, and as you seem to be in great difficulties in your Q.M.G.'s Department, I will push Holman out as soon as I possibly can.

How delightful it must be getting polo and pig-sticking instead of doing what I am here, sitting in an office all day long.

I will add a line to this letter tomorrow or Thursday before the post goes by which time I may have a little more gossip. I am sending over ten more battalions to Ireland this week and next week, and this leaves us very thin on the ground in England. At the same time I am convinced in my own mind that if this miserable Government will allow us to apply Martial Law thoroughly in Ireland for two or three months we will knock out the murder gang and get 90 per cent of the unfortunate men and women on our side in that country, for the whole of my information, as also my instincts, tell me that the vast bulk of the people in Ireland are sick to death of this murder campaign and will thank God when we have shot or hung the last of the filthy brutes.

Later

We spent three hours yesterday afternoon discussing whether or not we would have a truce with the Irish murderers.[59] Although my opinion was not asked I felt so strongly on the matter that I 'barged' in with some very strong and acid comments, and a thing happened that I have never heard before at a Cabinet meeting—my statement was greeted with loud cheers by some of the Members.

I enclose a copy of a letter I have written to Haldane by this mail, and you will see by that how the Cabinet is shaping at this end.

I hope to get off with Cecil to Biarritz in about ten days, going round by the Rhine for two or three days in order to give a lecture and present a lot of medals and decorations to the French . . .

1921

1921

The single most important correspondent in the 1921 selection—over a fifth of the letters—is Lord Rawlinson, the Commander-in-Chief in India. After Rawlinson went out to India in November 1920 he and the CIGS corresponded virtually every week, until Wilson left the War Office. Wilson's wide-ranging letters detail his day-to-day concerns with army business and also contain his own reflections on long term aspects of strategy and policy. They cover an extensive range of topics. The letter of 5 January [154], for example, among other matters touches on the evacuation of Persia, the appointment of Lord Reading as Viceroy of India (including a remark on the number of Jews in high places), the continuing struggle between the Greeks and the Turks, Allied policy towards Germany, and the position in Ireland. Rawlinson's letters to Wilson, of which parts of two are printed [166, 203] (their letters were frequently very long indeed), naturally concentrate on Indian matters and they record in detail the kinds of problems Rawlinson had to face as head of the Indian military establishment. To a very great extent these echoed Wilson's problems in London, including, as they did, the difficulty of reconciling military requirements with economic retrenchment. Like the CIGS, Rawlinson spent a lot of time resisting demands for the large-scale reduction of military expenditure, demands which in India were reinforced by the pressures of nationalism.[1] Wilson's own views on India predictably came down on the side of resolute 'government' to counteract the subversive impact of 'a small clique of talking, theoretical, sophistical, lawyer folk' [172].

A subject related to India recurs throughout 1921: that of the Dobbs Mission to Kabul [160, 164, 180, 185, 187, 197]. In the spring of 1920 Henry Dobbs, Foreign Secretary to the Government of India, had been given the task of negotiating an agreement with the Amir of Afghanistan. He eventually succeeded in November 1921, but only after the Afghans had played the Indian government and the Moscow Bolsheviks off against each other, and even initialled an agreement with Moscow in

March 1920. Wilson had little time for the seemingly endless talks. He felt that the Bolsheviks' ability to secure agreement with Kabul was a matter for British 'shame' and maintained that the Afghans 'like all other people, black and white, deep down in their hearts . . . only believe in force' [174].

Wilson's concern with Indian affairs during 1921 was undoubtedly stimulated by the fact that his closest military friend was Commander-in-Chief in India. Throughout the year, however, his primary concern was with Ireland. This is not entirely reflected in the present selection, since to represent fully the proportion of Wilson's correspondence devoted to Ireland would have resulted in a great deal of repetition. Even so, the subject is clearly predominant in the letters from Wilson which have been printed. The CIGS became increasingly obsessed with the fate of his homeland. 'Henry Wilson', wrote Lord Derby in December, 'has been quite mad on the subject of Ireland and has allowed that to taint all his work.'[2]

During the first half of the year Wilson believed that Lloyd George was at last going to take a really firm line in Ireland and allow the army a more or less free hand to crush the IRA [175, 178, 180]. The CIGS entirely favoured such a policy, but realistically appreciated that it could never succeed 'unless Great Britain is whole-heartedly in favour of it' [184]. Lloyd George, no doubt with precisely the same consideration in mind, concluded that British public opinion would not support full-scale repression in Ireland and instead he organised a truce and opened negotiations with the Irish nationalists. Wilson was appalled and disgusted [185, 187, 192, 193, 196, 197], as was Congreve [189]. Although the War Office continued to prepare for military action in case the negotiations broke down [190, 204, 205], on 6 December an agreement was signed between the British government and a delegation of southern Irish leaders. The Anglo-Irish Treaty provided for the establishment of a twenty-six-county Irish Free State with 'dominion status', equivalent to Canada [206, 208, 209].[3] Wilson nursed hopes that the agreement might break down, and if it did not he gloomily predicted civil war in Ireland [212].

A number of more specific Irish topics occur during 1921. In February Chetwode, who succeeded Harington as Deputy CIGS in October 1920, raised the problem of 'Tudor and his merry men', that is to say, the police.[4] In late 1920 policemen had indulged in reprisals and Chetwode was especially anxious, as was Wilson, to ensure that the army were not implicated in the matter [163]. In July 1921 Macready was driven almost to resignation when the Irish judiciary maintained that he had acted illegally under martial law [194, 195]. 1921 also saw the partition of Ireland and a separate administration being established in Belfast to govern the six counties of Northern Ireland. For the army special arrangements had to be made with the new government [158, 199, 201, 202]. Notwithstanding his contemptuous opinion of Irish nationalists, Wilson was not blind to the faults of the Northern Protestants [180]. In December, moreover, Radcliffe, the DMO, reported fears in Belfast of Protestant-led civil disorder [207]. On a more personal level, the destruction of country houses during the 'Troubles' raised the possibility of the Wilson home at Currygrane being burnt [189], a likely event which Wilson seems to have viewed quite fatalistically [192].

Wilson expressed his opinions on Ireland in undeniably vehement terms. Yet these private views contrast, in one case at least, with his 'official' opinions as demonstrated by his response to Sir James Craig's invitation to the opening of the Northern Ireland Parliament. Even though he personally supported the new institution, Wilson turned down the invitation on the grounds that it might 'bring politics into the Army' [182]. We find Wilson similarly adopting an official stance which conflicts with his privately-expressed views in connexion with an army order issued in Palestine. Worried that the order might imply an anti-Jewish bias on the part of the army, he wrote to Congreve suggesting its withdrawal. Congreve, however, refused to do this [213, 218].

During 1921 there was again serious industrial unrest at home. In the spring it seemed that there was going to be a coal stoppage and that the miners would be supported by their Triple Alliance allies in the railway and transport unions [168, 171, 172]. Wilson hastily reinforced the troops in Great Britain and even the Service Reserves were mobilised— a move which caused some unrest among the men concerned [174]. On 'Black Friday' (15 April), however, the Triple Alliance failed to come out and the great industrial crisis never materialised [183, 185].

On the international side Wilson attended conferences in Paris (January) and London (March) which addressed themselves principally to the problems of German reparations and the Graeco–Turkish conflict [160, 161, 164]. The CIGS also took a much-needed holiday in January and February when Chetwode took over at the War Office [155, 156, 158, 162, 163]. Despite the activity evinced by international conferences, Wilson castigated the government's general policy of drift which, he said, could well result in the emergence of 'a Militarist Germany or a Bolshevist Germany, led by an outstanding figure, raising the standard of patriotism' [191]. He still valued the maintenance of close Anglo-French relations and kept up his own personal entente with Foch [160, 171, 177, 178, 186].

The conflict between Greece and Turkey in Asia Minor continued to trouble Wilson. Recognising the fragility of Greece, he stressed the urgent need to come to an accommodation with Mustafa Kemal's nationalist Turks. One of his fears was that if the Greeks collapsed, it would leave Harington's troops at Ismid and Constantinople exposed before a Kemalist advance [158, 159, 164, 168].[5] Lloyd George's obstinately pro-Greek attitude [162], moreover, prevented a concerted policy with the French, who were keen to conclude an agreement with Kemal and during 1921 began making secret contacts with the nationalists. Harington learned of this through the British interception of French and Turkish diplomatic messages and the knowledge merely added to the frustration of his job at Constantinople [188]. By the end of the year Wilson had been relegated to the role of spectator. 'I am personally much crippled in the way of helping you', he wrote to Harington, 'because I don't appear to be on speaking terms with any of the Cabinet, unless by chance I offer them a meal at my expense' [209].

In February 1921 Churchill left the War Office and became Colonial Secretary. One of his principal new tasks was to sort out British policy in the Middle East [155, 161]. In order to do this most efficiently, he held a conference in Cairo during March. Sir Percy Radcliffe was the War Office representative and his letter to Wilson indicates the range of business covered at the meetings [165]. Churchill was particularly anxious to save money. One economy which he favoured was to replace expensive ground forces with a system of air policing, in which the RAF, rather than the army, would take primary responsibility for internal security. Wilson thought the idea dangerous and opposed it, vainly as it turned out [159, 170, 187, 200]. During 1921 the British presence in Mesopotamia was steadily reduced [157, 165, 170]. An incidental problem concerned the GOC in Baghdad, Haldane. Churchill and Lloyd George had no faith in the general and wanted to remove him [162]. Haldane, a rather temperamental man, was determined to resist any disparaging treatment [173]. In any case his tenure was extended when Ironside, who had been named to succeed him, was injured in an aeroplane crash and invalided home [170].

For Wilson there were some encouraging signs elsewhere in the Middle East. At the beginning of the year the Cabinet decided to evacuate Persia, a commitment the CIGS had long opposed [154]. He was less happy about the Palestine problem which he described as being 'exactly the same as the Irish—two different sets of people living in a small area, each hating the other "for the love of God"' [181], but in Egypt Allenby seemed to exemplify exactly the sort of imperial government Wilson thought absolutely necessary. In the face of civil unrest Allenby simply 'flourished the big stick' and deported the leading nationalist politicians [189, 197, 217]. But Allenby was the exception rather than the rule. Increasingly as the year went by, Wilson could only look impotently on while Lloyd George, as he believed, destroyed the empire. For Wilson the negotiations with De Valera were the final straw. When in July the Prime Minister invited him to meet the Irish leader, Wilson replied that he 'did not speak to murderers' and that if he met De Valera he would 'hand him over to the police'.[6]

Towards the end of 1921 the question of Wilson's successor began to be discussed. Wilson himself recommended Allenby [211], but in December the appointment was given to Lord Cavan, who was currently serving as British Military Representative at the Washington Conference on Naval and Far Eastern Affairs [214]. Lord Derby described him as 'a first class soldier but I should say he was anything but a good Staff man'.[7] Cavan's plain soldierly qualities and indifference to politics—contrasting sharply with Wilson—were probably exactly what recommended him to Lloyd George.

154

Wilson to Rawlinson

[Carbon]
Personal and Secret   5th January 1921.

I hope to push off to the Rhine on Saturday, and then about a week later go down with Cecil to Biarritz so you will not get a letter from me, I hope, for a month or five weeks.

You will see by the telegrams that the Cabinet have decided to come out of Persia, beginning to roll up from the Kasvin end at the commencement of April. Tiny [Ironside] ought therefore to be back at railhead at Khanikin somewhere about the beginning of June. The Cabinet have not decided whether to reduce our commitments in Mesopotamia by coming out of Mosul and remaining in Baghdad and Basra, or by coming out of Mosul and Baghdad and remaining covering Basra, or alternatively, standing on the line Basra–Mosul. Haldane, as you know, estimates that if Tiny does not get back to railhead at Khanikin until June he, Haldane, will not be able to get back to the Basra line, if that be decided upon, until March 1922. Our estimate here was that he might be able to get back to that line by about November or December of this year. The future of Mesopotamia, like the future of many another place, and many another man, lies in the laps of the Gods.

The Press seems to be pretty certain that Reading is coming out to you. You know him of course, and if it was not that he was a Jew I do not think that the appointment would be a bad one, but I confess that with Montagu, Meyer, Reading and Samuel the outlook for our Eastern possessions terrifies me. If the Cabinet would unship the 'Bull' [Allenby] and put a Jew in there the whole of the East, so far as we are concerned, would be in the hands of that very international people.

The Cabinet still appear to be going to back the Greeks as against the Turks. We here on the General Staff never lose an opportunity of rubbing in the vital importance, so far as the British Army is concerned, of getting the Turks and the Afghans on our side. The Cabinet on the other hand appear to think that the Empire is much safer with a hostile Turkey and a hostile Afghanistan. It is an astonishing frame of mind to be in.

I am afraid that in the coming meeting in Paris a fortnight hence, when we discuss the disarmament of the Bosches, we may get angry words from the French, and, so far as I can judge, the Foreign Office have succeeded beyond all expectation in antagonising every single nation, big and small, against the British Empire. It is a wonderful feat considering what friends we soldiers made with the soldiers of other countries during the war.

In Ireland the logic of events is proving too strong for the Cabinet and Martial Law is being gradually extended county by county. As you will remember the Cabinet refused to grant my request that Martial Law should be proclaimed over the whole of Ireland, including Ulster, at the same time, and Macready is being crippled in consequence—some counties being under Martial Law and others not. I have no doubt myself that M.L. will have to be extended, anyhow to the three provinces Munster, Leinster, and Connaught, and I personally would like to have seen it applied to Ulster also.[1]

So far as we can judge from the newspapers the United States seems to be determined to take command of the salt water. There is a Committee of Imperial Defence sitting, of which I am a Member, but it reminds me so forcibly of the meetings that I attended for four years—between 1910 and 1914—that I have little or no hopes of the 'Frocks' coming to a sensible decision.

However that may be, with the whole world in a state of profound peace, and above all with England a land full of heroes, and now made fit for heroes to live in, I can go to Biarritz with an easy mind and thoroughly enjoy my holiday.

No letter from you so far this week but I see by the papers you have run up to the North-West Frontier.

Montagu whispered to me yesterday that you were making a very favourable impression in India. I am not sure that I take this as a compliment to you . . .

155

Lieutenant-General Sir P. W. Chetwode
to Wilson

[War Office]
11th January, 1921.

I send you to-day (1) a letter from Harry Rawlinson with a postscript, (2) a letter from Congreve and (3) a letter to P de B. from Tiny Ironside.

Congreve seems to be thoroughly imbued with the Jewish "peril" idea and very scornful about Nebi's military proposals. Harry Rawlinson, as you will see by his letter, was very hopeful that he would overcome the financial objections of the Viceroy in Council, and a letter I had myself from Montgomery calculates that they would win by 4 votes, but as you will see from a cable and a personal telegram I send you to-day from Harry, they have been beaten. The matter is so serious and the reduction of the due proportion of white troops and natives in India is such a revolutionary proposal and so absolutely contrary to what all soldiers know to be necessary that I send you on a copy of it at once and also a copy to S. of S. although you are both on leave. I think they must be stark staring mad in India.[2]

You will realise also that we are already five battalions over and above our "Cardwell" requirements,[3] and two battalions leave Persia in April, making 7 and these further four battalions to be sent away from India will make us 11 battalions spare.

Of course we can put them into Palestine, Egypt, Black Sea, and thereby relieve a corresponding number of Indian units, which will actually result in a small saving to us in money, but as soon as these places are reduced to permanent peace garrisons we shall be confronted with an imperious demand from the Treasury to disband these units. This would be fatal as we should never see them again and if the demand comes A.G. and I both think that we should disband instead of them some of the 3rd and 4th battalions, of which there are 10 available. I also have a letter from Montgomery saying that he agrees to our suggestion to increase the number of yearly vacancies for Indian and British officers at Camberley and Quetta⁴ respectively to 8. This proposal to take effect from January, 1923, and that they will also consider later the possibility of increasing the accommodation at Quetta.

Tim [Harington] wires that his mails are arriving by ship. He is agitated because the French have announced that they are not going to feed Wrangel's troops and refugees after the 1st February, and as many of the former are still armed to the teeth he anticipates trouble. We have informed George Nathaniel [Curzon] of his fears and asked him to press the matter with the French. Obviously the latter are trying to shunt some of the cost on to us. [Added in holograph: 'we have also again pressed for Tim as C in C and the formation of the Gendarmerie'].

S. of S. has passed to us an agitated letter from Curzon enclosing a press cutting from America; very amusing. The writer says that the whole of Europe and America have been very intrigué all this past year because of the secrecy we maintain in Mespot and because we refuse to allow attachés or Standard Oil people or indeed anybody else access to the Garden of Eden. The writer says that he has now discovered that what we are really doing in Mesopotamia is using the unfortunate native[s] against whom we are operating for "intensive experiments with all the latest and most deadly weapons of modern war" with a view to the next world war which we consider will come in five years. He says we are making ghastly experiments with poison gas, air torpedoes, tanks, and all sorts of engines, and from our position in Mesopotamia are the only power able to do so without publicity. The writer thinks that his Government are aware of this which is one of the reasons why they are building so many ships!! Curzon thinks this should be categorically denied at once and D.M.I., who first advocated a very short answer, is now engaged in doing so.

Hankey writes to Creedy to say the Prime Minister has asked S. of S. [Churchill] to assume general direction of Mesopotamian affairs as from the 10th, and in order to carry out Cabinet decisions the responsibilities of the mandatoriate [sic] territory of Mesopotamia and Palestine should be concentrated under the

C[olonial]. O[ffice]. and an interdepartmental committee will be formed under S. of S. to outline steps to be taken to form a Middle East Department and a service for their administration, and prepare a time table for handing over to C.O. to report by February 1st. Creedy consulted me and I said we were indifferent except that we should strongly resent the new office forming a separate military department as in the Indian Office, as of course there is not the slightest need for it.

Finance have refused our demand to put G.O.C.-in-C. Mesopotamia, on the level of a 1st Class command for pay, and we are meeting in a day or two to have a go at C.H[arris]. about it, and other matters he is being naughty about.

Haldane wires that he agrees with you that we should not reduce in the first instance below two divisions and one Cavalry brigade, even though we concentrate on the Basra Baghdad Vilayet and agrees with you as to the probable consequence of evacuating Mosul. He considers 4 squadrons, R.A.F., would suffice.

S. of S. has ordered Trenchard to send at once a reserve squadron of aeroplanes from Egypt to Mesopotamia "to assist in the evacuation". Trenchard called yesterday to ask us to cable Haldane where he would like them sent. He hopes to be able to fly the machines over the desert.

* * *

156

Chetwode to Wilson

[Holograph]   War Office
                                                        13.1.21

* * *

Romer[5] tells me this morn: that Basil Thomson thinks there may be trouble in 2 months time over the Govt's proposal to de-control the mines — & also over the demand of Railway Workers to be represented as to a half on the Boards of Management—but even Romer could not get very excited about it.

The Greeks have made a small advance against slight opposition, and as far as we can make out have got control of a few miles of the Railway running South from Adabazar. This should help Tim's right flank and give him some more loads of potatoes.

I have told Mogg: to send you a copy of the Council of India's resolutions about the Esher Committee. Montagu asks for S of S comments, and as it is such a big subject I felt you would perhaps not like it to go to the Cabinet without your remarks. M.G.O. has already fired in a brochure on it to Creedy.

The Spaniards are attempting to recruit in Palestine for a foreign legion for Morocco—strong objections from Nebi. They must be d—d hard up.

D.M.I. says that provided the Conference in Paris is not off— He, Twiss,[6] & 2 Clerks will parade in Paris on Monday [17 January].

I do not understand this War Office—Godley and I agreed yesterday after a two hours talk on reduction of officers, that we had never so entirely wasted our time before. What the use is of discussing the possibility of lopping off a Vet: here or a doctor there or a M.G. Officer somewhere else, before we had settled our establishments, seems rather futile. We shall really have to tackle the establishments when you come back . . .

I hope you and the old Maréchal will succeed in getting these great ones to hold out a hand to Kemal.

Now you are away I wonder more every day how you ever found time to work. Q.M.G. & A.G. have transferred their affections to me. Q.M.G. talked for ½ hour today on the question of the issue of Mackintosh Capes on re-payment. I had to be very rude to him at last.

A.G. spent ¾ hour explaining how necessary it was to have 1 doctor to every 10 patients on the Rhine (which he has) on account of the diseased conditions of the German ladies! No news from Ireland of any importance . . .

157

Wilson to Congreve

[Carbon]
22 Rue de l'Elysée,
PARIS.
20th January, 1921.

Yours of January 7th reached me here in Paris last night. I have had to pull up in Paris on my way to Biarritz in order to attend a meeting of the Frocks next week. So far as I am concerned, as you know, I will never stop trying to pull out of Constantinople, Palestine and Persia, and pull back in Mesopotamia to railheads. In fact, if it was not for the oil at Ahwaz, I would like to pull out of Mesopotamia also, but the oil problem is a real difficulty, since the Admiralty insist on the vital necessity of covering those fields. Unfortunately, we cannot do it with less than about a Division and a half at a cost of 8 to 10 millions, and unfortunately again, the whole of the line from Ahwaz through Nasiryeh and then covering Basra is in a pestilential country; in fact, Leslie, who has been many years in Mesopotamia, told me the other day, that he very much doubted whether we could permanently quarter troops, either British or Indian, in so foul a climate. There is not a hill in the whole of that line as high as a tea table.

This rather inclines one to pull up and occupy Bagdad as well as Basra, but the difficulty of that again, is that it makes an increase of some 8 millions to the total cost of occupation. However, Winston, who proposed starting for Mesopotamia on the 7th February, can be guaranteed to box up the whole situation quicker than almost any other Frock I ever met. Give him my love as he passes through, for on the whole he and I have got on famously together, he has many good qualities, some of which lie hidden, and he has many bad ones, all of which are in the shop window.

* * *

158

Chetwode to Wilson

[War Office]
24th January 1921.

I have been away shooting on Saturday and find nothing much going on here today. Macready was with me for about an hour and did not seem in very good form. He is having great difficulties with Hamar [Greenwood]. He is talking with A.G. today on the question of what General shall sit on the combined enquiry under a Judge on the Cork outrages.[7]

He is very anxious to know what the position is with regard to Ulster when she starts her new Parliament,[8] vis-à-vis our troops.

He is trying to work out an organization for Ulster which will probably include a Brigade in the six counties, Donegal being a separate show, under the same Brigadier, but what he wants to know is who the troops will be under. He says nothing will induce him to give up control over them but thinks that the Ulster Government will demand that they should be under their orders in the same manner as troops are under our Cabinet here. He says Craig has got the wind up about Ulster but he has told him, and apparently Hamar agrees, that once Ulster gets its own parliament the Brigade will be all we shall give them and that it is their business to increase their 2,000 special police sufficiently to keep order within their own dominions.[9]

Tim wires this morning that his liaison with the Greeks during their recent operations has given him a less favourable idea of the Greek troops than he had. He says that the new Higher Command failed rather conspicuously and ought to have had a much better show than they did, and he wishes to modify the confidence he displayed in a previous telegram regarding the future of the Greek Army.

* * *

159

Wilson to Haldane

[Carbon]
24th January 1921
(Paris)

Yours of the 15th December reached me a couple of days ago and I have read it with the greatest interest, also the attachment on the functions of the Air Force, written by Sanders, Commanding the 17th Division.[10]

I had a long talk last night with Winston about this very thing, and I think he is gradually coming to realise that he cannot hold Mesopotamia with aeroplanes and a few odd garrisons dotted about. I cannot make out why he is taking the Colonies because it is going to be a much smaller job than the War Office. Last night, although he was talking rather wildly, I gathered that he was going to be given very little money, in which case he will certainly have to come back to Basra. He talked of reducing the Force as rapidly as he could, and of presently replacing you by Tiny Ironside, or somebody else, when the Force had got down to much smaller numbers.

Although both he and I, and others, have never ceased advocating a *rapprochement* with Kemal we have been quite unable to move either the P.M. or his Cabinet, and to me it seems absolutely certain that without such a *rapprochement* we will have a rough time in Mesopotamia, and in Palestine, and in Constantinople, and the French will have a rotten time in Syria. Why the P.M. goes on backing the Greeks in preference to the Turks, now that Venizelos has fallen off his perch, I am at a loss to understand.

Winston, who had thought of going out to Mesopotamia, starting on the 7th of next month, is now inclined to change his mind and to remain at home. I urged him to go out because I think that, especially with a man like him, it is everything to get impressions from the men on the spot, but I think he is afraid to go away for the necessary two or three months because the political outlook is so uncertain. Nothing has been decided about his successor but I understand that the House of Lords are pushing their claims very much for further representation in the Cabinet and it may be therefore that we shall have a peer instead of a commoner for our next S. of S.

I am writing this in Paris where we have collected up for a meeting which begins today and which I hope will finish within the week and give me a chance of going off to Biarritz for a little holiday.

Later. Since I wrote the foregoing Winston has developed an amazing plan of withdrawing Tiny through Teheran, by Ispahan and Shiraz. I am writing to Philip Chetwode to warn him to go very slow in showing any signs of approval, because it seems to me that a change of lines of communication of that description would be completely out of our power both as regards transport, time, and money. I just mention this because it may explain any telegrams which Winston may send you, the underlying idea being that if the Shah and his Government were to withdraw to Ispahan he could do so under cover of British bayonets, and that these same bayonets could remain in Ispahan for a little time in order to, as it were, establish the Persian Government in that town. The whole thing to me seems perfectly ridiculous . . .

160

Wilson to Rawlinson

[Carbon]   26th January 1921
Personal and Private   (Paris)

Yours of January 5th has just reached me. I am so sorry I let two mails go round without writing to you. I certainly did not do it out of villainy, or because of Christmas, because I did not even leave London, Cecil having had a bad operation on the 29th November and I was very anxious about her at the time. She is now at Biarritz where I hope to join her at the end of this cursed Conference which is now sitting in Paris. I want to keep her out there until April and am trying to let 36 [Eaton Place] so as to stop that bolt hole, otherwise when I return from Biarritz to London she is sure to want to come back also.

Mog writes you the office gossip so I will give you a little of our Conference news.

The 'Frocks' are frankly more hopeless than ever. They are totally unfit and unable to govern. They have no idea what they want and they have no idea where they are going, and the result is increasing chaos, increasing expenditure, and increasing discontent. A really very deplorable and dangerous situation. For example, the day before yesterday the 'Frocks' discussed for seven hours the question of disarming Germany. Being quite unable to arrive at any conclusion they handed over the thing to the Old Marshal and myself; we met yesterday and in one hour and a half decided every question, and in the course of yesterday afternoon drew up a note dealing with every point on all of which we were in absolute agreement. This note will go before the 'Frocks' this afternoon, and when I was coming away from the Old Marshal last night I asked him what he thought the 'Frocks' would do with our note — he said he felt sure they would send it to Constantinople!

Then yesterday the 'Frocks' discussed Austria. This was referred to a financial committee the Chairman of which came to see me last night and wanted to know what I thought of it and what would be the result if Austria fell down. I pointed out to him that it was not a question of Austria falling down but a question of the whole of Central Europe going crash owing to the 'Frocks' having 'Balkanised' it, and there was absolutely no possible means of preventing it, and that our course has always been quite clear, viz., pull out of the scrum and hang on to our own mufflers. It is a course which the 'Frocks' consistently go against.

Yesterday, also, the 'Frocks' discussed the Turkish and Greek question, and came to the truly marvellous decision to invite as many Turks and Greeks as would be good enough to accept our hospitality to London, and discuss somewhere towards the end of February what each of them will agree to . . .

Yesterday, also, they discussed Reparations. As, of course, no agreement was reached, they are going at it again this morning.

This afternoon they take our military paper on Disarmament.

Your trip on the N.W. Frontier seems to have been very satisfactory, and I am greatly pleased with your report on the troops, both British and Native. It is a wise precaution to give each British battalion of your fighting divisions a year's course up in that N.W. corner. I am very glad also to hear that the Khyber Railway is at last commenced.

Dobbs seems to be a man of high order. This seems natural to me seeing that he comes out of Kerry.[11] I hope he makes friends with the Afghans for if we had a friendly Turkey from Smyrna to Baku with a friendly Afghanistan from Kabul to the Caspian, joined together by a Turkish Fleet on the Caspian under a British midshipman, bos'ns mate, quartermaster and ship's carpenter we would have a real good barrier stretching from the Mediterranean to the Himalayas. There is just one point you might think over and that is I am not sure that the ship's carpenter is not senior to the midshipman—this might raise a delicate question.

* * *

161

Wilson to Chetwode

[Carbon]   27th January 1921
                                                        (Paris)

Do not forget that Winston in the course of a few days will no longer be Secretary of State,[12] and therefore with no responsibility at all for any of the amazing moves which he is inclined to make in Mesopotamia; nor when he becomes Colonial Secretary is he responsible for the safety of our troops in Mesopotamia which, unless he sets up a War Office of his own, will remain directly under us. I think myself it might be wise to prepare a short paper for the Cabinet asking for a decision as regards the relationship between Haldane and ourselves, on the one hand, and Haldane and the Colonial Secretary on the other.

I am glad you sent an H.W. to Haldane saying that Winston's repeated telegrams were of only academic interest. They would be quite enough to upset any ordinary soldier.

I am enclosing an H.W. wire to Tim in answer to the one he sent me [see below]. Will you please send it off for me! I think Tim will be well advised not even to see Repington nor to speak to him.[13]

I hope Macready gets his Martial Law extended to Dublin. As I have repeatedly said we shall do no good until we have it over, at any rate, the three provinces of Munster, Leinster and Connaught . . .

If Winston flies from Palestine to Baghdad the poor thing is very likely to be lost, and I will be sorry for this.

Here the 'Frocks' are in body grips over reparations, and at the moment neither side appear to be inclined to give in, but no doubt during the period between when the guard whistles and the train moves all these knotty questions will be solved.

I still hope to get off on Saturday . . .

[Enclosed]   *SECRET*

From—Field-Marshal Sir Henry Wilson
To—General Harington, Constantinople.

H.W. Personal 18th January 1921.
    Your C.H.H.29, January 25th.
    Repington is out from the Daily Telegraph. If you take my advice you will neither see him nor speak to him nor allow any of your Staff to do so either. The more he hates you the more certainly does he make your career. He succeeded even in making me Field Marshal.

Chetwode to Wilson

Rather a hectic two days. W.S.C. has been very difficile [*sic*]. My paper to him on the inadvisability of a Greek offensive at the moment, and the danger of our taking part in it, came back from the Cabinet scribbled all over by the P.M. who said "I am in favour of this offensive as if it succeeds Kemal will be easier to deal with, and if it fails the Greeks will be more amenable." And again, "We are not in a position to give any advice to the Greeks".

In spite of this cryptic utterance I got a definite decision that we could cable to Tim to say that in view of the coming Conference he was to take no part in any operation.

I told you in my last that I thought I had got W.S.C. straight about Haldane, but yesterday Creedy marched in with a cable in which W.S.C. congratulated Haldane on his work, but informed him his appt. terminated in May, when he was to hand over to Ironside. I at once formed a half section with Creedy and insisted on seeing him, & said he could not in practice remove Haldane the last day he held office—and before the logical conclusion of Haldane's task, viz: the reduction of the garrison to a Maj.-Genl's Command. He wriggled and got lower & lower in his chair, & said I surprised him, & that he had discussed it with you & that you were in agreement with him to get rid of Haldane. I replied I was sure you were when the latter's task was completed but not before.

He then showed his hand, & got angry & said he & the P.M. were convinced Haldane was purposely putting difficulties in the way of the Govt. policy. I replied that was impossible as Haldane had never been given a policy—nor anyone else—that stumped him. I said that if the Cabinet gave us a policy, we the Army Council, & not him (W.S.C.) would give Haldane his orders & the latter would presumably carry them out like any other Officer. But that so far Haldane had had nothing but a series of confusing telegraphic enquiries, & did not know what to do. I also said that if the evacuation of the heavy stores involved keeping a large garrison he should evacuate the troops which cost the money, and take over the stores as Colonial Minister & evacuate them as & when convenient. By this time the atmosphere was rather electrical, and Creedy was sweating visibly—but eventually W.S.C. agreed to put the matter of Haldane's supersession to the P.M. again today, but I feel I only gained a respite. He was in a bad mood.

* * *

Macready sends a long letter about M[artial]. Law. He is against putting it on in the Capital and not elsewhere, and does not seem very happy about his chances of getting Hamar to agree to a big extension. He strikes me as a little tired and dispirited. He has certainly had a horrible 10 days. One of the worst so far. The incendiary gang have started operations in England & there have been several mysterious fires; Bungo [?] whom I met at dinner last night, & who sees a lot of the under-world in connection with his ex service men's activities, is apprehensive about it. The Kemalists are sending a delegation to London & there have been several v. interesting "Jumbos"[14] between them & their pals at Constantinople. They will take a high line—and quite right too—They have certain people by the short hairs.

Another shock this morn. A F.O. wire to Paris authorizing Hardinge to "reopen the question of Silesia" on the "understanding that H.M. Govt. will not send more than 4 Battns." I had hoped it was dead. I have pointed out the expense & difficulties all over again. Meanwhile Switzerland has refused to allow troops to move through her country for Vilna or anywhere else, to the horror of the League of Nations. By the way Vilna is again coming to the front. We shall end by having the "Band & drums" left at Cologne and the French stepping in there.

10.2.21

Just had W.S.C.'s answer to my minute on the above. He professes to be astounded & directs that we should tell the F.O. to cancel the cable!! I dont quite see the A[rmy]. C[ouncil]. ordering George Curzon to cancel his wires. However we shall "request" them to do so.

A long talk this morn. to Congreve—Just arrived. He has interesting views on Palestine, Syria & thereabouts. And is very strong on making friends with Kemal—and with the Arabs. I am sending him to W.S.C. He has pointed out that our Garrison at Sollum[15] costs £100,000 p/a. and asked Allenby that Egypt should take it over. Allenby said they could not do so at the moment, but I take it they will have to eventually—or pay us to do it. If we leave it the Italians will be in next day and it is an important place for submarines. I do not think the frontier there has even been delimitated—or I cannot remember it if it has.

The question of Command in Egypt will come up soon. I think we must have a M. Genl. in Palestine, but Congreve and a M. Genl. in Egypt seem to rather crowd each other out.

I think Congreve had better go back to be present at Winston's Conference in Cairo early in March—to which he has summoned, Samuel, Cox, Haldane, Ironside & Aden.

No answer yet from Winston to my protest about Haldane . . .

163

Chetwode to Wilson

[Holograph]   War Office
                                              21.2.21

* * *

I send you herewith a memorandum on Ireland by Macready.[16] I have sent the original, at his request, to S. of S. Macready has also sent a copy to Hamar Greenwood. I think what is at the bottom of his mind all through is that Tudor and his merry men are a great deal more trouble than they are worth and that he is frightened of a collision between them and the troops. There is an Irish debate in the House this afternoon, & I just got in in time to

S. of S. to get him to try and get the recent accusations by de Valera against the troops quashed in public if he possibly could,[17] & also the decision of the Cabinet with reference to the Strickland Report,[18] viz: that it was to be suppressed, & in Parliamentary answers ministers were to confine themselves to saying that it revealed indiscipline in one "company" of men. I said we must insist that it was made quite clear that the word "company" did not refer to soldiers in any way. He informed me that Hamar Greenwood proposed to deny the de Valera accusations categorically, not that anyone will believe him, but an official denial was absolutely necessary or soldiers would have got out of hand I think . . .

The new S. of S. [Sir Laming Worthington-Evans] has impressed everyone so far, I think, with his desire to hear every point of view & not to dictate on subjects he does not know much about, & he has already supported our views quite strongly on certain matters, but of course he does not carry so many guns as Winston in the Cabinet. He is quite different to most of them to discuss things with.

* * *

164

Wilson to Rawlinson

[Carbon]   9th March 1921
Secret and personal

I find that the post goes out rather earlier than I thought and so I dictate in somewhat of a hurry. Yours of the 16th February from the Royal Train[19] reached me last night. Things seem to be marching pretty quickly in India and I think that at the end of four years you will have some difficulty in bowing yourself out as gracefully as did old Charlie Monro the other day. A cinema of the Commander-in-Chief getting the 'Order of the Boot', and a black 'Boot' at that, from the natives of India would fetch quite a big price in the United States of America, where England is always so popular.

I saw a telegram in yesterday from Dobbs saying that he played his last card and unmasked the Afghans by showing them that he knew of their trickery with the Bolsheviks.[20] I shall be very curious to see whether he can follow up the advantage gained by this surprise within the next few days, if he cannot I am sure he will have to return to India without having accomplished anything.

Here in London we are in the middle of another Conference. We bowed the Boches out the day before yesterday, and within twelve hours we were in occupation of Dusseldorf etc.[21] What this will mean in the way of cash nobody knows but it seems to me that in view of the fact that the 'Frocks' flung their armies out of the window $2\frac{1}{2}$ years ago that all that the Boches have got to do is to lie back on their traces and do nothing. With the exception of certain reprisals which we can take I do not myself see how we shall get any large sum of money out of the Boches, and if we do not I am afraid our little French friends will be in very serious trouble, for as you know, they have systematically banked on the fact that they need not pay any taxes themselves because the whole cost of the war would be defrayed by the Boches.

As regards the Turks, and the Greeks, I may have some further information for you in my letter next week, but at the present moment we stand at the four cross-roads, nobody knowing which road to take, we soldiers insisting on following the sign-post marked 'Turkey', L.G. and the other 'Frocks' inclined to follow the road marked 'Greece', with the result of course that nothing is decided. I had a long talk with L.G. the night before last and he seems to have moved a little in our direction, but so little that really it is not worth talking about. Meanwhile I would never be surprised to see the Serbs taking Salonika, after which the 'Old Turk' will have very little difficulty in taking Thrace, from that to the ejection of the Greek out of Smyrna is not a very long step, more especially as, so far as I understand the situation, the great bulk of the Greek nation would be only too glad to get out of their present commitments. Tim's report on the Greek Division under his command at Ismid is increasingly unfavourable. What will be tiresome will be if we get a solid block of Turks from Smyrna to Baku *hostile* to us, instead of what was quite easily to be arranged, a solid block from Smyrna to Baku friendly to us. Anything more deplorable than our foreign policy, whether as regards Russia, or the Turk, or the Greek, or Persia, or the United States, or our Home policy, whether as regards the Unions, or Ireland, or Egypt, or Mesopotamia, or India, I cannot well imagine.

Ireland, in my judgment, gets worse and worse, not so much in actual murders, which remain fairly constant in their numbers, in their atrocities, but by reason of the efflux of time which makes the English position increasingly difficult, and as I keep on telling the 'Frocks' if they do not settle up the Irish question in the next two years they will have America asking very difficult questions, with a fleet considerably greater than ours behind their hand. That will really be the beginning of the end of the last act.

* * *

165

Radcliffe to Wilson

[Holograph]   Cairo
                                                              21.3.21

I feel it is not much use writing a letter as mails are so erratic & take weeks to reach you, & you will have had the gist of affairs by telegram, from which you will have gathered that this conference has got through a lot of business. It has certainly settled questions that would have taken weeks & months to decide by correspondence & by bringing into personal contact all the conflicting interests has enabled much misunderstanding & many difficulties to be cleared up.

I have always had the feeling—ever since Haldane went out to Mespot—that things were not running smoothly. He did not seem to have a proper grip of the situation and appeared to be too much under the thumb of the Politicals, in the first instance A. T. Wilson, & later on Percy Cox. After seeing the latter & hearing from Haldane how things were run I am surprised that the results were not infinitely worse. Cox has never taken Haldane into his confidence & even now is asking for a "military adviser", in the shape of Gribbon, or Waters Taylor, or anybody in fact except the G.O.C. in Mesopotamia who is there for that purpose. It is not so much from malice prepense, I think, as from a certain shyness & reserve coupled with the most complete ignorance of everything to do with military affairs or even of the ordinary methods of business administration.

This in conjunction with Haldane's own rather curious temperament has led to continual friction & misunderstanding. H. would have done much better if he had taken you into his confidence & taken a stronger line vis-à-vis his 'Civils', but he himself is nervous, secretive & au fond *weak*. One notices the latter at these conferences & I have had to butt in myself once or twice when he has been inclined to agree to very unsound propositions.

I gather also that Percy Hambro was a great stumbling block to a good understanding with the civils. He & A. T. Wilson were scarcely on speaking terms, but since he was replaced by Frith towards the end of last year things have been much better. Frith has done a lot of useful work since he arrived & is a most capable officer. He used to have a reputation for being very disagreeable in the Canadian Corps but seems much pleasanter than he was.

Haldane & Ironside are on excellent terms I am glad to say & Haldane is quite agreeable to the idea that Ironside should succeed him in the autumn when the reductions now contemplated have taken place. In the meantime the idea is that Tiny should go back & take charge of the raising of the native levies which are to take over from British forces the outlying posts. I think the plan is a good one & both Haldane & Cox favour it. It is vital to get a real move on with these levies.

You will probably have received the whole scheme before you get this but in case you have not the reductions contemplated are in 5 stages:

(a) To the 33 battalion level now in progress.

(b) to—23 battalion level by the end of June.

(This I think is optimistic & shipping is hardly likely to permit of it)

(c) To a 16 battalion level in October, provided all has gone well & no recrudescence of revolt ensues during the hot weather.

(d) To a 12bn level later in the winter.

(e) The final situation, which can not be reached before April /22 or even much later, reduces the British forces to 1 Brigade at Basra & Amara, the latter being the healthiest spot available within supporting distance of Basra & securing its own communications with the base. The whole of the rest of the country including Baghdad would then be controlled by levies & Arab army & Air Force with the latter in command.

Long before this stage is reached we shall have gained experience showing how far the air force claims to be able to control the country are likely to be justified.

Personally I have throughout taken up the attitude that as long as British Forces were not being hazarded thereby I had no objection to the experiment being made. I told Trenchard that my present view was frankly agnostic, or to use an Americanism "I'm from Missouri—You got to *show* me!" But provided it did not endanger our troops I was all for his having a chance to show us. He on the other hand has modified the view he always maintained & agrees to trying the experiment on a modest & limited scale in the first instance—a thing which he never would agree to before, though I have urged it on him for the last year or more. So now he will begin to try his wings on the outlying districts such as Zakkho, N of Mosul, but under the general direction of the G.O.C. Troops, Trenchard was good enough to say I had helped him & I hope I may have been able to a bit—because quite apart from the local problem I have always felt that it is essential for the Air Force to be given some real live job to do in peace time or else they will simply wither & the next big war will find us with totally inadequate air forces in the field.

I am going up on 23rd to Palestine with the party & hope to get across the Jordan to Es Salt & Amman, the debatable land, which it is now agreed to occupy.[22] I have had to chuck my trip to Constantinople as time is short & I sail from Alexandria on the 31st arriving Genoa on April 4th. From there I pick up my car & my wife at Menton & drive home, & hope to be in London not later than 15th April.

This is a delightful place & I only wish you had been out here yourself. It should be a splendid holiday & they would all give you such a warm welcome. I haven't been able to see much of the troops as we have been all day & every day at work on committees, but I saw the R H A at practice in the desert & a very good show it was. The infantry also look well—nicely turned out & smart. It is a good training ground as you know and the more troops we can keep here the better.

The wire I sent you re the reserve to be kept here for the Middle East was intended to help fight the effort which they will make to wipe out altogether the units reduced from Mespot etc. It also forms a perfectly genuine & sound argument for use vis-à-vis the Egyptian Government in the forthcoming negotiations as to the future garrison.

For the time being I think we can meet the expense of the 2 British infy bns released from Mespot under the new reductions by sending back 2 or even 3 Indian bns from Egypt to India. Congreve is willing to do this. At present he has only 2 Indian Bns in Egypt as he exchanged 1 for a British Bn from Palestine. The reduction in the Black Sea ought to make it possible to save enough to square the account.

It was a great brainwave of Winston to make Congreve Chairman of the Committee on Mespot Garrisons—& conduced greatly to getting through business with the minimum of friction & loss of time.

As regards Palestine Congreve is very perturbed by the decision to raise a Jewish army, which in a few years time will have trained some 10,000 men. He regards with misgiving the attitude of the Jews when they feel themselves strong enough to stand on their own legs & thinks they are likely to become very aggressive & truculent with designs on Trans-Jordania & Syria. From the experience of the past year or two it is difficult not to be impressed with this danger. But Winston whom we have both talked to about it says that we are committed beyond reach to the policy which he thinks is a great stroke of business in enlisting the sympathies of the big Jew interests all over the world.

22nd March

Last night Winston had a big dinner party of the whole mission & their wives etc.—with the Allenbys as guests. After dinner speeches of the usual sort, good, bad & indifferent—but a cheery function all the same . . .

166

Rawlinson to Wilson

Commander-in-Chief's Camp,
India.
30th March, 1921.

I am on my way to Bombay with the Viceroy to bid him godspeed and to welcome Reading. I had to leave Delhi before I got my mail, so I have not got your last letter.

Chelmsford prorogued the Legislative Assembly yesterday in a speech which did not, I think, sufficiently rise to the occasion, but he is no great personality, with any extra gift for imagination, and I was not surprised that his speech fell rather flat. Having been here for five difficult years, his position is no easy one, particularly as he was responsible both for the Rowlatt Act[23] and for the Montagu–Chelmsford policy as a whole.

The general internal situation, as I said in my last letter, is not one that can be considered wholly satisfactory. There are indications of unrest in most areas, not all due to non-cooperation, many of them being attributable to industrial differences and to agrarian troubles, and we shall probably have sporadic outbreaks in various parts of the country during the next three or four months. However, Mr. Gandhi is less virulent in his propaganda than he was, and there are indications that he would like to effect a compromise, or, at any rate, have a round table conference with the Authorities. Chelmsford, in his position, could not countenance anything of this sort. Reading, who arrives with a clean slate, and will have a free hand to consider the whole situation from an impartial point of view, may quite possibly adopt a policy of compromise, which would turn non-cooperation into cooperation. It will be very interesting to watch the various phases through which Reading will go on his first arrival, for he will be torn asunder by very conflicting influences, will be badgered by all sorts of arguments put forward by different sections of the community, and will certainly have some difficulty in making up his mind. If he is wise, he will do nothing for the first three months. I suppose he will arrive imbued with all the Montagu doctrines, and, as he has proclaimed that justice only is his motto, we may expect him to adopt an attitude of friendliness and compromise towards Indians as a whole.

The financial aspect of India is one of the first subjects with which he will have to deal. The more I see of it the more persuaded I am that no one in this country really understands what economy means. The attitude of our rule in India is based upon swank and prestige. The sums of money which are spent in maintaining the glamour of state for the Viceroy, and for the Governors of Provinces, with the golden escorts and orderlies which swarm round the Heads of Government, are, to my mind, quite an unnecessary expense in modern India. I believe that a bold man who is prepared to scrap the pomp and ceremony of state would win much support from all classes of the community. But it will require a bold man to undertake it, and I doubt if Reading has the courage to push it through. However, I am going to do something in this direction in reference to my own establishment at Army Headquarters.

The day before yesterday the Legislative Assembly debated the Esher Report, and, on the whole, I was satisfied with the general tenor of the debate. The session has gone very well generally. A lot of the members have been extremely moderate, and the speeches, as a whole, compared favourably with those that one listens to in the House of Commons. In this Esher debate they put up fifteen resolutions, most of which we were able to accept. One member proposed that the Commander-in-Chief should no longer have a seat upon the Viceroy's Executive Council, and that he should be replaced by a Civil Army Member. We allowed the assembly to talk this out by themselves and the Government stood aside. I refused to speak being too closely implicated, and, after threequarters of an hour's debate, the House turned it down and strongly supported the maintenance of the position of Commander-in-Chief as a Member of the Viceroy's Executive Council.

Another resolution pressed for the creation of an Indian Sandhurst. I had intended to speak on this subject, but things went so quickly that I missed my opportunity, and the resolution was carried before I could get on my legs. However, though I am in favour of instituting a Government Preparatory School at Dehra Dun to allow Indians, and especially the sons of Indian Officers, to educate themselves and compete for Sandhurst, I am quite sure that we should be wrong ever to allow an Indian Sandhurst in this country. It could never be as efficient as the R.M.C., and would only end in supplying an indifferent class of officer to the Indian Army.

There was another resolution, in reference to the communications which you and I should be permitted to indulge in. I accused them of thinking that there was some low-down conspiracy between ourselves to subvert the interests of India to those of the War Office. I pointed out that there was nothing of the kind, that I had the interests of India wholly at Heart, and that we should continue between us to do our best for India and for the Indian Army.

I was attacked after the debate by an Anglo-Indian Member of the name of Colonel Gidney, because, whilst we admitted a certain number of Indians into Sandhurst, the clause of our regulations which only accepts candidates of purely European extraction knocks out the chances of any Anglo-Indian. He said it was not fair that Indians should be admitted into Sandhurst on favourable terms, and that Anglo-Indians should not be even allowed to compete in the open competition. There is something in what he said, and I told him that, if he would put it up to me in a letter, I would forward it to you. Personally, I think there are few

Anglo-Indians that are worth a damn, and fewer still who would ever be able to gain entrance in the open competition. However, I do not suppose that, even under these circumstances, there would be any chance of revising the existing regulations. I only send you on his letter for what it is worth.

Another resolution which they passed was that Indians should be allowed to enter freely into the scientific services, the Navy, and the Royal Air Force. By the scientific services they mean the Artillery and the Engineers. If Indians were allowed to compete for the entrance examination into Woolwich, their educational standard is so low that there would be no chance of any of them passing. I would strongly oppose their being allowed in on any other terms than those provided by the open competition. The Air Force, perhaps, is different, and there was a telegram some time ago from Trenchard asking whether we could supply any candidates for the Air Force. Monro, or rather Kirkpatrick, turned it down and said that, under no circumstances, would they recommend Indians for the Air Force. Personally, I do not agree with him. During the war there were one or two quite good Indian pilots, and I do not see why Indians should not be given opportunities to become pilots and observers, always provided that they pass through the required curriculum which the Air Force imposes. A small proportion of Indian pilots in the Air Force out here will certainly not have any detrimental effect on the squadrons themselves, nor will there be any danger of their taking part in, or joining, seditious movements. I am, therefore, prepared to support their entry into the Air Force.

I have been very pleased with the part that Sir Godfrey Fell has taken as Army Secretary in debating military questions in the Legislative Assembly. He is a very clever little fellow, speaks extremely well, and we get on very well together. Monro did not think he was to be trusted, but I do not agree with him, and am sure that the Army has a strong and faithful Ally in this clever little fellow.

Early next month I am sending a party of legislators up the Khyber to see something of the frontier. We are giving them about three or four days' trip from Peshawar, so that they may be able to realize some of our difficulties in dealing with the frontier tribes. I shall send them up to Landi Kotal to look over into Afghanistan and provide a show for them with our khassidars, who are tame Afridis, and will demonstrate to them a frontier raid. If I can't manage to get them sniped during their trip it will not be my fault, for none of them has the slightest idea of the conditions which prevail on the frontier. They are most of them Madrasees and Bengalis, who have quite an inordinate estimate of the value of their own skins, and a little sniping would do them an infinity of good. When they come back to the Assembly they will look upon frontier questions from quite a different angle of view.

We sent a telegram to you from the Viceroy the other day foreshadowing reductions next cold weather. I am going to have a stiff fight over this. I am pretty certain that, in the long run, we shall have to reduce the British troops in this country. How many I cannot say at present, but it looks as if the lowest limit will be three cavalry regiments, one brigade of field artillery, two medium batteries, and three battalions of infantry. If I am pressed very hard, I will go as far as this, but if they press me beyond this, I shall take off my cap and jacket and let them find another C-in-C. What my Hon'ble Colleagues urge is this. That the revenues of India, apart from those of the local governments, are really insufficient to meet the budget expenditure necessary. All other departments like Railways, Posts, Telegraphs, Commerce, and so forth, for which money is wanted, are remunerative services, and give a return on the capital outlay expended. The Army, on the other hand, is like pouring money down a sink, and no actual return is shown on the money laid out. It is pure insurance, and what they contend is that a military budget of 62.2 crores of rupees[24] is too high insurance to pay for the safety of India. The argument is not an easy one to refute. All one can do is to disagree with their opinion, and, having disagreed, there is nothing more to be said. If I refuse to accept responsibility for the defence of India with a less number of troops than this, I have no alternative but to pack up and come home. However, I am rather talking in the dark, because I do not know what view Reading will take of the military problem when he arrives, nor of what Montagu, you, and Charlie Monro have said to him before he left England. When we get to Simla at the end of April we shall go into these matters again. They will try and force me to give you warning of reduction in the number of British troops, somewhat similar to those I have already written above, and I think I shall probably refuse, because it is impossible to foretell what the situation is going to be twelve months hence, or at the end of next cold weather, when the actual reductions will have to be carried into effect. I am telling you this just to warn you of what is coming. Meanwhile, push on your tanks and armoured cars with all possible speed, because we must have plenty of these before the time arrives for sending home Brit: troops.

By this time next year your time will be up at the War Office. Have you considered who you are going to get to succeed you, or have you developed any new ideas on the subject? My own opinion is that you wont get out of it, and that you will have to stay on another year at least.

* * *

167

Wilson to Arnold Robertson

[Carbon]
Secret and personal   30th March 1921

My dear Frock

I was away at Easter, otherwise would have answered your letter of the 22nd before. I fully understand all you say, and theoretically I am in full agreement. As you know I am one of those like yourself who think that the only way of treating the Boche is to knock him down first and talk to him afterwards. If you talk to him first he will knock you down afterwards. Therefore I am all for putting the fear of God into the Boches, but I am brought up with this practical difficulty, that owing to the 'Frocks' having flung the British Army out of the window the day after the

Armistice, the British Empire at the present moment has no Army worth the name, and in addition such semblance of troops as we have are scattered in the most scandalous manner—the great bulk of them in Ireland; a very few in England; three battalions on the Rhine; four battalions in Silesia; one battalion at Gibraltar; two battalions at Malta; two battalions at Constantinople; two battalions in Palestine; seven battalions in Egypt; and two battalions on the sea coming back from the East. Was ever such a distribution of troops made in the face of an enemy? It is at least as bad as the distribution of troops on the 21st March 1918 under Generals Haig and Petain.

Now the picture that I see is this that if we are not careful we shall lose Ireland. If we lose Ireland we have lost the Empire. Therefore, to me, as a military gentleman, there is for the moment only one theatre of any importance, to wit, Ireland, and I would personally crowd into Ireland every single soldier that I have got on whom I could lay my hands, and amongst those would be the four battalions now in Silesia; the two battalions in Constantinople; the two battalions in Palestine; the two battalions on the sea; and one, two or three battalions from Malta and Egypt, with as many battalions as it was safe to spare from looking after London. I see nothing but disaster if we lose Ireland, even if we happen to be at that moment sitting in such delectable places as Silesia, Constantinople, Jewland, and Persia. To me, as you know because you heard me trying to give the lecture, to me the whole Treaty of Versailles is going to crash right under our eyes, and it must go crash because it is based on these different fallacies which I tried to point out when up in Cologne. And I keep on saying to the Cabinet, or to anybody else who is good enough to listen to me in a bus or tube, that the policy for England is quite quite simple and consists in this, get out of those places which do not belong to you and cling on like hell to those which do . . .

Yes, I promise you this, that if I form a National Party you shall be the first Foreign Minister. What chance you have of getting that appointment I leave you to judge . . .

168

Wilson to Rawlinson

[Carbon]
Secret and personal   2nd April 1921

I am afraid I have been treating you very badly these last few
weeks, but upon my honour and word what with this and what
with that there is jolly little time to write to a fellow like you!

Your Afghan business seems to be dragging, due to the
constant interference of Montagu, whose telegrams are so
nebulous that they act always in a negative and never in the
positive sense.

I am very glad Geoffrey [*sic*] Fell is working well with you; that
makes your work lighter and pleasanter than if he was pulling
contrary ways like two goats on an Irish road.

The Greek and Turkish position is equally scandalous, equally
amusing, and equally interesting. The 'Frocks' handed to the
Greeks and the Turks completely new terms when they were here
some few weeks ago. Both sides said that they would like to go
back to their countries and consult their superior persons. While
these whisperings in Greece and Turkey were going on the
Greeks with the full knowledge and suppressed approval of L.G.
have mounted an attack on the Turks. In order to keep quite clear
of so rotten an arrangement I got permission at once to wire to
Tim to hand over the Greek people he had under his command,
including the port and town of Ismid. So far, therefore, as we
soldiers are concerned we are free of all Greek entanglements.
The Greeks led off by a bloodless and victorious march which,
however, appears, yesterday, to have received some sort of a
check in front of Eskishehr, the Turks claiming that they have
knocked out one Greek division and routed two others, but
arithmetic has never been a strong point in the Turkish mentality.
However that may be it really will be most amusing, and from my
point of view very delightful, if the Turks hit the Greeks a really
good 'puck in the nose'; it will be still more amusing if by any
chance the Greeks set to work and run away, thus uncovering the

Peninsula of Ismid and poor Tim in Constantinople. It would bring the 'Frocks' up against the reality of things instead of living in a world of their own whisperings in that 'back parlour' in 10 Downing Street which has been and is so fatal for our Empire. I am afraid, however, it is more likely that the Greeks will occupy the line Eskishehr–Afium and very possibly push on in flying column fashion to Angora, in which case the turn for the Turk won't come for some few months.

* * *

5th April 1921
Since I began this letter, three days ago, I have received yours of the 16th March, and several other things also have happened . . .

I see that you think that I was taking a very pessimistic view of matters in Turkey and Greece. The course of events has more than justified my opinion when I wrote to you and since I began this letter, in fact only a couple of hours ago we received a telegram to say that the Greeks had not only taken a nasty knock in front of Eskishehr but were falling back in what appears to be some disorder to their original lines at Brussa. I am putting up a short note to the Cabinet pointing out that this retrograde movement on the part of their Greek friends, if really carried out, will entirely uncover poor Tim, and that he will find himself sitting in Constantinople with our friend Kemal facing him with a few odd guns stuck in the bushes having a shot at Tim, or anything else from a battleship to a jampot, from behind some cactus bushes and therefore quite invisible.

I repeat again for the thousandth time that the sooner we clear out of these places that do not belong to us and hang on to those that do the better for England.

What effect a Greek reverse will have on the Turk I do not know. Whether we will be able to induce the P.M. and his Cabinet to realise the state of affairs, and to make friends with Kemal before it is too late I do not know. But I confess that after two and half years of trying to get some sense into the Cabinet— since the Armistice—I cannot bring myself to be over-hopeful.

Apart from this change in the situation in Asia Minor, things here in England have developed with astonishing rapidity. Yesterday I was present at three Cabinet meetings and at each succeeding meeting the 'Frocks' became more and more certain that we were into a 'Red' revolution after midnight tomorrow night. Again I find it exceedingly difficult to believe this, but on the other hand there is no doubt that, although in my judgment not probable, it is certainly within the bounds of possibility.[25] So frightened were the 'Frocks' that I was given a free hand to move such troops as I wished and this included the withdrawal of the 4 battalions from Silesia to England, and if necessary even the other 4 battalions that are still on the Rhine; the shipment of 3 battalions from Malta to England; and the reinforcement of England by as many more troops from Ireland as I considered necessary. This was yesterday afternoon, and in accordance with the powers given to me I am moving 2 battalions from Ireland to Liverpool, to be followed by 2 more; I have recalled the 4 battalions from Silesia; I have told the Rhine they may have to send their 4 other battalions; the 3 battalions are getting into ships at Malta; and I am scraping up today 18 battalions of infantry, 6 regiments of cavalry, a lot of tanks, armoured cars etc. in London alone. At the present moment as I write the troops are pouring into London from Aldershot, Eastern and Southern Commands. It really seems incredible that our 'Frocks' should have reduced this Dear Old Country of ours to such a parlous condition while all the time preaching they were trying to make it a 'land fit for heroes to live in'. There certainly are plenty of heroes in England but I am afraid they do not live in 10 Downing Street.

I am very glad to hear of your opinion as regards the unlikelihood of serious disturbance in India. This is really good news, and although I have scarcely anything but bad news to give you, whether of Ireland, or of England or of Silesia, or of Constantinople, I have this, anyhow, to repeat, as I said at the Cabinet last night, that in the whole of this unfortunate, tormented country of England, and Ireland, the only contented body of men at the present moment is the soldiers and the sailors. I cannot imagine anything more creditable to the regimental officer in these times, nor anything more calculated to make one take an optimistic view of any troubles that may be coming, no matter how severe they are . . .

169

Wilson to Congreve

[Carbon]   13th April 1921
Secret and personal

I had a long talk yesterday with Winston. You can scarcely imagine how much pleasure it gave me to hear him praise you in the most generous and unstinted fashion. Considering what a bounder I know you are the pleasure was obviously all the greater.

Winston is anxious to plot out a road via Amman into Mesopotamia. He has a delightful plan of sending an aeroplane that would drop bombs which falling on to a white surface would penetrate into the black sub-soil which black material would blow up to the top, and the result would be, according to his description, a beautiful white surface with black dots along it, and an aeroplane would therefore find its way from Amman to Hit. If we could make the black material incandescent it would add to the facility of flying by night. You might ponder on this edition of Winston's.[26]

But, joking apart, I have always been in favour of making some arrangement by which we can fly from Egypt to Mesopotamia. In fact, so much has this been the case that just two years ago, now, in Paris, I remember writing a note to Milner to say that I was going to bring in a scheme of superior Inspector-Generals for the Army which was based on the fact that I hoped within the next few years an Inspector-General could interview the C.I.G.S. in his room at the War Office on Saturday morning, fly out to Delhi, discuss matters with the Commander-in-Chief in India, and be back again in the War Office on the following Saturday.

If therefore there is anything that you can do to help in investigating the possibilities of aeroplane flying, or motor car running, from Amman to Mesopotamia, let me know. Of course, as I said yesterday to Winston, all this sort of experiments depend on having friendly Arabs between the Jordan and the Euphrates. If the 'Squire' Abdullah, and the other local 'Squires' between him and Baghdad, will give our boys breakfast and lunch, or as we say in Ireland, lodging and entertainment, the task of plotting out for aeroplanes or motor cars will be much facilitated. That of course is obvious.

By the way, I telegraphed to you yesterday agreeing to the visit of aeroplanes now and again to Amman, provided you thought the operation was safe. But there is the danger that some poor little aeroplane man squatting at Amman may one night have his throat cut and drag us into some sort of military action which once again might increase our commitments. However, I am quite content to trust to you to do whatever you think is wise knowing that such action will be the right one under the circumstances.

We are in considerable trouble here at home but whether it is going to get worse or better we none of us know. Meanwhile the 'Frocks' are having the time of their lives because they are talking something like 18 hours out of the 24.

You will have had my wire telling you that in view of Allenby's report about the reception of Zaghloul etc.[27] I won't call on you for any of the three battalions which you so kindly offered to lend me. But when the two battalions which are presently coming back from Mesopotamia reach Egypt I think very likely the A.G. will ask you to swap them for a couple of others who are much higher on the roster for home service and push them on to us here, or I might even leave them with you for the minute or bring them to Malta. It depends on which of the many theatres, all of them more or less disturbed, requires most looking after at the moment . . .

170

Haldane to Wilson

G.H.Q., Mesopotamia,
14th April, 1921.

Thank you for your letter of the 24th January from Paris which I found on reaching Basrah on the 7th. Next day Ironside started by air for Baghdad, rather against my unexpressed wish. Cox had asked me for a plane for him and by air he would gain 24 hours. The wind was in the south of Basrah and the atmosphere very close which made me feel that flying conditions were not good. Next day when I was inspecting the new barracks at Shaiba I heard that his pilot had made a forced landing and Ironside had a broken thigh. An Air Force doctor had been sent off by plane at once to near Kidr where the accident had occurred, and I at once did all that was possible to ensure Ironside being taken either to Basrah or Baghdad. The doctors decided on the former, being nearer. Ironside must have had a trying night in the train but reached Basrah on the 9th. Next morning I saw him for a few minutes. He had slept badly in spite of a little morphia and looked tired. His back was a good deal bruised and his water-works only working by means of a catheter. That is not unusual owing to shock and no doubt is right by now. The leg has been X-rayed and the very slight error in junction of the fragments had been put right, Ironside declining an anaesthetic. It was hot at Basrah and I wished that he could have been moved to Baghdad, but moving him will be undesirable for some weeks, in fact until the break has joined. There has been some haemorrhage at the break but there have been no complications and the fracture is a simple one. I am communicating with him and I fancy that he will wish to go home to convalesce and it will be best.[28] I had to remain in Basrah for 3 days with Frith my D.Q.M.G., going into many questions regarding the reduction of the place to reasonable dimensions. That being arranged I left for Baghdad and got here on the 12th.

* * *

The instructions which I sent from Cairo, in continuation of orders issued before I went there, have been well carried out and from a ration strength of 190,000 on 1st January, we should be down to 55,000 on 30th June. That will bring me down to 23 battalions etc. Then there will be a pause as it is the dangerous season and the election for an Emir comes in July. Moreover that is the hottest season, and I prefer not to move troops. I will telegraph in plenty of time regarding diminution of shipping as may be necessary. By the end of June I shall probably be parting with 2 divisional commanders and staffs, and there will be reductions at G.H.Q. Such matters will be telegraphed very shortly. The Levies are now under me and I am settling their disposition etc., which is at present based on the civilian idea of dispersion! If the Levies are invested anywhere this summer they will have to do the best they can for themselves, and I should try to save the British personnel by plane if they will come away. I shall only have troops for very limited operations and whatever may happen nothing will be sent from overseas.

I still maintain that to hold this country a strong regular force (I mean not of the country) is necessary, otherwise it would be best to clear out from the greater part of it. It is a gamble to hold the country as is proposed, and all I have undertaken is to preserve my own troops in comparative safety. Unless one has lived here it is difficult to appreciate what a possible wasp's nest it can be. The tribes near Suq on the Lower Euphrates are giving trouble and I had a long talk with the political officer at Nasiriyeh on my way from Basrah on the subject and repeated the gist to Cox on my arrival. An aeroplane demonstration which is being made to-day and to-morrow may have a good effect and this will be a test of the value of the Air Service under similar conditions elsewhere in this country. The murder of a Sheikh, refusal to pay revenue and next, unless there is a show of force, anarchy and the tribe involved is as it is termed "out". It is perhaps even money whether peace can be maintained this summer, but one must hope for the best, though if there is trouble it might be fairly widespread. The tribes are busy buying arms in the Hillah and Suq districts and no doubt will get better quality ones than some we made them hand in. The road along the river from Shergat to Fatha will soon be fit for lorries which will give us a route other than that along the railway. Generally from the economical point of view affairs are going extremely well, and that this is so is greatly due to the fact that I got to work the moment that the state at which the insurrection operations had arrived permitted it.

It is disappointing that Churchill did not seem to appreciate the enormous difference in conditions between this country and the Sudan. He, and I think Lord Milner from something I read, does not understand why one British battalion is not sufficient for this country. If Churchill who is possessed of imagination cannot grasp what seems to me so utterly patent a fact how can one expect the ordinary politician to appreciate what we went through and did last summer.

I ask for credit from no one for doing my duty, but I did hope for understanding, and I found that after I had explained to Churchill that this was like a N.W. Frontier as regards tribesmen, who liked fighting and were well-armed, he put the same question to another soldier Colonel Joyce, who is to help to raise the Arab Army. I always understood that at the Battle of Khartoum the fighting men in the Sudan were wiped out which is far from being the case here. There are a dozen other differences between the two countries . . .

171

Wilson to Sackville-West

[Carbon]   14th April 1921
Secret

I will add a line to this tomorrow morning as I have lost today's post. Our position is as follows:

The P.M. tells me that we are practically certain to be up against the Triple [Alliance] tomorrow night. Once this game is unchained nobody knows what it means; where it will take us; or when it will end. What is certain is, if we are really into it the four battalions from the Rhine which are just arriving now at Dover will be required, and possibly I may have to call for the other four. Of course I won't do that unless I am in *extremis*. But I think you might read this letter to the Marshal so that he may know how I stand.

Our first two battalions from Malta arrived at Plymouth today, and will be followed by the other battalions in the course of a week, and then another three weeks or month, shipping having gone rather astray.

I have already taken four battalions from Ireland for Liverpool, and I am terribly anxious not to withdraw any more battalions from Ireland unless this country is in positive danger. My feeling is that having withdrawn already all I can from the Mediterranean, Mesopotamia and Persia; having none to spare in Constantinople or Egypt; and of course none from India, my next pull will have to be the Rhine, and after that Ireland. But as the Defence Force matures, and it is going on quite nicely, and as the Marines and Sailors, which the Admiralty are lending me and which amount to about 25 battalions, become available so I hope that what is still on the Rhine may remain there.
[Added in holograph]
Friday 15/4/21

We are in the melting pot again this morning! A wonderful people! . . .

172

Wilson to Rawlinson

[Carbon]   26th April 1921
Personal

Yours of 5th April, written on board ship going to Karachi, has just come in and is most interesting reading.

That the India of today is different from the India when we were there together as boys is certain. That we have encouraged the wrong class of education, in the wrong class of native, at the wrong time, and in the wrong way is equally certain. And the picture that I see is that the talking, lawyer mind is going to try and govern the silent, fighting mind. Up to a point that is always possible in any society and with men of any colour, but it is quite impossible for a long period of time, and more especially in times of strain and stress. Nor is it possible in a country like India, inhabited by races as different as the poles are asunder, governed by religions as far apart as the sun is from the earth. Nor is it possible for a small clique of talking, theoretical, sophistical, lawyer folk, practically all of one colour, one class, one caste, to govern the enormous number of other tribes of other colours, of other classes, of other castes. But the ludicrosity [*sic*] of it is emphasised when we remember that of a population of three hundred millions inside the boundary fence of India the reading, thinking, talking, characterless class which is seeking to impose its domination is not more than 2% of the three hundred millions, and, as I have said, coming all from one class, and one caste, it is probably not more than .00001 of the fighting, silent men of India. What absurd nonsense! It is claimed in England that 5% govern the 95%. It may or may not be so but in any case the five and the ninety-five are all one people, but in India, as I have just explained, it is the exact opposite. I come back therefore, always and ever, to the same thesis, which is that the English must govern India or clear out; they must govern the 98% because if the 2% try and govern the 98% you will have nothing but war and chaos. It is exactly the same with us here in England. The Government must either govern the Trades Unions or clear out. It is exactly the same in Ireland, it is exactly the same in Egypt, it is exactly the same in India.

I will add a line to this tomorrow about the position we are in here as regards miners, railways etc.

27th April

There is really nothing definite to report about the industrial situation here today. We go from one conference into another; everybody talks until they are exhausted; nobody takes any action;

but this of course suits the communists down to the ground and therefore does not suit us at all because every day's talking and no action, and therefore no coal, means increased unemployment and increased discontent, and we may, simply by dint of talking, find ourselves in a very dangerous situation. Why the Government keep on allowing this drift to continue passes my understanding. Everything that can be said for the mine owners, for the miners, for the railwaymen, for the transport workers, for the dockers, and for the Government has been said over and over again *ad nauseam*, and all the time this constant drift. Long before you get this letter the situation will be cleared, one way or the other, and we shall be either into serious trouble or have sailed out into at any rate temporary smooth water.

Monsieur Briand and the Old Marshal are coming over at the end of this week to discuss the occupation of the Ruhr, Hamburg, Bremen etc. The Boches have put in another proposal, this time to the Americans, and the 'Frocks' this morning are busy puzzling out what it means. The Boches of course by working through the Americans are hoping to make a split between us and the Frenchmen. However, this question of the occupation of the Ruhr will also be settled long before you get this letter[29] . . .

173

Haldane to Wilson

[Marked "Not Answered"]   General Headquarters,
                                                       Mesopotamia,
                                                   8th May 1921.

I do not know what the opinion of the Army Council may be regarding the rank of the G.O.C.-in-C. Mesopotamia, but it is evident that the S. of S. for the Colonies proposes to reduce it to that of Major General as soon as he can. According to a letter of his to me and telegrams received not long after I came to Mesopotamia, when he was War Minister, his intention was that the garrison of the country was to be gradually reduced, first to the equivalent of a division and a few months later the R.A.F. were to assume command. I now find that Churchill told Ironside at Cairo, that, on relieving me, he would be here for some five years, so that evidently the original scheme for air control shortly after my departure has undergone a considerable modification. Assuming that the summer passes quietly, and that by the raising of levies I can reduce my troops by October to 16 battalions and some other units, the force here—even putting out of consideration the command of the Levies, vested in me in time of trouble—will still considerably exceed those of other Lieut-Generals' Commands abroad, not to speak of those at home. Yet this Command—a post of exceptional responsibility for many reasons—is to be lowered in status.

The Army Council have been good enough to express their appreciation of my work here on several occasions, and have consistently agreed with and endorsed the policy I have followed.

The Operations last summer were of considerable magnitude, second only in my experience to the S. African War, and were carried out under circumstances of great difficulty. It is recognised here, and it is no exaggeration to say that we were for some months literally fighting for our lives, and an error of judgement or failure to accept risks on my part would have led to grave results. Yet these operations have been hushed up because the subject of Mesopotamia is unpopular. Despatches describing them are slow in appearing, if they are indeed to appear, and wherever I go I find officers who bitterly resent the way their services and those of their troops, have been kept out of the public eye. And now on the top of this it would seem that, as a reward for my services in carrying to a very thorough conclusion a campaign, pacifying a considerable portion of a turbulent country, and effecting reductions involving millions of money—in fact, putting things straight—I am, on the excuse of economy, to be required to efface myself to suit the whim of a Minister, here to-day there to-morrow, and submit to be superseded by a junior officer in what will still be a Lieut-General's Command. As regards the public, I have so successfully been kept in the background that they would hardly notice the change. But I cannot consent to leave Mesopotamia under what to me would be to do so under a cloud, and I am sure that you will understand that it is due to my honour as a soldier not to submit tamely to such treatment.

I have nothing but thanks to proffer to yourself and the Army Council for their support and encouragement to me as well as their appreciation of what has been accomplished here, and I cannot believe that they mean to abrogate their powers on the question of command to the S. of S. for the Colonies. Churchill, when writing to me last year about the air scheme stated that, if he left the War Office, he would leave on record a note that every effort was to be made to re-employ me, but what faith can one put in such a promise, any more than in the gratitude—held out in front of me at Cairo by him—of H.M. Government when treatment such as I foresee before me is to be meted out? You know how I have been treated as regards the question of grading—a matter affecting my staff as well as myself—and though Churchill has been home a month and took with him a note from me on the subject, nothing has happened. That, though perhaps a small matter, does not encourage one to trust promises on larger affairs. Mesopotamia is not a country that appeals to most of us who have to serve in it, and I would certainly for my own comfort and peace of mind have no objections to a Command elsewhere. However, even though there should be worse times ahead than I went through last year, and as I am as fit as I have ever been in my life, I have no desire to shirk the unknown and throw the load on other shoulders, however capable they may be.

There is a further point which I must mention, because it may be in Churchill's mind, viz: the idea that Sir P. Cox and I do not get on. I was a little annoyed with Cox at Cairo as he held back more than I felt was necessary in certain points that came up. He is excessively slow and so reticent as to make my task here more difficult despite every effort to create free intercommunication between the Military and Civil. I have realised since my return from Cairo that his staff is greatly responsible in the matter of lack of liaison—through ignorance and want of method. It is only fair to him and myself to say that we get on really well, and that he appears to have full confidence in my military judgement.

I am sorry to have to write at such length. It was only on my return here that it began to dawn on me that I was about to be treated in a manner perhaps common among politicians, but not among soldiers. There seemed to me to be a parallel between my case and that of a very great man, Sir John Moore, whose treatment by Castlereagh, or really by Canning, on his return from Sweden before he went on the Corunna Campaign, you may remember.[30]

I should be grateful for an early assurance that the Army Council are not going to see me cast into the dirt, as otherwise I must, however much I may dislike it, fight my own battle.

I wonder that Churchill does not appreciate the fact that there may be a hole in his armour when he is dealing with me![31] . . .

174

Wilson to Rawlinson

[Carbon]   11th May 1921
Personal

It is not easy to sit down and get a few quiet moments in which to write a connected story of what is passing. The communists appear, on the whole, to be gradually getting the upper hand, and if they succeed, as they evidently think they will, then I think we are in for a trial of strength between the law-abiding citizens and those who want to upset the King and Parliament and all known forms of law and order. We on our side have been terribly handicapped by the complete inertia of the Cabinet. As I have often said, I have seen no trace of governing in the Lloyd George Cabinet since the 11th November, 1918. This total lack of grip is bad enough in ordinary times but in times of stress and danger it leads headlong to ruin. I feel quite sure in my own mind that the great bulk of the people of England—and in this bulk I include the vast majority of the miners, railwaymen, transport workers, dockers etc.—are good sound Englishmen; first, law abiding and loyal, and only trades unionists second. But like all these whirlwind revolutions the majority, if untaught and unled, get swept off their legs by the minority. That is what happened in Ireland; that is what is happening in England; and in both cases, in my judgment, due from the start to the finish to the total inability to govern of Lloyd George and his Cabinet. We soldiers of course can do nothing at this stage except to try our best to keep our men contented, but our task is infinitely increased by the fact that the Government do not govern; that the Government do not take the Nation into their confidence; with the result that a very heavy propaganda amongst the troops has resulted in a sense of unrest—not more than that as yet—amongst the reservists in the Army, the Navy, and the Air Force at Aldershot and other centres where there are a large number of reservists. We have already had little troubles.[32] These would cease at once if the Government would only govern but if they won't then I am afraid the troubles will tend to increase. It is a very deplorable situation—pitiful and pitiable to a degree, because wholly unnecessary. What will happen in these coming weeks I do not know but there is one certain factor, I think, which is that if we don't govern other people they will govern us. That applies, as I have often said in my letters, to India, just as much as to England, Ireland or Egypt.

Your letter of the 16th April has just come in. What a jolly trip you had on the Frontier, and how much I would have enjoyed being with you. I will get a short General Staff paper written on your problem of the Frontier, but, broadly speaking, I think this, that just as in old days I never could see any use in the Afghans being a buffer state between us and the Russians, and then our having between ourselves and that buffer state a lot of turbulent tribes; just as in those days I always thought that our frontier and the Afghan frontier should be coterminous, so now that the Afghans are an independent people, made so by this wonderful Goverment of ours, I think that our frontiers should be coterminous with theirs, and, as regards our treatment of the Afghans, I am afraid that like all other people, black and white, deep down in their hearts they only believe in force. If they are more afraid of the Bolsheviks than they are of us, and they are, then so much the greater shame for us. If they insist on making a Treaty with the Bolsheviks to our detriment, and they are so insisting, then so much the greater shame for us. It puts the British Empire very low when we admit that the Bolsheviks can force a Treaty on the Afghans against our interests and we are unable to force a Treaty on the Afghans against the Bolshevik interest!

* * *

175

Wilson to Rawlinson

[Carbon]   18th May 1921
Personal

I won't try any more than a short letter this week.

Our strike in England continues to drag on its weary length; the Government taking no *offensive* action and just continuing their whispering in the 'back parlour'. It positively makes one cry, this total lack of power of governing.

In Ireland we have had one of the worst week-ends since the beginning of the rebellion, and it is perfectly clear to me that unless the 'Frocks' shout out at the top of their voices and get England on their side, and then really set to work to stamp out this vermin we shall lose Ireland, and with the loss of Ireland we have lost the Empire. I want permission from the 'Frocks', the moment England gets temporarily quiet again, to send over between 20 and 30 battalions, from here, some more cavalry, guns, aeroplanes, wireless, tanks, armoured cars etc. to place the whole of Ireland under Martial Law, and hand it all over to Macready. But even with this reinforcement no promise can be made that we can really knock out the murder gang in Ireland, all that I can say is that he is more likely to be able to do so after being reinforced than he is today before he is reinforced. But to go on as we are now, which is neither trying to knock out the murderers nor handing the country over to them as a present, is sheer madness, and when the weather breaks in September–October I am afraid we shall find that the troops, whoever they are, who have been separated from their wives and families for a couple of years, will be getting tired of the job and will say so, and then we shall be properly in the soup.

Since I began this letter, and when I got down to the bottom of the first page, the telephone rang and Curzon, who was at the other end, said that he and the P.M. agreed that I was to send five battalions back to Silesia. I told him that of course if he and the P.M. had settled the matter there was nothing more to be said about it except to send the battalions, but I would be failing in my duty if I did not tell him plainly that it was madness; that five battalions solved no problem; that they might get into a horrid mess; that we did not know how long they would be there; that they would be under the French Command, and quite possibly have a quarrel with the French troops; and so on and so forth; and then I finished up by saying that how anybody in their senses could dream of sending troops to Silesia when Ireland was in the condition she was in passed my understanding, and I told him categorically that in my opinion if we don't reinforce Ireland by every available man, horse, gun, aeroplane, that we have got in the world we would lose Ireland at the end of this summer, and with Ireland the Empire. I asked him of what avail would four or five battalions be in Silesia then! He has gone to speak to the P.M., who apparently won't see me for some reason, and I suppose I shall hear in the course of half an hour or so what those wonderful people have settled to do. It really is terrifying to have to deal with men who have so little idea of what is going on right under their noses . . .

The Japanese Prince, a rummy little card, is being breakfasted, lunched, and dined to death.[33] He may just pull through as he starts for Scotland tonight, but what a dose of haggis will do to him I don't know. If he would go to Galway for a turn he would not be under the necessity of buying a return ticket to Japan . . .

176

Wilson to Sir Laming Worthington-Evans

[Carbon]   23rd May, 1921
Secretary of State.

Marshal Foch having agreed to replace our 4 Battalions on the
Rhine by 4 French Battalions to be under General Morland's
command, I have to-day in accordance with the wishes of the
Government sent an order to General Morland to despatch his 4
British Battalions to Upper Silesia as quickly as possible there to
come under French Command.

I would be failing in my duty if I did not bring to the notice of
the Cabinet that it is an unwise, and possibly a dangerous move,
from the military point of view, to send a small detachment
unsupported, and probably unsupportable, such a distance from
its base, its Lines of Communication being in the hands of the
Germans.

177

Wilson to Sackville-West

[Carbon]   25th May 1921

I am trying to get you on the telephone this morning to tell you
that last night the Cabinet ordered me to send two more
battalions, in addition to those four that are going from the Rhine,
to Silesia. I have selected the Leinsters and the Connaughts, two
Irish battalions that I cannot employ in Ireland, and I am most
anxious that Marshal Foch should understand how it is I can
produce even those two battalions to strengthen the Silesian
garrison. The Cabinet informed me that the situation in England
was quieting down: that being so my attention is being at once
directed to Ireland and I am already preparing a plan for moving
over every available man, aeroplane, tank, etc., etc., from this
country to Ireland. Obviously the Roman Catholic Irish regi-

ments, like the Leinsters and the Connaughts cannot be sent to suppress the rebels in Ireland, and therefore, very much against my will, I am carrying out the orders of the Cabinet and am sending those two battalions straight through from here to Silesia, passing of course through Cologne.[34] In addition I am breaking up the six battalions into two brigades and sending Heneker as a sort of Divisional General in order to give our small force rather more standing than its actual numbers would indicate. I am sure the Old Marshal will understand all this, and make allowances for what may appear to be contradictory news sent by me from day to day.

I have asked Morland to find out from Degoutte whether he (Degoutte) would object to two batteries and 4 Tanks also being sent from the Rhine, as I think our poor little force must be as waspish as it can be made. If Degoutte does demur I will still ask Morland to send the guns and tanks and will replace, as best I can, from here.

The Old Marshal has been so wonderfully good to me that I want him told *everything* . . .

178

Wilson to Sackville-West

[Carbon]   28th May 1921

Yours of 26th received yesterday. I am hoping to hear this morning whether the Old Marshal is coming over for Cambridge, because if he is I propose to go down with him and see the undergrads rag him. He will have to tie his kepi on for sure. If he does not come I know you will thank him again for the way in which Degoutte is playing up to Morland. It really is the greatest pleasure to deal with men like the Old Marshal himself and his subordinates and I only wish, and I sincerely hope, that one of these days we may be able to do something to please him.

The 'Frocks' are, I verily believe, going to allow me to send over all the troops I have got in England to Ireland, my proposal being that every single battalion we have got except the Guard and five Irish battalions shall be shipped over to Ireland this coming month . . .

179

Wilson to The Reverend Thomas Hamilton

[Carbon]   3rd June 1921
Personal

I have delayed answering your letter in the hopes of having a talk with Marshal Foch. He was due over here last Tuesday, and I had arranged to take him down to Cambridge where he was going to be given a Degree, and I was going then to challenge him as regards coming over to Belfast next month. At the last moment he telephoned to me, and telegraphed, to say that he was infinitely sorry but it was quite impossible for him to come.

I am afraid that with the whole of Europe in its present state of increasing unrest and instability it is not safe to make a plan for the 15th July, nor indeed for any date, until we see a real sign of more peaceful intent on the part, not only of Germany and of Poland, but of the Balkans and of Turkey and Greece. In so far as I am concerned personally I might of course be able to go over, but I would be so sorry to have my Degree given to me without bringing over the Old Marshal, if by waiting a little longer we got a chance of both going together, and even as regards my move-ments it is quite true to say that I could not at the present moment go so far away as Belfast. There is not a single day that I have not been sent for two, and three, and even four times a day to meetings, and Cabinets, and matters affecting the forthcoming Imperial Conference, so that if you can possibly postpone the date *sine die* I will always let you know the first favourable opportunity that I see directly it reaches the offing. I am so sorry to be such an unsatisfactory person, and yet I am so in hopes of bringing the Old Marshal over with me one of these days that I think a further delay is well worth the inconvenience.[35]

Lord Stamfordham told me last night that in all probability The King would be going over to open your first Parliament, and this was real good news. If only our Royal Family had understood the Irish a little more, beginning during the reign of Queen Victoria, and had had a residence in Ireland, as they have in Scotland and in England, and had sent their young people over to hunt and shoot and fish I daresay we should not now be in the horrible mess we find ourselves . . .

180

Wilson to Rawlinson

[Carbon]   8th June 1921
Personal

* * *

How drearily drags the Dobbs' Mission! Some days your telegrams look more hopeful; some days they are more depressing; and at this distance it is impossible to forecast what the ultimate result may be, but that there should be any doubt at all, as I said I think in my last letter, as to which side Afghanistan ought to fall, either towards Simla or towards Moscow, is a crying reproach on our Simla and our India Office authorities.

We begin to ship troops over to Ireland next Monday. By the end of the month I hope to have got over about 20 battalions, plus a couple of thousand mounted gunners (Field Artillery who have been turned into mounted infantrymen) plus some battalions of marines, tanks, armoured cars etc., etc. Meanwhile the complexion of James Craig's Parliament becomes more apparent every day. As none of the Papists will take the Oath of Allegiance so the whole House is composed of Protestants, and the whole Police also of 'Black Protestants', so also will be the Laws, and if I mistake not, in the course of a very few years, so thorough will be the legislation in the Six 'Black Counties' that there won't be a Papish gentleman or lady resident in any of them. This no doubt will excite the Sinn Feins to do the same with the Parliament in Dublin, that is to say, murder and chase all the Protestants out of the Three Provinces . . .

181

Wilson to Rawlinson

[Carbon] 14th June 1921
Personal

Yours of the 25th May has come in just in time to answer. I think we can safely make up our minds that the Persians are an absolutely rotten people, far more rotten than even the Poles or the South-country Irish—and that puts them pretty low! Well, that being so you may take it from me that they will all go Bolshevik, not because they want to be Bolshevik but because they have got to be Bolshevik. On the other hand they will never be dangerously Bolshevik because they will never be dangerous no matter what they do, and a Bolshevik who is not dangerous is simply beneath contempt. Therefore, I have always looked upon Persia as certain to go a kind of soft Bolshevik, and it has never terrified me because the Bolsheviks will never be able to make real use of the Persians, and it is a great fat country to get across and the Bolsheviks will be continually a sort of butting into a pillow, a very tiresome process which leads nowhere.[36] On the other hand if the Afghans turned Bolshevik would be much more serious, because they are a venomous fighting lot of blackguards and would be a really dangerous element to have as neighbour. But the recent telegrams from Dobbs look more and more like a satisfactory conclusion, and if Dobbs and Muspratt pull the chestnuts out of that fire they ought to be made Peers, or 'Peeresses' or 'Peerlesses' or 'motors' of some description.

As regards Mesopotamia, I need not repeat again what I have several times said, beyond saying once more that you must either govern in Mesopotamia or come out, and as it is quite clear we are not going to govern so it is equally certain we shall come out, but I think we ought to hold the oil-fields, by which I imagine I mean in or about the Basra Vilayet.

The letters I get from Palestine all tend to show that there will be trouble there in the autumn. The Palestine problem is exactly the same as the Irish—two different sets of people living in a small area, each hating the other 'for the love of God'. In cases of that description, whether in Ireland, in East Prussia, in Silesia, in Croatia, in Palestine etc., if you want to have peace and quiet it can only be obtained by one over-riding authority, strong enough to knock either or both of these miseries on the head if either of them 'cocks a snook' at the other. In Ireland we call that the 'Union'; in East Prussia they call it 'The League of Nations'; in Croatia they call it 'Serbia'; in Poland they call it 'chaos'; in Palestine they call it 'Nebbi'.

* * *

As regards Ireland, nothing whatever has been decided.

182

Wilson to Sir James Craig[37]

[Carbon]   16th June 1921

I sent you a telegram this morning saying that I was afraid it was impossible for me to accept your invitation. As you may well imagine there are few things on earth that I would rather be present at than the Opening of your Parliament. I have an unlimited belief in our corner of Ireland, in fact so much so that I often tell these unfortunate English fellows that when they have made a hash of the Empire we Ulster boys will take over the show for them and let them see how to run a real Imperial idea! But I refused because of two reasons. First because, being the Senior Officer in the British Army, I do not think it would be right and proper for me to be present at the proceedings on the 22nd, unless the King had expressed a wish that I should be; and secondly, because in view of the fact that I am C.I.G.S. and that my opinions of the Irish Question are fairly well known, and in view of the fact that the Government appear to be determined to increase their pressure on the South and West in order to bring this Sinn Fein rebellion to an end, and that the orders for all the troops to go over will have to emanate from me, I think it would perhaps bring politics into the Army if as a preliminary to ordering thousands of troops over to crush the rebellion in the South and West, I was seen to take part in the opening of the Parliament in the North.

These are my two reasons and I am sure that you will agree that they are both good. On the other hand I send them to you with very real regret because it would in truth have given me immense pleasure to have seen this wonderful function on the 22nd.

Very many thanks to you personally for your letter and for your most kindly offer of care and hospitality . . .

183

Wilson to Sackville-West

[Carbon]   28th June 1921

I am delighted that you were decorated by the Old Marshal himself and that your 'citation' was a flattering expression of the work you have done. I am sure the Old Boy meant every word of it.

Was Eddie Derby at the 'Grand Prix' or was he in Dublin arranging for Valera to come over![38] He used to be excellent in old days in South Africa (was Eddie) for arranging a comfortable journey—sleeping cars, *lavabos*, carriages etc., so that Valera, Michael Collins, and any other murderers who care to come over, will I am sure have a comfortable journey both ways.

The Sinn Feins have had great fun pinching a letter of mine to James Craig in which, luckily, I made some flattering remarks about the English! This was to have been dealt with in the House of Commons last night but I have not heard what passed.[39]

The coal strike, with a *pour boire* of 10 millions looks like being settled. I suppose the settlement will last, with luck, for one or two months, and then we shall be into the mess again . . .

184

Wilson to Worthington-Evans

[Carbon]   29th June 1921
Secret

Secretary of State

As the time draws near for the final decisions of the Government as regards the military action to be taken in Ireland I, as your responsible military adviser, get more and more anxious.

The geographical position of Ireland turns all questions of the relations of that country to England into questions and problems of a Naval and Military character and if I speak quite openly on this subject it is entirely from the military point of view that I shall address my remarks.

For the last two years I have always thought and openly said that we have only two courses open to us in Ireland. One is to crush out the murder gang with a ruthless hand and restore law and order and the King's Writ, and the other is to clear out altogether, i.e., grant Independence. Now as regards the grant of Independence I am quite clearly of opinion that this will mean that we shall have a hostile Ireland in our rear and right athwart all our trade routes, and this again will mean that we shall have to reconquer Ireland *or* lose our Empire. I have therefore always been driven to advise the first of the two alternatives, viz., crush out the murder gang with a ruthless hand and restore law and order and the King's Writ.

But although I believe this to be proper, and indeed the only, course to pursue if we want to keep our Empire I have always said that it is an impossible course and one which should never be attempted unless Great Britain is whole-heartedly in favour of it. Now so far as I can judge Great Britain is *not* whole-heartedly in favour of ruthless suppression of crime in Ireland. I am judging by

275

the way in which the military authorities, even in the Martial Law area, are constantly being interfered with, I am judging by speeches and meetings of the Church of England, of the Labour Party, of the Liberal Party, and even of the House of Lords, but I am judging still more by the Press which appears to be almost unanimously in favour of more concessions and yet more concessions. If I am right in this then to embark on a ruthless campaign against the murderers in Ireland is a hopeless task. It is worse, it is suicidal, for without the whole-hearted support of Great Britain we shall fail, and if we fail we shall break the Army.

Can Great Britain be brought to approve and to adopt as her own the policy I have indicated above, a policy which can only be carried out by Martial Law and Blockade in their severest forms? I am one of those who believe that if Great Britain was really told of the appalling state of Ireland and of the savage, cruel murders perpetrated every day, murders of her own soldiers, her own police, and her own loyal subjects, she would not only approve of any measures, no matter how severe, but she would cry out for them. This however is a matter somewhat out of my province, but it is not out of my province, it is in fact my duty, to say that:

> Unless Great Britain is solidly in favour of severest measures in Ireland we soldiers are certain to fail and if we fail the Army will be broken.
>
> Therefore, until Great Britain is whole-heartedly crying for the severest measures, and determined to see this matter through to the end, I must warn you against using the Army in a campaign which is doomed to fail.

185

Wilson to Rawlinson

[Carbon]   6th July 1921
Secret and Personal

The miners' strike is by way of being over. Whether it *is* over or not I cannot tell you, and we won't know for a year or two at least, that is to say, we won't know whether the miners really mean to put their backs into it at reasonable wages or whether they don't. But for the moment everybody says the miners strike is over. On that I have to observe this, that in order to get it over we had to bribe them with 10 millions; now the railways become decontrolled next month, and unless I make a great mistake we shall have a railway strike, and probably a transport strike, which, again on the precedent of the miners will have to be bought off with 10, 20, 30 or 40 millions of your money and mine. Now this is the high road to ruin, to buy off importunate persons who have the ill manners to blackmail you!

Take the case, again, of Ireland. When Valera had only murdered five or ten policemen and soldiers he was thought of little account; when he had murdered 50 or 100 he was thought of more account; now that he has murdered 500 he is invited to lunch at Downing Street. In so far as I can judge Valera has not produced one single argument in favour of independence, except the argument of foul and cruel murders, and this argument has carried conviction to the Cabinet, headed by the Prime Minister, to the extent of asking him to come over to a conference. Valera's answer is from his point of view perfectly correct, he says he does not see any 'avenue of approach' or 'glimmer of light' or 'sun peak sunrise' or whatever these things are in a conference in London, and that he will therefore summon a conference of his own in Dublin. This he has done to selected idiots like Midleton and Woods, etc.[40] These gentlemen, having been given their orders by Valera came back again yesterday and have interviewed the Prime Minister. Meanwhile, to show the depth to which the present Cabinet have fallen Smuts is either sent over or allowed to go over to interview Valera, Valera himself refusing to come over here, and Smuts came back last night, and travelled under the name of 'Colonel Smith'.[41] Was ever anything more miserably cowardly than a Prime Minister talking to a murderer under the assumed name of 'Colonel Smith'? The real truth is, Henry, that we are in a fair way to lose Ireland first, then Egypt, and then India, and undoubtedly we shall lose all of them if we go on being governed by people who pay blackmail, of 10 millions to the miners, and blackmail of shaking hands with murderers.

I follow day by day your Mr. Dobbs and Mr. Muspratt, and again this week these poor fellows, who have struggled like heroes, who have been constantly interfered with, chiefly from London, appear to me on the whole to be rather further away than they were last week from a satisfactory treaty. I cannot help repeating once more what I told you about a month ago, that the fact that the Bolshevik can force a treaty on Afghanistan, should he do so, will be a sign of terrible weakness on our part.

Your Gandhi and Ali lunches[42] will lead you into the same mess that our Valera lunches are leading us into here. The proposal today, I understand in so far as Ireland is concerned, is to have a truce for a month, or what the Cabinet euphoniously describe as a 'gentlemanly undertaking'. I have nothing to add to those charming words.

* * *

Yesterday I sent you a telegram from Kitten Wigram on a proposal which Montagu made to him for taking over the internal security of India by gendarmerie. To me this is fantastic, and Kitten tells me that it would work out to a reduction of 28 battalions in India, and as you will readily understand, that will mean an equivalent number of battalions being abolished at home with a total loss to our poor little Army of 56 battalions. This again would mean that if those few troops that we still have on the frontier of India get into trouble with the Afghans or anybody else we shall be totally incapable of reinforcing them, and again as you can readily understand with 56 battalions less in our Army our reserves would dwindle down to something quite negligible so that even on mobilization we would be quite incapable of producing more than one or two divisions.

I am sorry we have been quite unable up to now to give you more than an indication of how many of your Native battalions we shall require in the ordinary times of peace. Touching those 'ordinary times of peace' my own belief is that you and I will never see them. I do not think that this unfortunate world of ours after its double upset, first by the Boche and then by my sainted

'Cousin' will recover under a period of 200 or 300 years. It took 300 years of constant European fighting to make the Hapsburg Empire, and I do not see why it should not take a like period to group up Europe into big empires once again, and now that every country in the world is so closely ramified with every other a constant state of war and restlessness in Europe will mean a constant state of war and restlessness all over the world.

Down at Constantinople Tim has written to Kemal to offer to have a talk with him and a cup of tea on board of one of His Majesty's ships.

Squibbie Congreve writes repeatedly warning us of coming troubles in Palestine, where the 'Frocks' in their wisdom set a Jew to govern Arabs.

In Mesopotamia things appear quieter but so long as we have the Turk either hostile or suspicious we shall never have comfort in Palestine, Egypt, Mesopotamia or India.

Yesterday I was invited to give an address to the Imperial Cabinet on the question of 'Imperial Strategy'. It was not altogether a success, chiefly because, so far as I could judge, I put a few unpalatable truths as, for example:

First. There is no dividing line between Imperial Strategy and Imperial Policy. The War Office is bound to tread on the heels and stamp on the toes of the Foreign Office just as the Foreign Office is bound to tread on the heels and stamp on the toes of the War Office.

Secondly. Neither the Imperial Cabinet nor the Cabinet of St. James's have ever indicated to the War Office who our possible enemies of the future may be, it has therefore been impossible for the War Office to make plans which will stand the test of war, because it is impossible to consider war in the abstract. We are therefore reduced in the War Office to having to select our own enemies without even the approval of the Foreign Office, otherwise we shall be making an army fit to fight France and suddenly finding that we were fighting the Afghans, or we shall be making a naval programme fit to fight the Japanese and suddenly finding that we were at war with America. I repeat that it is impossible to study war in the abstract.

Thirdly. The War Office is never given a standard up to which to work. In this respect we are greatly handicapped as compared to the Navy who have always had either a 2-power standard, a 1-power and 60% standard, or a 1-power standard. Soldiers have no standard but not only that, we have got a voluntary Army and no voluntary Army has any relation whatever to war. It is governed by two things, first the amount of money available to pay troops, and this obviously has nothing to do with war, and secondly the number of men who are willing to engage, and this also obviously has nothing to do with war. Therefore the unfortunate War Office is given an instrument which has no relation to any known or unknown war, is not informed of its possible enemies, has no standard up to which to work, and then is asked to make plans.

A few more truths of a like nature I brought out in a quiet but somewhat insistent voice, and the 'Frocks' got more and more uncomfortable and less and less inclined to listen. Poor 'Frocks', and still poorer Empire governed by such 'Frocks'.

We have had about 13 or 14 years now of no rain. My potatoes are about the size of marbles. I pass easily from a world problem—the world so far as I can make out from Winston has now been found out to be flat and not round—to potatoes which are a much more important topic at the moment . . .

186

Sackville-West to Wilson

[Holograph]   Paris
                                                                   July 6 [1921]

I & my fellows dined with Foch & the officers of his Staff as did the officers of the other delegations of the "Versailles" Committee, last night at the Cercle Militaire. I sat next to the old man, he will be 70 in October, & as usual he was most charming—I have seen a good deal of him lately what with dinners & garden parties etc. however he leaves today or tomorrow on leave for Morlaix. He told me he did not write to you as he had so much to say no letter would suffice & also for fear the letter fell into the hands of the Shin finns [*sic*]! but that you were in his thoughts always & he appreciated your difficulties. A mention by the way of your letter to Craig was in one of the French papers but with no comment.

He asked me was it true that the Battalions withdrawn from the Rhine would never return. I said I could not say whether or no the same Battalions would return but that I knew you intended to replace them as soon as you could as you liked for various well known reasons which I gave, having them there. I expect Foch got this idea from Morland's monthly report, Appendix III where he says "Three of the Battns despatched to England x x x x x have now been definitely transferred x x x & will not return to Cologne."[43] I dont know how Foch knew this & last night I had not read Morland's report—I said I thought it likely Irish Battalions would go to the Rhine rather than other ones. I attended a ceremony at Le Mans last Saturday laying of a foundation stone, speeches, luncheon etc. & 8 hours in a hot train.

We are not popular just now—there is an American boom going on but that is nothing for these mercurial little people—Meanwhile Aristide [Briand] is being heavily attacked in the Chambre on financial grounds. The State is d—d nearly bankrupt & the people very rich—the reverse of our position.

There are a few *very faint* indications of a beginning of social unrest—*very faint*—3rd International etc. & perhaps will die out but it is bound to arise in time, I think—however I must not write politics or your precious Marquess [Curzon] will be at me.

* * *

Frocks are amazing folk. How curiously exactly affairs in Asia Minor are turning out as you said they would & in spite of this a gentleman arrives to urge the Conference of Ambassadors to hand over Southern Albania to the Greeks. Its all because they will teach the young gentlemen at Balliol about Homer not to say Troy though in those days the Military gentlemen seemed to have the bigger say, anyhow they got the girls . . .

187

Wilson to Rawlinson

[Carbon]   12th July 1921
Personal

No letter in from you this week, thank goodness! But the Duke of Connaught sent me on one you had written to him full of mild and unintelligent platitudes which he appears to think are pungent and relevant truths.

You complain of hot weather in Simla, I wish you would come to London if you want to see the sun.

We have not got poor Toby out for you yet, and I am bothered if I know when we shall.[44] Tim has made a gallant effort to get into touch with Kemal but his pitch has been queered, so far as I can see by a gentleman called Hamid[45] who, according to Tim, is a play-boy of the first order.

As nothing has been finally settled in all the many points raised by the war, except possibly a paper promise from the Boche about reparations, so we are finding ourselves, in the month of July 1921, thoroughly well mixed up with the League of Nations, with America, with Egypt, with the Imperial Conference, with Silesia, with the Ruhr Valley, with the Greeks, with the Turks, with Palestine, with Egypt, with Mesopotamia, with Afghanistan, and no doubt presently with India. It is a wonderful performance on the part of the 'Frocks'. As nothing is ever decided, cleared up, rolled up, tidied up, tied up and put away on the shelf so everything crops up every day on every table, in every office in London. If we soldiers conducted war on the principles that the 'Frocks' conduct peace we would most assuredly get well thrashed for our pains.

I simply cannot write what I think about inviting Valera over. In your own cockney language, 'there ain't no bloody words for it'! We started the truce, so-called, in Ireland yesterday at 12 mid-day. What is going to happen I have not the faintest idea. We have something like 70 battalions over there now, and a whole lot of Field Artillery, without their guns, but mounted on their horses, as mounted infantry, and all the mechanical transport, aeroplanes, cavalry etc. that we can lay our hands on, but whether we are going to be told to withdraw the whole lot, or whether we are going to be told to carry out law and order, I have not the faintest idea, and to tell you a very great secret, no more has anybody else, except possibly, Michael Collins.

Tiny Ironside came in to see me yesterday most wonderfully well, and he says that he will be completely fit in another two or three months. I presume therefore that some time in the autumn he will go out and take over Mesopotamia, but as you know, I do not believe in Winston's ardent hopes of being able to govern Mesopotamia with hot air, aeroplanes and Arabs, nor, to my great satisfaction, does Tiny, and indeed he raised a point which I did not think of, and it is this; supposing that we put Feisal on the throne, and supposing that we try and keep him there by bombing any recalcitrant Arab villages who 'cock a snook' at him or at Percy Cox, Tiny says that what would happen would be this, the head Arab who owned that village would send in to Feisal to say that if his village or any other Arab village was bombed and any women and children killed, all the Arab tribes concerned would no longer owe allegiance to Feisal; on that Feisal would ask Percy Cox to issue orders that no village was to be bombed, but if the troops had been withdrawn, and if the levies were not sufficiently well-formed, well-disciplined, well-officered and well-led to hold the country by military force, as they most assuredly would not, then the whole hot-air, aeroplane and Arab scheme would fall to the ground. Tiny says further that the aeroplane officers out there, and indeed in a great many cases the same is true here, are not officers at all but chauffeurs, and that it would be quite impossible to put soldiers under their command, and that if this is so now when some of the senior posts in the Air Force are held by late military and late naval officers how much worse will it be later on when the only officers in the Air Force will be Air so-called officers who have never been brought up either as soldiers or as sailors. I was glad to find that Tiny, an eminently practical hard-headed soldier was so clearly of the same opinion about this matter as we are here, but I need not tell you that none of this sort of expressions of opinion by those who know have any effect whatever on the 'Frocks' who go on their way squandering millions and millions on an Air Force which gets steadily worse and which will get steadily worse and more out of touch with both soldiers and sailors as time goes on.

I got two days sailing last week in my little forty-tonner. The word sailing in your funny English language is grotesque, because I drifted out into the Channel midnight one night and I lay under a broiling sun two days, and by great and superior seamanship I got into a tide that brought me back in or about the place I started from 48 hours before. All the same I was not worried by any questions other than how I was to avoid sunstroke.

You will have seen in the papers that poor Craven was drowned in Cowes a couple of nights ago.[46] I suppose he lost his footing in some way on the deck of his yacht and fell overboard, got into that horrid 5-knot tide that runs round Cowes Point, and as it was just after midnight nobody saw or heard anything.

I have just come back from Woolwich where I carried out the annual inspection and where to my great delight I found a very nice looking lot of cadets, thoroughly well disciplined and in good heart under Gilly. I lunched in the Gunners' Mess where the Gunner Band played in their old full dress and where their powdered footmen carried out their duties in exactly the same way as they have done any time since William IVth dined there and decided on their dress.

Tomorrow I carry out the inspection of the Boys' College which is also going on famously, as also is the Staff College under Hastings. In all those sort of ways we are steadily and appreciably getting back to our 1914 form, and if in the course of our service we can get the Army back to the height of excellence at which we stood in 1914, supported of course by all recent inventions in the mechanical world, we really will have done something good for our country.

Poor Dobbs. Another week passed and no finality yet, and as I said last week, I am afraid every day that passes without a clinch is a day to the bad, and such a pity too because some three weeks ago it really looked as though he had got what he wanted. However, he and Muspratt are two first-rate men and as long as they remain in Kabul there must always be a chance . . .

188

Harington to Wilson

[Holograph]   General Headquarters,
                                     British Army in Constantinople.
                                             July 13 [1921]

    I'm afraid I am giving you a lot of trouble. What a mess the whole thing is in. I don't know whether I am a soldier, a diplomat, a bloody fool or a bloody rogue at present! There are too many crooked people here playing for their own ends. Grib's latest intercepts of Briand's & Bakir Sami's efforts in Paris fairly staggers me. I thought this was to be a problem in which England & France were to work together! If the French make a separate peace & clear out we could at least put up some commission which would be trusted & could then get the troops away which is what you want. The Greek offer of a Division is amusing. They are dreadful people — I wonder what will happen in their offensive. I hope they get beat. I am sick of the whole lot. I do not know if anybody is doing anything about our prisoners. At any rate I could have secured their release had I seen Mustapha [Kemal]. I could do it now if anyone wd. give me the job. I cannot follow this F.O. procedure. I wish to goodness they wd. keep my name out of the papers. I simply hate it especially all that nonsense abt. assassination which they made use of to save their faces vis-a-vis the Bolshies. I made 49 not out the day they were to catch me — What are the chances abt. Ireland? I never know what to believe. I won a Tennis Tournament a few days ago! Don't worry about us. All I want to know is the future policy & ought I to wire the Chanak line — What fun I seem to have caused over the Trade Delegation arrests. I must bag some more soon! . . .[47]

189

Congreve to Wilson

[Holograph]
General Headquarters,
Egyptian Expeditionary Force.
Cairo
14.7.21

Many thanks for copy of yr. most interesting letter to Rawly. These negotiations with de Valera & his scoundrels make me perfectly sick & seriously anxious for the Empire, for it is a direct incitement to everyone else to do the same to say nothing of the treachery to our friends & supporters—Mr. L.G. only wants Lenin in London at his Conference to complete the party and upon my word Lenin is no worse than de Valera so why not? We might get something out of him & buy a little peace somewhere & only at the small cost of sacrificing all our principles & honour! How sick you must be of politicians.

Here we are quiet. Adli compelled by the riots in Alexandria & propped up by Allenby flourished the big stick & down dropped Zaghlul flat, so once more is proved that the only thing an oriental respects is force & v. little of it suffices. When you talk politics with an Eastern you may be sure you will get the worst of it, kick him & he loves & respects you. I hear Reading has been v. clever with Ghandi [*sic*] in India, but what's the use? The general result will not be affected by diplomacy—force is the only thing & we still have plenty in India if diplomats & civilians will leave the soldier alone. In Palestine I hear the general impression is that the bottom has dropped out of the Jewish Home & certainly the example of Ireland will confirm the Arabs in resistance if they have not already shown enough. I wish to goodness we could get out of it, for it is a beastly country for soldiers—unhealthy. No barracks & nothing for them to do—they all hate it & when the garrison becomes all British there will be more to go sick & more to hate it.

I have got yr. Regt. here now, Ulster Rifles,[48] & v. good they seem to be. They are in the Citadel, quite happy & comfortable.

Poor Cooke-Collis is raging about his house at Fermoy having been destroyed & his old father & sister imprisoned in the stables to watch it burn[49] — no wonder — I can imagine no greater horror than to lose all one's family possessions, to me they are more precious than [illegible] — I hope the devils have not been at yr. brother.[50] I was v. glad to find myself once more a Rifleman[51] — it is odd that I shd. have fallen to the only battn. I had never been with. I feel rather ashamed of going ahead of Vic[52] & several other good Riflemen senior to me in the Regt.

* * *

190

Wilson to Worthington-Evans

[Carbon]   21 July 1921

If it has not been done already I think it would be a wise precaution to obtain from Valera some substantial guarantee that if the present 'conversations' fail in their object of obtaining peace we shall be given, at least, 24 hours notice by Valera before he once again initiates a campaign of murder against our soldiers, police and loyal citizens, otherwise we may be suddenly faced with the assassination of a number of our men.

191

Wilson to Arnold Robertson

[Carbon]   22nd July 1921
Personal

Yes, I quite agree that we are drifting into a very dangerous position vis-a-vis the French, vis-a-vis Silesia, vis-a-vis the coming of the Ruhr, vis-a-vis the passing away of Ireland, and beyond proving for the hundredth time that those who ought to be governing are not governing I do not think there is anything very new in all this. On the 17th March 1920 I wrote from Cologne to the Cabinet to say ". . . I can well imagine a Militarist Germany or a Bolshevist Germany, led by an outstanding figure, raising a standard of patriotism and the call of clearing Germany of all foreign invaders etc., etc.", and when the present Government in Berlin falls, as it certainly will, we shall be one step nearer to that Militarist Germany or Bolshevist Germany about which I wrote eighteen months ago.

* * *

192

Wilson to Congreve

[Carbon]   26th July 1921
Personal

Yours of the 14th just in. I knew you would view the present loathsome 'conversations' with Valera in exactly the same light as all of us here do. The strain that this class of work puts on the soldiers in Ireland is almost unendurable, and only yesterday young Bernard, who is G.S.O.(1) of the Cork Division told me that men that our soldiers knew to be murderers, and murderers of their own comrades, were allowed to walk about freely in the streets of Cork. You can imagine what our poor boys think of that class of work! I have had more experience in dealing with 'Frocks' than any other living, and possibly any other dead soldier, and I can say that I have a greater contempt for them today, for their abject surrender to the Irish murder gang, than I have ever had before. I shall be heartily glad when my time for working with them is up, and to tell you the truth it takes a good deal of strain to prevent me from cutting that period very much shorter.

Cuthbert Evans has just been in here telling me all about the Palestine story. It agrees with everything that you say and with everything which we thought here, and the surrender to the murder gang in Ireland is going to have a deplorable and very immediate effect on Palestine, Egypt, and India. So far as I can see Rawly will be the last Commander-in-Chief in India and you will be the last Commander-in-Chief in Egypt! It is a curious thing that ever since the Armistice I have been urging the Cabinet to "come out of those countries that do not belong to us and to hang on to those that do", and the Cabinet have consistently answered by doing the very opposite, i.e., coming out of those countries that do belong to us and hanging on to those that don't. They propose to come out of Ireland; they propose to come out of Egypt; and they are already thinking of coming out of India! Meanwhile they hang on to Silesia; they hang on to Constantinople; they hang on to Palestine; and they hang on to Mesopotamia. Can anything account for action of that description! Unless it be that they are determined to wreck the Empire.

My poor brother Jimmy has been hunted out of Ireland and is living in small lodgings, finding it difficult to pay for his very simple meals. Nor has he been able even now to get any of our things away from the old home. The roads between our old house and the railway are all cut and as we live miles and miles away from the station he has not been able to get any of the papers out of the safes, any of the pictures, the silver, and even the smaller ornaments. Every day he and I both expect to hear that the place has been burnt to the ground, with everything that we have got in the world that ties us to the past.[53]

* * *

193

Wilson to Rawlinson

[Carbon]   27th July 1921
Personal

First of all let me tell you how sorry we all are about poor Buddy; we had none of us heard that he had been ill nor had any of us any idea that he had heart trouble. I know well how grieved you personally will be at the loss of such a staunch ally and friend. As regards his successor, I sent you an 'H.W.' telegram a couple of days ago, and if the name of Van Straubenzee does not suit you and if there is anybody else that you want that we can get hold of you may be sure I will help to that end.

Of gossip I have this week but very little. Valera has not yet deigned to answer 'his obedient servant' D. Lloyd George. I take it that if he knows his business he will go on talking inanities until the weather breaks, after which he will probably say that he does not agree to the terms, and we shall be in a mess because we shall have some 70 battalions, a lot of cavalry and gunners in Ireland, and only barrack accommodation during the bad winter months for about a quarter of the force; we shall have lost the whole of the fine weather; and the short days, bad roads, and wet weather will make our task an exceedingly difficult one. I presume this will suit the Cabinet as well as Valera because I cannot help noting that the Cabinet having decided that we should start in on an intensive form of military operation on the 24th July invited Valera over quite suddenly four days before, making all military operations impossible. I presume therefore that the Cabinet do not intend, and probably never did intend, to have any intensive military operations. Be this as it may, I view the future as regards Ireland, and therefore as regards the Empire, with the very gravest concern. If the Cabinet grant what is euphoniously called 'Dominion Home Rule', but what is in hard fact complete independence, to Ireland, we shall have to withdraw all our troops, we shall lose the 16 Irish battalions,[54] and we shall lose all the Irish R.C. throughout the Army who after their soldiering may want to settle in Ireland for the rest of their lives. This will go very near breaking up the whole of our Glorious Old Army.

In Silesia nothing has yet been settled but it looks like a meeting of the Supreme War Council in Paris about a week hence.

In Anatolia the Greeks claim to have pushed the Turks about in a very savage way but as we have not yet been able to get anything at all authentic about captures of prisoners, numbers of killed, wounded and missing, either on the Greek side or on the

Turk side I personally am taking their reports with a good deal of salt. Probably by the end of next week we may have heard something worth recording.

In Egypt, nothing to report.

In Palestine, increasing animosity on the part of the Arabs against the Jews, and I feel confident that this will blaze out hither and thither, up and down, and with the small little garrison and the immobility of our troops we shall be quite unable to prevent local disorders, even local disorders of a serious nature.

In Mesopotamia as you know we are going on reducing, and Haldane now suggests leaving a garrison of only 8 battalions — 3 British and 5 Native. I am personally opposed to so small a garrison and am trying to pin him to the 12 battalions which was originally decided upon at the meeting in Cairo.

In India, poor Dobbs still struggles along. What a summer he must have had in Kabul! Only this moment I have been reading long telegrams from the Viceroy from which it is clear that up to yesterday nothing had been decided.

The Viceroy's lunch to Gandhi does not seem to have sweetened that gentleman for very long, and I prefer myself Allenby's way of treating Zaghloul which is, I am Allenby you are Zaghloul, if you open your beak I will hit you a knock on the side of the head that will astonish you. I say I prefer that to asking Zaghloul to lunch!

The Prime Ministers' Conference still goes on but I do not know that any remarkable decisions have been reached.

The American invitation to a Conference at Washington in November is rather hanging fire because in the first place our Government want to separate the question of disarmament from the question of the Pacific, and in the second place the Japs are asking the Americans some inconvenient questions. Until these two matters have been cleared up and decided one cannot say with any sort of certainty that there will be a meeting in Washington.

Tomorrow night I am going to dine at the Canada Club at a dinner given by the Club to The Honble. Lord Byng of Vimy, of whom perhaps you may have read. For some reason which I am quite unable to understand he appears to be going to Canada as Viceroy!

I saw Plumer yesterday. He came in here to see me and I thought he was looking quite well after his rather severe operation but a good deal thinner, and rather weak on his legs. He told me, however, that the 'medicines' say that he will be a great deal better and stronger than he has been for the last ten years, which is really good news.

There is no news of poor Toby, and no further attempt so far as I know on the part of our Government to make love to the Turks.

The Egyptian Delegation is in London.[55] Jimmy Watson is looking after their creature comforts, but as I have never been called in, nor so far as I know has David Beatty, I have no idea what the arrangements proposed will do to our military position, not only in Egypt but of course in Palestine and further away to the East. It is not the custom amongst well-bred 'Frocks' to consider the stupid, ignorant, and under-bred military butchers; it is however apparently their custom to sit in secret conference with murderers.

* * *

194

Chetwode to Wilson

[Holograph]
War Office
Saturday [30 July 1921]

Macready has just been in with his propeller racing at least 2 main bearings hot, which under the circumstances is not to be wondered at.[56]

He returns tonight, and desires me to say we shall receive his resignation on Tuesday—He is not sending it in today as he wants to be careful as to the wording of it.

He imagines Strickland must do the same but of course he will not make any attempt to influence him.

I cannot see that the Govt. will be able to induce any officer to take up either Appt. but you never know what some people will do . . .

195

Chetwode to Wilson

[Holograph]   War Office
                                                             2.8.21

Hankey wrote to S of S and asked that expert officers should be detached for the Paris Conference,[57] & that Marden should be wired for from Constantinople. D.M.I. had a copy of this letter & wired on his own for Marden. S of S sent for me & was v. sniffish about D.M.I. having done this without consulting him. He says the P.M. asked for Marden as the latter is Pro-Greek, & did not consult him. He made me send another wire to Tim saying Marden's presence was not essential & he was only to come if he could really be spared, in fact a strong hint not to send him.

S of S asked me what the military opinion was about the Macready affair & I told him it was just about as hot as you could make it.

He said he hoped we would keep calm as he thought he wd. have it all right in two or three days time. He had put in very strongly to the P.M. & Cabinet that the soldier's position in the affair was impossible & how it would re-act in Egypt, India, etc. and the P.M. had agreed.

S of S, Lord Chancellor & Attorney General are now composing an answer to a question in the House—which S of S said would state that the soldiers were right and the Master of the Rolls was wrong & that the answer would be one "in cold fact in our manual of Mil. Law". If this is so it is all right—but I shall wait till I see the answer. Macready is seeing the P.M. at Criccieth tomorrow, who I understand will tell him of this . . .

196

Wilson to Sackville-West

[Carbon]   11th August 1921
Personal

Many thanks for your long letter of the 9th and 10th and a copy of notes on a conversation with a Frenchman.

You and I are happily agreed that it doesn't matter a damn whether the 'Frocks' draw a line on a foreign Bradshaw map of Silesia or on a naval chart of the Caspian Sea in so far as the solution of the Silesian question is concerned. I would have thought that even the 'Frocks' would now see that people like the Boches and the Poles must work out their own salvation, but Philip Chetwode tells me that he is of opinion that the habit of interfering with other people's business, and of making what is euphoniously called "peace" is like "['hinder' crossed out] buggery", once you take to it you cannot stop. Do not let this letter be intercepted or if it is change Philip Chetwode's name into Chetwode Philip or something like that.

What is interesting me at the present moment, as I said the day before yesterday to the Secretary of State, is the form of words which L.G. will adopt when, at the muzzle of Valera's pistol, he lets out 5,000 rebel internees.

I hope you get down to Havre and have a sail on the brother's yacht. He very kindly asked me to race with him one day at Cowes but it was blowing so hard that we did not start and I got on the 'Joyette' and had a fine sail in her instead.

I quite agree as regards the future outlook, but I am inclined to think on the whole that about a 60 or 80-ton fine sea boat, auxiliary yacht, is perhaps the best headquarters we can make. I look forward in absolute terror to the future, not because any of the difficulties or any of the problems which face us are of themselves terrifying or insoluble but because we are, beyond all question, being governed by a Cabinet of cowards. It really is a thing to make the saints cry when one remembers that on the 11th November 1918, with the aid of the Old Marshal England stood absolutely at the top of the world, and I could not have believed that in three short years even cowards would have dragged the name of our Empire so deeply in the mud.

Keep me posted in what passes; if nothing else it still has a cynical interest for me. Give my love to the dear Old Marshal and to 'le petit Weygand' . . .

197

Wilson to Congreve

[Carbon]   16th August 1921
Personal

Your letter of the 20th July, which I have left too long unanswered. It seems to me quite clear from all the information you send, and from reports gathered from all sorts and conditions of men in Palestine, that we shall have trouble there, perhaps before the year is out, and that, unless we increase our forces we ought to clear out. What we have written repeatedly to the Cabinet, who, in this matter as in almost all others, simply ignore what we say to them, it may one of these days be useful to publish when the time comes to balance the plus/minus of Lloyd George and his Cabinet.

I agree about Lawrence being a dangerous little fellow, but of course if you have poor Winston at the top he naturally surrounds himself with men of a like kidney, with results which we have so often seen in places like Antwerp and the Dardanelles,[58] and the $12\frac{1}{2}\%$[59] and the Irish-Ulster pogrom of 1914 when the Fleet was ordered from Vigo to Lamlash to lay low Belfast with its guns.[60] Now poor Winston again—he has so many admirable qualities that it is a pity to see him making a continuous line of appalling blots through the whole length of his life—is now going to add another in the shape of trying to govern Palestine, Arabia and Mesopotamia with hot air, aeroplanes and Arabs.

Tit-Willow[61] is looking for an island where he can safely

sojourn and where pigs and chickens and vegetables will grow. In spite of my ducking I am considering a somewhat bigger yacht which, as I have pointed out to Tit-Willow, gives me a considerable range of action and allows you to pick your pig, choose your chicken and cook your vegetables—all these I may remark incidentally of course would belong to somebody else until the moment when they were being eaten, when they would belong to me.

Allenby came in to see me yesterday looking fit and well, and we had a long talk. He sees the future of Egypt in just the same light as I do, that is to say, if the Empire continues to be handled—I cannot use the word 'governed' because there is no sign of governing by the present Cabinet—we shall certainly lose the whole thing. Before long you will feel the reflex action of the course taken by the 'Cabinet of Cowards' in the matter of Ireland; their line of action is indeed quite simple and not the least difficult to understand, and consists in this, that the more murders there are in Ireland, and the more filthy those murders are, the better the terms L.G. gives to the murderers. One year of murders brought the Home Rule Bill, two years of murders brought Dominion Home Rule, three years of murders ought to bring complete Independence. If Valera really wishes to shorten that three years he has only got to enlarge the scope of his murders and include Cabinet Ministers—he will get his wish all the quicker.

Of other news I am afraid I have very little, except what you have seen in the newspapers. The 'Frocks' handing over the solution of Silesia to the League of Nations is as amusing as it is contemptible. That L.G. and M. Briand should at a given moment, owing to advancing years and a certain rotundity of person, become impotent is true; that they should unbutton their trousers in order to prove it to those who might pass is amazing.

I don't know whether you see telegrams and despatches passing between India and London; if not it will amuse you to hear that a certain Lord Rawlinson was made the head of a Committee which incidentally contained many 'Black' men to consider and report on the advisability of reducing the British garrison in India.[62] This Committee came to the unanimous conclusion—not at all agreed to by Lord Rawlinson but signed to by the same nobleman—that India could spare another five British battalions, three cavalry regiments and some trimmings. No sooner was this telegraphed home than it was followed by another telegram from Lord Reading, in which His Lordship said he in no wise agreed with the finding of the Committee, and refused completely to reduce by a single British unit. This again has been followed, only yesterday, by another telegram from the said Lord Reading shouting for drafts to fill up all the units he has got. The position of Lord Rawlinson, bowing to 'Black' men and signing at their dictation, and then being thrown over by an 'International', is really as amusing as it is undignified. I propose to write tomorrow and tell him so, not that he will mind, so I suppose there is no harm really done.

You may have noticed in the daily press that Russia, in spite of the Trade Agreement[63] does not appear to be very happy. A telegram from Moscow, from one of our people there, a couple of days ago, says that there are already 35 million people on the march. Poor devils! That will learn them to be governed by Jews! Talking of Jews how is Nebbi?

You may have seen, or may not, that poor unfortunate Dobbs seems to be very near the end of his tether, and that after months and months of competing against the Bolsheviks it now seems as though the Bolsheviks were stronger than the British Empire. I can well believe this because so far as I can judge by the trend of affairs, this Cabinet of ours is going to lose the Empire as fast as it possibly can. On the 12th November 1918 we stood higher, both in the estimation of people and in absolute power, than at any previous time in our history. I was asked at that time what I thought we should do, and my opinion then was, and still is, that we ought to come out of those places that did not belong to us and hold on like hell to those places that do. Now the action of the 'Frocks' from that date to this has been very curious—they have been coming out of those places that did belong to us and have been hanging on like hell to those places that don't, that is to say, they have been doing the exact reverse, not only of my advice but of what appears to me to be the elements of good government; they almost came out of England two or three months ago when we had to raise an army *ad hoc* and call up all the reserves; they have offered to come out of Ireland; they have agreed to come out of Egypt; and they are going to be kicked out of India. On the other hand, they cling on to Silesia, they cling on to Constantinople, they hold on like the devil to Palestine, and like grim death they clutch at Mesopotamia. Was ever anything more amazing!

Did I tell you that I fell into the Solent on a form of compulsion applied by a boom! Little Trench[64] and the two children were happily on board, and the children saw me disappearing over the side and set up the most terrific howling 'Oh the poor darling'. Little Trench, who did not see what had happened could not get either of the children to tell her what was the matter they simply went on shrieking 'Oh the poor darling' 'Oh the poor darling'. Anyhow the result was twenty minutes in a nasty sea and strong tide, in oils and long boots. My dear Squibbie, I only just pulled it, but whether that is a source of satisfaction or not I cannot tell you. You will be amused to hear that with the exception of George Nathaniel, Marquess Curzon, not one single Member of the Cabinet either wrote to me or telegraphed to me, or even sent word to me, to say that they were either glad or sorry that I had not been drowned! . . .

198

Colonel Price-Davies to Wilson

[Holograph]
Assistant Adjutant-General
Command Head-quarters
Aldershot
23 September 1921

I was talking to Perreau commanding 1st Bn R. Dub[lin]. Fus[iliers]. He is concerned about his men if things get bad in Ireland. The loyal men whose people are in the affected areas will feel they ought to be with their parents & Perreau thinks it should be considered whether Irishmen should not be given indefinite leave, or some other arrangement be come to, to enable them to look after them. It is a difficult question but the conditions are exceptional & are a strain on the men's loyalty & discipline. The Irish Guards were worried about their men too, from the mere fact that they cannot proceed to Ireland on furlough this winter ...

199

Craig to Wilson

Cabin Hill,
Personal & Confidential   Knock.
25th October, 1921.

I had Sir Nevile [*sic*] Macready to lunch last week, and he brought with him Major General Cameron who you had been good enough to appoint as Military Commander in Northern Ireland. I am grateful to you for having arranged that the Commander-in-Chief should come and see me, and to discuss his proposals in regard to Martial Law. It is certainly as well that he did so, frankly I must admit that his ideas showed an almost total lack of apprehension of conditions in Northern Ireland, and although I think that he is prepared to modify his views very considerably as a result of the conversation, I am still distinctly uneasy. His suggestions included practically the "scrapping" of two classes of our Special Constabulary and the disbandment of the third, in order to merge them into a Military organisation. He wished to raise a very large Military Force in Ulster, apparently for general service in Ireland, and to concentrate the existing Constabulary Force, thus leaving certain of our districts entirely at the mercy of Sinn Fein.

I believe that if his proposals had been carried out he would not have raised one-tenth of the numbers required in Ulster, and he would completely have disorganised the whole of the Loyalist party and probably have rendered the position of my Government entirely untenable.

General Cameron has come up from the South and is naturally imbued with the ideas that his experience has taught him there, and he does not yet quite realise the difference in Northern Ireland where the supporters of the Government are in a large majority, nor the necessity of ensuring the safety of the Loyalists in the six counties. I have no doubt that he will learn in time, just as General Bainbridge did, who, when he was leaving Ulster, stated quite frankly that his views had completely changed. The danger is that time may not be forthcoming, and that General Cameron may be called upon to act before he has gained the necessary local experience.

Another thing that makes me uneasy is, that General Cameron has come to the North from the South where there appears to be anything but harmony between the Military and Constabulary Authorities. Up here 80% at least of his Force will be Constabulary (raised locally), and it is vital that the machinery should work smoothly. Little incidents that have occurred even up here, show that there is a grave danger in this respect, but there appears to me to be one method of obviating this danger, if you can see your way to approve of it, that is, that the Chief Constabulary Officer shall also hold a Military appointment, under General Cameron, acting in a dual capacity. If you can see your way to having Colonel Wickham, Divisional Commissioner of the Constabulary, appointed to act as Senior General Staff Officer under General Cameron, in addition to his existing duties, I feel sure that this would be the best way to make things run smoothly. It is perhaps putting Colonel Wickham in rather a subordinate position, but I feel sure that we can rely upon his acquiescence in any arrangement which will prevent friction between the Military and Constabulary Forces. I feel sure that General Cameron would welcome the arrangement which would at once secure his position and give him as Staff Officer, one who has more general acquaintance with our local conditions, than perhaps anybody else. Colonel Wickham has gained the confidence of everybody up here as much by his tactful administrative ability, as by his refusal to countenance any interference with his discipline, no matter from what quarter it comes. Of course this appointment should not take effect until Martial Law comes into operation, but I think that its announcement now would solve many of our local difficulties.

I have not consulted either as to this! . . .

200

Haldane to Wilson

[Holograph]   G.H.Q. Mesopotamia
                                                     28th October 1921

Faisal[65] is now asking questions as to his position with regard to protection from outside aggression. The High Commissioner would like me to agree to employ all my force in conjunction with the Local Forces—or at least say that I would be prepared to do so—to repel external aggression. Major Young from the Colonial Office—who ought, having been a soldier, to know better—when dining with me a few nights ago said to one of my Staff that he could not understand why I would not agree to utilize every man I had for the purpose of meeting Turkish or Kurdish aggression as we were in a 'friendly' country. It seems to me that the Civil are inclined to throw dust in Faisal's eyes and live on a policy of pure bluff. The telegram which had been drafted in the High Commissioner's office to go to the Colonial Office, and in which I am sure Young has a finger, has just come back entirely reshaped as the result of an interview the Secretary had with me, and as there is an Air Mail tomorrow I merely write to say that I have concurred in it with a proviso as to the probable use of any troops that may be here when the R.A.F. takes over.

I have laid down that I am, now and later, not in a position to share in any action against external aggression, large or small, except by means of the R.A.F.

The situation when the R.A.F. take over will be that all Regular troops here will be required to protect aerodromes; but Cox in his telegram infers that the R.A.F. may be prepared to employ them with the Local troops in a manner which I now decline to do, if called upon. I think a strict limitation will have to be placed on the employment by the R.A.F. of the British and Indian troops that may be in this country when they take over.

If we are by that time not at peace with Turkey it may happen that strong pressure will be put on the G.O.C., or Air Force Commander, to help in case of trouble by the employment of troops. The matter might be put to him in such a form (danger to women, Christians, and so on) that it would be difficult for him not to yield unless he had imperative orders as to his conduct on the subject.

You know these politicians better than I do, and Cox is an out and out politician and not an administrator. They have lately put before me proposals for helping the Kurds to go for the Turks and incidentally put the nose of the French out of joint. The French don't seem to me to be playing straight with us in their dealings with the Kemalists, but I have stated that I will have nothing to do with any underhand proposal and that I feel sure that every means of coming to better terms with the Turks have not yet been exhausted. I don't think the telegram on this subject was sent, but at any rate it lacks my approval. I shall be glad to be clear of all this chicanery which is not at all in my line.

I am sorry that my typewriter is broken and my new one not arrived. I have had to write as the matter is 'deadly secret' I am told, and you ought to know it . . .

201

Craig to Wilson

SECRET & CONFIDENTIAL

Cabin Hill,
Knock,
Belfast,
ULSTER.
28th October, 1921.

General Cameron came to see me yesterday and we had a long conversation together. He is very anxious that I should write to you again, more especially with regard to the question of our two alternatives:

    (a) to re-raise the Ulster Division

or (b) to enrol into the Special Constabulary Forces already existing in Ulster.

He told me that he thought you were in favour of the former course, and that therefore my views that this was not practicable should be put before you.

I am afraid it must be admitted that the chances of making a success of raising a large Military Force in Ulster are not at all bright. I doubt whether you would obtain more than a very few hundred men to volunteer, and am sure that those who did so would not be of the type whom we should wish to enrol. There are various reasons for this; the first that the men would mistrust entering any Military Force even with a promise that they should not be required to serve outside the province, because when conscription was brought in an equally definite promise that they should only serve in the Ulster Division was broken, in spite of the fact that conscription did not apply to Ireland. Another reason is that the men are now accustomed to the Special Constabulary, which they look upon as being raised to protect their homes and they would not be prepared to leave their homes and enter into another Force where this purpose was not equally plain to their minds. Then of course there comes in the question of pay, the "A" Constabulary Force[66] being far better paid than the Military Forces, but I do not think that this will entail extra expense on the Government as the number of men required if raised on the Special Constabulary basis will, in our opinion, be not more than 3,000 or 4,000, whilst a Force of 12,000 is contemplated by the Military if raised as soldiers. Although anxious to help in every way possible it is no use my acquiescing in a course which I do not believe would be successful, and I know that you are as anxious as I am that Ulster should not be blamed for failure to support any scheme that the Government may put forward.

General Cameron pointed out that recruiting for the Special Constabulary might adversely affect recruiting for the Military Forces of the Crown, but there would be no possible objection to closing down the recruiting for the "A" Special Constabulary as soon as the numbers required were obtained, and I think that those definitely rejected for the Special Constabulary would be encouraged rather than otherwise to turn to the Army. In the Special Constabulary, who act very much in small bodies, only men of very high character are required. This is not so essential when the men form part of a large Unit in which their actions are always under supervision and strict discipline maintained.

General Cameron appears to have been most favourably impressed by the Special Constabulary whom he has seen, and I have impressed on him the necessity of maintaining the confidence of the people in Ulster at the start, so that they may feel that their homes will be protected if they enrol in the Forces of the Crown. I think that he has been convinced that the existing Forces should be distributed for this purpose, although I know that the latter hopes to be able to have greater concentrations in accordance with the methods adopted in the South of Ireland.

Another point which he raised was whether the Special Constabulary might not refuse to serve outside the border of the six Counties, but our experience has made it quite clear that they are anxious to do so in Counties Donegal, Cavan and Monaghan, and Colonel Wickham, I know, feels that there will be no difficulty in getting from the "A" Constabulary any number of volunteers required to serve just outside the six Counties for the better protection of our province. On the other hand, we are equally convinced that they would not join up for general service throughout Ireland.

General Cameron tells me that Sir Neville [sic] Macready is proposing to take him away to Dublin as soon as Martial Law is established. I am sorry to hear this, as it means that there will probably be a new General here totally inexperienced with local conditions at the time that our difficulties are greatest. General Cameron has already learned a great deal in the short time that he has been here of our peculiar conditions and is going down very well with the people who have accepted him as "a Scot with staunch Protestant views". We will be extremely sorry to lose him, but it is of the greatest importance that if a change is to be made it should be made *at once* in order that whoever has to go through with the operations should pick up all the local circumstances *before* the truce ends.

General Cameron told me that the Commander-in-Chief had been asked for his views as to whether Ulster should be made independent of him, the Local Commander, reporting direct to the War Office. Sir Nevile [*sic*] Macready is, not unnaturally, averse to this suggestion, but I personally am strongly in favour of it. I do not think that the Commander-in-Chief in Dublin need fear that there will be any lack of co-operation on the part of Northern Ireland in helping them to suppress Sinn Fein and I consider that he would be greatly relieved in his responsibilities if the duty of justifying our action up here, and of showing why a distinction is made in dealing with the Loyalists and with the Sinn Feiners, no longer rested upon him.

Sir Nevile Macready has, I think, thoroughly realized the importance of getting arms over in Ulster before the truce breaks down, and he writes that he hopes to get 13,000 quietly into Carrickfergus during the next few days. I hope there may be no question about this as previous promises have not been fulfilled and there would be very serious trouble if we lose a number of casualties at the beginning simply because arms are not available to let the people defend themselves. General Cameron told me that he was also exercised over the question of transport, which apparently is not making headway owing to the negotiations . . .

202

Wilson to Craig

[Carbon]   1st November 1921
Personal

Many thanks for your letter of the 28th which I got last night. There is of course a great deal in what you say about raising men for the Special Constabulary in place of the Regular Army, but there is a side to this which I do not like to discuss in a letter but which I will develop on Saturday morning when we meet . . .

As regards the arms, that is going forward and I think we shall be able to get what we want when you come over.

As regards the Six Counties being under a Command independent of the Commander-in-Chief in Dublin, I fully admit that you make a point which carries great weight with me, i.e., the point that it would be difficult for a Commander-in-Chief in Dublin to differentiate between the Three Provinces and Ulster, administering, as it were, one class of Martial Law to the Three Provinces and a different class of Martial Law to Ulster. At the same time there are many important issues which tend to incline one to the belief that on the whole it will be better to have only the one Commander-in-Chief for the whole of Ireland. This too is a subject which I very much want to discuss with you.

I have written to Macready by this post giving him your idea of the difficulty of differentiation, and by the time you come over I will have his answer.

* * *

203

Rawlinson to Wilson

the 15th November, 1921.

I am much obliged to yours of the 25th October. I am writing from the train on my way to Bombay to meet the Prince, who arrives the day after tomorrow,[67] and I may add to this in Bombay before the mail leaves. We are a little anxious as to what kind of reception may be accorded to him in Bombay, for the non-co-operators have issued an edict that there is to be a hartal and that all shops are to be closed. It is possible therefore that we may have trouble. It is very shortsighted policy on their part, for it can do no possible good and only get them the credit of showing discourtesy to the Monarchy throughout England and the British Empire. This must do great harm, not only to their own cause but also to

India as a whole and is a glaring example of the pettiness and shortsightedness of their policy.

Mr. Gandhi has now got himself into such a position that it is the tail wagging the dog, and he is gradually being pushed into taking definite action against the constituted Government by engaging in a policy of civil disobedience. The moment that he takes action we must put him in the 'jug' whether we like it or not, and he will then become a martyr! Many others will probably accompany him into the 'clink', but exactly when this will take place no one can say—not even himself, for he is showing distinct signs of indecision and is manifestly personally incapable of leading the 'frankenstein' which he has created.[68] It is always so with people who play with fire; and we may therefore have a lively time in the next month or two. My own personal opinion is that we are absolutely & perfectly capable of dealing with anything of this nature. Once the die is cast we shall proceed to govern, but it means of course that the Montagu Reforms will go by the board and that we shall return to the pre-war methods of government in India and push any idea of Swaraj into the dim distant future.

[Added in holograph:

'I have discussed this with the Viceroy and he is quite ready to take the strong line. The question is how long will he stick to it!! R.']

It is all very interesting, and the problem as it develops is most absorbing, but it does not in the least frighten me and I am quite sure that both politically and from the military point of view we are fully and amply capable of dealing with it.

In a letter I got from Haldane the other day he tells me that the idea is to reduce the garrison of Mesopotamia to 2 battalions by October 1922. If these battalions are to be Indian as I suppose they are, the Government of India will strongly object, and we shall say that they must either take 7 or 8 or none at all, for we see no reason to subject our Indian soldiers to the risks which would be entailed by 2 battalions sitting in the middle of a lot of fanatical Arabs five or six hundred miles from their base on the sea. I fancy we shall send a communication to the India Office on this subject in the course of the next few weeks.

I have written to Alec Godley about Archie Montgomery who wants leave up to the end of February. You might send me a cable about this when you get this letter.

The very drastic reductions in naval armaments which have been put forward by Mr. Hughes at the Washington Conference have been a surprise to us. If they can really agree to carry through such far-reaching measures and throw on to the scrap-heap more than a million tons weight of fighting vessels something may really be effected in this matter. I suppose the next thing will be similar cuts on the military side, though I fail to see how we, with a huge Empire to police all over the world, can possibly agree to similar wholesale reductions in soldiers. However, I foresee a danger in this, and you will have to use your utmost endeavours to stiffen the back of L.-G. and the Cabinet if we are not to get into a perilous position and lose the Empire.

The situation as regards Ireland looks no better, for I cannot believe James Craig and the Ulstermen will be able to give way sufficiently to enable a settlement to be arrived at. However, you know more of this than I do.

* * *

204

Wilson to Worthington-Evans

[Carbon]   30th November 1921

I see by the newspapers that December 6th may be an important day as regards the solution of the Irish question[69]. Neither General Macready nor I have been informed as to what the chances are of a breakdown of the present conference, nor what in the opinion of the Cabinet would follow if such a breakdown occurs. At the same time, as we are both responsible for the lives of our men and the security of Ireland in so far as we can ensure it I want to put before you as clearly as I can the problem which faces us, and the steps which appear to me to be necessary for its solution.

The two alternatives which I think face us are:

First. The restoration of law and order over the whole of Ireland.

Secondly. The withdrawal of all troops followed by civil war.

As regards the first alternative, at the meeting held in your room on the 7th November, you, the Prime Minister of Northern Ireland, Colonel Spender, and I being present, certain tentative decisions were reached for dealing with the problem of Ulster. These of course could only become operative with the approval of the Cabinet. They included, as you will remember, that no Martial Law should be applied to Ulster; that the Government of Northern Ireland should be responsible for its own law and order; that the War Office should lend senior and junior officers to help with the Constabulary; that the War Office should withdraw all its troops from Northern Ireland three days after the Truce had been broken off, except indeed those two battalions guarding Ballykinlar; that the War Office should supply arms, military material, and stores on requisition by the Ulster Cabinet; that an agreement as to coastal defence should be reached as between the Admiralty, the War Office, and the Northern Parliament; and that the expense of all special enlistments into the Constabulary, ammunition, arms, material etc. over and above the normal peace police garrison of the Six Counties should be borne by the Imperial Exchequer. If then the Conference breaks up on the 6th; if that is followed or is not followed by a period of 72 hours of warning of the termination of the Truce, we can easily find ourselves by the evening of the 9th December back in a state of war. As regards Ulster, therefore, what Macready and I want to know, and must know, as soon as possible, is whether the proposals tentatively reached in your room on the 7th of this month will be agreed to by the Cabinet. I may here mention that the Northern Government Authorities have already put in a requisition for 26,200 rifles and 5,240,000 rounds of SAA, that is to say, they are acting in accordance with subparagraph (e) of the notes of our meeting of November 7th.

As regards the rest of Ireland, what Macready and I will want to know, and must know as soon as possible, is whether all the arrangements which we drew up some months ago, and with which I think you generally agree, will be accepted by the Cabinet.

I ask you very earnestly to consider this matter and to let me have your views. If on the other hand the Government decide to accept the second alternative, that is to say to withdraw our troops from all Ireland except Ulster, then again both Macready and I must know at the earliest possible date so that we can make all the necessary arrangements.

I gather from the newspapers that there may be the possibility of the Conference breaking down but the Truce to continue. In that eventuality I agree absolutely with the following extract from a letter from General Macready which I received this morning, in which he says—"Valera will spend the time perfecting his organization and importing arms or stealing them from the Army. By the Spring when Michael Collins & Co. will not mind sleeping out the I.R.A. will be far more formidable than today and consequently more lives will be lost" and this view is strengthened by the Weekly Report for the week ending 26/11/21, which I have sent on to you this morning, in which you will see that General Macready says "that a large number of the I.R.A. consider that the rebel army is now a match for the British Army", and further down mentions the reports received of the landing of arms in Kenmare and Waterville . . .

205

Worthington-Evans to Wilson

[Copy] *SECRET*
C.I.G.S.

The only special importance to be attached to 6th December is, I think, because it is the day on or before which the full proposals of the British Government will be given to Sir James Craig.

The Conference may break down then or on any day.

I do not anticipate that the Conference will fail by reason of the rejection by Ulster of the British proposals; these proposals may, however, be refuted by Sinn Fein at any time.

If both sides accept the proposals, totally different arrangements will be required from any contemplated in 79/Irish/802, but in that case the atmosphere will be friendly, and no serious difficulties should arise.

If the Conference breaks down—whether notice is given or not given to terminate the truce—the Cabinet must give the decisions required on the paper prepared by the General Staff for the Cabinet in October last, and also upon the provisional arrangements discussed with Sir James Craig on 7th November.

I have tried to get these "decisions" in advance. It would obviously [be] more convenient to all those who have to act upon them, but the decisions themselves are of great importance and those who have to give them are entitled to the fullest knowledge of the latest phases of the situation both political and military at the time of giving the decisions, and this knowledge cannot be obtained in advance, and therefore it is that the Cabinet will wait until the Conference negotiations fail—if they are destined to fail—before giving the decisions.

With reference to the requisition which you say has been put in by the Northern Government for 26,200 rifles and 5¼ millions of SAA, I should like your advice; on previous occasions the number suggested was 12,000 rifles to arm the "A" class special constables. These I understand are on board ship ready to sail if the truce is terminated.

The question of the Truce continuing after the Conference has broken down is difficult. Judging from the many breaches even while the Conference is sitting, it would be almost impossible to avoid clashes between the troops and the I.R.A. and the R.I.C. and the Sinn Fein Police, and no doubt any interval would be used by some of the less responsible to obtain what advantage was possible by the I.R.A.

It is conceivable, however, that a breakdown might occur because time was wanted by the more moderate Sinn Feiners to gather support throughout Ireland against the more extreme elements — renewed warfare might thwart such a possibility.

So again until we know why the Conference fails, it is not possible to decide finally whether the Truce ought also to be terminated.

1st December 1921. (id) L.W.E.

206

Chetwode to Wilson

War Office
6th December 1921

S. of S. asked the Army Council to meet him this afternoon and announced that the terms signed by the Sinn Feins would be in the papers tomorrow morning, so he did not give us many details, he only wished to set our minds to work on the possible way in which it would affect us in the near future, i.e., the removal of the Irish Garrison and the question of the 16 Irish battalions.

Three of the rebels signed — the other two are supposed to sign this afternoon.

The form of the Oath is very weird: they swear true faith and allegiance to the Irish Free State and to be faithful to King George as Members of the Association of Nations etc. etc. [Added in holograph: 'Or something of that sort'.][70]

Ireland is to have the same Dominion Status as Canada etc. and her relations to the King with regard to Judicial Ctte. of the Privy Council are to be the same as other Dominions.

Ulster, I understand, has a month to come in or go out. If she goes out she remains exactly as she is today, i.e., the 1920 Act, with the exception that there will be a boundary commission which will settle the boundary in accordance with the wishes of the inhabitants! I understand the Sinn Feins did not sign this latter part of the Agreement. Ulster can come into the Irish Dominion at any time she likes.

There will be an interval during which there will be a Provisional Government, probably till Easter. We shall set up Crown Colony Government but instead of a Governor we shall have Sinn Feins and make them responsible!! They will enrol their own police but the King's Courts will function until they take over. They are allowed an Army of up to 30,000 strong. Parliament will be summoned probably on the 14th and the King will open it with great ceremony, and it will probably sit for three or four days to approve of the proposals and then be prorogued. The service of debt and pensions will apparently be the only contribution the Irish will make. It is thought that there may be a considerable amount of extremist S.F. opposition to the proposals.

We asked how soon we shall probably begin withdrawing troops. S. of S. said it was impossible to say. He told us we were to cease for the moment our preparations for War.

There will be a meeting on Friday of Military Members and Secretary (F) who will propound a series of questions for S. of S. to answer consequent upon the proposals.

S. of S. supposes that we shall probably get down to the normal garrison of Ireland during January, and that after Easter Ireland may ask us to take the two remaining divisions away. I know what your opinion is about this! There is nothing in the instrument about the Army remaining in Ireland, or about the 16 Irish regiments, and nothing as yet has been put in writing about either, I understand.

I am afraid this is very sketchy, but there was so much talk, especially on the part of Charley Harris, that it was difficult to grasp exactly what S. of S. meant.

We all promised to say nothing about anything that does not appear in the papers tomorrow . . .

207

Radcliffe to Wilson

[Holograph]   War Office
                                  Tuesday 6.xii.21

I got back this morning & as I hear you will not be here till Thursday am sending you a short account of my trip.[71]

I had breakfast with Macready on Sunday & after a short talk with him went on to Belfast where Cameron met me and took me out to Spender's house at Cultra, where he had arranged for me to sleep that night.

After lunch we then had a long talk & then went to Cabin Hill[72] where the P.M. gave us tea & had a long discussion with us & Wickham. Next morning (Monday) I spent in Wickham's office finding out about his organization etc. after which I went out to lunch at Cabin Hill & had another talk with the PM & Dawson Bates his Home Secy. I had decided that there was no need to see Macready in Dublin again as he was coming over for the selection board on Thursday—so came straight back by Larne last night.

Sir James is very anxious indeed to carry on as he is at present—this is with Wickham running the Constabulary organization, Cameron being at hand to advise & command the regulars. After going thoroughly into the whole think I think he is right. The situation at present is not a military but a police problem & the transition to a military line [?] will not be sudden but gradual. I am favourably impressed with Wickham & his arrangements. He is a man of 42—sober, level headed & practical—quite the reverse of what Macready led me to expect. He was a trifle reserved with me at first but by degrees expanded & told me everything that was in his mind, finally expressing great satisfaction at my having come over & had this talk.

I will keep the details till you come back—especially as it appears they have come to some sort of agreement with the murderers—so that it is unlikely that Cameron will be taken away for the present, and I will summarize by saying that the question of appointing a Military Adviser does not arise at present. Sir

James has authorized Wickham to correspond direct with me here on any points with regard [?] to which the W.O. can help & I said that I would slip over as often as they liked to have a talk & a general look round. I made no suggestion that you had me in mind as the future M.A. but should such an appointment prove necessary ultimately this could pave the way for it.

Wickham anticipates no difficulty in maintaining order in the counties but is frankly alarmed about Derry & Belfast, especially the latter. He is convinced that it would be very unwise to remove regular troops from there—not for fear of the rebels but for fear of what the black fellows[73] will do and I feel he is right. Cameron has carried golden opinions from everybody there & as long as he has enough troops there will be no serious catastrophe.

On the whole I think my flying visit was useful. It was intensely interesting to me & I have come back with even *more* confidence in Ulster than I had before which is saying a very great deal . . .

208

Morland to Wilson

General Headquarters,
British Army of the Rhine.
9th December, 1921.

Is there now any chance of your paying us a visit? I hope so, though it does not seem very probable.

I presume the so-called "settlement", if confirmed, will entail the withdrawal of all troops from Ireland shortly, in which case I presume we shall get some of them here. I see in the papers that the Silesian Commission are against the withdrawal of any British troops from the Force there.

There is no sign of trouble here at present: I can probably deal with any local strikes with 14th Hussars and Police. I have earmarked details of each to proceed in lorries if necessary, and would only need to call on the French if there were several outbreaks at same time. Personally, I do not anticipate trouble but while hoping for the best am prepared for the worst.

I can imagine what you think of the "settlement". Lloyd George has managed to get out of the mess, if not with honour, at least with considerable skill and éclat for himself. What the actual results will be—goodness knows. The Naval Staff seem satisfied as regards the harbours, etc. Not knowing the details, one cannot give an opinion, but it seems obvious that only a loyal Ireland would ensure their protection in time of war. One sees rumours of more cavalry reductions and possibly infantry reductions as well—and no doubt they will be made.

The frost here, which was severe, has now gone. The Rhine itself was blocked with ice and some of our supply barges were hung up; it is now quite mild again.

* * *

209

Wilson to Harington

[Carbon]   10th December 1921
Personal

Yours of 23rd and 28th November with enclosures. I sent you a telegram of appreciation of my friend Filoneau.[74] He is not a bad fellow, but with an English facade he has a French bedroom!

Time seems to be running round and the 'Frocks' as usual doing nothing about the Turks and Greeks. I am personally much crippled in the way of helping you because I don't appear to be on speaking terms with any of the Cabinet, unless by chance I offer any of them a meal at my expense. Winston indeed does talk to me but he seems to me to be getting wilder and wilder, according as he gets deeper and deeper into the bog. He is now proposing to withdraw our British troops from both Mesopotamia and Palestine, governing the former with 'hot air, aeroplanes and Arabs' and the latter with 'hot air, aeroplanes and Jews' with a backing of 'Black and Tans'.

Of Ireland you know as much as I do. Complete and absolute chaos reigns in 10 Downing Street, as in Dublin, and we cannot even find out, up to today, whether the murderers will let us withdraw any troops or whether they will order the whole lot of them out. We have to wait their pleasure!

We have written and are writing strongly to F.O. about the additional burden that you are now being loaded with in the shape of Cilician refugees[75] dumped in your unfortunate town, but it seems absolutely impossible to get the F.O. to take any action whatever.

My time is running out. I have only a little more than two months, and I am afraid when I make my bow that we will still be in occupation of Silesia, Burgenland, Constantinople, Palestine and Mesopotamia, in spite of three years of gallant efforts to get the 'Frocks' to come out, and we will on the other hand have practically given up Ireland and Egypt and be in a fair way of giving up India, so that the 'Frocks' have done the exact opposite to my advice, that is to say, they have come out of those places that do belong to them and have hung on like hell to those places that do not . . .

210

Wilson to Morland

[Carbon]   13th December 1921

Yes please! There is still a chance of my getting out to see you in January, but don't let this change any arrangements you and Miss Morlando may have made about taking a holiday, if so be that you want to get away in January.

The state of chaos in Downing Street and in Ireland increases every day, and there is no question at all that if the highest art and form of statesmanship is to reduce an absolutely peaceful, quiet, thriving country into a hell then Lloyd George is a master. Egypt will follow Ireland, and India Egypt, and then we shall be left with Silesia, Constantinople, Jewland and Mesopotamia. These will follow in succession and then we shall be left with England, that will follow in succession and then we shall be left with Ulster, and from there we shall have to start again and build an empire. Don't laugh, because bear in mind always that Portugal once had an empire, and even Venice . . .

211

Wilson to Allenby

[Copy]   14/12/21
Private

This really *is* rather a secret letter.

There is a certain amount of gossip, perhaps scarcely gossip but more floating ideas, that the F.O. may take the opportunity of the coming changes in Egypt to add to the number by changing the present High Commissioner (F.M. Viscount Allenby).

I really don't know how much weight to put on all this nor how much you know, but the object of my letter is this—that if you do leave Egypt and if you get the offer of coming into my chair I hope you will ponder well before refusing it. I have absolutely no idea as to who is going to succeed me, and as I have not seen Lloyd George since July 5th when I told him I would not sit with murderers I get very little gossip and my opinions are rarely called for, nevertheless I told Worthington Evans that you were the man for next C.I.G.S., and so if an offer is made to you I hope you will consider the matter very seriously . . .

212

Wilson to Cavan

[Carbon]   16th December 1921
Personal

Many thanks for yours of the 29th November and 2nd December. We follow with the greatest interest your work in Washington,[76] and David Beatty told us some truths when he came home three or four days ago.

I see the Old Marshal is coming home with two or three truck-loads of souvenirs, including a couple of motor cars. I must see if I cannot pinch one of the latter off him.

The mess in Ireland gets steadily greater, and tonight I am in doubts, thought I have great hopes, that Valera will beat Michael Collins, and fling the foul agreement into Lloyd George's face.[77] If that is not done I really see no alternative except civil war, which is a much worse and a more beastly arrangement.

In Egypt they don't seem to be able to get on with the new Cabinet, and so Congreve wires that matters are somewhat unsettled.

213

Wilson to Congreve

[Carbon]   16th December 1921
Personal

I send you out a copy of a paper I received last night which appears to be an order issued by your General Staff on the 29th October last. There are in it certain expressions which seem to me to be unfortunate and which I have marked. Since I got the paper, and before I got a moment to start this letter, Mr. Weizmann came to see me in a very disturbed state saying that he had seen this order and that it would be read on the one hand by the Jews as a stab in the back and as a withdrawal of necessary protection, and on the other hand by the Arabs as encouragement to their claims and as a manifest that the Army was on their side. I think it quite possible that this order may, if it became known, be the cause of some trouble, and so I write at once to ask you whether you had any reason, not explained in the order itself, for issuing it. I am inclined personally to think that when you read it quietly you may agree that although the intention undoubtedly was to get the Army to hold an even hand of justice, the wording of certain of the paragraphs might bias the intention of the whole. If you do think this perhaps it would be wise to withdraw the order. I only make this suggestion so as to try and avoid trouble which may possibly arise, although I have no particular reason to think that this trouble may come, and remember that this is entirely a *private* letter as between me and you and in no sort of sense official. It is in fact what I would say to you if you were sitting in the chair here in my room, and for a thousand reasons I wish you were.

You seem to be slow in setting up a new Ministry instead of Adly, and until you do I suppose the course of events in Egypt will be somewhat uncertain.

Ireland goes from bad to worse. The Cabinet are in another terrible fright that Valera may best Michael Collins and refuse to accept the agreement. I hope you read Carson.[78] It was straight from the shoulder but I could have made, and would have made with pleasure, a much more vehement speech myself. Happily I am neither in the Lords nor in the Commons, although I see the newspapers put me in both . . .

[Enclosure A]
C.I.G.S.

The attached is a copy of a document which was handed to me yesterday from a source which I should regard as unimpeachable. You will observe that the document emanated from the General Staff in Egypt. If it is authentic there are points in it which I think should be brought to your notice, since the two interested parties in Palestine may get to hear of it and even obtain copies.

T[ravers] C[larke]

15.12.21

Q.M.G.

[Enclosure B]
General Officer Commanding
Troops Palestine.

It is thought that an outline of the policy of H.M. Government in Palestine might with advantage be explained to the British

Garrison, who are liable at any time to be called upon to assist the civil Government in carrying out that policy.

Whilst the Army officially is supposed to have no politics, it is recognised that there are certain problems such as those of Ireland and Palestine, in which the sympathies of the Army are on one side or the other.

In the case of Palestine these sympathies are rather obviously with the Arabs, who have hitherto appeared to the disinterested observer to have been the victims of the unjust policy forced upon them by the British Government.

This policy based on the Balfour Declaration has now been defined by the High Commissioner's speech of the 3rd June last and Mr. Churchill's speech of the 14th June last, extracts from which are attached.[79] These two speeches represent the definite intentions of the British Government with regard to Palestine, and as such are worthy of study.

Whatever may be the opinions held by the various sections of the population of the justice or injustice of this declared policy, those responsible for its initiation are anxious that it should at least be clearly understood that their intentions are honest and that they would never countenance any policy which inflicted oppression or hardship on the Arab population. It is simply the considered opinion of the British Government that a National Home for Jews may be established in Palestine with a mutual advantage to all concerned and that, within the limits of the country's resources, Jews may be allowed to immigrate there without any hardship being inflicted on the Arabs.

The British Government would never give any support to the more grasping policy of the Zionist Extremist which aims at the establishment of a Jewish Palestine in which Arabs would be merely tolerated. In other words, the British Government has no objections to Palestine being for Jews what Great Britain is for the rest of the Empire, but they would certainly not countenance a policy which made Palestine for the Jews what England is for the Englishman.

The G.O.C. considers that the troops should thoroughly understand the policy of the British Government as outlined above, although it is the duty of the Army to support loyally whatever Government may be in power irrespective of personal opinions to which every individual is entitled.

Please therefore take steps to communicate the above to officers with all units and formations under your Command, who in their turn should explain to N.C.Os. and men the real aims and intentions of the British Government with regard to Palestine.

(Signed). B. J. Curling.
Lt. Col.
Act. Colonel on the Staff.
General Staff.

G.S., G.H.Q.
E, E. F.
29 Oct., 1921.

214

Cavan to Wilson

British Embassy
Washington
Dec 22 [1921]

[Holograph]

This is indeed a startling surprise! that a poor common semi-educated soldier—who has never held a W.O. appointment & never been to the Staff College & always hunted once a week & often more shd step into that great room! Well, well—

I only write to say thank you, & to tell you how sincerely I trust that I may be a worthy follower of so great a Chief as yourself.

I wont say any more now but will be up to see you as soon as possible after arrival about Jan 6 or 7 . . .

215

Wilson to Haldane

[Carbon]   22nd December 1921
Personal

This will be one of my last letters to you as C.I.G.S. because I step out on the 19th February, and I write less to you by far than any of the others partly because letters take so long to go that my news would be always stale, and partly because, owing to Winston the scenes and acts in the 'Mesopotamian Charade' pass so quickly that what is being spoken at the beginning of a scene is quite out of date when the curtain falls. We are now discussing whether or not it is safe to leave two British battalions in Baghdad with a somewhat uncertain line of communication for retirement and with an absolute certainty that they would be neither reinforced nor relieved if they got into trouble, and while I was in the act of putting down headings to maintain my objection to so dangerous a proceeding as leaving two battalions in Baghdad I was given Eric Geddes' Report[80] which if acted upon by the Cabinet will make quite certain that there will be no two battalions to leave there.

The pace at which we are throwing away our wonderful Empire is truly terrifying, and I have no hesitation in saying that if Lloyd George goes on for the next twelve months as he has been going on in the last twelve months we shall have no empire at all in 1923—either empire on the land or empire on the sea. It seems a pity but if under the tuition of Lloyd George the English have forgotten the art and power of government there is nothing else to be done.

Meanwhile the foul agreement which Lloyd George and his Cabinet came to with a band of 'murderers', an agreement in which even the word 'Allegiance' is left out with reference to The King, is now being criticised in Dublin, and I have great hopes that Valera may win in his refusal to sign, and that he will fling back the thing in Lloyd George's face. All this however will be stale news by the time you get my letter. Christmas and New Year also will be over, but there is no harm in my telling you before they arrive that I wish you well in both of them . . .

216

Wilson to Rawlinson

[Carbon]   23rd December 1921
Personal

Yesterday by chance I heard that Cavan had been offered and had accepted my post. I had no knowledge of this myself but I confess I was not in any way surprised, although I could not resist thanking the Secretary of State and asking him to convey my thanks to the Prime Minister, for their personal courtesy to me in not informing me. I sent you a wire directly I heard of it.

Of other news none. I am just off to Wynyard[81] for a week, and we are hard at work, or will be when I get back, on the Geddes' reductions which are simply terrifying . . .

217

Allenby to Wilson

[Holograph]   Cairo
                                                                24.XII.21

I have your letter of 14th Decr. and your cable of yesterday. I am very proud to know that you thought me worthy to succeed to the post of C.I.G.S., and that you recommended me to the Secy. of State. Personally I doubt if I am enough of a hard worker; or quick minded enough for such a responsible and difficult appointment. Anyhow, I am very grateful to you.

I wish you could have had an extension of the office you have held so well. I know little of Cavan, but that his record in the war has been consistently good.

The Foreign Office, to the best of my knowledge, have no

immediate intention of ousting me. Just now, we are undergoing
one of our political crises. Saad Zaghlul issued invitations to his
partisans to attend a political meeting on Friday last. I issued an
order that it was not to be held. He wrote a defiant letter to the
Press; & next day went to the Station to meet Makram, his
London agent, just returned, who had made a fiery speech on
landing. There were some riots in the streets; and, that night 2
British soldiers were shot in a lonely street—one killed. I then
ordered S.Z. & certain of his friends to take no further part in
politics. They defied me; & they are now at Suez, on the way to
Ceylon or the Seychelles. Some rioting followed on their arrest,
& a few rioters have come to an untimely end; however, I don't
expect such big trouble as we had in 1919. On the whole, the
country is really glad to get rid of S.Z. Schoolboys, lawyers &
professional agitators. They, of course, do take advantage of the
occasion for self assertion; but I can, I think, deal with them.

I have taken over Cairo under Martial Law. Adly's Government has resigned, & no other is yet formed, so I do what I like
just now. Best wishes . . .

218

Congreve to Wilson

General Headquarters,
Cairo,
30th December, 1921

Your letter of December 16th sending me copy of a paper
issued from my office signed by Curling re Jews and Arabs. What
it contains is substantially what I was asked to put about amongst
our officers in Palestine by Major Young of the Colonial Office
whom I met in Jerusalem in early October 1921.

Young said he was distressed to find so much anti-Zionist
feeling amongst Europeans in Palestine, which his own investiga-
tions proved were even more wide spread than I had reported to
you: that he was constantly being told that the Government was

being run by Zionists, which was an absolutely baseless and mischievous fiction: that no one in his office would one moment remain if they considered the policy meant "doing the dirty" (his own words) to the Arabs: that the declaration of Sir Herbert Samuel and Mr. Churchill made in June 1921, were the considered interpretation of the Balfour Declaration which H.M. Government was determined to carry through, as it considered it involved no injustice or hardship to any one and would meet the legitimate aspirations of a National Home for the Jews: that H.M. Government was in no way controlled by the Zionist Organisation and entirely dissociated itself from and disapproved of such expressions as were used by Dr. Eder before the Haycraft Commission[82] and by other speakers at the Zionist Conference at Stuttgardt.

The paper was forwarded to Sir Herbert Samuel and no criticism of it has ever been made by him, nor so far as I know by anyone else.

I do not think there is anything in my Memorandum which conflicts with the above, nor can I admit that it stabs the Jews or encourages the Arabs. If either side has an exaggerated idea of what H.M. Government policy means it may be able to get something from my paper to twist to its own ends, but so it will be with nearly everything written; and after all this paper was intended for soldiers only. I do not know how Weizmann comes to be in possession of it. I will stand or fall by it, for even if I agreed that it is wrong, I cannot now withdraw it, it is both too late and too undignified . . .

1922

1922

The 1922 letters are inevitably somewhat valedictory in tone since Wilson's four-year appointment ended in February. Even before the New Year, Wilson had begun to write 'last letters' as CIGS to his correspondents. His final weeks at the War Office were spent working on the army's response to the 'Geddes Axe'. In August 1921 Lloyd George had appointed a committee of businessmen, chaired by Sir Eric Geddes, to examine all aspects of government expenditure. In December Geddes issued an interim report which recommended that the army estimates could be reduced from £75 million to £55 million.[1] Wilson was appalled and thought what a 'perfectly horrible job' he was handing over to his successor [221, 222, 225]. In the end, however, the War office managed to secure a 1922 estimate of £62 million.[2]

The other main topic of concern at the beginning of 1922 was Egypt. Allenby's policy was a judicious mixture of stick and carrot. Having put down civil disorder and deported Zaghlul in December 1921, he now wanted to encourage moderate politicians with a unilateral British declaration of Egyptian independence. He believed that this would not in any way jeopardise imperial interests. If the government refused to adopt his policy, he was prepared to resign [223]. Allenby was summoned to London, where he arrived on 10 February, to be met at the station by Wilson himself.[3] The High Commissioner had to offer his resignation before the Cabinet eventually agreed to allow the publication of the 'Allenby Declaration', by which the British government conceded formal independence to Egypt, while reserving some matters, such as external defence and the security of imperial communications.

The other 1922 correspondence encompasses some of Wilson's more enduring concerns: his long friendship with Foch and desire for a close Anglo-French alliance [219]; his deep dismay at the state of Ireland and his biting criticism of 'the nerveless, cowardly hands of those who sit in 10 Downing Street' [224]. Wilson covers a number of these themes in his long letter to Rawlinson [225], in which he especially singles out the Prime Minister for harsh words: 'I know that as long as we keep Lloyd George it is certain that the Empire has gone'. Yet among Wilson's farewell notes was one to the Welshman. 'My last day as CIGS brings you very much to my mind and those glorious days when, together, in rough and boisterous times we fought for our Country', wrote the Field Marshal on 18 February. 'I cannot therefore let the day die out without a word of admiration for the part you then played and for the many kindnesses I then received from you'.[4]

Wilson told Rawlinson that he was going into parliament after he left the War Office, and so he did. On 21 February he was elected unopposed as Unionist Member for North Down. He addressed the Commons on a number of occasions, criticising the Geddes cuts and speaking on questions relating to Ireland. During March and April Wilson went to Belfast to advise the Northern Ireland government on security matters. He was also in demand as a political speaker who was unshakably opposed to Lloyd George, and for the rather melancholy task of unveiling war memorials. He was returning home from unveiling the memorial at Liverpool Street Station on 22 June 1922 when he was attacked and shot dead on his doorstep at 36 Eaton Place, Belgravia, by two Irish republicans.[5] He was granted a State funeral and is buried in the crypt of Saint Paul's Cathedral.

219

Sackville-West to Wilson

[Holograph]
Paris
Jan 2. 1922

Foch I know has written to you. He is anxious about the future — if only England & France hold together all will be well, if not the deluge. Meanwhile I suspect the Frocks & without you at the military helm I fear the soldiers of the two nations will gradually drift apart. No one seems to look very far into the future & of course the little Frenchmen are intensely irritating at times and then we get sulky. The Boches are *so* efficient & there are so many of them. *We* aren't really clever at soldiers & they are. They look at everything from such a different angle—they dread the economic recovery of Germany because they know it means their military recovery. What exactly has Lady Curzon done to get a G.B.E.? I didn't see de Valera's name in the honours list—was it omitted by mistake? I propose to come to England on the 9th to Bourne to see my children—London on the 16th to 19th. Then to Somerset to see my eldest sister & back here about 23rd.

I'll come & see you but will telephone & find out when you are free.

My job I suppose lasts 2 more years as Mil. Attaché & I have just paid 2 year's rent in advance—so long as I'm here I'll do my best to keep the soldiers together . . .

220

Wilson to Allenby

[Copy] 4/1/22

Thank you so much for your letter of the 24th.

Had I known about the Geddes Committee proposals when I wrote on December 14th I could not and would not have asked you to accept the post of C.I.G.S. I presume the Government will swallow *all* Geddes proposals and probably ask for more, but as they stand they are sufficiently drastic. We are to start with a reduction of 28 Battalions, 8 Cavalry Regiments, and a lot of Batteries etc. and then we are expected to be able to make further and considerable reductions! We won't keep our Empire long at this rate.

Valera has made Lloyd George a prisoner.

Gandhi has made Reading a prisoner and the one bright spot is that you have made Zaghloul a prisoner. And what a welter of chaos in Ireland! I keep hoping that within the next few days Valera will defeat Collins and throw the infamous Agreement back into Lloyd George's face!

And as you well say, all these agitations are got up by students, lawyers and professional agitators whether this is in Ireland, Egypt or India. One thing is certain, either we govern other people or they will govern us.

Best Wishes to you both . . .

221

Wilson to Plumer

[Copy]   7/1/22

Your letter of December 30th just received . . .

The Geddes bomb fell on us just before Xmas.

For your private eye I can roughly summarize: He calls for a reduction of £20,000,000. He suggests as a commencement the total abolition of 28 battalions, 8 cavalry regts. a mass of artillery, and all the etc. etc.!

On examination we find that even this deplorable cut will only mean a saving of £8,200,000! Where is the other £12,000,000 to come from?

I need not tell you that I am putting up a paper—my swan song—which will leave no one in doubt as to the military aspect and its determining factor in the loss of the Empire.

It is because of this very grave menace that we have asked you to hold your hand for the moment.[1] With a prospect of tens of thousands of men and thousands of officers—all regulars—flung out on to the side of the road, with the knowledge that if this is done we shall be forced to break our promises in a hundred directions we are trying to steady ourselves before the next move.

Cavan arrives home from Washington today and all this odious work is going to fall on his shoulders. I am dreadfully sorry for him, but I had no means of warning him as L.G. offered him my appointment without my having the slightest idea or knowledge of it.

I have not seen L.G. since July 5th when I told him to his face that I would not meet the Irish murderers.

Heigh-ho. What a curious world . . .

222

Wilson to Harington

[Carbon]   9th January 1922
Personal

Many thanks for yours of the 2nd, which I have this moment received, before post goes out. Our Geddes proposes an immediate reduction of 28 battalions, 8 cavalry regiments, with artillery and accompaniments to suit. To my horror two or three days ago Charley Harris informed me that this would mean a reduction of only eight millions; where we shall get the other twelve I have no idea at all.

Cavan returned on Saturday but having eaten something indigestible on board has had to go away for two or three days hunting to shake it up, shake it down, or shake it out.

Many thanks to you for your most kindly reference to me in your letter. I can assure you a trifle like Cavan's appointment without my knowledge has no effect whatever on my appetite, my sleep, or my outlook . . .

223

Allenby to Wilson

[Holograph]   Cairo
                                                          21.1.22

Thanks for your letter of the 4th inst. Geddes is not leaving much Army for Cavan to amuse himself with! My arrest & deportation of Zaghlul & his friends has had a splendid effect here. All the best Egyptians are solid in support of me. Even Z.'s old Wafd[2] are breaking up.

The important point now is that Z. & his co-exiles must not come back, and that H.M.G. makes no concession to him or his party. At the same time, I want then to put into effect the policy outlined in the letter to the Sultan, of 3rd. December: drop the word "protectorate", give them a constitution, retain all necessary safeguards, including British troops here, and make further concessions depend on circumstances.

I'll get a first class & friendly Ministry, and the Egyptian question will be far on towards settlement. Instead of the usual method of trying to conciliate our enemies, & carting our friends; we shall be conciliating our friends, rewarding those who have stood by us, and downing our enemies.

This being obviously the right thing to do, I can't get H.M.G. to do it. I've warned them that it's their last chance, & it will soon be too late even to do that. If I can't get it through, and that soon, I shall resign. Curzon is backing me, like a man . . .

224

Wilson to Harington

[Carbon]   6th February 1922
Personal

Three of your letters—10th January, 24th January, 31st January, are due for answer. I hope to see Marden before I leave the office. I have still thirteen days to put in!

I can well believe that you are getting tired of being pushed about from morning to night for no particular reason except increase of danger and loss of prestige. P. de B. [Radcliffe] I am sure filled you up with all the latest gossips that he took out with him, and since his departure nothing new has happened, although all the ill effects of three years of incompetence and cowardice become daily more accentuated.

The Turkish Agreement with the French[3] has once again sunk into the background, apparently because Lloyd George has not the slightest intention of doing anything except backing the Greek, and thus losing India and Egypt. Michael Collins has laid claim to three-quarters of the Six Counties[4] with the natural result that once more we are on the verge of civil war. Michael of course would be backed by Lloyd George and no doubt by all the other 'miseries' in his Cabinet. But just as in 1914 the rotters of that day got knocked out in the first round by a lot of determined devils who knew exactly what they wanted so now the very same fellows will knock out those 'miseries' who now frequent Downing Street, whether their names are those of cowards or murderers. But in truth the outlook in our poor country is exceedingly bad.

Then on the top of that we have Allenby returning home two or three days hence. Again in this case of Egypt Lloyd George by a policy of calculated drift had made it now certain that we shall have to give independence and sovereign rights to the Egyptians and presently remove our troops from there.

With Ireland gone, with Egypt going, the date for India is not far removed, and as I have often said to you, both in discussing these matters and in writing, it is not the problems which have ever frightened me, because none of them are insoluble, but it is the nerveless, cowardly hands of those who sit in 10 Downing Street.

Your letter of the 31st January is almost entirely devoted to thanking me for being nice to you. To tell you the truth it had nothing whatever to do with me. I have perpetually tried to be nasty, always to be headed off by your engaging personal smile or song. As I have just said to Haldane, in my last letter as C.I.G.S. to him, I cannot help feeling a little lonesome at the idea that my days as C.I.G.S. are so nearly run out, and surely no C.I.G.S. ever had a more interesting time, and certainly no C.I.G.S. ever had a Staff who in loyalty and in knowledge was comparable to all you boys!

If as you kindly say one of these days I can get a little time to travel, and if you are still in Constantinople, there is no trip I would rather take than pay you a visit, and then Squibbie [Congreve], and so home . . .

335

225

Wilson to Rawlinson

[Carbon]   13th February 1922
Personal

Here we go for my last letter to you as C.I.G.S., and it seems
only yesterday that I walked into this room, 'Wully' having walked
out without handing me over anything in particular; there was
indeed a box of matches in the top right-hand drawer and some
feathers for pipe cleaning, or the remains of some of the Staff.
And what a devil of a lot of water has flowed under the bridge
since the 19th February 1918. My only regret in leaving is that I
am handing over a perfectly horrible job to poor Cavan. I would
have been so much happier if he could have had a nice clean
healthy start. But indeed that is not my fault and I am sure he will
worry through if anybody can. He has been working here in the
office for about a month, and so is getting as soon a chance as he
can of keeping his tail up. Moreover he has Philip [Chetwode]
who is a great friend and will be a great standby.

Yours of the 26th just in. The Geddes Committee will soon be
up before the House of Commons. Instead of his 28 bns. and
eight cavalry regiments we are trying to get off with 24 and 5, and
something between 45 and 50 batteries, and of course an
enormous lot off the Q.M.G., A.G., and M.G.O. Our 24 are
made up as follows:

12 Irish
10 Third battalions, and the last two to make the 24 not yet
decided.

The cavalry question is also not yet decided. Cavan has a couple
of schemes on foot which are being examined to see whether we
can get the equivalent in money of 5 cavalry regiments without
disbanding any, but so far as I have seen his schemes I am afraid
they are not practicable or practical. If I am right in this then five
regiments will have to be abolished. My own proposal for that
would be amalgamating the 1st and 2nd Life into one regiment,
and then abolish two dragoons and two dragoon guards. We

would thus have abolished one Life Guard Regiment, two hussars, two lancers, two dragoons, and two dragoon guards.[5] I think on the whole this probably will be the fairest and the one which will meet with the greatest meed of approval by the Army. There were questions of abolishing Aldershot and amalgamating it with Salisbury but we fought this and won it. Philip will no doubt be abolished but it is agreed that he remains on until Cavan gets into the saddle.[6] Winston himself has killed the Ministry of Defence.

Jacob, who goes out this week will tell you of our latest Cabinet Committee meeting which took place three days ago and at which Lloyd George was in the Chair instead of Austen, and where absolutely nothing was decided about anything, Lloyd George having made an angry speech about people now-a-days saying that we might have to come out of India and adding that this even appeared to be the opinion of the Military Gentlemen—he was referring to Jacob—and I could not help writing on a slip of paper, and passing it to my neighbour, "I have heard this exact same speech made in exactly the same words about Ireland". However, Jacob will be able to tell you the whole of our gossip when he gets out. It amounts to nothing more than this, that we have a Cabinet in 10 Downing Street totally incapable of governing.

There was a rumour here yesterday that Gandhi was in the jug, but there are no telegrams in this morning to that effect, nor is there anything in the newspapers, but this is only Monday.[7] I will be adding a line later in the week.

You ask what I am going to do myself. It is devilishly difficult to tell you, but today I am situated as follows—I was offered St. Georges, Hanover Square [*sic*], and refused. Then the Member for North Down, a seat in the Imperial Parliament, became a Judge. I was approached as to whether I would take North Down and I agreed to do so under three conditions—first that it should be only for now until the General Election, possibly only a matter of weeks; second that I should be unopposed; third that it would only cost me from one hundred to two hundred pounds. I imagine that these conditions have been fulfilled but although I have had no word all the newspapers this morning registered the fact that I have been unanimously selected for North Down. If I find myself in the House of Commons next week, which is quite possible, either the Government or I will be in the tureen the week after. Of course in tureen swimming they are experts, whereas I may be drowned. On the other hand the case against them both at home and in Ireland, both in Egypt and in India, both as regards their debts and their unemployed, both as regards their ignorance and their extravagance, is so colossal that I cannot help thinking that a good hard puck somewhere about the lower rib would send them flying into eternity, or if they happen to be Buddhists, into oblivion.

I hope you got down to Bikanir for a week's shooting which would be both a rest and give you a jolly time.

I saw by the telegrams the other day that the Government had been defeated over making the Army Budget votable but I did not realise that the majority against the Government was as 54 to 27. Undoubtedly as you say that is the beginning of trouble.

15 Feb.

You will have seen by the wires that Morland goes to Aldershot. At the present moment he is down at St. Jean de Luz and does not come back to this country until the beginning of next month so I don't know what he will do about all your things.[8] Alec [Godley] goes to the Rhine, and Peyton succeeds Alec.

I am very sorry to see that Reading had screwed himself up to the point of arresting Gandhi and that Gandhi pretended that he was going to be a good boy. I am bothered if Reading has not run out again, just as though Gandhi's past is not enough to have him shot a dozen times over, let alone the present, and let alone the fanatical fool's future. However when Reading is cogitating over these events as Gandhi's prisoner he will have plenty of time to think over his appalling weakness.

Since I began this letter to you Ireland has gone steadily worser and worser [*sic*], and in very truth none of us can now see a way out of it except by the loss of Ireland and the proclaiming of a republic there, in which case we lose our Empire, or by the reconquest of the whole place. To me, as you know, these two alternatives have always been present—either govern Ireland or come out and lose your Empire—and I have never ceased saying so, with the result that practically none of the Cabinet will speak to me, but I knew I was right and now the damn fools know it too, and at a Cabinet meeting only yesterday I rubbed this in once again and Winston, who was in the Chair, admitted that he did not know where the devil we had got ourselves to. I know that as long as we keep Lloyd George it is certain that the Empire has gone.

Allenby is up before the Cabinet this morning and I hope to add a line of the result. I have had two talks with him. He is quite clear that either his proposals are adopted by the Cabinet or else he resigns, and seeing the appalling mess that Lloyd George and his 'miseries' have got themselves into in Egypt I think that Allenby is quite right. The Cabinet are angry with Allenby for presenting them with what they call an 'ultimatum'. Allenby remains quite unmoved and says 'you can take my plan or I walk out'. Knowing that cowardly crowd in 10 Downing Street I have personally no doubt that they will adopt Allenby's plan, which they have sworn, both in public and in private, over and over again, that they will not agree to. The oath in 10 Downing Street is simply not worth recording.

[Added in holograph]

Later

Allenby has won. Of course. Au revoir Henry dear. It's a long long time since we hunted Bo-shevey together in the Arrakans,[9] it is even 23 years since I, in the relieving column, flashed to you in Ladysmith "Both to Both"[10] and then put it in the clouds at night with the lamps. And now I step down before you and you must take your last fence alone. God be with you . . .

Notes

NOTES

Full publication details are given at the first mention of a particular book or article. In subsequent references only an abbreviated citation is given. Unless otherwise noted, the place of publication is London.

INTRODUCTION

1 The main biographical sources for Wilson are Sir C. E. Callwell, *Field Marshal Sir Henry Wilson, His Life and Diaries*, 2 vols., Cassell, 1927; H. de Watteville's essay in the *Dictionary of National Biography*; Basil Collier, *Brasshat*, Secker and Warburg, 1961; and Bernard Ash, *The Lost Dictator*, Cassell, 1968.

2 Patrick Buckland, *Irish Unionism I: The Anglo-Irish and the New Ireland 1885 to 1922*, Gill and Macmillan, Dublin, 1972, p. xv.

3 The house had once been the home of Lord Edward FitzGerald, a leader of the United Irishmen in 1798.

4 Callwell, *Wilson*, I, p. 8.

5 John Gooch, *The Plans of War: the General Staff and British Military Strategy c. 1900–1916*, Routledge and Kegan Paul, 1974, chapters 2–4, is indispensable for the development of the General Staff before and during the early part of World War I.

6 This was particularly so since the Director of Staff Duties, Maj.-Gen. H. D. Hutchinson was not an assertive character.

7 Wilson diary, 31 December 1906, quoted in Callwell, *Wilson*, I, p. 66.

8 The letters 'W.F.' were sometimes wrongly thought to stand for 'Wilson-Foch', an understandable error. *See* 'The "W.F." Plan and the Genesis of the Western Front: a previously unpublished account by General Sir Percy Radcliffe', in *Stand To!*, no. 10, Spring 1984, pp. 6–13.

9 Hankey to Reginald McKenna, 15 August 1911, Hankey MSS (Churchill College, Cambridge), HNKY 7/3.

10 Both Lloyd George and Churchill afterwards asserted that this was a crucial point in the political acceptance of the British commitment to

343

France. The policy had, nevertheless, been developing for some years. *See* Michael Howard, *The Continental Commitment*, Penguin Books, Harmondsworth, 1974, pp. 45–8.

11 Wilson diary, 13 March 1913, Wilson MSS.

12 The best recent account of the Curragh crisis is in Patricia Jalland, *The Liberals and Ireland: the Ulster Question in British Politics to 1914*, Harvester Press, Brighton, 1980, chapter VII.

13 Wilson diary, 21 March 1914.

14 Ibid., 29 March 1914.

15 Anthony Farrar-Hockley, *Goughie: the Life of General Sir Hubert Gough*, Hart-Davis, MacGibbon, 1975, p. 112.

16 John Connell, *Wavell: Scholar and Soldier*, Collins, 1964, p. 87.

17 The circumstances surrounding Murray's replacement are covered in Richard Holmes, *The Little Field Marshal: Sir John French*, Jonathan Cape, 1981, pp. 266–7.

18 Wilson to his wife, 31 January 1915, quoted in Callwell, *Wilson*, I, p. 204.

19 Wilson diary, 1 July 1915, ibid., p. 236.

20 See, for example, Haig diary entries for 18 December 1914, 26 January and 12 April 1915, and 23 June 1916, in Robert Blake (ed.), *The Private Papers of Douglas Haig 1914–1919*, Eyre and Spottiswoode, 1952, pp. 81, 85, 90–91, 149.

21 David Lloyd George, *War Memoirs*, Odhams edn., n.d., vol. II, pp. 1687–8.

22 Wilson diary, 27 November 1916, quoted in Callwell, *Wilson*, I, p. 299.

23 Wilson's term for politicians, derived from 'Frock coats'. Soldiers were 'Brasshats'.

24 Sir William Robertson, *From Private to Field Marshal*, Constable, 1921, p. 329.

25 Lord Hankey, *The Supreme Command*, Allen and Unwin, 1961, vol. II, p. 770.

1918 INTRODUCTION

1 Rawlinson to Wilson, 19 August 1918. Haig said the same to Lord Esher, Esher to Wilson, 17 July 1918. Wilson MSS. HHW 2/13A/26 and 2/34A/17.

2 The Maurice affair and its context are covered in: 'The Maurice Case', in John Gooch, *The Prospect of War: Studies in British Defence Policy, 1847–1942*, Frank Cass, 1981, pp. 146–63; and David R. Woodward, 'Did Lloyd George starve the British army of men prior to the German offensive of 21 March 1918?', *The Historical Journal*, 27, 1 (1984), pp. 241–52.

3 Harold Nicolson, *King George the Fifth*, Constable, 1952, pp. 321–2.

4 *See* Richard H. Ullman, *Intervention and the War*, Princeton University Press, 1961.

1918 CORRESPONDENCE

1 Although Weygand was the French Permanent Military Representative at the Supreme War Council, Foch was chairman of the Executive War Board and was thus concerned with troop movements between theatres.
2 Viscount Duncannon, Personal Assistant to Sir Henry Wilson, 1916–19.
3 General Sir Herbert Plumer was in Italy at the time. After the Italian defeat at Caporetto in October, 1917, Plumer had been put in command of a Franco-British force sent to reinforce the front in north-east Italy. This having been done, he was to return to the command of the 2nd Army in France, which he did on 13 March.
4 Headquarters of the 2nd Army.
5 Georges Clemenceau.
6 Haig and Pétain.
7 Executive War Board.
8 On 28 March Gough was relieved of command. He was replaced by Rawlinson who amalgamated the remnants of Gough's 5th Army into the 4th Army. There is a vivid account of the German offensive in Farrar-Hockley, *Goughie*, pp. 271–312.
9 On 9 April the Germans had launched a fresh attack south of Ypres with the intention of driving towards the coast. Portuguese and British troops under the command of Sir Herbert Plumer took the brunt of this attack. By 16 April, although the momentum of the German advance had slackened somewhat, Plumer was urgently requesting reinforcements from the French to relieve his exhausted troops. Foch, who had already reinforced Plumer's 2nd Army with five French divisions, was reluctant to commit any more troops in the north. Wilson took a very gloomy view of the position on 17 April and pressed Foch to provide more troops. The alternative, he argued, having consulted Plumer and Haig, was to draw the left flank of the Allied Armies in Flanders back to the line of inundations running through St Omer to the coast. This would protect Calais but involve giving up Dunkirk and the remaining strip of Belgium, which Foch absolutely refused to do. In the end Foch was proved correct and the Allied line held. The renewed German offensive is covered in detail in Sir James E. Edmonds, *Military Operations, France and Belgium*, 1918, Vol II, Macmillan, 1937.
10 Haig.
11 Plumer's headquarters.

12 Ellipsis in original.

13 Wigram had written on 19 April 1918: 'His Majesty only longs to see harmony amongst the higher commanders and a unified General Staff without any sects, schisms or dissensions'. Wilson MSS. HHW 2/31/2.

14 The nickname 'Long Job' dated from Wilson's period as Assistant Military Secretary to Lord Roberts in 1900. This had originally been a short, temporary appointment, but it was extended on a number of occasions. Lord Roberts' daughters teased Wilson about his protracted stay by calling him 'Long Job'. The nickname was also adopted by some of his friends from those days.

15 Derby and Lloyd George never got on very well. The Prime Minister felt that Derby while Secretary for War supported the policies of Robertson and Haig too uncritically. Derby thought that Lloyd George interfered too much in military affairs. Lloyd George records that Derby resigned three times in twenty-four hours during the events which led up to the replacement of Robertson by Wilson in February 1918. Lloyd George, *War Memoirs*, vol. II, pp. 1689–90.

16 A counter-attack on the evening of 24 April succeeded in recapturing the whole of Villers-Bretonneux. Sir F. Maurice, *The Life of Lord Rawlinson of Trent*, Cassell, 1928, pp. 218–19.

17 For four days, 27 to 30 March 1918, Allied forces including a brigade from the 60th (London) Division attempted in vain to take Amman. Unusually heavy rain during the last fortnight of March caused the Jordan to flood and the consequent delays in crossing the river gave time for the Turkish forces defending Amman to be reinforced. Allenby's troops withdrew, and Amman was not finally captured by the Egyptian Expeditionary Force until 25 September. Sir Archibald Wavell, *Allenby: a Study in Greatness*, Harrap, 1940, pp. 248–9, 282.

18 It had been suggested that the Australian Light Horse attached to Allenby's forces in Egypt and Palestine should be dismounted and used to provide reinforcements on the western front.

19 Sir Eric Geddes.

20 The attack was launched from the British front east of Amiens, with eight divisions, led by the Canadian Corps, and 350 tanks. Rawlinson noted that the advance was so rapid that some armoured cars penetrated through the German lines and surprised the headquarters of a German Corps at breakfast. Over two days Allied troops advanced some ten miles. Maurice, *The Life of Lord Rawlinson*, pp. 227–8; Sir J. E. Edmonds, *Military Operations, France and Belgium, 1918*, vol. IV, His Majesty's Stationery Office, 1947, chapters I–VIII.

21 Foch's headquarters, April–June 1918.

22 Foch had complained that the British were not using all the men they

could. 'He presently said that we did not send wounded back to the front. I jumped in at once. I said he totally ignored our efforts in other theatres, our Navy, mercantile marine, coal, industries, etc., and that his observation about our wounded was untrue.

'I pretended to be much more annoyed than I really was, and it did him good . . . It was nice and breezy while it lasted, but it did good, and we were as good friends as ever after it'. Wilson diary, 11 Aug. 1918.

23 Byng's 3rd Army began an advance on 21 August. No great gains were made until two days later when the Army advanced two miles and took five thousand prisoners. Edmonds, *Military Operations, France and Belgium, 1918*, vol. IV, chapters X–XV.

24 At the end of August Wilson sent a wire to Haig warning him that the Cabinet 'would become anxious if we received heavy punishment in attacking the Hindenburg Line, without success'. Haig, whose forces were advancing strongly, regarded the message as offensively pusillanimous. 'The object of this telegram is, no doubt, to save the Prime Minister (Lloyd George) in case of any failure', he wrote in his diary on 29 August. 'So I read it to mean that I can attack the Hindenburg Line if I think it right to do so . . . If my attack is successful, I will remain on as C. in C. If we fail, or our losses are excessive, I can hope for no mercy! I wrote to Henry Wilson in reply. What a wretched lot of weaklings we have in high places at the present time!' Blake, *The Private Papers of Douglas Haig, 1914–1919*, pp. 325–6.

25 Haig was scarcely reassured by this letter. 'How ignorant our present Statesmen are of the principles of war', he commented. 'In my opinion, it is much less costly in lives to keep on pressing the enemy after several victorious battles than to give him time to recover and organise a fresh line of defence.' Haig diary, 3 Sept. 1918, ibid., p. 326.

26 On 30 August 10,000 of the 19,000 Metropolitan Police went on strike in support of the right to form a union, and for improved pay and conditions. The Prime Minister did not concede the former demand, but an immediate pay rise was granted and the strikers were persuaded to return to work within a very few days. Sir Nevil Macready, the Adjutant-General, replaced Sir Edward Henry as Commissioner of the Metropolitan Police. See G. W. Reynolds and A. Judge, *The Night the Police went on Strike*, Weidenfeld and Nicolson, 1968.

27 Wilson never got on very well with Macdonogh. This seems to have stemmed, in part at least, from the 'Curragh Crisis' in March 1914 when Macdonogh, subordinate to Wilson in the Directorate of Military Operations, had taken a studiously neutral line with regard to events in Ireland, in sharp contrast to Wilson's own apparent threat of resignation. Wilson, too, reflecting his Ulster Presbyterian roots, mistrusted Roman Catholics,

especially one such as Macdonogh, who had begun as a Methodist and was a convert to Catholicism.

28 Wilson and his friends jokingly referred to the United States' President as Sir Henry's 'cousin'.

29 In September 1918 Spears was passed over as Military Attaché at the Paris Embassy in succession to Le Roy-Lewis. Maj.-Gen. Sir David Henderson was appointed and specifically named as being superior to Spears. On 18 September Lord Derby reported to Wilson that Spears was 'very sore' about the whole affair. Wilson MSS HHW 2/3A/25.

30 Hussein, King of the Hedjaz, 1916–24.

31 Allenby laid down that the administration of conquered Syria and Palestine should be as follows: O.E.T.A. (Occupied Enemy Territory Administration) South, comprising all of Palestine, under a British general; O.E.T.A. North—coastal Syria and Lebanon—under French administration; and O.E.T.A. East under Arab administration was a somewhat indeterminate area to the east of the French zone, including Aleppo and Damascus. Lord Wavell, *Allenby in Egypt*, Harrap, 1943, pp. 28–9.

32 Pressed by the Supreme War Council and the British GOC in Italy, Cavan, the Italian High Command were planning an offensive across the river Piave, which was eventually begun on 23 October. Some difficulties were encountered due to flood conditions, but bridge heads were secured across the river and within a week the Allied forces were pursuing 'a beaten army in full retreat'. Cyril Falls, *The First World War*, Longman, 1960, pp. 365–6.

33 The Australian Corps had played a major role in the Allied advances begun with the offensive of 8 August. Exhausted and denied rest after a week's continuous fighting, Australian officers and men had briefly mutinied on 14 September. Anxious to save the 'Australian Imperial Force' from destruction, in October Hughes had successfully insisted that Australian units be drawn out of the line in order to recuperate. G. St. J. Barclay, *The Empire is marching*, Weidenfeld and Nicolson, 1970, pp. 76–8.

34 A number of arrangements were made during the war for the post-war disposal of the Ottoman Empire. Among them was the Treaty of London (April 1915) which offered Italy territory on the Mediterranean littoral of Asia Minor. The Sykes–Picot Agreement (May 1916) effectively divided the northern Arab provinces of the Ottoman Empire between Britain and France. The Balfour Declaration (October 1917) announced that His Majesty's Government viewed with favour 'the establishment in Palestine of a national home for the Jewish people'. The British government had also made various agreements with Arab nationalists regarding the establishment of an independent Arab Kingdom. British wartime policy, with its

contradictions, is summarised in Elizabeth Monroe, *Britain's Moment in the Middle East*, Chatto and Windus, 2nd edn. 1981, ch. 1.

35 In August 1914 the modern German cruiser *Goeben* and the light cruiser *Breslau* escaped from the Mediterranean fleet and found refuge in the Dardanelles. After Turkey entered the war both ships engaged in raiding until January 1918 when the *Breslau* was sunk and *Goeben* seriously damaged by British mines in the Aegean Sea.

36 The Committee of Union and Progress was a radical group which played a major part in the 'Young Turk' Revolution of 1908. The Committee effectively ruled Turkey, 1909–12 and 1913–18. Over time it became less and less reformist, and by 1914 it was a repressive military oligarchy.

37 These were just two of the bewildering series of forms arising from the elaborate demobilisation scheme.

1919 INTRODUCTION

1 Wilson diary, 6 January 1919.

2 S. R. Graubard, 'Military demobilisation in Great Britain following the First World War', in *Journal of Modern History*, xix (1947), pp. 297–311.

3 Lloyd George to Churchill, 16 February 1919, Lloyd George MSS. (House of Lords Records Office), F/8/3/18.

4 There is a good account of this in Lord Ironside, *Archangel 1918–19*, Constable, 1953.

5 This was first made in February 1919. *See* Inter-departmental Conference on Middle Eastern Affairs, 6th meeting, 13 February 1919. Curzon MSS. (India Office Library and Records), F.112/275.

6 Among the other high military honours were an earldom and £100,000 for Haig; a viscountcy and £50,000 for Allenby; £50,000 for French; a barony and £30,000 each for Rawlinson, Byng and Plumer (all Army Commanders; Gough got nothing); a barony and £10,000 for Robertson.

1919 CORRESPONDENCE

1 During early 1919 there was widespread unrest among troops impatient to be demobilised. One of the principal outbreaks occurred at Folkstone on 3 January where some 10,000 soldiers in transit camps refused to return to their units in France. Details of post-war protests can be found in Andrew Rothstein, *The Soldiers' Strikes of 1919*, Macmillan, 1980, and a general account of demobilisation difficulties in Robin Higham, *Armed Forces in Peacetime*, G. T. Foulis, 1962, pp. 9–19.

2 The Lloyd George family home near Caernarvon in North Wales.

3 Beaverbrook controlled the *Daily Express*, not the *Daily News*. Both the *Express* and the *News*, however, were critical of demobilisation arrangements.

4 Herbert Asquith.

5 One of the results of the demobilisation crisis was that Lloyd George replaced Milner with Churchill as Secretary for War and Air. He took over the office on 10 January 1919.

6 The Emperor Charles I (b. 1887) succeeded to the imperial throne in November 1916. He abdicated in November 1918 and was afterwards permitted to go to Switzerland where he died in 1922.

7 The appointment of Clarke to the QMG was widely criticised by Wilson's friends. See letters from Percy Radcliffe (17 Mar. 1919, HHW 2/44A/3) and George Harper (17 Mar., HHW 2/90/110) who wrote: 'To put in T.C. as Q.M.G. is a *bad* effort, and you will soon get the D.H. incompetents everywhere.'

8 The Fontainebleau conference, 22–24 March, between Lloyd George and his principal advisers, Hankey, Kerr, General Smuts and Wilson, resulted in proposals 'which exercised considerable influence on the eventual Treaty of Peace with Germany'. Lord Hankey, *The Supreme Control at the Paris Peace Conference*, Allen and Unwin, 1963, pp. 99–102. The 'Fontainebleau memorandum' argued that too harsh treatment of Germany would drive it towards Bolshevism.

9 General Haller commanded a Polish Army in France during the latter part of the war. Much time was spent at the Peace Conference discussing the practical difficulties of returning these troops to Poland. In the end they travelled through Danzig and arrived at Warsaw in late April 1919.

10 Lemberg (now Lvov in the USSR), in the former Austrian province of Galicia, was threatened by an anti-Bolshevik Ukrainian army. Foch was anxious for the Allies to equip Polish and Rumanian forces to defend the town, but the Supreme War Council confined itself merely to recommending a ceasefire. Lemberg remained in Polish territory between the wars, when it was known as Lwow. R. H. Ullman, *Britain and the Russian Civil War*, Princeton University Press, 1968, pp. 138–9.

11 Cowans resigned as QMG early in 1919 to take up a career in the oil business. D. Chapman-Huston and O. Rutter, *General Sir John Cowans*, Hutchinson, 1924, vol. II., p. 291.

12 Beginning in December 1918 a mainly French force of some 80,000 troops had built up in Odessa. By the following spring, Odessa was threatened by Bolshevik forces, choked with refugees and short of supplies. The final decision to evacuate the port was made in Paris at the end of March. J.

Silverlight, *The Victors' Dilemma*, Barrie and Jenkins, 1970, pp. 107–8, 203–7.

13 The former German Supreme HQ was at Spa. Foch had been instructed to meet a German plenipotentiary there in order to settle the problem of moving Haller's Polish Army back to Poland. B. H. Liddell Hart, *Foch: Man of Orleans*, Penguin edn., Harmondsworth, 1937, vol. II, p. 439.

14 At the end of the war there was widespread support for the idea of joining together Constantinople and the Straits into a new state, which could be put under an American Mandate. This was provisionally agreed at the Peace Conference by mid-May 1919. But in the end the United States refused to take on any mandates at all. There is a useful account of the peace-making with Turkey in Michael L. Dockrill and J. Douglas Goold, *Peace without Promise*, Batsford, 1981, chs. 4 and 5.

15 This was a dinner for Wilson, given by Lloyd George and other Members of the House of Commons. It was eventually held on 24 July 1919, when over 200 MPs attended.

16 Throughout 1919 and early 1920, discussions were held regarding the precise post-war functions and constitution of the Territorial Force. In order to counter criticisms about the delay in deciding the future of the force, Churchill met Territorial representatives on 1 April 1919 and reassured them that the Territorials would be retained as a reserve formation. Peter Dennis, 'The reconstruction of the Territorial Force 1918–1920', in Adrian Preston and Peter Dennis (eds), *Swords and Covenants*, Croom Helm, 1976, pp. 196–7.

17 On 3 April Churchill had secured Lloyd George's approval to send extra volunteer British troops to North Russia in order to cover the evacuation of the British force already there. Martin Gilbert, *Winston S. Churchill*, vol. IV, Heinemann, 1975, pp. 273–4.

18 During April 1919 there was a nationalist-inspired strike of government officials in Egypt.

19 'Troopers, London' was the telegraphic address of the War Office.

20 The King's Birthday Honours were published on 3 June each year. The 'Peace' list was not published until August 1919.

21 Plumer, Allenby and Wilson were all promoted to Field Marshal on 31 July 1919.

22 Milne did not get the Command, which was given to Lieut.-Gen. Sir Beauvoir De Lisle on 1 October 1919.

23 The Treaty of Versailles was presented to the German Delegation on 7 May. Count Brockdorff-Rantzau, the chief German delegate, made a speech which Hankey described as 'a strange mixture of cringing and insolence', and which was particularly badly received by the French. Hankey, *The Supreme Control*, pp. 150–5.

24 This was somewhat optimistic. The last British troops did not leave Batum until July 1920.

25 'The Military Situation throughout the British Empire, with Special Reference to the Inadequacy of the Numbers of Troops Available', memorandum by CIGS, 26 April 1919, circulated to Cabinet, 3 May. PRO CAB 24/78 G.T. 7182.

26 Feisal had gone to put the Arab case before the Peace Conference.

27 The Peace Conference planned to send a joint Allied Commission to investigate the problems of Syria and Palestine. Realising their unpopularity with the Arabs the French refused to appoint any representatives. British representatives were named but never joined the investigation which ended up as the all-American 'King-Crane Commission'. Dr Henry C. King and Mr Charles Crane visited the Middle East during June to August 1919. Its final recommendation that Syria, including Palestine and Lebanon, should be incorporated into a single Arab state under Emir Feisal was ignored by the Peace Conference. Doreen Ingrams, *Palestine Papers 1917–1922*, John Murray, 1972, ch. 5.

28 The 'Third Afghan War' began when Afghan forces crossed the Indian frontier on 5 May 1919. After a rapid response from Anglo-Indian units, including the aerial bombing of Jalalabad, the Emir sued for an armistice on 31 May. Peace was signed on 8 August 1919. 'Despatch by Gen. Sir C. C. Monro, CinC India, on the Third Afghan War 1919', 1 Nov. 1919, PRO WO 106/58.

29 Lord French's book, *1914* was serialised in the *Daily Telegraph* during April and May 1919. He particularly criticised Sir Horace Smith-Dorrien's decision to stand and fight at Le Cateau in August 1914 during the retreat from Mons. *See* Holmes, *The Little Field Marshal: Sir John French*, pp. 222–4, 359–60.

30 In March 1919 a coalition of socialists and communists led by Bela Kun established a Bolshevik regime in Hungary. It was driven out of power in July by Rumanian forces which invaded Hungary and occupied Budapest.

31 The plan to join together the anti-Bolshevik forces in North Russia and Siberia depended on about half of the 60,000-strong Czech Corps under the French General Janin co-operating with Kolchak's offensive towards Archangel. In the event, Janin refused and the scheme came to nothing. Ullman, *Britain and the Russian Civil War*, pp. 183–90.

32 German troops had occupied the Baltic provinces of Latvia, Lithuania and Estonia since the collapse of Russia in 1917. While they acted against Bolshevik forces in the region during 1919, they also appeared to represent renewed German ambitions when a group of Baltic Germans seized power in Latvia in April. By the end of the year, however, the Allies had succeeded

in evacuating all German forces from the provinces. Dockrill and Goold, *Peace without Promise*, pp. 119–21.

33 The wartime reduction in the number of white troops in India, the strain of fighting the Afghan War and problems of internal security, especially in the Punjab, prompted the CinC India to press for the British garrison to be brought back up to establishment levels.

34 The post-war IRA campaign effectively began with the killing of two Irish policemen at Soloheadbeg, near Tipperary, in January 1919. During the spring there were arms raids and some attacks on soldiers and police, two more of whom died at Knocklong, county Limerick on 13 May. Nevertheless, by June 1919, while Ireland, perhaps, exhibited symptoms of 'lawlessness', violence had not yet begun in earnest. *See* Charles Townshend, *The British Campaign in Ireland 1919–1921*, Oxford University Press, 1975, pp. 16–20.

35 Wilson got his way and Knox remained in Russia until the collapse of the anti-Bolshevik forces.

36 See note 31 above.

37 This was part of the plan to join up with Kolchak's forces.

38 The Council of Four had instructed Foch to be ready to march into Germany should the Germans refuse to sign the Treaty of Versailles. To the annoyance of the statesmen, Foch had stressed the difficulties of doing this. Liddell Hart, *Foch*, vol. II, p. 447. On 28 June 1919 the Germans signed the Treaty of Versailles.

39 Churchill and Lloyd George also favoured the establishment of a Ministry of Defence, and discussed it on a number of occasions during 1919, but nothing came of the scheme. According to Lloyd George, one of the chief difficulties was moving Walter Long, the First Lord of the Admiralty. Gilbert, *Churchill*, IV, pp. 211–13.

40 M.O.5 was the branch of the Directorate of Military Operations with responsibility for questions relating to 'Russia, the Far East, Scandinavia and Holland'.

41 The peace negotiations with Bulgaria did not prompt much 'trouble', and the Treaty of Neuilly was signed on 27 November 1919.

42 Most of the offices for the British Delegation were in the Hotel Astoria on the Place de l'Etoile at the corner of the Avenue des Champs-Elysées.

43 Fiume, formerly Austrian, was disputed between Italy and Yugoslavia. In September 1919 it was seized by a party of Italians, led by the patriotic poet Gabriele D'Annunzio. The 'Free State of Fiume' was set up in 1921, but in 1924 the town was annexed by Italy. It was transferred to Yugoslavia after the Second World War.

44 The actual scope of Milne's command as GOC, Army of the Black Sea, in charge of Allied troops in Constantinople and the Bosphorus area,

was questioned by the French, whose General Franchet D'Esperey was CinC Allied Forces in the East. In the eyes of the British government, however, D'Esperey's remit did not extend to the exclusive British interests in Turkey. The problem of command in Constantinople was further complicated by the existence of High Commissioners representing each Allied Power. *See* Graham Nicol, *Uncle George*, Reedminster, 1976, pp. 228–40.

45 Sir Boyle Roche (1743–1807) was an Irish MP noted for outrageous remarks. On one occasion in the House, quoting from Jevon's play, *The Devil of a Wife*, he said, 'Mr. Speaker, it is impossible I could have been in two places at once, unless I were a bird.'

46 This minute was circulated to the Cabinet by Churchill on 20 August 1919 under the title 'The Future of the Army'. PRO CAB 24/87 G.T. 8039.

47 Churchill was on holiday in Scotland.

48 The establishment of new nation states—particularly Poland—in eastern and Central Europe entailed the drawing of new international frontiers. In a number of instances under the auspices of the League of Nations plebiscites were arranged to determine the wishes of the local inhabitants. The provision of Allied troops to police these plebiscites was a fruitful source of Anglo-French irritation.

49 Wilson suffered a serious attack of whooping cough in September–October, 1919.

50 Wilson's own house was at Grove End, Bagshot, Surrey. He also rented 36 Eaton Place, London, S.W.1.

51 In May 1919, with the approval of the 'Big Three' in Paris (Lloyd George, President Wilson and Clemenceau), Greek troops landed at Smyrna. Over the next few months the Greeks advanced into Anatolia, encountering fierce resistance from the Turks. Early in October Milne, the British GOC in Constantinople, laid down a limit to the Greek advance which ran close to the town of Aidin. Despite fears to the contrary, the 'Milne Line' held until July 1920. *See* Dockrill and Goold, *Peace without Promise*, pp. 190–216.

52 In July Churchill had offered Robertson the Irish Command when it fell vacant. Churchill to Robertson, 21 July 1919, Robertson Papers (Liddell Hart Centre for Military Archives, King's College London) I/31/2. When Churchill did consult Lloyd George about the appointment, the Prime Minister refused to allow Robertson to have the job.

53 The Congreve family home was Chartley Hall in Staffordshire.

54 There was a national railway strike in Great Britain from 27 September to 5 October 1919. Quite elaborate arrangements were made to mitigate the effects of the stoppage. In the end the government settled the strike on the railwaymen's terms. Keith Jeffery and Peter Hennessy, *States of Emergency:*

British Governments and Strikebreaking since 1919, Routledge and Kegan Paul, 1983, pp. 15–19.

55 In February 1919, at Lloyd George's instigation, an invitation was broadcast to representatives of all sections of Russian opinion, Bolshevik and anti-Bolshevik, to attend a conference with the Allies in order to try to bring the Russian civil war to an end. The suggested venue was Prinkipo, a group of islands used as a summer resort a few miles from Constantinople. The initiative failed in the face of White Russian and French opposition. Speaking at the Lord Mayor's Banquet in the Guildhall on 8 November 1919, Lloyd George concentrated on the continuing need to establish peace in Russia, and implied once again that a conference might be arranged. Although he did not mention Prinkipo by name, *The Times* report of his speech included the sub-headline 'Prinkipo Again'. The speech was received critically by the Conservative press. Ullman, *Britain and the Russian Civil War*, pp. 99–117, 304–7.,

56 Inter-Departmental Conference on Middle Eastern Affairs, commonly known as the 'Eastern Committee', and chaired by Lord Curzon, 32nd meeting, 18 November 1919. There is a set of Eastern Committee minutes in the Curzon Papers (India Office Records) MSS. Eur. F.112/275.

57 The Government of India Act, 1919, embodied the so-called 'Montagu–Chelmsford Reforms', named after the Secretary for India and the Viceroy respectively. Scheduled to begin operating in 1921, the reforms brought a measure of home rule to India and included the establishment of a largely-elected legislative assembly, and the inclusion of indigenous Indians in the Viceroy's Council.

1920 INTRODUCTION

1 R. H. Ullman, *The Anglo-Soviet Accord*, Princeton University Press, 1972, pp. 60–88, 311–13.

2 Conference of Ministers, 18 January 1920, PRO CAB. 23/35 S.11.

3 The operation was completed on 9 July 1920. Nicol, *Uncle George*, p. 214. Keith Jeffery, *The British Army and the Crisis of Empire, 1918–22*, Manchester University Press, 1984, p. 138, erroneously states that the evacuation was completed on 9 June.

4 Wilson diary, 16 January 1920.

5 Macready himself was not particularly keen on the job. He later asserted that only the desire of his 'old Chief', Lord French, had persuaded him to accept it. Sir Nevil Macready, *Annals of an Active Life*, Hutchinson, 1924, vol. II, p. 425.

6 Macready had experience of commanding troops 'in aid of the Civil Power'

both in South Wales in 1910 and Belfast during 1914. He was Commissioner of the Metropolitan Police at the time of his appointment to the Irish
Command.

7   Memorandum by the DMO, 10 December 1920, PRO CAB. 24/116
C.P. 2275.

8   The impact of the Amritsar massacre and the Hunter Committee is
covered in Sir Algernon Rumbold, *Watershed in India, 1914–1922*, Athlone
Press, 1979, especially pp. 197–203.

1920 CORRESPONDENCE

1   This coal was to facilitate Denikin's withdrawal in the face of Red Army
advances. By the end of 1919 it had become clear that Denikin's White
Russian forces were destined for defeat. *See* Churchill to Wilson (2 letters),
31 December 1919, in Martin Gilbert, *Winston S. Churchill*, Companion
Volume IV, Heinemann, 1977, Part 2, pp. 986–7.

2   This idea was not quite as far-fetched as it might seem. For a year from
mid-August 1918, there was a British naval squadron in the Caspian. At its
largest it comprised 9 armed ships, 4 aircraft carriers of a rudimentary type
and 12 torpedo boats with 1,200 officers and men of the Royal Navy and
RAF. D. Norris, 'The British Navy in the Caspian, 1918–19', *Journal of
the Central Asian Society*, vol. X (1923), pp. 216–40.

3   This was the ratification of the Treaty of Versailles, which actually took
place on 10 January 1920. Under Articles 88, 94 and 96 of the Treaty parts
of Upper Silesia and East Prussia were to be allocated according to a
plebiscite of inhabitants.

4   The Triple Alliance was a loose formation of the miners, railwaymen, and
transport workers, pledged to co-ordinate industrial action on important
issues.

5   On 12 February 1920, Wardrop, the British High Commissioner in the
Caucasus, prematurely reported to the Foreign Office that the evacuation
of Batum had begun. Curzon, who had specifically asked Wilson for a
temporary postponement of any withdrawal, at once wrote to complain.
Curzon to Wilson, 12 February 1920, (2 letters), telegram from Mr
Wardrop enclosed, Wilson MSS. HHW 2/20A/26.

6   Allenby had recommended that the Allied Powers should acknowledge the
'sovereignty of Feisal over an Arab nation or Confederation embracing
Syria, Palestine and Mesopotamia, the Administration of Syria being
secured to [the] French, and that of Palestine and Mesopotamia to [the]
British'. Allenby to Curzon, 18 March 1920, *Documents on British Foreign
Policy 1919–1939*, 1st ser., vol. XIII, HMSO, 1963, no. 223.

7 Lord Milner headed the Special Mission to Egypt, which visited Egypt and Palestine from December 1919 to March 1920.

8 On 25 March Churchill sent a note to Wilson's Secretary with the instruction that a formal letter should be written to Sir Nevil Macready offering him the Irish Command. Wilson MSS. HHW 2/18B/31.

9 Congreve's son, a Lieutenant-Commander R.N., who was ADC to his father 1920–21.

10 Churchill and Lord Rawlinson spent a fortnight's holiday together over Easter 1920 on the Duke of Westminster's estate at Mimizan, south of Bordeaux.

11 The San Remo inter-Allied Conference was held from 19 to 26 April 1920. The principal British representatives were Lloyd George, Curzon, Hankey and Wilson. The main business involved settling the terms of the Turkish peace treaty.

12 Meinertzhagen had written to the Foreign Office criticising Allenby for not doing enough to fulfil the promises of the Balfour Declaration. For this action Allenby immediately dismissed him. Meinertzhagen, who remained on good terms with Allenby after the incident, observed to him at the time: 'I suppose you realize that you would have had to give your housemaid longer notice'. Wavell, *Allenby in Egypt*, p. 33.

13 The request was refused.

14 Recruitment did not improve and the Territorial Army remained below establishment throughout the 1920s.

15 Congreve's left hand was shattered by a shell at Vimy Ridge in 1917. It was subsequently amputated.

16 See note 9.

17 In January 1917 Wilson was promoted temporary General when he was appointed Chief Military Representative on the British Mission to Russia. He reverted to Lieutenant-General in March 1917 when he became Chief Liaison Officer with the French Army.

18 This was the result of Wilson's 'war game' at the beginning of the year. These conclusions were accepted by a meeting of the Eastern Committee on 12 January 1920. This was, however, one of the few such meetings from which Lord Curzon was absent. Inter-Departmental Conference on Middle Eastern Affairs, 34th minutes, Curzon MSS. (IOR) Eur. F. 112/275.

19 A telegram from the British Military Attaché in Rome, dated 15 May 1920.

20 On 17 May the thousand-strong British garrison at the Persian port of Enzeli on the Caspian Sea withdrew in the face of a Bolshevik advance from the north. *See* Jeffery, *The British Army and the Crisis of Empire*, p. 142.

21 The War Office telegram of 25 February 1920 instructed the GOC, Mesopotamia, to 'make arrangements with your force in North Persia to offer a bold front to Bolsheviks should they threaten Enzeli and endeavour

by bluff to prevent them seriously attacking that place. At the same time, if seriously attacked, there is no intention of holding on to Enzeli . . .', quoted in 'Summary of events in North-West Persia, 20 May 1920', appendix C, PRO F.O. 371/4904/C11.

22 Wilson, however, added to this: 'who are obviously bent on reasserting their sway in North Persia on pre-war lines, but *unless His Majesty's Government are prepared to go to war with Russia* [original italics], there is little chance of our being able to prevent them doing so'. Memo. by Wilson, ibid., appendix D.

23 Wilson's London house.

24 One of Curzon's three country houses.

25 'British Military Liabilities', circulated to the Cabinet on 15 June 1920, PRO CAB. 24/107 C.P. 1467.

26 From the summer of 1919 a Turkish nationalist movement had developed. Based in Anatolia, it was led by Mustapha Kemal who was deeply opposed to the Constantinople government. The nationalists were determined to resist any attempt by the Allies to partition Turkey.

27 In July 1920 a special Trades Union Congress meeting passed a resolution calling for a truce in Ireland and the withdrawal of the 'army of occupation', but the motion never prompted any direct action. Late in 1920 a Labour Party Commission visited Ireland and delivered a report sharply critical of the government's Irish policy but again this stimulated little more than rhetorical support for the Irish nationalists. *See* D. G. Boyce, *Englishmen and Irish Troubles: British Public Opinion and the Making of Irish Policy 1918–22*, Jonathan Cape, 1972, pp. 62–3, 66–7.

28 Lieutenant-Colonel A. T. Wilson.

29 Under the Defence of the Realm Act, during 1918–19 'Special Military Areas' had been established in parts of south-west Ireland. Within them the local military commander had powers to impose extensive restrictions, but by the autumn of 1919 their effectiveness was being questioned. Townshend, *The British Campaign in Ireland*, pp. 7–8, 11, 23, 25, 31.

30 The Irish Situation Committee was set up on 24 June. Chaired by Walter Long, it included A. J. Balfour, Lord Birkenhead, Churchill and H. A. L. Fisher (President of the Board of Education), Cabinet Minutes, PRO CAB. 23/21/37(20).

31 From 1 to 11 July Wilson was away at the Spa Conference (Belgium), where the Allied and German leaders met to discuss matters such as reparations payments.

32 On 26 June the IRA captured Brigadier Lucas while he was on a fishing trip with two other officers near Fermoy, Co. Cork. Lucas escaped after about a month. Townshend, *The British Campaign in Ireland*, p. 88.

33 Moggridge sent these notes to Wilson on 5 July.

34 During the unrest which preceded the shooting at the Jallianwala Bagh a lady missionary, Miss Sherwood, was attacked and left for dead. General Dyer ordered that any Indian who wished to pass the spot where she fell must go on 'all fours'. The order remained in effect for about a week. Sir C. W. Gwynn, *Imperial Policing*, Macmillan, 1934, pp. 46, 56–7.

35 Wilson noted in his diary on 12 July 1920 that Churchill had been 'trying to get me—on paper—to express a political opinion' regarding Ireland.

36 The results were not quite the same. According to Harington's own memoirs, 'At the time of the Belfast Riots in 1898 . . . we were a fortnight in the streets amongst the brickbats. Luckily we never had to fire . . .' Sir Charles Harington, *Tim Harington Looks Back*, John Murray, 1940, p. 19.

37 Milne in fact came to England in August 1920, according to his biographer, 'ostensibly to see Claire [Milne's wife] who had had an operation, but in reality to get his GCMG and to hand over to Harington who was to succeed him'. Nicol, *Uncle George*, p. 249. Milne did not return to Constantinople. The Command temporarily passed to General Sir H. F. M. Wilson until Harington took over in November 1920.

38 During the Spa Conference the Polish government appealed to the Allies for support against advancing Bolshevik armies which threatened Warsaw. An Anglo-French Mission was appointed to assist the Poles. The British representatives included D'Abernon, Hankey, and Radcliffe; the French, M. Jusserand and General Weygand.

39 The French government had provided the Mission with a special train 'provisioned and prepared for them to live in for some time'. Stephen Roskill, *Hankey: Man of Secrets*, vol. II, 1919–1931, Collins, 1972, p. 183. Despite this apparently agreeable domestic arrangement, Lord D'Abernon contracted dysentery in Warsaw. D'Abernon, *An Ambassador of Peace*, vol. I. Hodder and Stoughton, 1929, p. 71.

40 Wilson's yacht.

41 The Mesopotamian Rebellion was in full swing.

42 Cox was in any case being hurried out to Baghdad to replace the Acting High Commissioner, Arnold Wilson, whose elaborate administration in Mesopotamia was believed by some to have contributed to the outbreak of rebellion. Jeffery, *The British Army and the Crisis of Empire*, pp. 150–2.

43 Churchill was holidaying in France, again based at the Duke of Westminster's house at Mimizan, but this time with his wife.

44 During the summer of 1920 a Soviet Russian Trade Mission was in London for talks with Lloyd George's government. British Intelligence intercepted the Mission's communications and the deciphered messages appeared to indicate duplicity on the part of the Russians, and that they had indulged in Bolshevik propaganda. Churchill, strongly supported by Wilson, waged a powerful campaign to expose this and publish some of the

intercepts in the press. A few were eventually published but to Churchill's disgust, Lloyd George refused to make a public issue of the matter and the trade talks continued more or less uninterrupted. There is a summary of the affair in Gilbert, *Churchill*, vol. IV, pp. 422–30.

45 Terence MacSwiney, Sinn Fein MP for Mid Cork and Lord Mayor of Cork, began a hunger strike when he was arrested on 12 August 1920. He died in Brixton prison on 25 October. The other two men, Michael Fitzgerald and Joseph Murphy, who were hunger-striking in Cork gaol, also died. Townshend, *The British Campaign in Ireland*, p. 122.

46 The report of the Milner Mission, published in August 1920, proposed a modest degree of independence for Egypt. The circumstances of the Mission and its report are detailed in John Darwin, *Britain, Egypt and the Middle East: Imperial Policy in the Aftermath of War, 1918–1922*, Macmillan, 1981, chapters 4 and 5.

47 Rawlinson was on his way East to take up the appointment of CinC, India.

48 Actually twelve officers and two civilians. During that afternoon, Sunday, 21 November, twelve civilians were killed by Auxiliary Police firing into the crowd at Croke Park football stadium. No bout of Irish troubles is complete without a 'Bloody Sunday'.

49 Field Marshal Lord William Gustavus Nicholson (1845–1918), CIGS, 1908–12.

50 Lord Birkenhead, known as 'F.E.'.

51 On 9 October 1920, the semi-independent Polish General Zeligowski seized Vilna from the Lithuanians. Although the Polish government officially disowned his action, the town remained under Polish rule. This state of affairs continued until the Soviet invasion of September 1939. Vilna (now Vilnius) is today the capital of the Soviet Republic of Lithuania.

52 The Cabinet agreed to spend £20,000 and let the British CinC in Constantinople assist in relief measures for the refugees. Silverlight, *The Victors' Dilemma*, p. 359.

53 Venizelos was heavily defeated in the Greek elections of November 1920, which followed the death of King Alexander as a result of a bite by a pet monkey.

54 Wilson's wife, Cecil, had a serious operation at the end of November 1920.

55 Approximately £46.7 million. A crore is ten million rupees.

56 Following the 3rd Afghan War in 1919, Henry Dobbs was given the unenviable task of negotiating an agreement with the Afghans which would ensure peace on the frontier, secure the maintenance of British access to the country and maintain Afghanistan as a buffer against Russian expansion.

57 This memorandum, dated 16 December 1920, is reproduced in Gilbert, *Churchill*, Companion Volume IV, Part 2, pp. 1267–9.

58 In June 1920 Lord Esher's Committee on the Army in India had recommended that, in order to promote imperial efficiency, the Indian Army should be placed directly under the authority of the CIGS in London. The proposal was still-born as Delhi refused even to consider such an arrangement. For the Esher Report and Indian reactions to it, see V. Longer, *Red Coats to Olive Green: A History of the Indian Army, 1600–1974*, Allied Publishers, Bombay, 1974, pp. 177–86.

59 Despite the date on the letter (28 December) this seems to refer to the special Cabinet Conference on Ireland on 29 December (PRO CAB. 23/23/79A (20)). See also Wilson diary, 29 December 1920.

1921 INTRODUCTION

1 *See* Maurice, *The Life of Lord Rawlinson*, chapter 13.

2 Derby to Rawlinson, 31 December 1921, Derby MSS. (IOR) MSS. Eur. D.605/15.

3 Lord Longford (Frank Pakenham), *Peace by Ordeal*, Sidgwick and Jackson edn., 1972, contains an authoritative account of the Anglo-Irish negotiations and treaty.

4 General Tudor was head of the police in Ireland who in 1921 comprised three main categories of men: the rump of the old RIC, British recruits brought in to the regular Constabulary since late 1919, and the 'cadets' of the Auxiliary Division, established in July 1920. Elements from the latter two groups became known popularly as 'Black and Tans'.

5 This is eventually what happened at Chanak in the autumn of 1922. Harington describes the course of events in his memoirs: *Tim Harington Looks Back*, chapter XII.

6 Wilson diary, 5 July 1921.

7 Derby to Rawlinson, 31 December 1921, as n. 2.

1921 CORRESPONDENCE

1 On 10 December 1920 martial law was proclaimed in the four Irish counties of Cork, Tipperary, Kerry and Limerick. On 4 January 1921 it was extended to Clare, Kilkenny, Waterford and Wexford. But despite Wilson's urging, the government refused to extend it any further. See Townshend, *The British Campaign in Ireland*, chapter V.

2 During December 1920 and the early part of the following year Rawlinson was under strong pressure in the Viceroy's Council to cut the Army budget, which meant reductions in the number of British troops in India. The

proposal caused alarm in London and in the end the question of troop reductions was postponed until the spring of 1922 when some economies were made. Maurice, *The Life of Lord Rawlinson*, chapters 13 and 14.

3 The 'Cardwell system', named after Edward Cardwell, Secretary for War 1868–74, demanded that there should be at least as many battalions at home as overseas in order to provide a constant flow of replacements and reliefs. The difficulties of maintaining the system in the inter-war period are discussed in Brian Bond, *British Military Policy between the Two World Wars*, Clarendon Press, Oxford, 1980, pp. 99–126.

4 The Indian Staff College.

5 From February 1920 to July 1921 General Romer headed a temporary section called MO4(x) within the Directorate of Military Operations. He was specially responsible for duties relating to internal security. The War Office's post-war organisation for internal security is covered in detail in K. Jeffery, 'The Army and Internal Security 1919–39', *Historical Journal*, vol. 24, no. 2 (1981).

6 Colonel Twiss was head of MI3, the French, Central European and Scandinavian Section of the Directorate of Military Intelligence.

7 On 11 December 1920, as a reprisal for an IRA ambush, members of the Auxiliary Division of the RIC (popularly known as 'Black and Tans') set fire to a number of buildings in the centre of Cork, including the City Hall.

8 The Government of Ireland Act, 1920, which became law in December 1920, provided for separate parliaments in Dublin and Belfast to be elected at some time between January 1921 and March 1922. At the end of 1920 it was decided to hold the elections in May 1921.

9 In Ulster the RIC had been reinforced by a part-time Special Constabulary which had been set up in October 1920. The background and organisation of the Special Constabulary is fully covered in Michael Farrell, *Arming the Protestants*, Pluto Press, 1983, chapters 1–4.

10 Sanders' memorandum, while noting the undoubted 'great moral effect' which intensive aeroplane bombing had on the inhabitants of towns and villages, emphasised that aeroplanes by themselves could not be relied on to reduce bands of armed insurgents. 'Aeroplanes', he wrote, 'like other arms must be used in co-operation with Infantry but it is the Infantry attack at close quarters which still decides the battle.' Memo. by Major-General G. A. T. Sanders, 10 December 1920, Wilson MSS. HHW 2/55/7.

11 There seems to be no justification for this assertion. The Dobbs' family home was in Cappoquin, county Waterford.

12 Churchill gave up the Secretaryship of War on 13 February 1921.

13 Repington had formerly been a brother officer and friend of Wilson in the Rifle Brigade. He resigned his commission in 1902 because of a threatened scandal involving another man's wife. There seems to be no truth in the

widely-circulating story that Wilson hounded Repington out of the Army. Nevertheless by the time of the First World War, neither man regarded the other with any affection and Repington's sometimes unscrupulous methods as a military journalist were frequently criticised by Wilson and his friends.

14 Short for 'Black Jumbo' (sometimes abbreviated to 'B.J.'), a nonsense term used for intercepts of foreign wireless or cable messages.

15 On the Mediterranean coast of Egypt, adjacent to the frontier with Libya, then an Italian colony.

16 In his paper Macready argued the urgent necessity for reorganising the Irish police and establishing unity of command between the civil security forces and the military.

17 During the Irish debate, Hamar Greenwood did as Chetwode hoped. He drew particular attention to a letter issued by de Valera which not only reiterated 'the usual accusations against the Government', but also contained the 'allegation that our soldiers and policemen in Ireland have been guilty of outrages on women. That', asserted Greenwood, 'is the most serious charge that can be laid at the door of any white man.' He categorically denied the accusation. 21 February 1921, *Hansard* 138 H.C. Deb. 5s., col. 627.

18 The Strickland Report blamed a number of policemen for the Cork burnings in December 1920. Townshend, *The British Campaign in Ireland*, p. 139.

19 The Duke of Connaught, uncle of King George V, visited India in the spring of 1921.

20 On 29 February 1921 Afghanistan concluded a treaty of friendship with Soviet Russia. Anxious to avoid exclusive dependence on one major power, the Afghans attempted to keep a balance between Britain and Russia. Relations between Russia and Afghanistan are covered in Harish Kapur, *Soviet Russia and Asia, 1917–27*, Michael Joseph, 1966, chapter VIII.

21 In response to the German rejection of Allied terms for the payment of reparations, the Allies broke off negotiations, occupied Dusseldorf, Dinsburg and Ruhrort and imposed a customs cordon between the occupied area and the rest of Germany. There is an account of the reparations problem in G. M. Gathorne-Hardy, *A Short History of International Affairs, 1920 to 1938*, Oxford University Press, new edn. 1938, chapters III and IV.

22 Transjordan was to be constituted an Arab province of Palestine under an Arab governor responsible to the British High Commissioner in Jerusalem. In order to establish a settled government in the area, the conference recommended its immediate military occupation. Churchill later rescinded

this decision after consulting with the Emir Abdullah at the end of March. Since Abdullah asserted that he could keep control with no more than 'aerial support', the idea of a military occupation was dropped. *Report on Middle Eastern Conference held in Cairo and Jerusalem, March 12 to 30, 1921*, April 1921, PRO CAB 24/122 C.P. 2866.

23 The 'Rowlatt Acts' of early 1919 extended emergency wartime legislation which allowed the courts to try political cases without juries and gave the Indian provincial governments the power of internment without trial. A committee chaired by Mr Justice Rowlatt in 1918 had recommended the measures. Sir Algernon Rumbold, *Watershed in India, 1914–1922*, Athlone Press, 1979, pp. 135–8.

24 622 million rupees, approximately £41.5 million.

25 Sir Maurice Hankey, in contrast to Wilson's views as expressed to Rawlinson, blamed the CIGS himself for the Cabinet's alarm. Apparently Wilson had travelled up from the country with Austen Chamberlain and Hankey believed Wilson had infected the other with his own panic. Thomas Jones, *Whitehall Diary* (ed. Keith Middlemas), vol. I, Oxford University Press 1969, p. 137.

26 According to his biographer, the idea originated with Sir Hugh Trenchard, the Chief of the Air Staff. Andrew Boyle, *Trenchard, Man of Vision*, Collins, 1962, p. 384.

27 Sa'ad Zaghlul, the Egyptian nationalist leader, had recently returned to Egypt from discussions in London and was currently undermining Allenby's efforts to establish a stable Egyptian government under the moderate Adly Pasha Yeghen. The difficulties attending Egyptian policy-making at this time are very fully covered in Darwin, *Britain, Egypt and the Middle East*, especially chapter 5.

28 Ironside indeed went home, and he never took over command at Baghdad. Both his legs were damaged, the right one was badly fractured and the other splintered in two places. He recovered almost completely, although he afterwards walked with a limp and lost over an inch in height. He counted himself very fortunate to have 'fallen into the hands of a very able surgeon, Major McVicker of the RAMC and an Ulsterman'. *High Road to Command: the Diaries of Major-General Sir Edmund Ironside 1920–22*, edited by Lord Ironside, Leo Cooper, 1972, p. 200.

29 Plans had been made for the military occupation of the Ruhr should the Germans still refuse to accept the Allied reparation terms, but in the end the revised terms were accepted.

30 In 1808 Moore, who had held independent commands in Sicily and Sweden, was peremptorily instructed by the government to go out to Portugal subordinate to two other officers, one of whom had never been employed as a general in the field. Moore strongly believed that the

government had not treated him at all well. Details from the *Dictionary of National Biography*.

31 This probably refers to Haldane's experience when he was imprisoned with Churchill and two other officers in Pretoria during the South African War (November–December 1899). Haldane sporadically maintained that Churchill in escaping on his own had deliberately abandoned his companions. It seems unlikely that this was so. The matter is discussed in Randolph Churchill, *Winston S. Churchill*, vol. I., Heinemann, 1966, pp. 499–502.

32 The most serious trouble occurred late in April when two companies of a Royal Fleet Reserve battalion, stationed at Newport, Monmouthshire, refused to parade. They both objected to coercing fellow trade unionists and complained about their sub-standard living conditions. Jeffery and Hennessy, *States of Emergency*, p. 65.

33 The Crown Prince of Japan, later the Emperor Hirohito, visited Great Britain in May 1921.

34 The four battalions already earmarked for Silesia were also Irish. On 26 May Wilson assured General Morland that they were 'all good—two of them north country battalions, Royal Ulster Rifles and Inniskilling Fusiliers, and two of them jolly good battalions, specially selected for the unfortunate Experimental Brigade that we were to have had this summer, i.e. Royal Irish Fusiliers and the Dublin Fusiliers'. Wilson MSS. HHW 2/57/35.

35 Foch never received his honorary degree from Queen's University, Belfast. Wilson, however, received his in March 1922.

36 In February 1921 the Persians signed a treaty of friendship with Soviet Russia. It was not ratified by the Persian parliament until December 1921. Kapur, *Soviet Russia and Asia*, pp. 130, 186.

37 Wilson's letter was intercepted by Irish nationalists between Dublin and Belfast. It was published in the republican *Irish Bulletin*. See correspondence in Wilson MSS. HHW 2/63/1.

38 Lord Derby was a very well-known horse racing enthusiast. The Grand Prix de Paris was run at Longchamps on Saturday 25 June. It was won by Mr J. Watson's Lemonora. In April 1921 Derby, disguised with special glasses and calling himself Mr Edwards, engaged in a bizarre mission to Dublin where he interviewed de Valera in an at the time vain attempt to open negotiations with the Irish nationalist leader. On 24 June, however, Lloyd George publicly invited de Valera and Sir James Craig to a conference in London. Longford, *Peace by Ordeal*, pp. 64–71.

39 Although Irish questions were taken on 27 June, the case of Wilson's letter did not come up.

40 Lord Midleton and Sir Robert Woods were moderate southern Irish

Unionists. De Valera conferred with them over four days, 4–8 July 1921, and the meetings resulted in his agreeing to enter into negotiations with Lloyd George. Buckland, *Irish Unionism: I*, pp. 236–46.

41 Smuts spent 5 July negotiating with de Valera in Dublin. The South African travelled over *incognito* in the hope of keeping his mission secret, but the news of his arrival at Kingstown (now Dun Laoghaire) was widely publicised. W. K. Hancock, *Smuts 2: The Fields of Force 1919–1950*, Cambridge University Press, 1968, pp. 56–8.

42 The Ali brothers, Mohammed and Shaukat, were vigorous leaders of Muslim opinion. During May 1921 the Viceroy, Lord Reading, met Gandhi, who acted as an intermediary with the Ali brothers. Lord Reading, *Rufus Isaacs* vol. II, Hutchinson, 1945, pp. 193–200.

43 Ellipsis in original.

44 Rawlinson's younger brother, Toby, was imprisoned by the nationalist Turks in eastern Turkey from March 1920 to October 1921. *See* A. Rawlinson, *Adventures in the Near East 1918–22*, Cape, 1923.

45 Probably Hamid Hasancan Bey, Administrator of the Ottoman Bank, 1912–25, and Constantinople Agent of the Angora government, 1921–22.

46 The fourth Earl of Craven, a member of the Royal Yacht Squadron, died on 9 July 1921.

47 Early in July Harington arrested 52 persons, mostly Russians, ostensibly members of a trade delegation. They were suspected of fomenting revolution and being involved in a plot to assassinate Harington. Harington to the Secretary, War Office, 6 July 1921, Wilson MSS. HHW 2/46B/15.

48 Wilson was Colonel of the Royal Irish (Ulster from 1 January 1921) Rifles from 1915 until his death.

49 Cooke-Collis's father, Colonel William Cooke-Collis, was 73 years old when the family home, Castle Cooke, was destroyed.

50 Wilson's eldest brother, James Mackay Wilson, who had inherited the family home at Currygrane, was a prominent southern Unionist.

51 Congreve was appointed Colonel-Commandant of the 1st Battalion, Rifle Brigade, in 1921.

52 Probably Major-General Sir Victor Couper (1857–1938) who was Colonel-Commandant of the 4th Battalion, Rifle Brigade, 1921–22, and of the 1st Battalion, 1927–29, in succession to Congreve.

53 Ironically, the Wilson house survived unscathed until after Sir Henry's death when it was burnt down as a reprisal for the execution of his murderers.

54 After the Anglo-Irish treaty of December 1921 the five Irish regiments (ten battalions) with an exclusively southern Irish domicile were disbanded.

55 In July and August 1921 a series of meetings on the question of Egyptian self-government were held in London with a delegation of moderate

Egyptian nationalists led by Adly Pasha Yeghen. Darwin, *Britain, Egypt and the Middle East*, pp. 120–1.

56   On 26 July 1921 the Master of the Rolls in Ireland allowed a writ of habeas corpus for two IRA men who had been sentenced to death by military courts-martial under Martial Law. Macready refused to release the men, arguing that civil jurisdiction did not apply in the case, whereupon the Master of the Rolls issued a writ of attachment against Macready and a number of other officers, including General Strickland. The problem was solved, although not entirely to Macready's satisfaction, by Lloyd George ordering the prisoners' release on the grounds of political expediency. Macready, *Annals of an Active Life*, vol. II, pp. 586–92.

57   This was the 'Third Paris Conference', which was due to discuss both the problem of Upper Silesia and the continuing conflict between Greece and Turkey.

58   Churchill, then First Lord of the Admiralty, was widely blamed for the fall of Antwerp to the Germans in October 1914, at a cost of over 2,500 men from the Royal Naval Division, killed, wounded or captured. He was also blamed for the failure of the Dardanelles campaign in 1915. Robert Rhodes James, *Churchill: A Study in Failure 1900–1939*, Penguin edn., Harmondsworth, 1973, pp. 81–100.

59   In the autumn of 1917 in order to counteract widespread industrial unrest, Churchill, then Minister of Munitions, persuaded the government to restore pay differentials between skilled and unskilled munitions workers by granting an increase of wages to the skilled men. This was eventually settled at $12\frac{1}{2}$ per cent. But it did not solve the problem since the unskilled workers proved to have sufficient bargaining power to secure substantial increases for themselves. The affair prompted some not entirely justified public criticism of Churchill for granting the increase in the first place. Henry Pelling, *Winston Churchill*, Macmillan, 1974, pp. 234–5.

60   Many Unionists, such as Sir Henry Wilson, believed that in 1914 Churchill planned to use the Navy to break the Ulster Unionists' resistance to home rule. Rhodes James, *Churchill*, pp. 59–64.

61   General Sir Charles Sackville-West.

62   The Indian Military Requirements Committee reported in July 1920. Jeffery, *The British Army and the Crisis of Empire 1918–22*, Manchester University Press, 1984, pp. 105–6.

63   In March 1921 an Anglo-Soviet Trade Agreement had been signed.

64   Wilson's niece, Mrs Coote.

65   In August 1921, following the decisions of the Cairo Conference, Sherif Hussein's son, Feisal, was installed as King of Mesopotamia (Iraq).

66   There were three grades of the Special Constabulary. The 'A Specials' performed full-time duties and the 'B Specials' part-time. A further group,

the 'C Specials' comprised a register of volunteers prepared to perform part-time duties if necessary.

67 The Prince of Wales visited India from mid-November 1921 until mid-March 1922.

68 Gandhi was eventually arrested on 10 March 1922. The event caused little excitement. Rumbold, *Watershed in India*, p. 285.

69 On 29 November 1921 the British negotiators had announced that they would present their final proposals to Sir James Craig and the Southern Irish delegates on 6 December. Longford, *Peace by Ordeal*, p. 202.

70 The actual wording of the Oath to be taken by members of the Parliament of the Irish Free State is: 'I . . . do solemnly swear true faith and allegiance to the Constitution of the Irish Free State as by law established, and that I will be faithful to H.M. King George V, his heirs and successors by law, in virtue of the common citizenship of Ireland with Great Britain and her adherence to and membership of the group of nations forming the British Commonwealth'. The treaty is reproduced in Longford, ibid., pp. 288–93.

71 Radcliffe had been sent to Belfast to report on the military position in Northern Ireland.

72 Craig's house.

73 I.e. 'Black (Protestant) Ulsterman'. In his report, Radcliffe wrote that Wickham was 'averse to the withdrawal of Regular troops from Belfast; not for fear of what the rebels may do, but because he is terrified of wholesale reprisals by the Unionists, which would be disastrous to the Ulster cause'. Wilson MSS. HHW 2/44B/5.

74 Filoneau, a Frenchman, had recently been appointed President of the Sub-Commission of Gendarmerie in Constantinople. His mother and one grandmother were English, and he spoke English as if it were his native language.

75 Resulting from the advances of the Turkish nationalist armies.

76 Cavan headed the military section of the British Delegation to the Washington Conference.

77 From 14 December 1921, a bitter debate was conducted in the *Dáil Éireann*. Opposition to the treaty was led by de Valera. On 7 January 1922 the *Dáil* agreed to ratify the treaty by 64 votes to 57. Dorothy Macardle, *The Irish Republic*, Corgi edn., 1968, pp. 555–83.

78 There was a debate on the Irish Treaty in the House of Lords on 14 December 1921. Lord Carson made his maiden speech as a peer and spoke eloquently of the 'defeat and humiliation' represented by the agreement. *House of Lords Debates*, 5th ser., vol. 48, col. 36–53.

79 Sir Herbert Samuel had explained that the intention of the Balfour Declaration was that Jews would be allowed to settle in Palestine 'within the limits which are fixed by the numbers and interests of the present

population'. On 14 June Churchill told the House of Commons that Jewish immigration to Palestine was being 'very carefully watched and controlled both from the point of view of numbers and character'. Ingrams, *Palestine Papers*, pp. 127–31.

80 The so-called 'Geddes Axe' recommended large cuts in the armed services.

81 Lord Londonderry's house near Stockton-on-Tees.

82 The Haycraft Commission of Inquiry had been set up to report on the Jaffa riots of May 1921. In giving evidence to it, Dr Eder, head of the Zionist Commission, had asserted that there could only be one National Home in Palestine, and that a Jewish one. Ingrams, *Palestine Papers*, pp. 133–5.

1922 INTRODUCTION

1 Interim Report of the Committee on National Expenditure, December 1921, PRO CAB. 24/131 C.P. 3570

2 Jeffery, *The British Army and the Crisis of Empire*, p. 23.

3 Wavell, *Allenby in Egypt*, p. 75.

4 Wilson to Lloyd George, 18 February 1922 (typescript copy), Wilson MSS. HHW 2/10B/13.

5 The circumstances of Wilson's death are fully examined in Rex Taylor, *Assassination: the Death of Sir Henry Wilson and the Tragedy of Ireland*, Hutchinson, 1961.

1922 CORRESPONDENCE

1 Since early 1920 Plumer had been pressing the War Office to approve the establishment of a local infantry unit in Malta, but to his increasing frustration the approval had been withheld on the grounds of expense. See Wilson-Plumer correspondence in Wilson MSS. HHW 2/56/1–9.

2 The *Wafd* or 'Delegation' party had been formed by Zaghlul in November 1918. The name reflected the Egyptian nationalists' desire to send a representative delegation to the peace conference.

3 In October 1921, after conducting secret negotiations for several months, the French concluded a unilateral agreement with the nationalist Turkish government at Ankara. Christopher M. Andrew and A. S. Kanya-Forstner, *France Overseas: the Great War and the Climax of French Imperial Expansion*. Thames and Hudson, 1981, p. 223.

4 Under the Anglo-Irish Treaty a Commission, comprising representatives from the North and the South, was to be established to determine the

boundary between Northern Ireland and the Irish Free State. Collins contended that if the wishes of the inhabitants were followed the counties of Tyrone and Fermanagh, together with large areas in Down, Londonderry and Armagh, should be transferred to the Free State. Macardle, *The Irish Republic*, p. 599.

5   The cavalry was eventually reduced—partly by amalgamations—by eight regiments. There is a summary of the Geddes cuts in Bond, *British Military Policy*, pp. 26–7.

6   The post of Deputy Chief of the Imperial General Staff was abolished in the autumn of 1922.

7   On 8 February the Government of India had issued orders for Gandhi's arrest, but the action was postponed in the hope that Congress would suspend the civil disobedience campaign. This proved to be a vain hope and in the end Gandhi was arrested on 10 March. Rumbold, *Watershed in India*, pp. 283–5.

8   Presumably a reference to some of Rawlinson's possessions, left behind at Government House, Farnborough, official residence of the GOC, Aldershot Command.

9   Wilson and Rawlinson had first met in December 1886 when they were both part of a force endeavouring to capture a leader of the Burmese Bo tribe called Shewe. Maurice, *The Life of Lord Rawlinson*, pp. 13–16.

10   'Both to Both' or 'b. to b.' was invariably how Wilson and Rawlinson signed off their letters to each other.

APPENDIX I
BIOGRAPHICAL NOTES

Abdullah Ibn Hussein (1882–1951), Son of Hussein, Emir of Mecca. A leader of the Arab revolt against Turkey, 1915–18; Emir of Transjordan, 1921–46; first King of the Hashemite Kingdom of Jordan, 1946 until his assassination in 1951.

Adly Pasha Yeghen (1865–1933), Turkish aristocrat and Egyptian politician. Governor of Cairo, 1902; Vice-President of Legislative Assembly; Minister of Foreign Affairs; collaborated loyally with the British during and after World War I in the hope of concessions to the Nationalists; Prime Minister, 1921.

Ali Riza Rikabi, Military Governor at Damascus of Occupied Enemy Territory Administration, 1918.

Allenby, Edmund Henry Hynman (1861–1936) 'the Bull'. Educated Haileybury and Sandhurst; entered Army (Inniskilling Dragoons), 1882; served Bechuanaland Expedition 1884–85; Zululand, 1888; South Africa, 1899–1902; Maj.-Gen. 1909; commanding 1st Cavalry Division, BEF, 1914; Cavalry Corps, 1914–15; 5th Army Corps, 1915; knighted, 1915; commanding 3rd Army, 1915–17; CinC Egyptian Expeditionary Force, June 1917–Oct. 1919; created Viscount, 1919; High Commissioner for Egypt and the Sudan, Mar. 1919–1925; Field Marshal, 1919.

Anderson, Chandler Parsons (1866–1936), American lawyer. Attached to State Department, 1910–18; member, Special Mission to London and Paris, 1918; hon. Colonel; counsel to International Red Cross Commission, 1919.

Anderson, (Warren) Hastings (1872–1930). Educated at Marlborough and Sandhurst; Cheshire Regiment; served South Africa, 1899–1902; European War, 1914–18 (promoted Maj.-Gen.); Commandant, Staff College, 1919–22; knighted, 1922; Maj.-Gen. G.S., Allied Forces in Turkey, 1922–23; QMG, 1927–31.

Asquith, Herbert Henry (1852–1928). Educated at City of London School and Balliol College, Oxford; Liberal MP, 1886–1918 and 1920–24; Home Secretary, 1892–95; Chancellor of the Exchequer, 1905–08; Prime Minister, 1908–16, and Secretary for War, Mar.–Aug. 1914; leader of the Liberal Party, 1908–26; created Earl of Oxford and Asquith, 1925.

Asser, (Joseph) John (1867–1949). Entered Army (Dorsets Regiment), 1887; served Sudan, 1897–99; retired as Colonel, 1914; restored to active list as Maj.-Gen., 1916; GOC line of communications, in France and Flanders,

1916–19; knighted, 1917; GOC, British Troops in France and Flanders, 1919; Governor and CinC, Bermuda, 1922–27.

Badoglio, Pietro (1871–1956), Italian General. Lieut.-Gen., 1917; Chief of Army General Staff, Nov. 1919–Feb. 1921 and 1925–27; Ambassador to Brazil, 1923; Chief of Supreme General Staff, 1925–40; Prime Minister, 1943–44.

Bainbridge, (Edmond) Guy Tulloch (1867–1943). Educated at Marlborough and Sandhurst; entered Army (The Buffs), 1888; served Dongola Expedition, 1896; Nile Expeditions, 1897, 1898; South Africa, 1899–1908; European War, 1914–18; Maj.-Gen., 1917; commanding 25th Division; GOC 1st Division, in northern part of Ireland, 1919–June 1921, and Aldershot 1921–23.

Bakir Sami, Turkish soldier. Commanding 56th Nationalist Division in Anatolia, 1920–21; Kemalist delegate to London Conference, Feb.–Mar. 1921; representative of Kemal in Italy and France, June–July 1921.

Balfour, Arthur James (1848–1930). Educated at Eton and Trinity College, Cambridge; Conservative MP, 1874–1922; President of the Local Government Board, 1885–86; Secretary for Scotland, 1886–87; Chief Secretary for Ireland, 1887–91; First Lord of Treasury, 1891–92 and 1895–1905; Prime Minister, 1902–05; First Lord of the Admiralty, 1915–16; Foreign Secretary, 1916–Oct. 1919; Lord President of the Council, 1919–22 and 1925–29; created Earl, 1922; President, National Cyclists' Union.

Barnes, George Nicoll (1859–1940). General Secretary of Amalgamated Society of Engineers, 1896–1906; Glasgow Labour MP, 1906–22; Minister of Pensions, 1916–17; Minister without Portfolio, 1917–20; Member of War Cabinet, 1917–19; resigned from the Labour Party in 1918 when it withdrew from the Coalition so that he might take part in the Peace Conference.

Barrès, Maurice (1862–1923), French novelist, essayist and politician. Entered Chamber of Deputies, 1889; became president of the *Ligue des Patriotes* during World War I; chief ally of Alexandre Millerand in creating the *Bloc National*, which won a landslide victory in the Nov. 1919 elections.

Beadon, Roger Hammet (1887–1945). Educated at Clifton College; entered Army Service Corps from Devon Militia, 1907; attached to Supreme War Council, Versailles, 1917–18; senior representative of QMG at Peace Conference, 1918–20; Brevet Lt.-Col., 1918; Assistant Adjutant and QMG, Allied Military Committee of Versailles, 1920–21; Instructor RASC Training Establishment, 1923–25; attached to Iraq Army, 1925–28; retired, ill health, 1929.

Beatty, David (1871–1936). Entered Navy, 1884; served Sudan, 1896–97, 1898; China, 1900; Rear-Admiral, 1910; knighted, 1914; commanding 1st Battle Cruiser Squadron, 1912–16; Grand Fleet, 1916–19; 1st Sea Lord,

Nov. 1919–1927; created Earl Beatty and Viscount Borodale of Wexford, 1919.

Beaverbrook, Lord, William Maxwell Aitken (1879–1964). Educated at Harkins Academy, Newcastle, New Brunswick, Canada; Conservative MP, 1910–16; knighted, 1911; Canadian Government Representative at the front, 1916–17; invested in *Daily Express*, 1912, took controlling interest, 1916; created Baron, 1917; Chancellor of the Duchy of Lancaster and Minister of Information, 1918; Minister for Aircraft Production, 1940–41; Minister of State, 1941; Minister of Supply, 1941–42; Lord Privy Seal, 1943–45.

Benson, William Shepherd (1855–1932). Entered U.S. Navy, 1877; Rear-Admiral, 1915; Chief of Naval Operations, 1915–18; Naval Adviser to American Peace Commissioners in Paris, 1919.

Bernard, Denis John Charles Kirwan (1882–1956). Educated at Eton and Sandhurst; entered Army (Rifle Brigade), 1902; served World War I at Gallipoli, Salonika and France; GSO 1 (Lieut.-Col.), 6th Division (Cork) Ireland, 1920–22; Maj.-Gen., 1933; GOC 3rd Division, 1936–39; knighted, 1939; Governor and CinC, Bermuda, 1939–41; retired to the family home, Castle Hacket, Co. Galway.

Berthelot, Henri Mathias (1861–1931), the 'fat General'. Assistant Chief of Staff to Joffre, 1914; reorganised Rumanian Army, 1917; commanded an Army in Champagne, 1918.

Berthelot, Philippe (1866–1934). Entered the French Foreign Ministry, 1904; served as Liaison Officer between the Allied Staffs, 1914–18; Head of Political Department, Foreign Ministry, 1919–20; Secretary-General, 1920–21 and 1924–32.

Birkenhead, Lord, Frederick Edwin Smith (1872–1930). Educated at Birkenhead School and Wadham College, Oxford; Conservative MP, 1906–19; a strong supporter of the Irish Unionists; Solicitor-General, 1915; Attorney-General, 1915–19; knighted, 1915; Lord Chancellor, 1919–22; Secretary for India, 1924–28; created Baron, 1919; Viscount, 1921; Earl, 1922.

Bliss, Tasker Howard (1853–1930). Entered U.S. Army, 1875; Brig.-Gen., 1901; Chief of Staff, 1917; American Military Representative on the Supreme War Council, Versailles, 1917–19; American Commissioner, Paris Peace Conference, 1919; honorary knighthood, 1918.

Block, Adam Samuel James (1856–1941). Educated at Clifton College; entered Diplomatic Service, 1877; served in Ottoman Empire; knighted, 1907; representative of British Bondholders on Council of Administration of Ottoman Public Debt 1903–29; President of British Chamber of Commerce, Constantinople, 1907–18.

Bols, Louis Jean (1867–1930). Entered Army (Devon Regiment), 1887; served Burma, 1891–92; Chitral Relief Force, 1895; South Africa, 1899–1902; France, Flanders, Palestine and Syria, 1914–19; Maj.-Gen., knighted, 1919;

CGS, EEF, 1917–19; Chief Administrator, Occupied Enemy Territory in Palestine, 1920; Divisional Commander, Southern Command, 1920–24; Governor and CinC, Bermuda, 1927–30.

Bonar Law, Andrew (1858–1923). Born in Canada; educated at Glasgow High School; Conservative MP, 1900–10 and 1911–23; Parliamentary Secretary to the Board of Trade, 1902–05; Colonial Secretary, May 1915–Dec. 1916; Chancellor of the Exchequer, 1916–Jan. 1919; member of the War Cabinet, Dec. 1916–Oct. 1919; Lord Privy Seal, 1919–Mar. 1921; Prime Minister, Oct. 1922–May 1923; Leader of the Conservative Party, 1911–21 and 1922–23. 'A queer fishlike sort of creature', Milner to L. S. Amery, 26 Feb. 1921, quoted in *The Leo Amery Diaries* (ed. J. Barnes and D. Nicholson), vol. I, Hutchinson, 1980, p. 269.

Boris III, (1894–1943). King of Bulgaria Oct. 1918–Aug. 1943; succeeded on the abdication of his father, King Ferdinand.

Bowes, William Hely (1858–1932). Entered Army (21st Foot, Royal Scots Fusiliers), 1879; served Burma, 1885–87; N.W. Frontier, 1897–98; European War, 1914–18; Brig. Gen. 1915; Chief of Military Mission, Siberia, 1918–19.

Brémond, Colonel Edouard. Served in French Africa before World War I; Corps Chief of Staff on the western front; Head of French Military Mission to Hussein at Jeddah, 1916–18; Chief Administrator, Occupied Enemy Territory in Cilicia, 1918–19.

Briand, Aristide (1862–1932), French politician. Six times Prime Minister: 1909–10; 1913; 1915–17; Jan. 1921–Jan. 1922 (also Foreign Affairs); 1925–26; 1929; Minister of Foreign Affairs, 1925 and 1926–32; awarded Nobel Peace Prize for his part in the Locarno Agreements, 1926.

Bridges, (George) Tom Molesworth (1871–1939). Entered Army (Royal Artillery), 1892; served South Africa, 1899–1901; Somaliland, 1902–04; Lt.-Col. 4th Hussars, 1914; Head of British Military Mission with the Belgian Field Army, 1914–16; Maj.-Gen. commanding 19th Division, 1916–17; Head of British War Mission, USA, 1918; Head of British Mission, Allied Armies of the Orient, 1918–20; knighted, 1919; Governor of South Australia, 1922–27.

Briggs, Charles James (1865–1941). Educated at Sandhurst; entered Army (King's Dragoon Guards), 1886; served South Africa, 1899–1902; Natal, 1906; Brig.-Gen. commanding 1st Cavalry Brigade, 1913–14; Lt.-Gen. commanding 16th Army Corps at Salonika, 1916–19; knighted, 1917; Chief of British Military Mission to South Russia, Feb.–June, 1919; Special Duty, War Office, June 1919–Jan. 1920.

Briggs, F. C. C. Entered Army (The King's (Liverpool) Regiment), 1909; Captain, 1915; Brigade Major 45th Jullundur Brigade, 1918; died on N.W. Frontier, 1919.

Buchanan, George William (1854–1924). Educated at Wellington College;

entered Diplomatic Service, 1876; Minister, Bulgaria, 1903–08; knighted
1905; Netherlands, 1908–10; Ambassador, Russia, 1910–18; Italy,
1919–21.

Budenny, Simon Mikhailovich (1884–1973), Soviet General. A former
sergeant-major in the Imperial Russian Army; from 1918 commanded Red
Army cavalry formations, with particular success against Denikin's forces in
1919, and the Polish Army in the summer of 1920; member of Soviet Military
Council 1921–22; commanding Red Army Cavalry, 1924–37; Marshal of the
Soviet Union, 1935; Deputy People's Commissar of Defence, 1939–41;
Army Commander, 1941–43; Commander of Cavalry, Soviet Army,
1943–53.

Budworth, Charles Edward Dutton (1869–1921) 'Buddy'. Educated at
Woolwich; entered Army (Royal Artillery), 1888; served South Africa;
European War 1914–18; Brig.-Gen. RA, BEF, 1915–16; Maj.-Gen. RA
France, 1916–19; Divisional Commander, 1919; attached to Indian GS,
1920–21.

Byng, Julian Hedworth George (1862–1935), 7th son of 2nd Earl of Strafford.
Entered Army (10th Royal Hussars), 1883; served Sudan, 1884; South
Africa, 1899–1902; Maj.-Gen. 1909; GOC Egypt 1912–14; commanding
3rd Cavalry Division, 1914–15; Cavalry Corps, 1915; knighted 1915; 9th and
17th Army Corps, 1916; Canadian Corps. 1916; 3rd Army, 1917–19; created
Baron, 1919; Governor-General of Canada, 1921–26; created Viscount,
1926; Commissioner Metropolitan Police, 1928–31.

Byron, John (1872–1944). Educated at Woolwich; entered Army (Royal Artil-
lery), 1892; served Malakand Field Force, N.W. Frontier, 1897; South
Africa, 1900; Deputy Director of Artillery, War Office, 1916–18; Brig.-Gen.
RA 23rd Division, Italy, 1918–19; GSO 1 (Liaison Officer) GHQ, Egyptian
Expeditionary Force, 1919; Brig.-Gen. commanding RA in Egypt and
Palestine, 1920–24.

Calthorpe, Somerset Arthur Gough- (1864–1937). Entered Royal Navy, 1878;
Rear-Admiral, 1912; commanding 2nd Cruiser Squadron, 1914–16; Second
Sea Lord, 1916; knighted, 1916; CinC Mediterranean, 1917–19, and also
British High Commissioner at Constantinople, 1918–19; CinC Portsmouth,
1920–23; Admiral of the Fleet, 1925.

Cameron, Archibald Rice (1870–1944). Entered Army (The Black Watch),
1890; served South Africa, 1899–1902; European War, 1914–18; Brig.-
Gen. GS, France and Rhine, 1915–19; Brigade and Divisional (Maj.-Gen.)
Commander, Irish Command, 1920–22; GOC Northern Ireland District,
1923–25; Director of Staff Duties, War Office, 1926–27; GOC 4th Division, 1927–31; Scottish Command, 1923–37.

Capel, Arthur, 'Boy'. Sir Edmund Allenby's interpreter in 1915. 'An Englishman of wealth, living in Paris, and a great friend of M. Clemenceau's. Wilson came to know him well . . . His health broke down and he had to resign his interpretership in the field. He died shortly after the close of the struggle.' Callwell, *Sir Henry Wilson*, vol. I, p. 205.

Carson, Edward Henry (1854–1935). Educated at Portarlington School and Trinity College, Dublin; a barrister; Unionist MP, 1892–1921; knighted 1900; Solicitor-General, 1900–06; Attorney-General, 1915; First Lord of the Admiralty, 1917; Member of War Cabinet, 1917–18; Lord of Appeal in Ordinary, 1921–29.

Cavallero, Ugo (1888–1943), Italian General. Attached to Gen. Cadorna's staff, 1916; Member of Italian Delegation to Peace Conference, 1919; left Army, 1920; became a Director of Pirelli; Under-Secretary for War, 1925–28; Chief of Comando Supremo, 1940–43; believed to have shot himself in German HQ, Frascati, Sept. 1943.

Cavan, Earl of, Frederick Rudolph Lambart (1865–1946). Entered Army (Grenadier Guards), 1885; succeeded father as 10th Earl, 1900; Maj.-Gen. commanding 4th (Guards) Brigade, Sept. 1914–June 1915; commanded Guards Division, Aug. 1915–Jan. 1916; XIV Corps in France and Italy, Jan. 1916–18; GOCinC, Aldershot Command, 1920–22; head of War Office Section of the British Delegation at the Washington Conference, 1921; CIGS in succession to Sir Henry Wilson, 1922–26; Field Marshal, 1932. 'Ignorant, pompous, vain and narrow, but a nice man and a fine fighting soldier', diary of Sir Henry Wilson (Imperial War Museum), 11 Jan. 1922.

Caviglia, Enrico (1862–1945), Italian General. GOC of 8th Army, North Italy, 1918; promoted to Marshal, 1926.

Cecil, (Edgar Algernon) Robert Gascoyne (1864–1958). Educated at Eton and University College, Oxford; became Lord Robert Cecil in 1868 when his father became 3rd Marquess of Salisbury; Conservative MP, 1906–23; Parliamentary Under-Secretary of State for Foreign Affairs, 1916–19; Minister of Blockade, 1916–18; created Viscount Cecil of Chelwood, 1923; Lord Privy Seal, 1923–24; President of the League of Nations Union, 1923–45; Chancellor of the Duchy of Lancaster, 1924–27; Nobel Peace Prize, 1937.

Chamberlain, (Joseph) Austen (1863–1937). Educated at Rugby and Trinity College, Cambridge; Liberal Unionist MP, 1892–1906; Conservative MP, 1906–37; Civil Lord of the Admiralty, 1895–1900; Financial Secretary to the Treasury, 1900–02; Postmaster-General, 1902–03; Chancellor of the Exchequer, 1903–05 and Jan. 1919–Apr. 1921; Secretary of State for India, 1915–17; member of War Cabinet, 1918–19; Lord Privy Seal and Leader of the Conservative Party, Mar. 1921–Aug. 1922; Foreign Secretary, 1924–29; knighted, 1925; First Lord of the Admiralty, 1931.

Charpy, Charles Antoine (1869–1941). Entered French Army, 1888; Chief of Staff to CinC Allied Armies of the Orient (Salonika), 1917–19; Général de Brigade, 1918; GOC French Troops, Constantinople, 1920–22; Chief of French Military Mission to Poland, 1926.

Cheetham, Milne (1869–1938). Entered Diplomatic Service, 1894; Counsellor Cairo, 1911–19 (acting High Commissioner in Allenby's absence, 1919); knighted 1915; Minister, Peru and Ecuador, 1919–20; Paris, 1921–22; Switzerland, 1922–24; Athens, 1924–26; Copenhagen, 1926–28.

Chelmsford, Lord Frederic John Napier Thesiger (1868–1933). Educated at Winchester and Magdalen College, Oxford; succeeded father as 3rd Baron, 1905; Viceroy of India, 1916–21; created Viscount, 1921; First Lord of the Admiralty, 1924, during first Labour government.

Chetwode, Philip Walhouse (1869–1950). Educated at Eton; entered Army (19th Hussars), 1889; succeeded father as 7th Baronet, 1905; served Burma, 1892–93; South Africa, 1899–1902; European War, 1914–19; Maj.-Gen., 1916; commanding Desert Corps, Egypt, 1916–17; 20th Army Corps, 1917–18; Military Secretary, War Office, 1919–20; Deputy CIGS, Oct. 1920–Sept. 1922; GOCinC Aldershot, 1923–27; CinC India, 1930–35; Field Marshal, 1933; created Baron, 1945.

Chicherin, Georghy Valentinovich (1872–1936). Russian diplomat and politician, successively Social Democrat, Menshevik and Bolshevik; lived in Paris and London, 1908–17; expelled from Britain, Jan. 1918, in exchange for the British Ambassador in Petrograd, Sir George Buchanan; succeeded Trotsky as People's Commissar for Foreign Affairs, Mar. 1918; replaced by Litvinov, 1930.

Churchill, Winston Leonard Spencer (1874–1965). Educated at Harrow and Sandhurst; entered Army (4th Hussars), 1895; served with Spanish forces in Cuba, 1895; Malakand Field Force, 1897; Tirah Expeditionary Force, 1898; Sudan, 1898; resigned from Army 1899; Lieutenant, South African Light Horse, 1900; *Morning Post* war correspondent, South Africa, 1899–1900; Conservative MP, 1900–04; Liberal MP, 1904–22; Under-Secretary for the Colonies, 1905–08; President of the Board of Trade, 1908–10; Home Secretary, 1910–11; First Lord of the Admiralty, 1911–15 and 1939–40; Chancellor of the Duchy of Lancaster, 1915; served on Western Front, 1915–16; battalion commander, 6th Royal Scots Fusiliers; Minister of Munitions, 1917–Jan. 1919; Secretary for War and Air, 1919–Feb. 1921; Colonial Secretary, 1921–Oct. 1922; Conservative MP, 1924–64; Chancellor of the Exchequer, 1924–29; Prime Minister, 1940–45 and 1951–55; knighted, 1953.

Clarke, Travers Edwards (1871–1962). Entered Army (Royal Inniskilling Fusiliers), 1891; served Tirah Expedition, 1897–98; South Africa, 1900–02; Maj.-Gen., 1917; QMG, British Armies in France, 1917–19; knighted,

1919; QMG, Mar. 1919–Mar. 1923; Deputy Chairman and Chief Administrator, British Empire Exhibition, Wembley, 1923–25.

Claudel, Henri (1871–1956), French General. Served in West Africa: Mauretania, 1908, and Morocco, 1912; CGS, Group of Armies of the East, 1915; aide-major to General Joffre, 1916; GOC 2nd Army Corps 1918; commanding French Army of the Orient, Constantinople, 1919–20; Inspector-General of Colonial Troops, 1925–36.

Clemenceau, Georges (1841–1929), 'the Tiger'. Mayor of Montmartre, 1870; Member of the Chamber of Deputies, 1876–93 and 1902–29; radical journalist; Minister of the Interior, 1906; Prime Minister, 1906–08; Prime Minister and Minister for War, Nov. 1917–Jan. 1920.

Cobbe, Alexander Stanhope (1870–1931). Educated at Wellington College; entered Army (South Wales Borderers), 1889; served Chitral Relief Force, 1895; South Angoniland Expedition, 1898; Kwamba Expedition, 1899; Ashanti, 1900; Captain, Indian Staff Corps, 1900; served Somaliland, 1902–04 (V.C., 1903); Great War, 1914–18; Mesopotamia, 1915–16 (promoted Maj.-Gen.); knighted, 1917; Secretary of Military Department, India Office, 1920–26; GOCinC, Northern Command, India, 1926–30; Military Secretary, India Office, 1930–31.

Collins, Michael (1890–1922). Educated at National School, Clonakilty, Co. Cork; worked as a clerk in London, 1906–16; fought in the General Post Office, Dublin, during Easter Rising, 1916; AG of the IRA, 1917–18; Minister of Home Affairs and Finance Minister in Sinn Féin Government, 1918–21; a signatory of The Anglo-Irish Treaty, Dec. 1921; Chairman of the Provisional Free State Government, 1922; killed in an ambush by anti-Treaty forces.

Congreve, Walter Norris (1862–1927), 'Squibbie'. Educated at Harrow and Pembroke College, Oxford; entered Army (Rifle Brigade), 1885; served South Africa, 1899–1902 (won V.C. at Colenso, 1900); Brig.-Gen. 1911; commanding 18th Infantry Brigade, UK and France, 1911–15; Maj.-Gen. commanding 6th Division, France, 1915; GOC XIII Corps, 1915–17; VII Corps, 1918; knighted, 1917; GOC British Troops in Egypt and Palestine, 1919–23; GOCinC, Southern Command, 1923–24; Governor and CinC, Malta, 1924–27. His son was killed in action on the Somme, July 1916, and was awarded a posthumous V.C.

Cooke-Collis, (William) James Norman (1876–1941). Educated at Cheltenham; entered Army (Royal Irish Rifles), 1900; served South Africa, 1900–02; European War, 1914–18; Military Governor of Batum, 1919; commanding 11th Infantry Brigade, 1927–31; Maj.-Gen. commanding T.A. Division, 1934–35; GOC N. Ireland District, 1935–38; knighted, 1937; chief organiser of Civil Defence in N. Ireland, 1940–41.

Cornwallis, Kinahan (1883–1959). Educated at Haileybury and University

College, Oxford; Sudan Civil Service, 1906–14; Egyptian Civil Service, 1914–24; seconded by Egyptian Government; temporary commission (acting Major, 1918); Director, Arab Bureau, Cairo, 1916–20; Assistant Chief Political Officer, EEF, 1919; Colonel, Special List; seconded to Iraq Government, 1921; Adviser to Ministry of Interior, Iraq, 1921–35; knighted, 1929; retired, 1935; Foreign Office, 1939–41; Ambassador in Baghdad, 1941–45.

Cory, George Norton (1874–1968). Born in Nova Scotia; entered Army (Royal Dublin Fusiliers), 1895; served South Africa, 1899–1902; Aden hinterland, 1903; European War, 1914–18; Maj.-Gen. GS, Salonika, 1917–19; Divisional Commander in the Caucasus, 1919; Mesopotamia, 1920–21; Deputy CGS, India, 1922–26; knighted, 1925; GOC 50th Northumbrian Division (TA), 1927–28.

Cowans, John Steven (1862–1921). Educated at Dr Burney's Academy, Gosport, and Sandhurst; entered Army (Rifle Brigade), 1881; Maj.-Gen., 1910; QMG, 1912–Mar. 1919.

Cox, Percy Zachariah (1864–1937). Educated at Harrow and Sandhurst; entered Army (The Cameronians), 1884; Indian Staff Corps, 1889; Indian Political Department, 1890; consular appointments in and around Persian Gulf, 1899–1914; knighted, 1911; Foreign Secretary to Indian Government, 1914; Chief Political Officer, MEF, 1914–18; Maj.-Gen. 1917; Acting Minister to Persia, 1918–20; High Commissioner in Mesopotamia, 1920–23.

Craig, James (1871–1940). Born in Dublin; educated at Merchiston School; army career (Capt. Royal Irish Rifles); served South Africa, 1899–1902; Unionist MP, 1906–21; served South-West Africa, 1914–15; created Baronet, 1918; Parliamentary Secretary, Ministry of Pensions, 1919–20; Financial Secretary, Admiralty, 1920–21; first Prime Minister of Northern Ireland, from June 1921 until his death; created Viscount Craigavon, 1927.

Creedy, Herbert James (1878–1973). Educated at Merchant Taylor's School and St John's College, Oxford; entered War Office, 1901; Private Secretary to successive Secretaries for War, 1913–20; knighted, 1919; Member and Secretary, Army Council, 1920–39; Permanent Under-Secretary for War, 1924–39.

Crowe, Eyre Alexander Barby Wichart (1864–1925). Born in Leipzig; educated in Germany; entered Foreign Office, 1885; knighted, 1917; a British plenipotentiary at the Peace Conference, 1919; Permanent Under-Secretary, Foreign Office, Nov. 1920–25.

Cuninghame, Thomas Andrew Alexander Montgomery (1877–1945). Educated at Eton and Sandhurst; entered Army (Rifle Brigade) 1897; succeeded father as 10th Baronet, 1897; served South Africa, 1900–01; member British Military Mission, French GHQ, 1914–15; Military Attaché, Athens, 1915–

16; Chief British Military Mission and Military Attaché, Vienna and Prague, 1920–23; retired with rank of Colonel, 1923.

Curling, Bryan James (1877–1955). Educated at Eton and Magdalen College, Oxford; entered Army (King's Royal Rifle Corps), 1899; served South Africa, 1899–1902; European War, 1914–19; temporary Brig.Gen., France, 1918–19; GSO2 Egypt, 1920–22; War Office, 1922–24; retired with rank of Brig.-Gen., 1927.

Curzon, George Nathaniel (1859–1925). Educated at Eton and Balliol College, Oxford; Conservative MP, 1886–98; Under-Secretary for India, 1891–92; Under-Secretary for Foreign Affairs, 1895–98; Viceroy of India, 1898–1905; created Baron, 1898; Earl, 1911; Lord Privy Seal, 1915–16; President of the Air Board, 1916; Lord President of the Council, 1916–19 and 1924–25; member of War Cabinet, 1916–19; Foreign Secretary, 1919–24; created Marquis Curzon of Kedleston, 1921. Lloyd George's 'gilded door mat'.

D'Abernon, Edgar Vincent (1857–1941). Educated at Eton; entered Army (Coldstream Guards), 1877; resigned, 1882; Conservative MP 1899–1906; created Baron, 1914; Ambassador to Germany, 1920–26; Member of Anglo-French Mission to Poland, July–Aug., 1920; created Viscount, 1926.

Davies, Francis John (1864–1948), known as 'Joey'. Educated at Eton; entered Army (Worcestershire Militia), 1881; Grenadier Guards, 1884; served Suakin Expedition, 1885; Jebu Expedition, 1892; South African War 1899–1901; Maj.-Gen., 1913; European War (France, Dardanelles and Egypt), 1914–16; knighted, 1915; Military Secretary to Secretary for War, and Secretary to Selection Board, 1916–June 1919; GOCinC, Scottish Command, 1919–23; Lieutenant of the Tower of London, 1923–26.

Davies, John Thomas (1881–1938). Educated at Bangor Normal College and London University; Private Secretary to Lloyd George, 1912–22; knighted, 1922.

Defrance, Albert (1860–1936), French diplomat. Minister in Cairo, 1910–18; Brussels, 1918–19; High Commissioner at Constantinople 1919–21; Ambassador in Madrid, 1921–23.

Degoutte, Jean M. J. (1866–1938), French General. Commanded Moroccan Division on Somme and in Champagne, 1916; XXI Corps, 1917; 6th Army, 1918; Chief of Staff to King Albert of the Belgians, 1918; CinC, Allied occupation forces in Rhineland, 1920–25.

Denikin, Anton Ivanovitch (1872–1947). Entered Russian Army 1887; General commanding Iron Division in World War I; commanding anti-Bolshevik White Russian Army in North Caucasus and Ukraine, 1918–20; defeated by Red Army, 1920; lived in exile in France and USA.

de Piépape, P. Colonel in command of *Détachement Français de Palestine et Syrie* during World War I; Military Governor at Beirut, 1918.

Derby, The Earl of, Edward George Villiers Stanley (1865–1948), known as 'K.G.'. Educated at Wellington College; Lieutenant, Grenadier Guards, 1885–95; Conservative MP, 1892–1906; Postmaster-General, 1903–05; succeeded father as 17th Earl, 1908; Director-General of Recruiting, Oct. 1915–July 1916; Under-Secretary for War, July–Dec. 1916; Secretary for War, Dec. 1916–Apr. 1918; Ambassador to France, 1918–20; Secretary for War, Oct. 1922–Jan. 1924; Member of the Jockey Club.

De Robeck, John Michael (1862–1928). Born in Ireland; 2nd son of 4th Baron De Robeck (a Swedish title); educated at HMS *Britannia*; entered Navy, 1875; Rear-Admiral, 1911; commanding Eastern Mediterranean Squadron at Gallipoli, 1915–16; knighted, 1916; CinC Mediterranean, 1919–22; High Commissioner for Constantinople, 1919–20; CinC Atlantic Fleet, 1922–24; Admiral of the Fleet, 1925.

de Valera, Eamon (1882–1974). Born in New York of a Spanish father and an Irish mother; educated at Blackrock College and University College, Dublin; a teacher of mathematics; fought with Irish Volunteers during Easter Rising, 1916; Sinn Féin MP, 1917–22; President of Sinn Féin 1917–26; Prime Minister, Irish Free State, 1932–48 and Irish Republic, 1951–54; President, 1959–73.

Devonshire, Duke of, Victor Christian William Cavendish (1868–1938). Educated at Eton and Trinity College, Cambridge; Liberal Unionist MP, 1891–1908; succeeded father as 9th Duke, 1908; Governor-General of Canada, 1916–21; Colonial Secretary, 1922–24.

de Wiart, Adrian Carton (1880–1963). Born in Brussels; educated at The Oratory School, Edgbaston and Balliol College, Oxford; entered Army, 1899; served South Africa; 2nd Lieut. 4th Dragoon Guards, 1901; served in Somaliland, 1914–15 (lost eye); Western Front, 1915–18 (lost a hand); V.C. in 1916; Brig.-Gen., 1918; Head of British Military Mission to Poland, 1918–23; retired from Army with rank of Maj.-Gen., 1923; recalled, 1939; Head of Military Mission to Poland, 1939; served Norway; taken prisoner in North Africa, 1941; freed, 1943; British Military Representative with Chiang Kai-Shek, 1943–46; knighted, 1945.

Diaz, Armando (1861–1928). Educated at Military Academy, Turin; served Libyan War, 1912; European War; CinC of the Italian Armies, 1917–19, at defence of Piave, 1917, and battle of Vittorio Veneto, 1918; for which he was made 'Duke of Victory'; Minister for War in Mussolini's first cabinet, 1922–24; Marshal, 1924.

Dillon, John (1851–1927). Educated at the Catholic University, Dublin; Surgeon; Nationalist MP, 1880–83 and 1885–1918; Chairman of Irish Nationalist Party, 1918.

Dobbs, Henry Robert Conway (1871–1934). Educated at Winchester and Brasenose College, Oxford; entered Indian Civil Service, 1892; Political

Officer, Mesopotamia, 1915–16; Foreign Secretary, Indian Government, 1919; Head of British Mission, Kabul, 1920–21; knighted, 1921; High Commissioner and Consul-General, Iraq, 1923–29.

Du Cane, John Philip (1865–1947). Entered Army (Royal Artillery), 1884; served South Africa, 1899–1902; BGGS, 1914; Maj.-Gen., 1915; knighted, 1916; commanded XV Corps, Oct. 1916–Apr. 1918; British Representative with Marshal Foch, 1918; MGO, Jan. 1920–Sept. 1923; GOCinC, Western Command, 1923–24; British Army of the Rhine, 1924–27; Governor and CinC, Malta, 1927–31; subsequently a director of several South African mining companies and Chairman of De Beers Consolidated Mines.

Duncannon, Viscount, Vere Brabazon Ponsonby (1880–1956), 'the Lord'. Educated at Harrow and Trinity College, Cambridge; Conservative MP, 1910 and 1913–20; served at Gallipoli, 1915; Personal Assistant to Sir Henry Wilson, 1916–19; succeeded his father as 9th Earl of Bessborough, 1920; Governor-General of Canada, 1931–35.

Dundonald, 12th Earl of, Douglas Mackinnon Baillie Hamilton Cochrane (1852–1935). Educated at Eton; entered Army (2nd Life Guards), 1870; served Nile Expedition, 1884–85; South Africa, 1899–1900; promoted Maj.-Gen.; Chairman Admiralty Committee on Smoke Screens, 1915.

Dunsterville, Lionel Charles (1865–1946), the model for Kipling's 'Stalky'. Educated at the United Services College, Westward Ho, and Sandhurst; entered Army (Royal Sussex Regiment), 1884; transferred to Indian Army, 1889; served in Waziristan, 1894–95; N.W. Frontier, 1897–98; China, 1900; France, 1914–15; commanding a Brigade on N.W. Frontier, 1915–17; GOC, 'Dunsterforce' in north Persia and the Caucasus, 1918; Brigade commander in India, 1918–20.

Dyer, Reginald Edward Harry (1864–1927). Born in India; educated at Middleton College, Co. Cork and Sandhurst; entered Army (The Queen's Royal West Surrey Regiment), 1885; served Burma Field Force, 1886–87; Indian Army, 1887; Waziristan Expedition, 1901–02; commanding Operations in East Persia, 1916; Brig.-Gen. commanding Jullundur Brigade (India), 1918–19; 5th Brigade, 1919–20; relieved of his command, 1920, following the death of over 370 Indians at the Jallianwala Bagh, Amritsar, in April 1919.

Enver Pasha (1881–1922). Turkish soldier and politician; appointed himself Maj.-Gen. and Minister of War, 1914; commanding Turkish Army in the Caucasus, 1914–15; fled to Germany, 1918; assisted Denikin against the Bolsheviks, 1919; supported Bolsheviks as director of Asiatic Bureau, Moscow, 1920; turned against the Bolsheviks and killed fighting at the head of an anti-Bolshevik force in Turkestan, as a champion of 'Pan-Turanianism'.

Esher, Reginald Baliol Brett (1852–1930). Educated at Eton and Trinity College, Cambridge; Liberal MP, 1880–85; Secretary, Office of Works, 1895–1902; succeeded his father as 2nd Viscount Esher, 1899; permanent member of the Committee of Imperial Defence, 1905–18; Liaison Officer between British and French War Offices, 1915; President of London County Territorial Force Association, 1912–21; chairman of Army in India Committee 1919; an intimate of the royal family and an influential adviser on military affairs to successive governments.

Evans, Cuthbert (1871–1934). Educated at Winchester and Woolwich; entered Army (Royal Artillery), 1891; served South Africa, 1899–1902; World War I in France and Italy; Brig.-Gen. G.S. 10th Army Corps, France and Rhine, 1918–19; GSO 1 3rd Division, Egypt and Palestine, 1920–23.

Farnham, Samuel (b. 1880). Royal Engineer, Warrant Officer, Class 1, 1918; Superintending Clerk in CIGS's office, 1919–25; left Army, 1925.

Feisal Ibn Hussein (1885–1933). Third son of Hussein, Sherif of Mecca; a member of the Turkish Parliament, 1913; leader of the Arab Revolt against the Turks, 1916–18; proclaimed himself King of Syria and Palestine, Mar. 1920; deposed by the French and fled from Damascus, July 1920; elected under British protection to the throne of Mesopotamia (Iraq), 1921.

Fell, Godfrey Butler Hunter (1872–1955). Educated at Eton and Magdalen College, Oxford; entered Indian Civil Service, 1894; knighted, 1918; Secretary Government of India, Army Department, 1921–23.

Foch, Ferdinand (1851–1929), the 'Old Marshal'. Born in Tarbes; entered French Army 1875; Professor at *Ecole Supérieure de Guerre*, 1894–1900, and General commanding, 1907–11; commanded 9th Army at Battle of the Marne, Sept. 1914; Deputy to CinC, 1914; honorary knighthood 1914; commanded Armies of the North 1915–16; deprived of command after Battle of the Somme; recalled; Generalissimo of Allied Forces, France, Mar.–Nov. 1918; Marshal of France, Aug. 1918; British Field Marshal, 1919.

Foulon, General (d. 1920). Commanded Macedonian Gendarmerie before World War I; Head of Inter-Allied Mission to manage Gendarmerie, 1919–20.

Franchet D'Esperey, Louis Félix Marie François (1856–1942). Born in Algeria; entered French Army, 1876; served Indo-China, 1886; China, 1900; Divisional General, 1912; active service on the Western Front, 1914–17, commanding 5th Army, 1914–16, Group of Armies of the East, 1916, Group of Armies of the North and North-East, 1916–17; CinC of Allied Armies of the East, with HQ at Salonika and Constantinople successively, June 1918–Nov. 1920; commanding the French Forces in Odessa, 1919; Marshal of France, 1921. Nicknamed 'Desperate Franky' by British colleagues.

Franklin-Bouillon, Henri (1870–1939). French journalist and politician; member of Chamber of Deputies, 1910–19 and 1923–36; Minister of State in Charge of Propaganda, 1917; Chairman of Chamber's foreign affairs commission, 1918–19; Chairman of *Congrès Français de la Syrie*, 1919; in charge of secret French negotiations with Mustafa Kemal, 1921–22; known as 'boiling Frankie' to the British in Constantinople.

Fremantle, Sydney Robert (1867–1958). Entered Royal Navy, 1881; Rear-Admiral, 1913; commanding Aegean Squadron, 1917–18; Deputy Chief of the Naval Staff, 1918–19; knighted, 1919; commanding 1st Battle Squadron, 1919–21; CinC, Portsmouth, 1923–26.

French, John Denton Pinkstone (1852–1925). Educated as naval cadet, HMS *Britannia*, Dartmouth; entered Army (Suffolk Artillery Militia), 1871; 19th Hussars, 1874; served in Sudan, 1884–85; Maj.-Gen., commanding 1st Cavalry Brigade, 1899; South Africa, 1899–1902; knighted 1900; CIGS, 1911–14; Field Marshal, 1913; CinC Expeditionary Forces in France and Flanders, 1914–15; Home Forces, 1916–18; Lord Lieutenant of Ireland, 1918–21; created Viscount, 1915, Earl of Ypres, 1921.

Frith, Gilbert Robertson (1873–1958). Born in Canada; educated at Upper Canada College and Royal Military College, Canada; served South Africa, 1899–1902; Nigeria, 1903; European War, 1914–18; France and Germany, 1917–20; Brig.Gen. i/c Administration, MEF, 1920–22; retired, 1923.

Gandhi, Mohandas Karamchand (1869–1948). Born in India; called to Bar, London, 1889; practised in South Africa, 1889–1908; leader of campaign for Indian settlers' rights in South Africa, 1908–14; raised an Ambulance Corps for service in France, 1914; started Non-Co-operation Movement in India, 1918; delegated by Congress to lead the national movement, 1921; inaugurated Civil Disobedience Campaign, 1930; assassinated, 1948, within six months of India and Pakistan gaining independence.

Geddes, Eric Campbell (1875–1937). Educated at Oxford Military College and Merchiston Castle School, Edinburgh; a railway engineer; brought into government by Lloyd George; Deputy Director-General of Munitions Supply, 1915–16; knighted, 1916; Inspector-General of Transportation, 1916–17; hon. Maj.-Gen. and hon. Vice-Admiral, 1917; Conservative MP, 1917–22; 1st Lord of the Admiralty, 1917–19; Member of Imperial War Cabinet, 1918; Minister of Transport, 1919–21; President of the Federation of British Industries, 1923–24. His brother, Sir Auckland Geddes, was also a government minister, 1917–20.

Gillman, Webb (1870–1933), 'Gilly'. Educated Dulwich College and Woolwich; entered Army (Royal Field Artillery), 1889; served South Africa, 1899–1900; Nigeria, 1902; European War, 1914–18 (promoted Maj.-Gen.); knighted, 1919; Commandant, Woolwich, 1920–24; Inspector of Artillery, 1924–27; MGO, 1927–31.

Godley, Alexander John (1867–1957). Educated at Royal Naval School, Haileybury, United Services College and Sandhurst; entered Army (Royal Dublin Fusiliers), 1886; served Rhodesia, 1896; South Africa, 1899–1901; transferred to Irish Guards, 1900; Maj.-Gen. commanding New Zealand Forces, 1910–14; knighted, 1914; commanding Division and Army Corps, Dardanelles, Egypt, France, Belgium and Germany, 1914–19; Military Secretary to Secretary of War, 1920–22; GOCinC Rhine, 1922–24; Southern Command, 1924–28; Governor and CinC Gibraltar, 1928–33; commanded Home Guard platoon, 1939–45.

Gough, Hubert de la Poer (1870–1963). Educated at Eton and Sandhurst; entered Army (16th Lancers), 1889; served Tirah, 1897–98; South Africa, 1899–1902; Instructor, Staff College, 1904–06; Maj.-Gen. 1914, commanding 3rd Cavalry Brigade; resigned commission during the 'Curragh Incident', Mar. 1914; commanding 2nd Cavalry Division, France, 1915; 1st Army Corps, 1916; 5th Army, 1916–18; removed from his command after German breakthrough of March 1918; Chief, Allied Mission to the Baltic, 1919; retired with rank of General, 1922, and took up a business career thereafter; in 1936 Lloyd George exonerated him from blame for the events of March 1918.

Grant, Charles John Cecil (1877–1950). Entered Army (Coldstream Guards), 1897; served South Africa, 1899–1902; European War; Brigadier-General, 1917–18; General Staff, 1918–19; Liaison Officer with Marshal Foch, 1918; Egypt, 1921–25; GOC, London District, 1932–34; GOCinC, Scottish Command, 1937–40; knighted, 1937.

Graziani, Jean César (1859–1932), French General. Divisional commander, 1914; Chief of Staff, Army of the Interior, 1915; commanding French troops on Italian Front, 1917–18; French Military Commissioner in Budapest, 1919–20.

Greenwood, Hamar (1870–1948). Born in Canada; educated at Whitby High School, Ontario, and the University of Toronto; an officer in the Canadian Militia for seven years; came to England, 1895; Liberal MP, 1906–22; Conservative MP, 1924–29; commanded a battalion on Western Front, 1915–16; created Baronet, 1915; returned to politics, 1916; Under-Secretary for Home Affairs, 1919; Secretary for Overseas Trade, 1919–20; Chief Secretary for Ireland, Apr. 1920–Oct. 1922; created Baron, 1929; Viscount, 1937.

Grey, Edward (1862–1933). Educated at Winchester and Balliol College, Oxford; succeeded father as 3rd Baronet, 1882; Liberal MP, 1885–1916; Under-Secretary for Foreign Affairs, 1892–95; Foreign Secretary, 1905–16; created Viscount Grey of Fallodon, 1916; temporary Ambassador to USA, 1919.

Gribbon, Walter Harold (1881–1944). Educated at Rugby School; entered

Army through Leicester Militia; 2nd Lieut. King's Own Royal Regiment, 1901; served Mesopotamia, 1914–16; on staff in War Office (Directorate of Military Intelligence), 1916–20; on staff of Army of the Black Sea (i/c Intelligence), 1920–23 (Col., 1921); Brigade commander, Egypt, 1931–32.

Haig, Douglas (1861–1928). Educated at Clifton, Brasenose College, Oxford, and Sandhurst; entered Army (7th Hussars), 1885. Served Sudan, 1898; South Africa, 1899–1902; Maj.-Gen., 1904; Chief of Staff, India, 1909–12; GOC, Aldershot, 1912–14; knighted 1913; commanding 1st Army, 1914–15; CinC, Expeditionary Force in France and Flanders, 1915–19; Forces in Great Britain, 1919–20; created Earl, 1919.

Haking, Richard Cyril Byrne (1862–1945). Entered Army (Hampshire Regiment), 1881; served Burma, 1885–87; South Africa, 1899–1900; Brig.-Gen. 1908; commanding 5th Brigade, 1914; 1st Division, 1915; XIth Corps, 1915–18; knighted, 1916; Chief of British Section, Armistice Commission, 1918–19; commanding British Military Missions, Russia and Baltic Provinces, 1919; Allied Troops Plebiscite Area, East Prussia and Danzig, 1920; High Commissioner, League of Nations, Danzig, 1921–23; GOC, Egypt, 1923–27.

Haldane, (James) Aylmer Lowthorpe (1862–1950). Educated at Edinburgh Academy, Wimbledon School and Sandhurst; entered Army (Gordon Highlanders), 1882; served Chitral, 1895; Tirah, 1897–98; South Africa, 1899–1900; imprisoned with Winston Churchill in Pretoria 1900; Military Attaché with Japanese Army during Russo–Japanese War, 1904–05; served throughout World War I; Maj.-Gen., commanding 3rd Division, 1914; 6th Corps, 1916; knighted, 1918; GOCinC Mesopotamia and Persia, Feb. 1920–May 1922. A cousin of R. B. Haldane (Viscount Haldane), the Liberal politician.

Haller, Jozef (1873–1960), Polish General and politician. Served in Austro-Hungarian Army, 1891–1918; joined Allies and commanded the 50,000-strong Polish Army in France, 1918; returned with Army to Poland, 1919; commanding Polish Volunteer Army in operations against Russians, 1920; retired from Army, 1926; active in politics, 1926–39; Minister of Education in Polish Government in Exile (London), 1940–43; died in London.

Hambro, Percival (Percy) Otway (1870–1931). Educated at Eton; entered Army (15th Hussars), 1892; served South Africa, 1899–1900; European War, 1914–19; DA & QMG, France and Rhine, 1915–19; DA & QMG, MEF, 1919–21; knighted, 1921; Director of Movements and Quartering, India, 1921–24; Maj.-Gen. i/c administration, Aldershot, 1925–27; Divisional Commander, Northern Command, 1927–31.

Hamilton, Thomas (1842–1925). Educated at Royal Academical Institution and Queen's College, Belfast; Natural Scientist, Antiquarian and

Presbyterian Clergyman; President and Vice-Chancellor, The Queen's University of Belfast, 1908–23.

Hankey, Maurice Pascal Alers (1877–1963). Educated at Rugby; entered Royal Marine Artillery, 1895; Captain, 1899; retired, 1912; Secretary to Committee of Imperial Defence, 1912–38; Lt.-Col. Royal Marines, 1914; Secretary to the War Council, 1914–15; to Dardanelles Committee, 1915; to Cabinet War Committee, 1915–16; to War Cabinet and Cabinet, 1916–38; knighted, 1916; created Baron, 1939; Minister without Portfolio, 1939–40; Chancellor of the Duchy of Lancaster, 1940–41; Paymaster-General, 1941–42.

Hardinge, Charles (1858–1944). Educated at Harrow and Trinity College, Cambridge; entered Foreign Office, 1880; knighted 1904; Ambassador at St Petersburg, 1904–06; Permanent Under-Secretary for Foreign Affairs, 1906–10 and 1916–20; created Baron Hardinge of Penshurst, 1910; Viceroy of India, 1910–16; Ambassador to Paris, 1920–22.

Harington, Charles Harington (1872–1940), known as 'Tim'. Educated at Cheltenham College and Sandhurst; entered Army (King's Liverpool Regt.), 1892; served South Africa, 1899–1900; BEF during retreat from Mons, 1914; BGGS, Canadian Corps, 1915–16; Chief of Staff to Sir Herbert Plumer, 2nd Army and Italian Expeditionary Force, 1916–18; Maj.-Gen., 1918; DCIGS, 1918–20; knighted, 1919; commanding Army of the Black Sea, 1920; GOC, Allied Forces of Occupation in Turkey, 1920–23; Northern Command, 1923–27; Western Command, India, 1927–31; Aldershot Command, 1931–33; Governor and CinC, Gibraltar, 1933–38. A very keen games player; playing member of the MCC; reserve for Irish international hockey team.

Harper, George Montague (1865–1922), 'Daddy'. Entered Army (Royal Engineers), 1884; served South Africa, 1899–1900; Henry Wilson's junior in Directorate of Military Operations, 1910–14; Head of Operations Branch, BEF, 1914; served European War; commanded 51st Highland Division; promoted Maj.-Gen.; GOC Southern Command from 1919 until his death.

Harris, Charles (1864–1943). Educated at Bradford Grammar School and Balliol College, Oxford; civil service career from 1886; Joint Secretary and Permanent Head of Finance Department, War Office, 1920–24.

Henderson, David (1862–1921). Entered Army (Argyll and Sutherland Highlanders), 1883; served in the Sudan, 1898; South Africa, 1899–1900; Director-General of Military Aeronautics, 1913–18; Maj.-Gen. 1914; knighted, 1914; Vice-President of the Air Council, Jan. 1918; resigned, April 1918, after a disagreement with the Air Minister, Lord Rothermere; Military Attaché, Paris, Oct. 1918–June 1919; Director-General League of Red Cross Societies, Geneva, 1920–21.

Heneker, William Charles Giffard (1867–1939). Entered Army (Connaught

Rangers), 1888; served Nigeria, 1902; European War, 1914–18; commanding 54th Infantry Brigade, 1915; 190th Brigade, 1916; 8th Division, 1916–18; Maj.-Gen. 1917; knighted 1919; GOC Rhine Garrison, 1920–21; commanded British Upper Silesian Force, 1921–22; GOC 3rd Division, 1922–26; Southern Command, India, 1928–32.

Henry, Edward Richard (1850–1931). Entered Indian Civil Service, 1873; Inspector-General of Police, Bengal, 1891–1900; on special duty, South Africa, 1900–01; Assistant Commissioner Metropolitan Police, 1901–03; Commissioner, 1903–18; replaced as result of Police Strike; knighted, 1910; created Baronet, 1918.

Henrys, Paul Prosper (1862–1943), French General. GOC, French Army of the East, 1917–19; Head of French Military Mission to Poland, 1919–20.

Holman, Herbert Campbell (1869–1949). Educated at Dulwich College and Sandhurst; entered Army (Devonshire Regiment), 1889; served Burma, 1891; China, 1900; Attaché with Russian Forces in Manchuria, 1905; served on Western Front, 1914–19; Maj.-Gen., 1919; Chief of Military Mission to South Russia, 1919–20; knighted, 1920; Divisional Commander in India, 1924–27; served as a Private in the Home Guard, 1940–44.

Horne, Henry Sinclair (1861–1929). Educated at Harrow and Woolwich; entered Army (Royal Artillery), 1880; served South Africa, 1899–1902; Brig.-Gen., 1912; commanding Artillery, 1st Corps, 1914; Maj.-Gen. Oct. 1914; commanding 2nd Division, 1915; went to Egypt to devise a scheme for defence of Suez Canal, 1915; commanding XV Corps in France, 1916; knighted, 1916; CinC 1st Army, 1917–18; created Baron, 1919, GOCinC, Eastern Command, 1919–23; refused several offers of colonial governorships after 1923.

Horthy de Nagybanya, Nicholas Vitéz (1868–1957). Naval ADC to Emperor Franz Joseph I of Austria, 1909–14; naval commands, 1914–17; Admiral; Minister of War in Hungarian counter-revolutionary Government and CinC Hungarian National Army, 1919; Regent of the Kingdom of Hungary, 1920–45; deported to Germany, Oct. 1944; captured by Allies, 1945; released, 1946.

Huggett, Colonel; Allenby's 'financial expert' does not appear in any of the standard reference works. He was presumably a temporary appointment on Allenby's staff. A James Huggett was Comptroller and Auditor-General for Northern Ireland in 1921.

Hughes, William Morris (1864–1952), born in London. Educated at Llandudno Grammar School and St Stephen's Church of England School, London; emigrated to Australia, 1884; Labour MP in the first Federal Australian Parliament; Minister for External Affairs, 1904, 1921–23 and 1937–39; Attorney-General, 1908–09, 1910–13, 1914–21 and 1939–40; Prime Minister of Australia, 1915–23; Member of Imperial War Cabinet and

Delegate to Paris Peace Conference; Minister for Health and Repatriation, 1934–35 and 1936–37; for Industry, 1939–40; for the Navy, 1940–41.

Hussein (c. 1854–1931). Emir of Mecca, 1908–16; King of the Hedjaz, 1916–24; defeated by Ibn Sa'ud, 1924, and abdicated; in exile in Cyprus, 1925–30; awarded an honorary knighthood; died in Transjordan (which was then ruled by his son Abdullah).

Ironside, (William) Edmund (1880–1959), 'Tiny' (Ironside was 6 feet 4 inches tall). Educated at Tonbridge School and Woolwich; entered Army (Royal Artillery), 1899; served South Africa, 1899–1902; Western Front in France, 1914–18; Brig-Gen. commanding 99th Infantry Brigade, 1918; Maj.-Gen. commanding British Troops, Archangel, 1918–19; knighted, 1919; Head of British Military Mission to Hungary, 1920; commanding Ismid Force, Turkey, 1920; North Persian Force, 1920–21; Commandant of Staff College, 1922–26; QMG, India, 1933–36; Governor and CinC, Gibraltar, 1938–39; Head of British Military Mission to Poland, Aug. 1939; CIGS, 1939–40; CinC Home Forces, 1940; Field Marshal, 1940; created Baron, 1941.

Izzet Pasha, Ahmed; Turkish politician. Grand Vizier, Oct.–Nov. 1918; Minister of Interior, 1920–21; Foreign Minister, 1921; used by British as intermediary with Nationalist Turks, 1920–21.

Jacob, Claud William (1863–1948). Educated at Sherborne School and Sandhurst; entered Army (Worcestershire Regiment), 1882; transferred to Indian Army, 1884; served Zhob Valley, 1890; N.W. Frontier, 1901–02; Brigade Commander, BEF in France, 1914–15; Maj.-Gen. commanding Division, 1915–16; II Army Corps, 1916–19; knighted, 1917; CGS, India, 1920–24; CinC India, 1925; Field Marshal, 1926; Secretary of Military Department, India Office, 1926–30.

Janin, Pierre Thiébaut Charles Maurice (1862–1946). Entered French Army, 1882; served Western Front, 1914–16; General, 1915; Head of French Military Mission to Russia, 1916; Head of Franco–Czechoslovak Mission in Siberia, 1918; commanding Czech Army in Siberia, 1918–19; CinC Allied forces in Siberia, 1918–19; GOC French 8th Army Corps, 1921–24.

Jeudwine, Hugh Sandham (1862–1942). Educated at Eton and Woolwich; entered Army (Royal Artillery), 1882; served South Africa, 1899–1902; France and Flanders, 1914–18; Maj.-Gen. commanding 55th Division, 1916–19; knighted, 1918; British Army of the Rhine, 1919; commanding 5th Division in Ireland, 1919–22; temporary GOCinC Ireland, Nov.–Dec. 1920; Director-General, Territorial Army, 1923–27.

Joffre, Joseph Jacques Césaire (1852–1931). Entered French Army during Franco-Prussian War, 1870–1; served China, Indo-China, Formosa,

Sudan, Madagascar; General of Division, 1905; Chief of the French General Staff, 1914; CinC of the French Armies, 1915–17; promoted Marshal.

Joyce, Pierce Charles (1878–1965). Born Galway; educated at Beaumont College, Old Windsor; entered Army (Connaught Rangers), 1900; served South Africa, 1900–02; attached Egyptian Army, 1907–16; European War, 1915–18; served Gallipoli, EEF; promoted Lieut.-Col.; Military Adviser to the Iraq Government, 1921.

Judenitch, see Yudenitch.

Jusserand, (Jean Adrien Antoine) Jules (1855–1932), Diplomat and writer on English Literature and History. Entered French Foreign Office, 1876; Minister to Denmark, 1898; Ambassador to USA, 1902–25; Member of Anglo-French Mission to Poland, 1920.

Kemal, Mustafa (1881–1938), Turkish soldier and politician. Served at Gallipoli, 1915; in the Caucasus, 1916; in Syria, 1917–18; assumed leadership of Turkish National Movement, 1919; first President of the Turkish Republic from 1923 until his death; known as Atatürk.

Kerr, Philip Henry (1882–1940). Educated at The Oratory School, Birmingham and New College, Oxford; worked as a civil servant in South Africa, 1905–08; editor of *The Round Table*, 1910–16; Secretary to Prime Minister, 1916–21; succeeded cousin as 11th Marquess of Lothian, 1930; Chancellor of the Duchy of Lancaster, 1931; Ambassador in Washington, 1939–40.

Kiamil Pasha, Mahmud. Deputy Head of the War Department, Constantinople, 1914; General commanding 3rd (Caucasus) Army at time of Armenian Deportations of 1915, when 500,000 people were deported to Mesopotamia, of whom only 90,000 survived the war; exiled by the British to Malta, 1918; died in 1922, shortly after his return to Turkey.

Kirke, Walter Mervyn St George (1877–1949). Educated at Haileybury and Woolwich; entered Army (Royal Artillery), 1896; served Waziristan Campaign, 1901–02; Western Front and Salonika, 1914–18; Brig.-Gen., 1918; Deputy DMO, War Office, 1918–22; Maj.-Gen., 1924; Head of British Naval, Military and Air Force Mission to Finland, 1924–25; Deputy CGS, India, 1926–29; GOCinC, Western Command, 1933–36; knighted, 1934; Director-General of Territorial Army, 1936–39; Inspector-General of Home Defences, 1939; CinC, Home Forces, 1939–40.

Kirkpatrick, George Macaulay (1866–1950). Educated Haileybury, Royal Military College, Canada; entered Army (Royal Engineers), 1885; served South Africa, 1899–1902; European War, 1914–15 (promoted Maj.-Gen.); knighted, 1917; DMO, India, 1914–16; CGS, India, 1916–20; GOC, China, 1920–21; GOCinC, Western Command, India, 1923–27.

Klotz, Louis Lucien (1868–1930). French Finance Minister, 1910–11, 1911–13, 1917–20; Chairman of Reparations Committee at Peace Conference.

Knox, Alfred William Fortescue (1870–1964). Educated at St Columba's College, Dublin and Sandhurst; entered Army (Royal Irish Rifles), 1891; transferred to Indian Army, 1898; ADC to Lord Curzon, Viceroy of India, 1899–1900 and 1902–03; served N.W. Frontier, 1901–02; Military Attaché Petrograd Embassy, 1911–18; temporary Maj.-Gen., 1918; Chief of British Military Mission to Siberia, 1918–20; knighted, 1919; Conservative MP, 1924–25.

Kolchak, Alexander Vasilievich (1870–1920). Served in Russian Imperial Navy; Vice-Admiral CinC of Black Sea Fleet, 1916–17; Minister of War in anti-Bolshevik Siberian 'All Russian Government', 1918; declared himself 'Supreme Ruler', Nov. 1918; resigned leadership of anti-Bolshevik forces in favour of Gen. Denikin, Dec. 1919; shot by Bolsheviks, Feb. 1920.

Lenin, Vladimir Ilich, original surname Ulyanov (1870–1924). Founded Russian Social Democratic Labour Party, 1898; lived in exile from Russia, 1900–17; returned to Russia, Apr. 1917; Chairman of the Council of People's Commissars (Prime Minister), Oct. 1917–24.

Le Rond, General. French soldier; Head of Inter-Allied Commission in Upper Silesia, 1920–21.

Le Roy-Lewis, Herman (1860–1931). Educated at Eton and Trinity College, Cambridge; Captain on the Reserve of Officers from 1892; served with the Imperial Yeomanry, South Africa, 1900–01; Brig.-Gen. commanding 1st South-Western Mounted Brigade, 1908–13; Military Attaché, Paris, with rank of Colonel, 1915–Sept. 1918.

Leslie, George Arthur James (1867–1936). Educated at Dulwich and King William College; entered Army (Royal Engineers), 1887; served Tirah, 1897; Chitral, 1900; West Africa, 1909–12; Maj.-Gen. commanding 17th Indian Division in Mesopotamia, 1918–20; retired, 1923.

Lindley, Francis Oswald (1872–1950). Educated at Winchester and Magdalen College, Oxford; entered Foreign Office, 1897; Counsellor of Embassy, Petrograd, 1915–17; Commissioner in Russia, June 1918; Consul-General in Russia, 1919; High Commissioner and Minister, Austria, 1919–20; Minister, Greece, 1922–23; Norway, 1923–29; knighted, 1926; Ambassador, Portugal, 1929–31; Japan, 1931–34.

Livesay, Robert O'Hara (1876–1946). Educated at Wellington College and Sandhurst; entered Army (The Queen's Regiment), 1896; served South Africa, 1899–1902; left Army Feb. 1914; recalled Aug. 1914; served European War; commanding 1st Infantry Brigade, Aldershot, 1919; retired with rank of Brig.-Gen., 1920.

Lloyd, George Ambrose (1879–1941). Educated at Eton and Trinity College,

Cambridge; Conservative MP, 1910–18 and 1924–25; served European War in Egypt, Gallipoli, Mesopotamia and the Hedjaz (Captain); knighted, 1918; Governor of Bombay, 1918–23; created Baron, 1925; High Commissioner for Egypt and the Sudan, 1925–29; Colonial Secretary, 1940–41.

Lloyd George, David (1863–1945). Liberal MP for Caernarvon Boroughs, 1890–1945; President of the Board of Trade, 1905–08; Chancellor of the Exchequer, 1908–15; Minister of Munitions 1915–16; Secretary for War, 1916; Prime Minister, Dec. 1916–Oct. 1922; created Earl, 1945.

Long, Walter Hume (1854–1924). Educated at Harrow and Christ Church, Oxford; Conservative MP, 1880–1921; President of the Board of Agriculture, 1895–1900; of the Local Government Board, 1900–05 and 1915–16; Chief Secretary for Ireland, 1905; Colonial Secretary, 1916–19; First Lord of the Admiralty, 1919–21; created Viscount, 1921.

Lucas, Cuthbert Henry Tindall (1879–1958). Educated at Marlborough and Sandhurst; entered Army (Royal Berkshire Regiment), 1898; served South Africa; France, 1914; Gallipoli, 1915; France, 1917–18; Brig.-Gen. Irish Command, Oct. 1919–Oct. 1923; Aldershot Command, 1924–27; Rhine Army, 1927–29; Maj.-Gen. 1929.

Macdonogh, George Mark Watson (1865–1942). Entered Army (Royal Engineers), 1884; barrister-at-law, Lincoln's Inn, 1897; served in B.E.F., 1914–16; Maj.-Gen. 1916; DMI, 1916–18; AG, Sept. 1918–Sept. 1922; member of Royal Commission on Local Government, 1923–29; President, Federation of British Industries, 1933–34.

MacLay, Joseph Paton (1857–1951), shipowner. Educated at Glasgow High School; member of Glasgow Town Council; Commissioner for Taxes, City of Glasgow; created Baronet, 1914; Shipping Controller (later Minister of Shipping), 1916–21; member of Committee on National Expenditure, 1921; created Baron, 1922.

MacMunn, George Fletcher (1869–1952). Educated at Kensington School and Woolwich; entered Army (Royal Artillery), 1888; served Burma, 1892; Kohat Field Force, 1897; Tirah, 1897–98; South Africa, 1899–1902; Gallipoli, 1915; Mesopotamia, 1917–18; Maj.-Gen. 1917; knighted, 1917; GO CinC, Mesopotamia, May 1919–Jan. 1920; QMG, India, 1920–24.

Macready, (Cecil Frederick) Nevil (1862–1946). Educated at Marlborough and Cheltenham; entered Army (Gordon Highlanders), 1881; served Egypt, 1882; South Africa, 1899–1902; Maj.-Gen., 1910; knighted, 1912; GOC Belfast, 1914; AG, BEF, 1914–16; AG to the Forces, 1916–18; Commissioner Metropolitan Police, Sept. 1918–April 1920; GOC Ireland, 1920–23; created Baronet, 1923.

Maistre, Paul André Marie (1858–1922), French General. Général de Brigade, 1914; CGS, 4th Army, 1914; commanding 21st Corps, 1914–16; 6th Army,

1917; 10th Army in Italy, 1917–18; GOC reserve divisions in France, 1918.

Malcolm, Neill (1869–1953). Educated at Eton and Sandhurst; entered Army (Argyll and Sutherland Highlanders), 1889; served N.W. Frontier, 1897–98; Uganda, 1898–99; South Africa, 1899–1900; Somaliland, 1903–04; European War, 1914–18; Maj.-Gen., 1918; Chief of British Military Mission, Berlin, 1919–21; GOC, Malaya, 1921–24; knighted, 1922.

Malleson, Wilfrid (1866–1946). Educated at Wimbledon and Woolwich; entered Army (Royal Artillery), 1886; Indian Army, 1904; Inspector-General of Communications, East Africa, 1914–15; special mission to Belgian Congo, 1915; Brig.-Gen. commanding troops in British East Africa, 1915–16; Head of British Military Intelligence Mission to Turkestan, 'Malmiss', 1918–20; knighted 1920.

Marden, Thomas Owen (1866–1951). Educated at Berkhamsted School; entered Army (Cheshire Regiment), 1886; served Burma, 1887–89; South Africa, 1900; European War, 1914–18; Maj.-Gen. commanding a Division, France and Rhine, 1917–19; Black Sea and Turkey, 1920–21; GOC, British Troops, Constantinople, 1921–22; Divisional Commander, Turkey, 1922–23; Welsh Division, 1923–27; knighted, 1924.

Marsh, Edward Howard (1872–1953), known as 'Eddie'. Educated at Westminster and Trinity College, Cambridge; entered Colonial Office, 1896; Private Secretary to Churchill, 1905–15, 1917–22 and 1924–29; to successive Colonial Secretaries, 1929–36; knighted, 1937.

Marsh, Frank Graham (1875–1957). Entered Indian Army, 1897; served N.W. Frontier, 1897–98; European War, 1914–18; Brig.-Gen., 1918; War Office representative to the Baltic States, 1919.

Marshall, William Raine (1865–1939). Educated at Repton and Sandhurst; entered Army (Sherwood Foresters), 1886; served N.W. Frontier, 1897–98; South Africa, 1900–02; France, commanding 1st Sherwood Foresters, 1914–15; Gallipoli, 1915; Maj.-Gen. commanding Divisions at Gallipoli and Salonika, 1915–16; 3rd Indian Army Corps, Mesopotamia, 1916–17; GOCinC, Mesopotamian Expeditionary Force, 1917–19; Southern Command, India, 1919–23.

Maurice, Frederick Barton (1871–1951). Educated at St Paul's School and Sandhurst; entered Army (Derbyshire Rgt.), 1892; served Tirah, 1897–98; South Africa, 1899–1900; Instructor at the Staff College, 1913–14; Staff Officer, BEF, 1914–15; DMO, Dec. 1915–Apr. 1918; Maj.-Gen., 1916; knighted, 1918; he was retired from the army, 1918, following his letter to the press accusing Lloyd George of deceiving Parliament about the strength of the British army on the Western Front; a close friend of Sir William Robertson; Principal, Working Men's College, St Pancras, 1922–33; Professor of Military Studies, London University, 1927; Principal, Queen Mary

College, London, 1933–44; a prolific writer on military and historical subjects.

Maxse, (Frederick) Ivor (1862–1958). Educated at Rugby and Sandhurst; entered Army (7th Fusiliers), 1882; served Sudan, 1897–99; South Africa, 1899–1902; Brig.-Gen., 1910; commanding 1st Guards Brigade, Aug. 1914; Maj.-Gen. commanding 18th Division, 1915–17; XVIII Army Corps, 1917–18; knighted, 1917; Inspector-General of Training in France, 1918; GO CinC Northern Command, 1919–23; retired 1926 and successfully took up commercial fruit-growing.

Maynard, Charles Clarkson Martin (1870–1945). Educated at St Paul's School and Sandhurst; entered Army (Devonshire Regiment), 1890; served in Burma, 1889–92; Tirah campaign, 1897; South Africa, 1899–1902; Staff appointments in European War; Brigade Commander, 1915–17; GO CinC, Allied Forces, Murmansk, 1918–19; knighted, 1919; Maj.-Gen., 1923; retired, 1925.

Meinertzhagen, Richard (1878–1967), of Danish origin. Educated at Harrow; entered Army (Royal Fusiliers), 1899; King's African Rifles, 1902; served in East Africa, Palestine and France, 1914–18; Colonel commanding Field Intelligence Section, EEF, 1917–18; Chief Political Officer in Palestine and Syria, 1919–20; Military Adviser, Middle East Department, Colonial Office, 1921–24; published a number of books on ornithology.

Mercier, Captain. French Liaison Officer with Feisal, 1918.

Midleton, Earl of, St John Freemantle Broderick (1856–1942). Educated at Eton and Balliol College, Oxford; Conservative MP, 1885–1906; Secretary for War, 1900–03; for India, 1903–05; succeeded father as 9th Viscount, 1907; served on Irish Convention, 1917–18; created Earl, 1920; an important English landowner in Ireland and a leader of the Southern Irish Unionists.

Milne, George Francis (1866–1948). Educated at MacMillan's School, Aberdeen; Aberdeen University and Woolwich; entered Army (Royal Artillery), 1885; served Sudan, 1898; South Africa, 1900–02; Brig.-Gen. commanding 4th Division Artillery, 1913–14; Lt.-Gen. commanding British Forces at Salonika and the Army of the Black Sea, May 1916–Nov. 1920; knighted 1918; Lieutenant of the Tower of London, 1920–23; GO CinC Eastern Command, 1923–26; CIGS, 1926–33; Field Marshal, 1928; created Baron, 1933.

Milner, Alfred (1854–1925). Educated in Germany, King's College, London, and Balliol College, Oxford; Under-Secretary for Finance in Egypt, 1889–92; Chairman, Board of Inland Revenue, 1892–95; knighted, 1895; High Commissioner for South Africa, 1897–1905; created Baron, 1901; Viscount, 1902; member of the War Cabinet, Dec. 1916–Apr. 1918; Secretary for War, 1918–Dec. 1919; Colonial Secretary, 1919–Feb. 1921.

Moggridge, Harry Weston (1879–1960). Educated at Radley College and Corpus Christi College, Oxford; served with 40th Imperial Yeomanry, South Africa, 1900–01; entered War Office, 1904; Private Secretary to successive Chiefs of the Imperial General Staff, 1908–16; on the Staff, GHQ, France, 1916–18 (Lt.-Col.); Private Secretary to Maj.-Gen. J. E. B. Seely at Ministry of Munitions and Air Ministry, 1918–19; Civil Assistant to Sir Henry Wilson, April 1919–Oct. 1921; Assistant Secretary, War Office, 1927–46.

Mombelli, Ernesto (1867–1932), Italian General. Allied Military Commissioner at Budapest, 1919; GOC Italian Forces at Constantinople, 1921–23.

Monash, John (1865–1931). Educated at Scotch College and University, Melbourne; civil engineer; served in Australian Citizen Forces from 1887; Brig.-Gen., 1915; Gallipoli; Maj.-Gen. commanding 3rd Australian Division in France, 1916–18; Lt.-Gen. commanding Australian Army Corps, 1918; knighted, 1918; Vice-Chancellor of Melbourne University, 1923–31.

Money, Arthur Wigram (1866–1951). Educated at Charterhouse; entered Army (Royal Artillery), 1885; served Zhob Valley expedition, 1890; Isazai, 1892; N.W. Frontier, 1897–98; South Africa, 1899–1902; Zakka Khel expedition, 1908; Mohmand expedition, 1908; Maj.-Gen. and CGS Indian Expeditionary Force and Mesopotamian Expeditionary Force, 1915–17; knighted, 1917; Chief Administrator, Occupied Enemy Territory Palestine, Mar. 1918–Aug. 1919; retired, 1920.

Monro, Charles Carmichael (1860–1929). Entered Army 1879; served N.W. Frontier, India, 1879–80; South Africa, 1899–1900; Maj.-Gen. commanding 2nd Division, 1914; I Corps 1914–15; 3rd Army, 1915; knighted, 1915; CinC, Eastern Mediterranean Forces (Gallipoli and Salonika), 1915–16; GOC 1st Army, 1916; CinC, India, 1916–20; Governor, Gibraltar, 1923–28.

Montagu, Edwin Samuel (1879–1924). Educated at Clifton, City of London School and Trinity College, Cambridge; Liberal MP, 1906–22; Parliamentary Secretary to Chancellor of the Exchequer, 1906–08; to Prime Minister, 1908–10; Under-Secretary of State, India, 1910–14; Chancellor Duchy of Lancaster, 1915; Financial Secretary to Treasury, 1914–16; Minister of Munitions, 1916; Secretary of State for India, June 1917–Mar. 1922.

Montgomery, Archibald Armar (1871–1947), assumed name of Montgomery-Massingberd, 1916. Born Fivemiletown, Co. Tyrone; educated at Charterhouse and Woolwich; entered Army (Royal Artillery), 1891; served South Africa, 1899–1902; European War; Chief of Staff to Rawlinson with IV Corps and 4th Army, 1916–18; promoted Maj.-Gen.; knighted, 1919; Deputy CGS, India, 1920–22; commanding 1st Division, 1923–26; GOCinC, Southern Command, 1926–31; AG, 1931–33; CIGS, 1931–36.

Morland, Thomas Lethbridge Napier (1865–1925). Entered Army (King's Royal Rifle Corps), 1884; served Nigeria, 1897–98, 1901–03; Maj.-Gen.,

1914; European War, 1914–18; knighted, 1915; GOCinC, British Army of the Rhine, Mar. 1920–Mar. 1922; Aldershot Command, 1922–23.

Murdoch, Keith Arthur (1886–1952). Educated at Camberwell Grammar School, Australia, and the London School of Economics; journalist; war correspondent with the Australian Forces throughout the war; editor and manager of the United Cable Service; newspaper proprietor; knighted, 1933.

Muspratt, Sydney Frederick (1878–1972). Educated at United Services College and Sandhurst; entered Indian Army; served N.W. Frontier, 1908; European War in France, 1914–18; member of the British Mission to Kabul, 1920–21; DMO, India, 1927–29; Maj.-Gen., 1929; DCGS, India, 1929–31; Secretary, Military Department, India Office, 1931–33 and 1937–41; GOC Peshawar District, 1933–36; knighted, 1937.

Natsarenus, S. P. (1883–1938), Lithuanian Communist. Bolshevik Special Military Commissar for Murmansk–White Sea region and Petrograd District, 1918; Commissar, Kharkov District, 1919–21; Soviet Representative in Turkey, 1921; later career in government service; arrested and died in prison, 1938.

Newman, Charles Richard (1875–1954). Entered Army (Royal Artillery), 1895; served N.W. Frontier, 1897–98; France, 1915–19; Colonel, 1919; Assistant Military Secretary, Rhine, 1919–20; BGGS, Egypt, 1920–21; Maj.-Gen., 1929; District Commander Madras, India, 1930–34.

Northcliffe, Viscount, Alfred Charles William Harmsworth (1865–1922). Educated at Stamford Grammar School, Lincolnshire; newspaper proprietor; purchased *Evening News*, 1894; founded *Daily Mail*, 1896; *Daily Mirror*, 1903; owned *The Times*, 1908–22; Chairman of the British War Mission to the USA, 1917; Director of Propaganda in Enemy Countries, 1918; created Baronet, 1904; Baron Northcliffe, 1905; Viscount, 1917.

Peel, William Robert Wellesley (1867–1937). Educated at Harrow and Balliol College, Oxford; Conservative MP, 1900–06 and 1909–12; succeeded father as Viscount Peel, 1912; Under-Secretary of State for War and Member of Army Council, 1919–21; Chancellor of the Duchy of Lancaster and Minister of Transport, 1921–22; Secretary for India, 1922–24 and 1928–29; created Earl, 1929; Lord Privy Seal, 1931.

Pellé, Maurice César Joseph (1863–1924), French General. Chief of Staff to Joffre, 1914; commanding 15th Corps, 1917–18; Head of French Military Mission in Czechoslovakia, 1919–20; French High Commissioner at Constantinople, 1921–22 and in Syria, 1923–24.

Perreau, Charles Noel (1874–1952). Educated at Harrow and Sandhurst; entered Army (Royal Dublin Fusiliers), 1895; served South Africa; European War; acting Commandant and Commandant, Royal Military College,

Canada, 1915–19; Lt.-Col. commanding 1st Battalion Royal Dublin Fusiliers, 1919–22; C.O. 166 Infantry Brigade (T.A.), 1923–27.

Pershing, John Joseph (1860–1948). Educated at Kirksville Normal School and U.S. Military Academy; entered U.S. Army (6th Cavalry), 1886; served in Apache and Sioux campaigns, 1886, 1890–91; Spanish–American War, 1898; General, 1906; commanded U.S. troops sent into Mexico, 1916–17; CinC, American Expeditionary Forces in Europe, June 1917–Sept. 1919; Chief of Staff, U.S. Army, 1921–24.

Pétain, Henri-Philippe Benoni Omer Joseph (1856–1951). Educated at Ecole de St Cyr; Lieutenant in the Infantry, 1878; commanding an Infantry Regiment, Aug. 1914; 33rd Army Corps, Oct. 1914; 2nd Army, June 1915; in charge at the siege of Verdun, 1916; CGS, Apr. 1917; CinC of the French Armies, May 1917–Nov. 1918; Inspector-General of the French Army, 1922–31; War Minister, 1934; Prime Minister, June 1940; negotiated armistice with Germany; Chief of State, 1940–44; condemned to death after the liberation of France, 1945; sentence commuted to life imprisonment.

Peyton, William Eliot (1866–1931). Educated at Brighton College; entered Army (7th Dragoon Guards), 1885; served Dongola Expeditionary Force, 1896; Sudan 1897 and 1898; South Africa, 1899–1900. Maj.-Gen., 1914; served Gallipoli and Egypt; knighted 1917; Military Secretary in War Office, 1916–18; commanded 40th Division in France and Flanders, June 1918–Mar. 1919; 3rd Indian Division, Meerut, 1920–22; Military Secretary to Secretary for War, 1922–26; GO CinC, Scottish Command, 1926–30.

Picot, François Georges-, French diplomat. Consul-General, Beirut, 1914; signatory on behalf of France of Sykes–Picot Agreement, May 1916; High Commissioner and Chief Political Adviser to Allenby in zone of French influence in Lebanon and Syria, 1918–19.

Pilsudski, Jozef Clemens (1867–1935), Polish nationalist leader. President and CinC Army, 1918–22; Chief of the General Staff, 1923; retired from public life, 1923; led military *coup d'état*, 1926; Minister of War, 1926–35; Prime Minister, 1926–28 and 1930; Finance Minister, 1931–32.

Plumer, Herbert Charles Onslow (1857–1932). Educated at Eton; entered Army (York and Lancaster Regt.), 1876; served Sudan, 1884; South Africa, 1899–1902; Maj.-Gen., 1902; QMG, 1904–05; knighted 1906; GOC, Northern Command, 1911–14; commanded 5th Army Corps, 1915, and 2nd Army, BEF, France, 1915–17 and 1918; GOC, Italian Expeditionary Force, 1917–18; refused the post of CIGS in succession to Sir William Robertson, Feb. 1918; Army of the Rhine, 1918–19; created Baron, 1919; Governor and CinC, Malta, 1919–24; High Commissioner, Palestine, 1925–28; created Viscount, 1929; president of the Marylebone Cricket Club, 1929.

Plunkett, Edward Abadie (1870–1926). Lincolnshire Regiment; served, Nile Expedition, 1898; Head of British Military Mission to Royal Serbian Army,

1918; Military Attaché, Belgrade, 1918–20; Inter-Allied Commissioner of Control, Bulgaria, 1920–22; retired with hon. rank of Brig.-Gen., 1922.

Poole, Frederick Cuthbert (1869–1936). Entered Army (Royal Artillery), 1889; served Tirah Expedition, N.W. Frontier, 1897–98; South Africa, 1899–1902; Somaliland, 1903–04; France, 1914–16; Brigadier-General, 1916; specially employed on Mission to Russia, 1917; temporary Maj.-Gen., 1917; commanding Archangel force, 1918; British Military Mission in the Caucasus, 1918–19; knighted, 1919; retired, 1920.

Price-Davies, Llewelyn Alberic Emilius (1878–1965), known as 'Mary'. Educated at Marlborough and Sandhurst; entered Army (King's Royal Rifle Corps), 1898; served South Africa, 1899–1902, V.C., 1901; married Henry Wilson's sister, Eileen, 1906; Brigade Commander 1915–18; liaison officer at Italian GHQ, 1918; President, Standing Committee of Enquiry regarding Prisoners of War, 1918–19; ADC to the King, 1920–30; AAG, Aldershot Command, 1920–24; commanding 145th Infantry Brigade, 1924–27; AA and QMG, Gibraltar, 1927–30.

Radcliffe, Percy Pollexfen de Blaquiere (1874–1934). Educated Winchester and Woolwich; entered Army (Royal Artillery), 1893; served South Africa, 1899–1900; France and Flanders, 1914–18; BGGS, Canadian Corps, 1916; DMO, Apr. 1918–Mar. 1922; Maj.-Gen. 1918; mission to Poland, 1919, assisting General Weygand in reorganisation of Polish Army; knighted, 1919; Divisional Commander, 1923–27; GOGinC, Scottish Command, 1930–33, and Southern Command, 1933–34; generally known in the Army as 'P. de B.' to distinguish him from General Sir Charles Delmé-Radcliffe.

Rawlinson, Alfred (1867–1934), 'Toby', brother of Henry Seymour Rawlinson. Lieutenant, 17th Lancers; served European War as Lieutenant-Commander, Royal Naval Volunteer Reserve, and Lt.-Col., Royal Garrison Artillery, 1914–16; in charge of Anti-Aircraft Defence of London, 1916–18; Special Mission in Persia and the Caucasus, 1918–19; Special Intelligence Service, Army of the Black Sea, 1919; prisoner of the Turks in eastern Turkey, Mar. 1920–Oct. 1921; succeeded his brother as 3rd Baronet, 1925.

Rawlinson, Henry Seymour (1864–1925), 'Rawly'. Son of Maj.-Gen. Sir Henry Rawlinson, Bt.; educated at Eton and Sandhurst; entered Army (60th King's R. Rifles), 1884; served alongside Henry Wilson in Burma campaign, 1887–88; on Lord Kitchener's staff in the Sudan, 1898; South African War, 1899–1902; Maj.-Gen. commanding 4th Division, Sept. 1914; 7th Division and 3rd Cavalry Division, Oct. 1914; IV Corps, Dec. 1914.–Dec. 1915; knighted 1914; Lt.-Gen. commanding First and Fourth Armies, Dec. 1915–Feb. 1918; General, 1917; British Representative, Supreme War Council (in succession to Sir Henry Wilson), Feb.–Mar. 1918; commanding Fourth

Army, Mar. 1918–Mar. 1919; GOC, North Russia, Aug.–Nov. 1919; created Baron, 1919; GOCinC, Aldershot, Nov. 1919–Nov. 1920; CinC India, Nov. 1920–Mar. 1925.

Reading, Lord, Rufus Daniel Isaacs (1860–1935). Educated at University College School; Liberal MP, 1904–13; knighted, 1910; Solicitor-General, 1910; Attorney-General, 1910–13; Lord Chief Justice, 1913–21; Viceroy of India, 1921–26; Foreign Secretary, 1931; created Baron, 1914; Viscount, 1916; Earl, 1917; Marquess, 1926.

Redmond, John Edward (1851–1918). Educated at Clongowes Wood, and Trinity College, Dublin; Nationalist MP, 1881–1918; Chairman of Irish Parliamentary Party from 1900. His brother Maj. William Redmond, Nationalist MP for East Clare, was killed in action on the Western Front in 1917.

Repington, Charles à Court (1858–1925). Educated at Eton and Sandhurst; entered Army (Rifle Brigade), 1878; served Afghanistan, 1878–79; Burma, 1888–89; on Kitchener's staff (Lieut.-Col.) in the Sudan, 1898; South Africa, 1899–1900; Military Attaché, Brussels and the Hague, 1899–1902; forced to resign his commission because of a personal indiscretion involving another man's wife; Military Correspondent of *The Times*, 1904–18; of *The Daily Telegraph*, 1918–25.

Richardson, Wilds Preston (1861–1929). United States General; graduated from West Point, 1884; served on Western Front, 1918; commanding US forces at Murmansk, 1919; retired, 1920.

Robertson, (Malcolm) Arnold (1877–1951). Educated at Marlborough; entered Foreign Office, 1898; Diplomatic Service, 1903; Deputy High Commissioner on Inter-Allied Rhineland Commission, 1919–20; High Commissioner, 1920–21; Agent and Consul-General, Tangier, 1921–24; knighted, 1924; Minister, Argentina, 1925–27; Ambassador, 1927–29.

Robertson, William Robert (1860–1933), 'Wully'. Educated at a private school; entered Army (16th Lancers) as a private, 1877; commissioned into 3rd Dragoon Guards, 1887; Chitral Relief Force, India, 1895; served in South Africa, 1900; Maj.-Gen., 1910; Commandant, Staff College, 1910–13; Director of Military Training, War Office, 1913–14; knighted 1913; QMG, BEF, 1914–15; Chief of Staff, BEF, 1915; CIGS, 1915–18; GOCinC, Eastern Command, 1918; CinC, Home Forces, 1918–19; British Army of the Rhine, 1919–20; created Baronet, 1919; Field Marshal, 1920.

Romer, Cecil Francis (1869–1962), 'Romeo'. Entered Army (Royal Dublin Fusiliers), 1890; served South Africa, 1899–1902; European War, 1914–18 (promoted Maj.-Gen.); CGS, Forces in Great Britain, 1918–20; Maj.-Gen., G.S., War Office, 1920–21; Director of Staff Duties, 1922–25; knighted, 1925; GOCinC, Western Command, 1928–31; Southern Command, 1931–38; AG, 1933–35.

Rumbold, Horace George Montagu (1869–1941). Educated at Eton; entered Diplomatic Service, 1888; succeeded father as 9th Baronet, 1913; Minister, Switzerland, 1916–19; knighted, 1917; Poland, 1919–20; High Commissioner and Ambassador, Turkey, 1920–24; Ambassador, Spain, 1924–28; Germany, 1928–33.

Rupprecht, Crown Prince of Bavaria (1869–1955). Eldest son of King Ludwig III; commanding 6th Army in Alsace-Lorraine and northern France 1914; Field Marshal and CinC of Army Group on right wing of Western Front, 1916–18.

Sackville-West, Charles John (1870–1962), 'Tit Willow'. Entered Army (King's Royal Rifle Corps), 1889; served Manipur, 1891; Burma, 1891–92; South Africa, 1899–1900; twice wounded on the Western Front, 1914–16; Maj.-Gen., 1917; British Military Representative on the Allied Military Committee, Versailles, 1918–19; knighted, 1919; Military Attaché, Paris, 1920–24; Lieutenant-Governor of Guernsey, 1925–29; succeeded his brother as 4th Baron Sackville, 1928.

Samuel, Herbert Louis (1870–1963). Educated at University College School and Balliol College, Oxford; Liberal MP, 1902–18 and 1929–35; Chancellor of the Duchy of Lancaster, 1909–10 and 1915–16; Postmaster-General, 1910–14 and 1915–16; President of the Local Government Board 1914–15; Home Secretary, 1916 and 1931–32; High Commissioner for Palestine, 1920–25; knighted, 1920; created Viscount, 1937. Nicknamed 'Nebbi' by Wilson and his friends.

Sanders, Gerard Arthur Fletcher (1869–1941). Educated at Rossall School and Woolwich; Royal Engineers; served Burma, 1892–93; Dongola Expedition, 1896; European War, 1914–19; temporary Maj.-Gen. commanding 17th Division, Mesopotamia, 1920–21; retired, 1923.

Shoubridge, (Thomas) Herbert (1871–1923). Educated at Blundell's School, Tiverton; entered Army (Dorsets Regiment), 1893; served Tirah Expedition, 1897–98; South Africa, 1899–1902; GSO 2, BEF, 1914; Maj.-Gen. commanding 7th Division, France and Italy, 1917–19; Shorncliffe Barracks, near Folkestone, Jan.–June 1919; East Lancashire Division, 1919–23; Commandant Staff College, 1923.

Shuttleworth, Digby Inglis (1876–1948). Educated at Bedford School; entered Indian Army (3rd Gurkha Rifles), 1898; served World War I; GSO 1 North-West Persia Force; commanded 39th Infantry Brigade, Caucasus; 83rd Infantry Brigade, Army of the Black Sea, 1919; President Allied Commission of Control, Ottoman War Office, 1920; commanded 83rd Infantry Brigade, Chanak, Dardanelles, 1920–23; Maj.-Gen., 1929.

Sikorski, Wladyslaw (1881–1943), Polish soldier and politician. Chief of Polish General Staff, 1921–22; Prime Minister, 1922–23; Minister of Military

Affairs, 1923–25; CinC, Polish Army and Prime Minister of Polish Government in exile, 1939–43.

Smith-Dorrien, Horace Lockwood (1858–1930). Educated at Harrow; entered Army (Sherwood Foresters), 1876; served Zulu War, 1879; Egypt and the Sudan, 1882 and 1884–86; Chitral Relief Force, 1895; Tirah Campaign, 1897–98; Sudan, 1898; Maj.-Gen. commanding a Brigade and a Division, South Africa, 1900; knighted, 1904; GOCinC, Aldershot, 1907–12; Southern Command, 1912–14; 2nd Army Corps and 2nd Army, BEF, 1914–15; East African Forces, 1915–16; Governor, Gibraltar, 1918–23.

Smuts, Jan Christian (1870–1950), South African soldier and politician. Educated at Victoria College, Stellenbosch, and Christ's College, Cambridge; commanding Boer forces in South African War, 1899–1901; commanded troops in East Africa, 1916–17 (hon. Lieut.-Gen.); member of Imperial War Cabinet, 1917–19; Prime Minister of South Africa, 1919–24 and 1939–48; Field Marshal, 1941.

Sonnino, Baron Sidney (1847–1922), born in Egypt of a Florentine father and an English mother. Prime Minister of Italy, 1906 and 1909–10; Foreign Minister, Nov. 1914–June 1919; Italian Delegate at Peace Conference, Jan.–June 1919; a distinguished Dante scholar and bibliophile.

Spears, Edward Louis (1886–1974). Original surname Spiers, changed spelling to Spears in mid-September 1918. Educated privately, joined Kildare Militia, 1903; Captain, 11th Hussars, 1914; Liaison Officer with French 10th Army, 1915–16; Head of British Military Mission to French Government, 1917–20; hon. Brig.-Gen.; National Liberal MP, 1922–24; Conservative MP, 1931–45; Maj.-Gen., 1940; Churchill's personal Representative with French Prime Minister, May–June 1940; Head of British Mission to Gen. de Gaulle, July 1940; Head of Mission to Syria and the Lebanon, July 1941; First Minister to Republics of Syria and the Lebanon, 1942–44; knighted, 1942; created Baronet, 1953; a close friend of Winston Churchill.

Spender, Wilfrid Bliss (1876–1960). Educated at Winchester; entered Army (Royal Artillery), 1897; served World War I on staff of Ulster (36th) and 31st Divisions and GHQ, (Lieut.-Col.); re-raised and commanded Ulster Volunteer Force (later Special Constabulary) 1920; first Secretary to Cabinet of Northern Ireland, 1921–25; Head of Northern Ireland Civil Service, 1925–44; knighted, 1929.

Stamfordham, Lord, Arthur John Bigge (1849–1943). Entered Army (Royal Artillery), 1869; served Zulu War, 1878–79; entered Royal Household, 1880; Private Secretary to Queen Victoria, 1895–1901; to Prince of Wales, 1901–10; to King George V, 1910–31; created Baron, 1911.

Stokes, Claude Bayfield (1875–1948). Educated at St John's School, Leatherhead, and Sandhurst; entered Army (East Kent Regiment), 1895; Indian Army (Skinner's Horse), 1897; served N.W. Frontier, 1897–98; Military

Attaché, Teheran, 1907–11; served European War, 1914–18; Lt.-Col., 1918; Political Officer at Baku, 1919; Chief British Commissioner in Trans-Caucasia, 1920–21; retired, 1922; British Vice-Consul, Nice, 1931–40.

Studd, Herbert William (1870–1947). Educated at Eton and Trinity College, Cambridge; entered Army (Coldstream Guards), 1891; served South Africa, 1899–1902; commanding 180th Brigade, 1915–16; Brig.-Gen. G.S., 1916–17; Chief of Staff, British Section Supreme War Council, 1917–19; commanding Coldstream Guards, 1919; retired, 1923.

Sykes, Mark (1879–1919). Educated at Beaumont; Ecole des Jésuites, Monaco; Institut St Louis, Brussels; Jesus College, Cambridge; Yorkshire Regiment; served South Africa, 1902; Lt.-Col., 1911; Member North Riding Territorial Association; Conservative MP from 1911; succeeded father as 6th Baronet, 1913; served on missions to Balkan states, Russia and Mesopotamia in World War I; advocate of Arab independence and signatory on behalf of Britain of the Sykes–Picot agreement, May 1916; Assistant Secretary to the War Cabinet secretariat, 1916–19.

Teodoroff, Todor (1858(?)–1924). Prime Minister of Bulgaria, Nov. 1918–Oct. 1919.

Thomas, James Henry (1874–1949). Educated at Council schools; railwayman; Labour MP, 1910–31, National Labour, 1931–36; General Secretary, National Union of Railwaymen, 1918–24 and 1925–31; Colonial Secretary, 1924 and 1935–36; Lord Privy Seal, 1929–30; Dominions Secretary, 1930–35.

Thomson, Basil Home (1861–1939). Educated at Eton and New College, Oxford; entered Colonial Service, 1881; acting PM of Tonga, 1890; transferred to Home Office (Prison Service), 1896; successively Governor of Dartmoor and Wormwood Scrubs Prisons, 1901–08; Assistant Commissioner, Metropolitan Police, 1913–19; knighted 1919; Director of Intelligence, Home Office, 1919–21.

Thomson, Christopher Birdwood (1875–1930). Educated at Cheltenham and Woolwich; entered Army (Royal Engineers), 1894; temporary Military Attaché with Serbian Forces, 1912–13; staff appointments, 1914–15; temporary Military Attaché, Bucharest, 1915–17; Divisional Commander Royal Engineers, Egyptian Expeditionary Force, 1917–18; BGGS, Supreme War Council, Versailles, 1918–19; retired from Army, 1919; created Baron Thomson of Cardington, 1924; Secretary for Air, 1924 and 1929–30; died in the R101 airship disaster.

Thwaites, William (1868–1947). Educated at Wellington and Woolwich; entered Army (Royal Artillery), 1887; served South Africa, 1899–1900; Western Front, 1914–18; Maj.-Gen., 1918; DMI, War Office, Sept. 1918–Apr. 1922; knighted, 1919; DMO and I, Apr.–Sept. 1922; GOC 47th

Division (TA), 1923–26; GOCinC, British Army of the Rhine, 1927–29; Director-General of the Territorial Army, 1931–33.

Tomasini, Francesco. Italian Minister to Poland, c. 1920–c. 1923.

Trenchard, Hugh Montague (1873–1956). Educated at Hill Lands Army crammers, Wargrave, Berkshire; entered Army (Royal Scots Fusiliers), 1893; served South Africa, 1899–1902; West African Frontier Force, 1903–10; GOC, Royal Flying Corps in the Field, 1915–17; Maj.-Gen., 1916; Chief of the Air Staff, 1918–29; knighted, 1918; Air Marshal, 1919; Marshal of the RAF, 1927; Commissioner of the Metropolitan Police, 1931–35; created Viscount, 1936.

Trotsky, Lev Davidovich (born Bronstein) (1879–1940), Russian Revolutionary. Head of Petrograd Soviet, 1917; Commissar for Foreign Affairs, 1917–18; for Military Affairs, 1918–25; expelled from Communist Party, 1927; exiled from Soviet Union, 1929; assassinated in Mexico.

Tudor, Henry Hugh (1871–1965). Entered Army (Royal Artillery), 1890; served South Africa, 1899–1902; Brig.-Gen. commanding Artillery, 9th (Scottish) Division on Western Front, 1916–18; Maj.-Gen. commanding 9th Division, 21–24 Mar. 1918; Police Adviser, and later Chief of Police, Ireland, 1920–21; GOC, Palestine Gendarmerie, 1922, with rank of Air Vice Marshal; knighted, 1923; retired, 1923. A long-time acquaintance of Churchill.

Twiss, William Louis Oberkirch (1879–1962). Educated at Bedford School and Sandhurst; entered Army, 1898; served North China, 1900–01; Tibet Expedition, 1903–04; France, 1914–17; Army HQ, India, 1917–19; GSO 1 Directorate of Military Intelligence, War Office, 1919–21; commanding 2/9th Gurkha Rifles, 1921–23; DDMI, India, 1923–24; DMO, India, 1924–27; Maj.-Gen., 1929; GOC, Burma, 1936–39; knighted, 1938.

van Straubenzee, Casimir Cartwright (1867–1956). Entered Army (Royal Artillery), 1886; served Ashanti, 1895–96; European War, 1914–18; Maj.-Gen. RA, 5th Army in France, 1918–19; Rhine Army, 1919; Divisional Commander, Northern Command, 1923–27; GOC, Malaya, 1927–29; knighted, 1928.

Venizelos, Eleutherios (1864–1936). Cretan and Greek politician and nationalist; Prime Minister of Greece, 1910–15; 1917–20; 1928–32 and 1933.

von Sanders, Field Marshal Otto Liman (1855–1929). Prussian Cavalry General; Head of German Military Mission to Turkey, 1913; Inspector-General of Turkish Army, 1914; commanding Turkish 5th Army at Gallipoli, 1915; commanding Army group in Syria, 1918.

Wardrop, (John) Oliver (1864–1948). Educated at Balliol College, Oxford; entered Diplomatic Service, 1892; served in Russia, Poland, Rumania, Tunis,

Haiti; retired, 1910; rejoined Service, 1914; Consul-General at Bergen, 1914; Moscow, 1917; Chief British Commissioner in Georgia, Armenia and Azerbaijan, 1919–20; Consul-General at Strasbourg; knighted, 1922.

Waterfield, Arthur Charles Malleson (b. 1866). Entered Army (1st Dragoon Guards), 1887; Lt.Col., Indian Army, 1913; GSO 1 (Liaison Officer) Egypt, 1917–18; retired, 1920.

Waters Taylor, Bertie Harry (1874–1946). Lived in South Africa, 1893–1902; served in Cape Mounted Riflemen; commissioned into Royal Berkshire Regiment during South African War; transferred to South Staffordshire Regiment; served Nigeria, 1909–10; World War I; with ANZAC, 1915; Egypt, 1916–18; Acting Military Governor, Jerusalem and Tiberias, 1918–19; Colonel on Staff of Occupied Enemy Territory Administration, Palestine, 1919–20; attached to EEF, 1920–23.

Watson, James Kiero (1865–1942), 'Jimmy'. Educated at Clifton College and Sandhurst; entered Army (King's Royal Rifle Corps), 1885; served Burma; attached Egyptian Army, 1894–99; ADC to Sirdar, Dongola and Khartoum Expeditions; South Africa, 1899–1901; retired from Egyptian Army, 1905; served European War, 1914–16; Military Attaché, Egypt (Lieut.-Col.), 1916–19.

Wavell, Archibald Percival (1883–1950). Educated at Winchester and Sandhurst; entered Army (The Black Watch), 1901; served South Africa; N.W. Frontier, 1908; France, 1914–16; Military Attaché with Russian Army in Caucasus, 1916–17; Egyptian Expeditionary Force, 1917–20 (BGGS, 1919–20); Assistant AG, War Office, 1921–23; Maj.-Gen., 1933; CinC, Middle East, 1939–41; knighted, 1939; CinC, India, 1941–43; created Viscount, 1943; Field Marshal, 1943; Viceroy of India, 1943–47; created Earl, 1947.

Webb, Richard (1870–1950). Educated at Fonthill, Wiltshire, and HMS *Britannia*; Midshipman, 1885; on Admiralty War Staff, 1914–17; commanded *New Zealand*, 1917–18; Rear-Admiral, 1918; Assistant High Commissioner to Turkey, 1918–20; knighted, 1920; Rear-Admiral in 4th Battle Squadron, Mediterranean Fleet, 1920–22; Head of Naval Mission to Greece, 1924–25; President, Royal Naval College, Greenwich, 1926–29.

Weizmann, Chaim (1874–1952). Born in Russia; educated in Germany; Reader in Biochemistry, Manchester University, 1906; naturalized British subject, 1910; Director Admiralty Laboratories, 1916–19; President World Zionist Organization, and of Jewish Agency for Palestine, 1921–31 and 1935–46; Adviser to Ministry of Supply, London, 1939–45; First President of Israel, 1949–52.

Wemyss, Rosslyn Erskine (1864–1933). Entered Navy, 1877; Rear-Admiral Commanding 12th Cruiser Squadron, 1914; commanding squadron at Gallipoli, 1915; knighted, 1916; CinC, East Indies and Egypt, 1916–17; First

Sea Lord, Jan. 1918–Nov. 1919; created Baron Wester Wemyss, 1919; Admiral of the Fleet, 1919.

Weygand, Maxime (1867–1965). Entered French Army (Cavalry), 1887; Chief of Staff to General Foch, 1914–23; French Military Representative at Versailles, 1918; Member of Anglo-French Mission to Poland, 1920; French High Commissioner, Syria, 1923–24; CinC, French Army, 1931–35 and 1940; Minister of National Defence, 1940; Governor-General of Algeria and Vichy Government Representative in French Africa, 1940; prisoner of the Germans, 1942–45; imprisoned in France, 1945–48.

Whigham, Robert Dundas (1865–1950). Educated Fettes College, Edinburgh and Sandhurst; entered Army (Royal Warwickshire Regiment), 1885; served Sudan, 1898; South Africa, 1899–1902; DCIGS, 1916–April 1918; Maj.-Gen., 1916; knighted, 1917; commanded 62nd Division in France, 1918; AG, 1923–27; GOCinC, Eastern Command, 1927–31.

Wickham, Charles George (1879–1971). Educated at Harrow; entered Army (Norfolk Regiment), 1899; served South Africa, 1900–02; European War, 1914–18; Assistant Provost Marshal, France, 1915–16; Lieut.-Col. with Gen. Knox's Military Mission, Vladivostock; Divisional Commissioner, Royal Irish Constabulary, 1920; Inspector-General, Royal Ulster Constabulary, 1922–45; knighted, 1922.

Wigram, Clive (1873–1960). Educated at Winchester; entered Army (Royal Artillery), 1893; served N.W. Frontier of India, 1897–98; ADC to Lord Curzon, Viceroy of India, 1899–1904; Assistant Private Secretary to King George V, 1910–31; Private Secretary, 1931–35; Brevet Lt.-Col., 1915; knighted, 1928; created Baron, 1935.

Williamson, Archibald (1860–1931). Educated at Craigmount School and Edinburgh University; Liberal MP, 1906–18; Coalition Liberal MP, 1918–22; Member of Mesopotamian Commission, 1916; created Baronet, 1909; Financial and Parliamentary Secretary to the War Office, and Member of the Army Council, 1919–21; created Baron Forres, 1922.

Willingdon, Lord, Freeman Freeman-Thomas (1866–1941). Educated at Eton and Trinity College, Cambridge; Liberal MP, 1900–10; Junior Lord of the Treasury, 1905–12; created Baron, 1910; Governor of Bombay, 1913–19; of Madras, 1919–24; Governor-General of Canada, 1926–31; Viceroy of India, 1931–36.

Wilson, Arnold Talbot (1884–1940). Educated at Clifton College and Sandhurst; entered Army (Wiltshire Regiment), 1903; Indian Army, 1904; Indian Political Department, 1909; on duty in Persia, 1907–13; Deputy Chief Political Officer, Mesopotamian Expeditionary Force, 1915; Deputy Civil Commissioner, 1916; Acting Civil Commissioner, Mesopotamia, and Political Resident in the Persian Gulf (rank of Lt.-Col.), Mar. 1918–Oct. 1920; knighted 1920; Adviser to Anglo-Persian Oil Co., 1921–32; Conservative

MP, 1933–40; Pilot Officer (Air Gunner), 1939–40; killed in action over France, May 1940.

Wilson, Henry Fuller Maitland (1859–1941). Educated at Eton and Sandhurst; entered Army (Rifle Brigade), 1878; served Afghanistan, 1878–79; Mahsud Waziri Expedition, 1881; South Africa, 1899–1900; Maj.-Gen. commanding 4th Division, France, 1914–15; knighted, 1915; GOC, XII Army Corps, Salonika, 1916–18; GOC, Allied Forces Gallipoli, 1919–20. Known as 'Fatty'.

Wilson, Henry Hughes (1864–1922). Educated at Marlborough; entered Army (Longford Militia), 1882; Royal Irish Regiment, 1884; transferred to Rifle Brigade, 1884; served Burma, 1886–87; South Africa, 1899–1901; DMO, 1910–14; Maj.-Gen., 1913; Assistant CGS, BEF, 1914–15; Chief Liaison Officer with French Army, 1915; knighted, 1915; GOC IV Army Corps, 1916; British Military Representative, Supreme War Council, 1917–18; CIGS, Feb. 1918–Feb. 1922; Ulster Unionist MP, 1922; assassinated, 1922.

Wilson, Woodrow (1856–1924). Educated privately and at Princeton, the University of Virginia and Johns Hopkins University; Professor of History and Political Economy, Bryn Mawr College, 1885–88; Wesleyan University, 1888–90; of Jurisprudence and Politics, Princeton University, 1890–1910; President of the University, 1902–10; Governor of New Jersey, 1911–13; President of the United States (Democratic Party), 1913–21. Sir Henry Wilson jokingly referred to the President as 'my cousin'.

Wingate, (Francis) Reginald (1861–1953). Educated at Woolwich; entered Army (Royal Artillery), 1880; joined Egyptian Army, 1883; Nile Expedition, 1884–85; Governor Red Sea littoral and O.C. troops, Suakin, 1894; DMI during Dongola campaign, 1896; Nile Expedition, 1897; Sudan, 1898–99; knighted, 1898; Maj.-Gen., 1903; Pasha of Egypt; Sirdar (CinC) of the Forces of Egypt and Governor-General of the Sudan, 1899–1916; High Commissioner, Egypt, 1917–19; dismissed in favour of Sir Edmund Allenby after nationalist riots, March 1919; created Baronet, 1920.

Woods, Robert Henry (1865–1938). Educated at Wesley College and Trinity College, Dublin; a surgeon; independent Unionist MP for Dublin University, 1918–22.

Worthington-Evans, Laming (1868–1931). Educated at Eastbourne College; a solicitor; Conservative MP, 1910–31; created Baronet, 1916; Minister of Blockade, 1918–19; of Pensions, 1919–20; without Portfolio, 1920–21; Secretary for War, Feb. 1921–Oct. 1922 and 1924–29; Postmaster-General, 1923–24.

Wrangel, Baron Peter Nikolaevich (1878–1928). Imperial Russian cavalry officer; served in Russo-Japanese War and World War I; joined Denikin's army, 1918; took over command, March, 1920; 'recognised' by French government, Aug. 1920; by Nov. 1920 he had been defeated and his followers were being evacuated from the Crimea by the French; he died in Brussels and was buried in Belgrade.

Young, (Charles) Alban (1865–1944). Entered Diplomatic Service, 1890; Minister, Central American Republics, 1913–19; knighted, 1918; Minister, Yugoslavia, 1919–25.

Young, Hubert Winthrop (1884–1950). Educated at Eton and Woolwich; entered Army (Royal Garrison Artillery), 1904; transferred to Indian Army (116th Mahrattas), 1908; served N.W. Frontier, 1915; Mesopotamia and Hejaz, 1915–18 (Major); attached to Foreign Office, 1919–21; Assistant Secretary, Middle East Department, Colonial Office, 1921–27; knighted 1932; Governor, Nyasaland, 1932–34; Northern Rhodesia, 1934–38; Trinidad and Tobago, 1938–42.

Yudenitch, Nikolai Nikolaevitch (1862–1933). Entered Russian Army, 1879; Chief of Staff, 1912; commanding Russian Forces in the Caucasus, 1915 and 1917; commanded anti-Bolshevik North Western Army in attack on Petrograd, Oct.–Nov. 1919; fled to Estonia after failure of attack; died in France.

Zaghlul, Sa'ad (1860–1927), Egyptian nationalist politician. A lawyer by profession; Vice-President of the Legislative Assembly, 1914; pressing for Egyptian independence, 1918; arrested and deported to Malta, 1919; negotiated in London with Milner and Adly Pasha, 1921; deported again from Egypt, to Aden, the Seychelles and Gibraltar successively, 1921–23; Prime Minister of Egypt, 1924; President of the Council of Deputies, 1925–27.

APPENDIX II
SENIOR OFFICE-HOLDERS IN
THE BRITISH ARMY 1918–22

Dates of appointment are given and, after the last officer named, that of relinquishing the appointment. Otherwise it may be assumed that officers relinquished their positions on the day before their successors took office. Military ranks are not given, but every person listed held a rank of Major-General or above at the time of his appointment.

Sources: War Office and Army Lists 1918–22

1. Military Members of the Army Council[1]

Chief of the Imperial General Staff

Sir W. R. Robertson	23 December 1915
Sir H. H. Wilson	19 February 1918
The Earl of Cavan	19 February 1922–18 February 1926

Quarter-Master-General

Sir J. S. Cowans	8 June 1912
Sir T. Clarke	16 March 1919–15 March 1923

Adjutant-General

Sir C. F. N. Macready	22 February 1916
Sir G. M. W. Macdonogh	11 September 1918–10 September 1922

Master-General of the Ordnance

Sir W. T. Furse	4 December 1916
Sir J. P. Du Cane	1 January 1920–30 September 1923

2. Department of the CIGS

Deputy Chief of the Imperial General Staff

Sir R. D. Whigham	23 December 1915
Sir C. H. Harington	29 April 1918
Sir P. W. Chetwode	30 October 1920–10 September 1922

Director of Military Operations[2]

Sir F. B. Maurice	23 December 1915
Sir P. P. de B. Radcliffe	22 April 1918–30 March 1922

Director of Military Intelligence[2]
Sir G. M. W. Macdonogh 3 January 1916
Sir W. Thwaites 11 September 1918–10 September 1922

3. Principal Commands of the Army

Home Forces[3]
Viscount French 19 December 1915
Sir W. R. Robertson 30 May 1918
Sir D. Haig 15 April 1919–31 January 1920

Ireland[4]
Sir B. T. Mahon 15 November 1916
Sir F. C. Shaw 13 May 1918
Sir C. F. N. Macready 14 April 1920–17 February 1923

British Armies in France
Sir D. Haig 19 December 1915–1 April 1919

British Army of the Rhine
Sir H. C. O. Plumer 2 April 1919
Sir W. R. Robertson 22 April 1919
Sir T. L. N. Morland 3 March 1920
Sir A. J. Godley 25 March 1922–16 June 1924

Egypt and Palestine
Sir E. H. H. Allenby[5] 28 June 1917
Sir W. N. Congreve 14 October 1919–15 April 1923

Mesopotamia and Persia
Sir W. R. Marshall[6] 17 November 1917
Sir G. F. MacMunn 2 May 1919–28 January 1920
Sir J. A. L. Haldane 9 February 1920–3 May 1922

Army of the Black Sea
Sir G. F. Milne[7] 10 May 1916
Sir C. H. Harington 2 November 1920–31 October 1923

4. Commander-in-Chief of the Army in India
Sir C. C. Monro[8] 10 October 1916
Lord Rawlinson 21 November 1920–28 March 1925

Notes
1 During the war, and for a time thereafter, the DCIGS was included among the Military Members, as also was the Director-General of Military Aeronautics (February 1916–March 1918).
2 The Directorates of Military Operations and Intelligence were amalgamated in April 1922. Thwaites held the joint post from April to September 1922.
3 From August 1918 this Command was called GHQ Forces in Great Britain. It was wound up on 1 February 1920.
4 Wound up in February 1923.
5 GOCinC, Egyptian Expeditionary Force.
6 GOCinC, Mesopotamian Expeditionary Force.
7 Originally GOCinC, British Salonika Force.
8 Strictly CinC East Indies.

LIST OF DOCUMENTS AND SOURCES

INDEX

Abdullah Ibn Hussein, 255, 371
Aden, 237
Adly (or Adli) Pasha Yeghen, 286, 320, 325, 371
Afghanistan: 3rd Afghan War (1919), 105, 352; Bolsheviks and, 133, 136, 266, 272, 278, 363; and defence of India, 146, 233, 265-6, 278; policy towards, 211-12, 222-3, 251; mentioned, 248, 279, 282; *see also* Dobbs, Sir Henry
Agadir Crisis, 7
Ali brothers, Mohammed and Shaukat, 278, 366
Ali Riza Rikabi (Pasha), 55, 371
Allenby, General Sir Edmund (Lord), the 'Bull': career, 371, 410; letters to Wilson, 54-6, 61, 98-9, 101-3, 324-5, 333-4, from Wilson, 42-3, 51, 64-5, 154-5, 318, 331-2; Middle Eastern policy, 23, 54-6, 61; exchange of congratulations with Wilson, 61, 64-5; on post-war situation in Middle East, 69, 71, 101-3; at Constantinople, 82; at peace conference, 88; question of succeeding Wingate, 89; on Egyptian situation (1919), 98-9, 101-2; promotion to Field Marshal, 100; views on Syria, 126; predicts that Egypt might become 'another Ireland', 144, 202 296; row with Meinertzhagen, 163, 166, 357; Wilson approves of policy, 221, 291, 339, and recommends for CIGS, 221, 318, 324; and question of Sollum garrison, 237; resolute policy, 286, 291, 325, 333-4, 339; threatens to resign, 329, 334; Allenby Declaration (1922), 329; post-war honours, 349, 351; mentioned, 105, 130, 146, 206, 222, 244, 255, 335
Amery, Leopold, 4
Amritsar, 144; *see also* Dyer, Brig.-Gen. Reginald
Anderson, Chandler, 107, 371
Anderson, Maj.-Gen. Hastings, 284, 371

anti-semitism, 141-2
Arabs, policy towards, 55, 212, 237; national aspirations, 71, 102-3, 157; *see also* Mesopotamia, Palestine, *and* Syria
Archangel: British troops at, 51, 52, 85, 105; policy towards, 85, 90, 113; American troops at, 94; evacuation of, 70; mentioned, 45, 112, 119
Armenia: Milne's jaundiced views on inhabitants, 77, 79; massacres in, 123, 124-5; Armenian refugees, 129-30; discussed at San Remo, 161, 162
Arnold-Forster, Hugh, 5
Asquith, H. H., 'Squiff': career, 371; and Curragh Crisis, 10; mistrusts Wilson, 11-12; forms Coalition, 12; consults Wilson, 13; resigns as PM, 14; and the 'Maurice case', 22; denounces Lord French, 106; mentioned, 7, 9, 74, 105
Asser, Lt.-Gen. Sir Joseph: career, 371; letter from Wilson, 103-4; warned by Wilson not to take Churchill too seriously, 72, 103-4; mentioned, 109
Australia: troops in action, 40, 48-9; proposed disbandment of Australian Light Horse, 44-5; deployment of troops, 58-61
Austria: army, 30, 32; peace treaty with, 71; future of ex-Emperor, 87; situation in (Feb. 1920), 151; financial crisis, 232
Azerbaijan: Milne's views on, 77, 79; policy towards, 127, 141, 148; discussed at San Remo, 161, 162

Badoglio, General Pietro, 162, 372
Bainbridge, Maj.-Gen. Guy, 300, 372
Bakir Sami, 285, 372
Baku: Milne's views on, 77-8; Italians and, 93; proposal to retain British troops in, 124, 148; and defence of India, 138, 169, 176; mentioned, 51, 211, 233
Balfour, A. J.: career, 372; and Allenby, 89; on diplomacy, 117; and Gen. Malcolm, 119; the 'old fool', 128; and Danzig,

opinion of Persian people, 272; mentioned, 42, 105, 178, 179, 204, 217, 228, 240, 250, 259

Pétain, General Henri-Philippe: career, 397; letter from Wilson, 60; mentioned, 15, 43, 250

Peyton, Maj.-Gen. Sir William, 28, 338, 397

Picot, François Georges-, 61, 129, 397

Pilsudski, Marshal Jozef, 192, 196, 397

plebiscite areas: supply of troops for, 127, 134, 147, 205–6, 236, 267, 268; Wilson's views of, 138; drafts for, held back because of domestic situation, 149; Wilson keen to withdraw troops, 177–8, 191; see also Silesia

Plumer, General Sir Herbert (Field Marshal Lord): career, 397, 410; letter to Wilson, 193–4, from Wilson, 332; commanding in Italy, 25, 33, 345; on difficulty of holding the line, 35, 345; offered CIGS-ship, 17; promotion to Field Marshal, 100, 351; and Irish Command, 159; believes a Labour government would help 'clear the air', 194; health of, 292; post-war honours, 349; mentioned, 28, 36, 42, 59

Plunkett, Brig.-Gen. Edward, 152, 397–8

Poland: post-war policy towards, 57, 84, 93; problem of Haller's troops, 91, 92, 94, 350; Anglo-French Mission to (1920), 143, 192–3, 194–7; supply of material to, 200; and Danzig, 210; mentioned, 114, 127, 134, 273, 295; see also plebiscite areas

Poole, Maj.-Gen. Frederick: career, 398; letter to Wilson, 45–6, from Wilson, 46; high hopes for success of Allied intervention in Russia, 46; is like the 'daughter of the horse leech', 52

Portugal, 318

Price-Davies, Brig.-Gen. Llewelyn: career, 398; letter to Wilson, 298–9; mentioned, 37

Prinkipo, proposed conference at, 83, 133, 355

Quetta (Indian Staff College), 225

Radcliffe, Maj.-Gen. Sir Percy: career, 398, 409; letters to Wilson, 194–7,

240–4, 314–15; wanted by Wilson as DMO, 28; and Anglo-French Mission to Poland, 192, 194–7, 200; report on visit to Belfast, 219, 314–15; report from Cairo conference, 220, 240–4; mentioned, 90, 91, 94, 174, 212, 334

Rawlinson, Lt.-Col. Alfred ('Toby'), 123, 282, 292, 366, 398

Rawlinson, General Sir Henry (Lord), 'Rawly': career, 398–9, 410; letters to Wilson, 30–2, 39–40, 59, 244–9, 306–8, from Wilson, 25–6, 122–3, 204–6, 210–13, 222–3, 231–3, 251–4, 259–61, 264–6, 266–7, 271–2, 272–3, 276–80, 282–5, 289–92, 324, 336–9; early contacts with Wilson, 2, 4; Commandant of Staff College, 4, 5; hands over command of IV Corps to Wilson, 13; succeeds Wilson at Supreme War Council, 21, 24–6; reports opening of German spring offensive (1918), 30; views on Armistice Day, 59; a good companion, 159; regular correspondence with Wilson, 217; praised by Montagu, 223; difficulties with finance in India, 224, 245; and Indian military affairs, 245–9, 296–7, 307; visit of Prince of Wales, 306–7; valedictory letter from Wilson, 336–9; post-war honours, 349; mentioned, 3, 58, 289

Reading, Lord: career, 399; as Viceroy of India, 211, 217, 244–5; and Gandhi, 286, 338; and military policy, 297; mentioned, 222, 248–9, 331

Redmond, John, 162, 399

Regiments:
11th Hussars, 156, 158
14th Hussars, 315
16th Lancers, 130
20th Hussars, 156, 165
Connaught Rangers, 268
Highland Light Infantry, 180
Irish Guards, 299
Leinster Regiment, 268
Longford Militia, 2
Middlesex Regiment, 209
Rifle Brigade, 2, 366
Royal Dublin Fusiliers, 298
Royal Horse Artillery, 243
Royal Inniskilling Fusiliers, 365
Royal Irish Regiment, 2

The Army Records Society has been launched with the aid of an appeal supported by the following institutions and individuals:

The Wolfson Foundation

A C Taylor-Knight Esq
Tozer Kemsley & Millbourn
  (Holdings) Ltd
United Scientific Holdings PLC
Westland PLC
Williams & Glyn's Bank PLC
The George Wimpey Charitable
  Trust
The Household Cavalry
1st The Queen's Dragoon Guards
The Royal Scots Dragoon Guards
4th/7th Royal Dragoon Guards
5th Royal Inniskilling Dragoon
  Guards
The Queen's Royal Irish Hussars
9th/12th Royal Lancers
The Royal Hussars
13th/18th Royal Hussars
17th/21st Lancers
Royal Tank Regiment
Royal Regiment of Artillery
Grenadier Guards
Scots Guards
Welsh Guards
The Royal Scots
The King's Regiment
The Green Howards
The Cheshire Regiment
The King's Own Scottish Borderers

The Royal Irish Rangers
The Gloucestershire Regiment
The Worcestershire and Sherwood
  Foresters Regiment
The Duke of Wellington's
  Regiment
The Queen's Lancashire Regiment
The Royal Hampshire Regiment
The Staffordshire Regiment
The Duke of Edinburgh's Royal
  Regiment
The Parachute Regiment
The Queen's Gurkha Engineers
The Royal Green Jackets
Army Air Corps
Royal Corps of Transport
Royal Army Ordnance Corps
Corps of Royal Electrical and
  Mechanical Engineers
Corps of Royal Military Police
Royal Army Pay Corps
Small Arms School Corps
Royal Army Educational Corps
Army Physical Training Corps
Territorial Auxiliary and Volunteer
  Reserve Association for Wales
Territorial Auxiliary and Volunteer
  Reserve Association for Western
  Wessex

438